Strategic Software Production With Domain-Oriented Reuse

For a listing of recent titles in the *Artech House Computing Library,* turn to the back of this book.

Strategic Software Production With Domain-Oriented Reuse

Paolo Predonzani
Giancarlo Succi
Tullio Vernazza

Artech House
Boston • London
www.artechhouse.com

Library of Congress Cataloging-in-Publication Data
Predonzani, Paolo.
Strategic software production with domain-oriented reuse /Paolo Predonzani, Giancarlo Succi, Tullio Vernazza.
p. cm. — (Artech House computing library)
Includes bibliographical references and index.
ISBN 1-58053-104-0 (alk. paper)
1. Computer software—Development. 2. Computer software—Reusability.
I. Succi, Giancarlo, 1964–. II. Vernazza, Tullio. III. Title.
IV. Artech House computing library

QA76.76.D47 P73 2000
005—dc21 00-055884
CIP

British Library Cataloguing in Publication Data
Predonzani, Paolo
Strategic software production with domain-oriented reuse. —
(Artech House computing library)
1. Computer software—Reusability. 2. Computer software—Development.
I. Title II. Succi, Giancarlo III. Vernazza, Tullio
005.1′2

ISBN 1-58053-104-0

Cover design by Wayne McCaul.

International Standard Book Number: 1-58053-104-0
Library of Congress Catalog Card Number: 00-055884

10 9 8 7 6 5 4 3 2 1

This work is dedicated to our parents, who instilled in us the love of knowledge and supported our studies with deep passion, absolute commitment, and hard work.

Contents

Preface

Software reuse is one of the most common buzzwords in software engineering today. We know that through reuse we can achieve quality, productivity, reliability, flexibility, low costs, and all kinds of benefits. Unfortunately, in most cases we do not know how to achieve reuse.

The fact is that software reuse is a pervasive property of software systems. We can reuse code as well as design documents, requirements, even the overall development process. Attempting to achieve reuse through mere effort, however, is quite like trying to find analytic solutions to a tenth-order polynomial equation—it can be considered an act of good will. People have published countless papers and obtained numerous academic degrees in such attempts. However, it is simply not possible, due to the very nature of the problem.

This book proposes a Copernican revolution in the way we perceive software reuse. Rather than figuring out how to modify the software development process to include "reuse-related" activities, it discusses how software reuse can be integrated into the "usual" development process. Reuse is no longer viewed as an abstract state to achieve; it becomes the lens through which we view the problems we encounter.

Reuse starts at the very beginning of the development process—when we determine what products to develop and how they are related to one another. It ends at the very last stages of the development process—when we update the code that we have developed and make corrections to the common parts and product-specific parts of the software system. Reuse always occurs within the framework of an application domain. That is why this book is centered on domain analysis and engineering. It is our experience that software reuse can be achieved if a domain perspective is taken—that is, if we try to determine how to take advantage of multiple applications running in the same domain.

Sherlock precisely categorizes the relations between the products of a domain and generates a tangible asset: the domain framework. This framework constitutes the basis of real software products.

This might look bizarre. People in software engineering have always striven to make things simple, using a "divide-and-conquer" approach to complex problems. The reality is that it is important to separate the problem of understanding how to effectively cluster different software systems that share common features from the problem of making the design and the development of these systems as simple and easy as possible. Sherlock aims to hit these two birds with a single stone, by proposing a model for the analysis of application domains, in which the different features of the products and their mutual relations are deeply revised. It uses the latest methodologies to develop the resulting software systems, targeting the construction of reusable frameworks organized around domain architectures.

This book is aimed at a wide audience. It will be of interest to software managers that have to decide how to define their products in order to achieve maximum synergy among them. It is relevant for software engineers interested in implementing such synergy. Professors and students interested in software reuse will also find much of interest in this book. Examples and case studies are used to help explain how to apply the book's core ideas to the work site in a very concrete and effective way. With a sound and well thought-out theoretical framework, it sets the basis for an academic study. Early versions of this work have already been used as both a reference guide and a textbook.

This book is intended to be a clean and well-structured entry point for people interested in Sherlock. However, the entire Sherlock body of knowledge cannot be contained within a single book. The Sherlock Web site (http://www.lips.dist.unige.it/Sherlock) is the ideal complement to this book. It contains the latest Sherlock development news, FAQs, summaries, and syntheses from ongoing projects.

We've divided this book into three parts. Chapters 1 to 6 are introductions to software reuse and domain analysis and engineering in Sherlock, and to the examples that we use throughout the book. Chapters 7 to 11 contain detailed descriptions of Sherlock. Chapters 12 to 15 present real cases where Sherlock has been applied.

Acknowledgments

At the end of this effort, we would like to acknowledge the help we have received in the course of this study.

First, this work could not have been conceived without the inspiring guidance of Enrico Zaninotto. Enrico introduced us to the theory of network economies, tutored us, showed us the way, and kept repeating something we understood only at the end: "the key to the game is mix-n-match and bundling."

A special acknowledgment goes out to Arrigo Frisiani. His scientific leadership and personal ethics have served as reference points for us in the years of hard work that have resulted in this book.

We would like to thank a number of other people who have helped make this work possible (presented here in alphabetical order): Aronne Armanini, Luigi Benedicenti, Charles Brown, Stefano De Panfilis, Alberto Giordano, Ron Johnston, Eliseo Mambella, Michele Marchesi, Andrea Valerio, who contributed to the early phases of this work, and Chan Wirasinghe. We would also like to thank the Canadian Natural Sciences and Engineering Research Council, the European Commission, the Government of Alberta, and the Italian Ministry of University and Research for funding our research. We thank Barbara at Artech House for keeping us on schedule with nice e-mails that never put us under pressure, and we thank Judi for her very accurate proofreading of the material. We thank all the students who used early versions of this work and diligently reported all the problems they faced. And we would like to thank WaveRider Communications, Inc. for allowing us to use their experience as the core case study for this book.

> *"Cum omnia procedant ex voluntate Divina, omnia suo modo per appetitum inclinator in bonum, sed diversimode."*
>
> —Thomas Aquinas, *Summa Theologica*, I, 59, 1

CHAPTER

1

Introduction

In academic and industrial groups substantial interest has been directed toward understanding the fast-growing industry of software through the study of its products. By *product* we mean the concept, the code, the data, and the documentation that constitute a homogeneous unit and that can be sold in several copies. These kinds of studies focus on several issues, including technical, user, and commercial ones. For instance, some studies show how a product works, what benefits it delivers to the user, and how it is selling in the market. Addressing these issues for single products gives some interesting results. However, single products give partial information on the software industry. A more complete view requires that we focus on groups of products. There are visible reasons for this: software firms generally produce more than one software product and users generally use more than one software product.

These characteristics are also common to other industries—automakers produce more than one car model and car users use more than one car model. However, they assume a higher relevance in the software industry. Producing several products rather than one is better because there are advantages to reusing experience and software across the products. Using several products rather than one is better because it is possible to assemble better and more complex software systems from different products.

This is an extreme approach that does not work. In the multitude of available software products, we may think that any product is somehow connected to any other product and that all the products must be considered together. This "group all" approach is of little use, much like the "single product" approach: It is impossible to deal with all products at once. The solution is to recognize that there are "domains" which gather software products into groups of reasonable size. The analysis of these domains yields interesting results for those who wish to understand the software industry.

In its simplest definition, a *domain* is a collection of related products. Relatedness of products is a very broad and manifold concept. Products can be related if they perform similar tasks, if they use similar technologies, or if they are used in similar contexts. *Domain analysis* is the analysis of products in a given domain. *Domain engineering* is the production of products in a given domain. The distinction between domain analysis and domain engineering is not very sharp, because analysis and production are closely related. While the distinction exists in literature, most people now refer to a single concept: domain analysis and engineering (DA&E). This book describes the theory and the application of Sherlock, a methodology for DA&E.

Traditionally, the motivation for doing DA&E has been to foster software reuse. Reuse means that software artifacts—like requirement and design documents, code, documentation, and so forth—are used in several products, which is the scope of DA&E. The reuse approach requires (1) the creation of reusable artifacts and (2) the integration of those artifacts into final systems. In current practice, firms perform both the creation and the integration. The proportion between creation and integration varies, covering the full range between pure creators (e.g., library producers) and pure integrators.

Software reuse tackles the issues of productivity in software engineering and is seen as one of the most promising approaches to software production. Its potential benefits range from decreased development time and increased product quality to improved reliability and decreased maintenance costs. As an investment, reuse works only if the software fits a variety of situations and is actually reused many times. The larger the variety, the greater the potential for reuse and to reap the benefits of that reuse. However, dealing with variety bears some risks, like the fact that unknown or unforeseen requirements can challenge the reusability of software, or that quality can decrease as a consequence of adaptations. Variety is generally the result of variability, a leitmotiv of this book.

Variability comes from many sources: customers' unique needs, differences between versions, mutability of the environment, localization, and so on. All of these can potentially disrupt the efforts of reuse. A fundamental task of DA&E and Sherlock is to explore all the sources of variability within a domain. Sherlock is the recognition that variability is a characteristic of modern software that every software firm needs to confront. In this way, variability is no longer a source of trouble and unpleasant surprises. Rather, from a competitive viewpoint, it is a feature to exploit more effectively than your competitors.

Variability is a crucial part of decision-making in all software projects. Variability shows that a project can be undertaken in different ways–adopting one of several alternative solutions, or implementing different strategies. Decisions determine the purpose and shape of the final products, and thus determine their impact on the market. Decisions can be made on a range of possible alternatives—which derive, for instance, from the market positioning, the technology, and the software architecture. Sherlock finds the benefits and the costs of the alternatives and provides the tools to evaluate these alternatives objectively. Moreover, it finds the interactions between the various aspects of variability—market, technology, architecture, and so on—which are often critical but also very difficult to dominate. In this way, Sherlock gives the DA&E practitioner the tools and confidence to make clear-cut decisions about software product strategies.

Decisions are made at all levels. Using a top-down approach, the following is a list of areas where decisions are encountered:

1. *Strategic positioning in the market.* Decisions concern the role of the firm and its products in the market. The elements to consider are the competitive relations in the market. The alternatives to choose from are those that allow the DA&E practitioner to achieve its long-term goals.

2. *Definition of the strategic positioning in terms of product lines.* Product lines are the ultimate implementation of a strategy. A product line

is the combination of products that embeds a strategic idea. A product line has the breadth to support a strategy over a long period of time. Decisions here should determine the shape of the product lines, considering the relations between them and competing product lines. Decisions should also make clear how many product lines are necessary and, in case there is more than one, what different objectives they address.

3. *Definition of product lines in terms of products.* This is the DA&E practitioner's tactic. Here, decisions are made with regard to the articulation of each product line in terms of products. Decisions should evaluate the best options to ensure that products are cohesive in terms of the product line's strategy. Products should also support each other, exploiting the synergies (or network externalities) between them and other products. The result of these decisions can be a plan for the development and coordination of the product line's products.

4. *Development of products.* The decisions should determine which design and implementation solutions best support the development of the products. Development is conducted exploiting the benefits—like synergies and reuse—of working in the larger context of product lines.

By taming variability, Sherlock also makes it more friendly to reuse. More precisely, it formalizes variability into manageable schema through which reuse is possible. A major difficulty in the practice of software reuse is that reusability of a software artifact is difficult to assess. Reusability can only be proved in the future: A piece of software is not reusable until it is actually reused! A piece of software may seem reusable in the current situation, but, if the assumptions of the current situation change, reusability can be compromised. In stable domains, assumptions rarely change, which results in predictable levels of reusability. However, not all domains are stable.

Instability may come from several sources, such as immature technology or competition between firms pulling the domain in different directions. The goal of Sherlock is to foster software reuse in domains with high variability. On one hand, this is a matter of tracking the evolution of the domain, so that changes in the assumptions do not come as an unpleasant surprise. On the other hand, it is also a matter of influencing the evolution of the domain according to a plan and exploiting all the strengths that a software firm has, such as network externalities, compatibility, coordination, installed bases, and so on. Of course, Sherlock cannot foresee the unpredictable. However, Sherlock is a valid guide for spotting variability, evaluating the variants, and picking the choices that are thought to be most profitable and least risky. In this sense, Sherlock improves the quality of decision-making in software development.

From a practical point of view, Sherlock delivers a set of documents describing the domain and a strategy to use to move within the domain. In addition to this, Sherlock delivers a software framework on which developers can build a variety of applications in the domain, thus exploiting reuse. Object orientation is the underlying paradigm of the documentation and the framework.

This book assumes the DA&E practitioner to be the central point of the discussion. The DA&E practitioner is surrounded by the entities that are typically present in a domain—namely products, competitors, and partners. This book teaches the DA&E practitioner how to perform certain activities, which are organized in phases. The activities may follow different paths, depending on the DA&E practitioner's decisions and the situation of the domain. We provide examples, criteria, and templates to address a large variety of situations.

Throughout the book we assume an entire software firm to be the DA&E practitioner. This is reasonable because of the multitude of the required skills and activities. For this reason, readers of this book can be more than one person in the firm and the profile of those readers is manifold. Certainly, a lot of decision-making is involved in Sherlock; competence is needed to set the strategy for the development of the firm's products. Other skills are also essential. Knowledge of the firm's products should reside with the architects and builders of the products. Mastery of the technology is usually with those who research it, or at least know its trends. Knowledge of sales and network externalities lies with the marketing experts. Potentially, any person who envisions, studies, plans, or designs the products is likely to participate in DA&E. Practice shows that these competencies and activities belong to high or medium-high roles within the firm.

Sherlock shares some aspects with other DA&E methodologies. As Arango [1] points out, a basic scheme is common to all DA&E methodologies. The differences between Sherlock and other methodologies are evident in its form and substance. The formal differences involve the use of different terminology and representation techniques. As to the substantial differences—in the authors' opinion, most of the other DA&E approaches focus too much on modeling the domain and too little on the characterization of the products. Moreover, very few of them give guidelines as to how to move from the analysis to the development of actual software. Conversely, Sherlock precisely characterizes the relations between the products in the domain and generates a tangible asset—the domain framework—which constitutes the basis of real software products.

As mentioned, Sherlock characterizes the relations between the products in the domain. Informally, some examples of the considerations that this characterization may generate are as follows:

- Competition is not a pure marketing matter. Product features can be designed to defeat competitors.
- There is little space for a new product that does not offer radical improvements over the existing products in an established domain.
- Even a poor product produced in a timely manner can be highly profitable in a domain with high demand and little competition.
- Coordinated products can help each other penetrate hostile markets.

A clear understanding of phenomena like these sets the stage for the development of any successful software product—one who starts out on the right foot is already halfway there! Such understanding is essential in DA&E. DA&E aims at multiproduct development and, without a very clear strategy regarding what each product should do and how they should interact, coordination, synergy, and economies of scope will not happen.

Once the domain is characterized, it is necessary to select the functional and nonfunctional features the products should have. This selection process is a core part of DA&E. More precisely, for the products to be developed, the selection process determines which characteristics should be constant in all products, which should vary, and which may vary even though such variability is not implemented right away. Sherlock obtains relevant information from the study of the target firm and the market. It then builds a variability space that allows existing products to be analyzed, which leads to planning for future strategies.

The variability space visualizes the space of available choices. Products are the result of choices, so products can be positioned on the variability space. The variability space has rules to determine how products on it are related to each other in terms of users, competition, coordination, and movement. For instance, a typical problem is to determine how a product in a certain position on the variability space can be moved to another position to attract more users from a competing product. The construction of the variability space, the positioning of the products, the assessment of the rules, and the planning of the movements are all incremental activities for which Sherlock provides clear specifications. A Sherlock practitioner with a military background has compared Sherlock to military procedures in the sense that "you know what to do next."

This book contains many concepts—from market analysis to technical implementation, decision-making to object-oriented modeling. It is meant to be a self-contained package that explains the benefits of DA&E from the very beginning to the very end, and shows how to obtain those benefits. We did not want a theory book or a book only for DA&E "hackers." Moreover, Sherlock is not a "toy" methodology—it has already been applied with extreme success in several firms. In this book we have tried to provide all the material needed to replicate our experience in other contexts.

Understanding by means of examining examples is easier than learning from pure theory. The last part of this book contains four case studies obtained from the analysis of three different domains—telecommunications, neural networks, and control systems. In addition to these case studies, simpler examples accompany the presentation of the concepts, pointing out difficulties and proposing workable solutions. We want readers to be able to start practicing DA&E now!

Reference

[1] Arango, G., "Domain Analysis Methods," in *Software Reusability,* W. Schaefer, R. Prieto-Diaz, and M. Matsumoto, Eds., New York: Ellis Horwood, 1994.

CHAPTER

2

Contents

Domain analysis and engineering: the definition

Domain analysis and engineering (DA&E) is the synergetic analysis and engineering of products in a given domain. Normally products in the same domain share something—a concept, a technology, users, certain artifacts, etc. This sharing makes products related. The analysis of related products as a whole has the potential to provide unique insights that are not obtainable from the analysis of each product individually.

Domains exist not only in software. Examples of nonsoftware domains include the transport system, the telephone system, and the banking system. Each domain has firms producing different products. In the transport system domain, for example, a firm may produce cars for private use or bus routes for public use. Within these domains, products are related according to the definition given above—products in the transport system domain, for example, move people or goods from one place to another, possibly using the same roads and similar technology.

The definition of the domain in terms of products is very handy because (1) it defines exactly what producers consider to be feasible or not feasible in the domain, and (2) it reflects the user's perception of the domain. Let us consider the transportation domain: people can fly from Paris to Berlin, but do not even think of booking a flight from Paris to the moon. This evidences (1) that airlines (the producers) know what flights (the products) can be offered, and (2) that travelers are well aware of this. Products also evidence an important characteristic of domains: competition. In this sense, domain and market are frequently interchangeable terms.

Software domains comply with the given definitions and characteristics. In addition, they exhibit very high potentials for synergistic development. First, enormous complexity and variety are seen in the relations between software products (interoperability, compatibility, and so on). Second, users can assemble "ideal" software systems from the combination of separate products picked from a domain containing many products. Third, software is frequently a way through which users communicate: users attach high value to networks of communicating users. Although these points partially hold also for nonsoftware domains, they are most highly present, with the highest complexity, in software domains.

Traditionally in software domains, the sharing of common software artifacts has been the basic definition of domain and the motivation for DA&E. Software artifacts are all the products and by-products of software development, including requirements, design, code, test cases, and even ideas, pictures, comments, and notes. As Prieto-Diaz [1] says, DA&E identifies, collects, and organizes all the artifacts used in software development in a particular domain so as to make them available for the development of other products in the same or different domains. This view of domains and of DA&E coincides with the goals of software reuse—rather than reinventing solutions and redoing things several times in many products, it is better to do them only once and reuse them across all products.

A note is necessary to explain the difference between "sharing" and "reuse." The two concepts are similar. However, sharing can occur even by chance, while reuse is the result of an explicit intention. For instance, two firms that do not communicate at all can produce two very similar products: They share a common idea, although the idea is developed independently in two different places. On the contrary, if the two firms share a software library, the sharing is the result of an (agreed-upon) intention to reuse such a library.

Sherlock provides full support for the reuse-oriented view of DA&E. However, Sherlock also focuses on the structure and dynamics of the products in the market. As mentioned before, products compete in a domain. A firm that produces more than one product in a domain has a cutting edge over the competition—its products have the potential to "help" each other or, more technically, to "coordinate" events. Coordination works because products that are used by many users attract new users; this attraction leads to more coordinated products. As a result, products have the potential to attract more users when they are coordinated. There are interesting cases of software firms that, practically neglecting reuse, have exploited these characteristics to conquer the users of a domain.

To summarize, DA&E deals with the following aspects of software production:

1. Determination of the requirements at domain level, considering the needs of a network of users;
2. Assessment of the competitive relations between products and visualization of what opportunities are available for the development of successful products;
3. Establishment of a domain-based approach to software development, ensuring that the technology meets the business.

Informal practices of DA&E that fulfill some of these points are widespread. Many programs aimed at the introduction of reuse in software firms resemble DA&E. However, to be repeatable and to produce durable results, these practices should become systematic through a defined methodology. At any rate, DA&E is an incremental learning process and all firms that have already started informal DA&E or reuse practices have a good ground for practicing successful, systematic DA&E.

2.1 DA&E and competition in the domain

So far we have talked of products within a domain without regard for who produces the software. However, for a software firm there is a major distinction between products made by the firm itself and products made by competitors. This is an intriguing issue; on one hand, DA&E requires coordination between products; on the other hand, the domain is the "battlefield" of competing products that do not coordinate. Simple evidence of this is that reuse of software artifacts across competing products is, at least, an unusual practice. Keep in mind, however, that coordination and competition are not contradictory. First, DA&E effectively explores and exploits the competitive relations within the domain; second, there is still a huge possibility of coordination among the products of the same firm.

The analysis part of DA&E can consider all products of a domain—the firm's products as well as the products of others. There is no reason to restrict the scope of analysis. Knowing what others have done is as valuable as the experience on one's own. On the other hand, the synthesis part of DA&E is clearly competitive—it produces products that most probably won't be shared with competitors.

2.2 Typical skills in DA&E

Utilizing DA&E requires the recognition that products share something. We call the shared part the commonalities, and the nonshared part the differences. Commonalities are important for the production of abstractions and generalizations of the domain. The ideal person to manage commonalities should have good abstraction skills, the capability to explore various and variable scenarios, and the competence to move between several products.

Differences are as important as commonalities, especially in the synthesis of final software products. Differences can be subtle and tricky to handle, because differences arise from environmental factors—installation, integration with other tools, and so on—that may not be flexible at all and thus difficult to accommodate. The ideal person for manage differences should be product oriented, with synthesis skills and knowledge of the environment in which the products will be used. The two profiles—the "commonalities" person and the "differences" person—should both be present in the personnel of a firm practicing DA&E.

Reference

[1] Prieto-Diaz, R., "Domain Analysis: An Introduction," *ACM SIGSOFT Software Engineering Notes,* Vol. 15, No. 2, 1990, pp. 47–54.

CHAPTER

3

Contents

An overview of Sherlock

Sherlock is a fully developed object-oriented DA&E methodology targeted at the development of products within a domain. It covers all aspects of DA&E, from market analysis to coding. Its focus is on variability, which is a fundamental characteristic of domains and a crucial issue faced by software producers every day.

Sherlock addresses the development of multiple products. To achieve this, it groups such products into product lines according to a coherent strategic idea, and develops them in a coordinated way. Coordinated products strengthen each other—what is gained from the development of one product in terms of market, experience, and code can be exploited in the other products. Through Sherlock, the DA&E practitioner learns how to make the best use of multiple product production, effectively coping with the difficulties of variability.

Sherlock can also be applied to the development of single products. This is not contradictory with the focus on variability. Even single products go through several versions or experience a maintenance phase to accommodate changing requirements. Moreover, a firm may want to develop one initial product alone because the domain is undergoing rapid changes and it is risky to invest in other products. Later circumstances may clarify the situation and evidence the need for the development of more products. In this case, it is important to ensure that the initial product be an advantage, not a burden. What is important is not to limit the perspective to a single product, hindering future opportunities.

Sherlock consists of five phases. The flow of execution of the phases is not sequential and may follow several paths, depending on the situation under analysis and, possibly, on the existing software development practices. A standard path of execution is presented in this book; it is based on the experience of the authors in the application of Sherlock. The five phases have strict relationships with the traditional activities of software engineering. For instance, one of Sherlock's phases is related to what traditional software engineering calls *requirements acquisition.* In this sense, Sherlock can be seen as an augmentation of the traditional software process with an emphasis on the domain. In this way, software developers do not have to subvert previously established practices in order to introduce Sherlock.

This chapter presents an overview of the phases of Sherlock and a description of how to move between them.

3.1 A brief tour of the phases

The five phases of Sherlock are: (1) domain definition, (2) domain characterization, (3) domain scoping, (4) domain modeling, and (5) domain framework development. Each phase defines a group of activities and generates a set of deliverables. Some deliverables are only intermediate by-products of DA&E; others are an integral part of the final products that are developed. The deliverables serve also as a means of communication between the phases.

Table 3.1 presents the five phases and an outline of the activities performed in each phase. The table is introductory; it familiarizes readers with the terminology and sets the basis for a deeper discussion. Each phase has a well-defined rationale and is very useful because it provides a means to define a path throughout DA&E. However, in real life there are no shock boundaries between the phases. The activities defined by the phases communicate with each other in very complex ways that depend on the structure of the target domain.

Table 3.1
Sherlock's Phases and Their Activities

Phase	Activities
Domain definition	Works as the "information central" of DA&E, collecting and organizing information on the domain. Defines the borders of the domain. Performs a feasibility analysis.
Domain characterization	Characterizes the domain considering the products and their relations. The focus is on the domain as a market.
Domain scoping	Works as the "variability central" of DA&E. Manages variation points.
Domain modeling	Captures requirements from an analysis of the products in the domain. Identifies commonality and variability in the requirements. Formalizes the requirements in use cases and in object-oriented analysis models.
Domain framework development	Synthesizes a framework to support the development of several products in the domain.

Domain definition is the first phase of DA&E. Subsequent phases can rely on the first one, but the first phase does not rely on anything to start. Domain definition collects and organizes information from external sources, like product descriptions, market surveys, interviews with experts, and so on. This information may already be available or can be generated specifically for DA&E. Domain definition also addresses issues pertaining to DA&E as a project of a firm. It defines the focus of the domain and performs a feasibility analysis. Finally, domain definition defines a domain vocabulary. As DA&E progresses, domain definition is revised as new information is collected on the domain. For instance, the domain vocabulary is updated each time a new term is used in the domain.

Domain framework development is the final phase of DA&E. It focuses on the design and development of the actual framework, which is then used to develop products. Domain framework development is final in the sense that it does not provide direct input to the other phases. However, it may influence the other phases. It may introduce new terms, thus requiring an update of the domain vocabulary. It may result in a better understanding of the domain itself, as well as the products and the cost of developing the software. This also impacts the other phases.

Domain characterization, domain scoping, and domain modeling are the three core phases of DA&E; this is where most decisions are made. The three phases are interdependent; each phase uses information from the other phases, processes it, and makes it available to the other phases for further refinement.

Domain characterization, domain scoping, and domain modeling set up a loop responsible for the market and technical analysis of the domain. More specifically, the loop identifies, describes, and evaluates the interesting products in the domain. Domain characterization provides the study of complementary and competing products in the market analysis, so that the products can be positioned properly in the market. Domain scoping manages the variability between the products. Domain modeling models the products from the perspective of requirements.

These three phases depend heavily on the concept of a variation point. A *variation point* is a source of variability within the domain. It is a common feature implemented in different ways in different products or in a single product. Domain characterization and domain modeling find the variation points. Domain characterization seeks them in the market; domain modeling identifies them through a model of the products and of the domain. Domain scoping organizes the variation points, creating a variability space on which choices and strategies can be visualized and evaluated.

The order in which we introduce these phases identifies dependencies among them that we found in most applications of Sherlock:

- Domain characterization is a natural starting point. We look around for what is available.
- Domain scoping is the "variability central" of a process based on the analysis of variability. Domain scoping is thus the fulcrum of DA&E.
- Domain modeling deepens the initial model of the domain with a unique formalization.

Figure 3.1 depicts the five phases of Sherlock. The following sections discuss the five phases considering the required activities in greater detail.

3.1.1 Domain definition

The domain definition phase collects information about the domain. The sources of information are currently available documents, which might

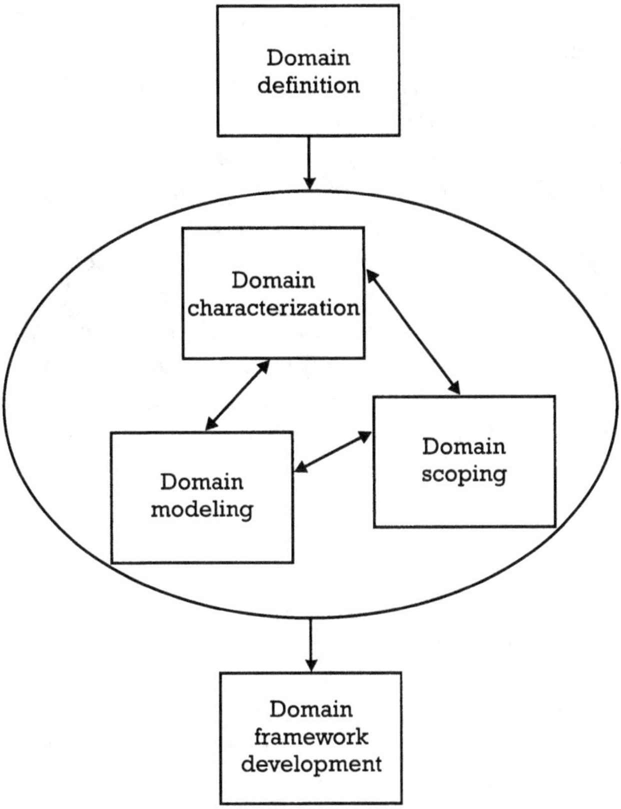

Figure 3.1 Sherlock's five phases.

have been previously produced for other purposes, and expertise from relevant people. Typical sources of information include interviews with clients, market surveys, reports from domain and market experts, product documentation, and project summaries.

Domain definition classifies the collected information into three categories: user's perspective, market/strategy, and information technology. The classified information feeds the subsequent phases of Sherlock.

DA&E's major interest is in products. Given a domain, products have a different relevance for it: Some are critical, others marginal. A product is critical to a domain if it is a best seller or if it has features that significantly characterize the domain. A product is marginal for a domain if it has only minimal features of the domain or if it plays a marginal role with respect to the other products in the domain. Time also determines the relevance of products. Old and new products are not weighted the same and older products are generally less relevant.

Domain definition classifies the relevance of the products into three domains: feasible, strategic, and current domain. The current domain contains the products with the highest relevance at the time of the analysis, and generally includes the firm's current products along with their direct competitors. The strategic domain includes products that are relevant on a wider time range. Strategic products planned for the future belong to the strategic domain. Finally, the feasible domain includes products that may be relevant but are unlikely to become strategic.

Domains usually represent market or technology sectors. The language used in the domain might not be widespread and it might be difficult to understand. Moreover, inconsistent or ambiguous use of the terms may lead to confusion. Domain definition generates a vocabulary containing the domain-specific and nondomain-specific terms that can generate misunderstandings.

Domain definition is done as preparation for what could be a complex and expensive DA&E. Due to its exploratory nature, the exact results of DA&E are not known when DA&E is started. Generally, costs and advantages are incurred with DA&E. Costs are seen in terms of the time and effort spent on the activities. Advantages are reaped with regard to the potential economies of scope resulting from the application of DA&E. Domain definition includes a feasibility analysis to determine whether it is useful and profitable to continue with DA&E.

3.1.2 Domain characterization

Domain characterization describes the domain from a market perspective. The focus is on the products and their competitive relations.

Domain characterization determines what products should be developed. It puts the products in a development plan, sequencing the products according to a coherent strategy line and finding the right market segments that will accept them. Domain characterization performs an analysis of the value of the products, as perceived by their users. The goal is to maximize the success of the products in the market.

Users base their decision of what product to buy not only on the internal features of the products, but also on how the products allow them to interact with other products and users. This diversification of the decision leads to the concepts of internal and external value. The internal value depends on features and quality. A user can evaluate the internal value of a product using the product alone. Domain characterization determines the internal value through the analysis of the features performed in domain modeling. On the other hand, the external value depends on the ability of the product to do the following:

- Interact with other products.
- Allow the user to interact with other users.
- Provide users with confidence that the product will grow and be supported in the future. This is equivalent to ensuring that interoperability of products and users will also be possible in the future.

The external value puts the user in a larger context: a network of users and products considered over a long time period. The external value depends significantly on the size of the network, both present and future. The term *installed base* refers to the size of the network. The term *network externalities* refers to the extra value perceived as a consequence of a large installed base.

A firm creates the internal value by working to produce a good product that performs the right functionality. A firm creates the external value by improving the present and future interoperability opportunities for the users of the product.

Domain characterization gives a summary of all the aspects of value for the products in the domain. It then analyzes network externalities in greater detail.

DA&E aims at the production of several coordinated products. Network externalities are relevant because the coordination of several products can achieve a higher impact on the market than separate, uncoordinated products. Domain characterization ensures that this coordination exists and is reflected in a strategy for product development. To do this, domain characterization considers all the products—those of the firm, those of the competitors, and those of the partners—and looks for possible interactions that generate network externalities.

The most relevant interactions occur through compatibility elements. Compatibility elements are elements that make two or more products compatible, such as data formats, APIs, protocols, and user interfaces. Through compatibility elements, products interact and connect their installed bases. For instance, if two products comply with the same data format, then users of one product can interoperate with users of the other product through the common data format; the installed bases are connected and network externalities occur.

3.1.3 Domain scoping

Variability permeates the whole DA&E and is the justification of the variety of products in the domain. Domain scoping is the phase that coordinates the analysis of variability.

Variability is a consequence of the variety of products within the domain. Products in a domain are similar in some ways and different in others. The similar aspects are the commonalities of the domain. Commonalities give a general idea of what the products do. Commonalities omit the details of specific products. The details are in the differences—or peculiarities—of the individual products.

Variation points are the link between commonalities and differences. A variation point is a feature of the commonalities that can be implemented in different ways. For instance, the currency is a typical variation point in the domain of accounting products: All products use a currency but the currency is different for each country. A variant is a specific implementation of a variation point. A variant represents a specific choice for the variability that the variation point represents. The variants of the "currency" variation point are the U.S. dollar, the British pound, the German mark, and so on.

Variation points and variants define a variability space. This is a multidimensional space where variation points are the dimensions and the variants are the possible values for the dimensions. A point in the variability space represents a unique choice of variants. Domain scoping is not responsible for finding the variation points. Domain characterization (from a market perspective) and domain modeling (from a technical perspective) find the variation points. Domain scoping is the "variability central" that supervises the quest for variation points and analyzes the variability space.

Domain scoping maps products onto the variability space. A product usually implements several variants for each variation point and thus looks like a "blotch" on the variability space (Figure 3.2).

A strategy is the idea or motivation behind the development of a product. Technically, a strategy is a choice of variants on the variability space. Strategies are similar to products. The difference is that products can include more than one strategy. A product typically starts from a strategy and then grows, incorporating other strategies. A product moves between strategies trying to achieve certain effects on the market. Several

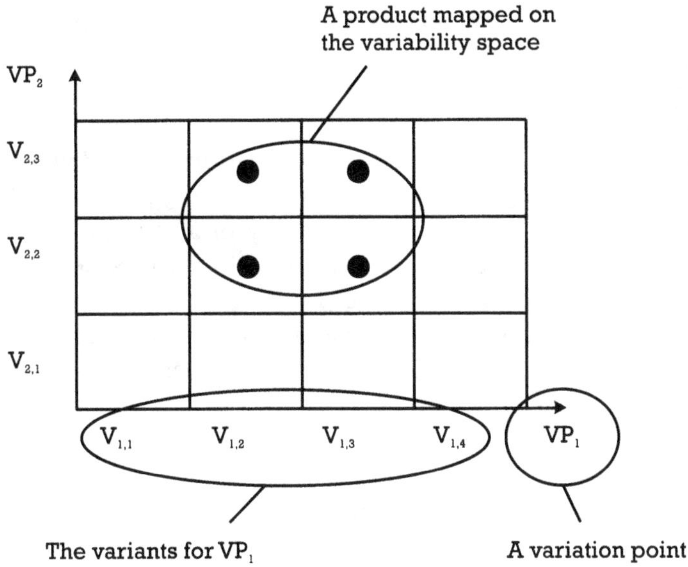

Figure 3.2 A product mapped on the variability space.

approaches exist to choose the strategies to implement. Sherlock uses the *move*, the *bridge*, and the *push*.

Domain scoping defines a set of attributes applicable to the variation points. An attribute is a visible feature of the product. Typically, attributes represent nonfunctional requirements such as performance and reliability. Different variants produce different values for the attributes. For instance, some variants that affect performance may produce a low, medium, or high value of performance. Strategies may define constraints on the attributes. A constraint limits the acceptable values of an attribute. For instance, a constraint may limit the value of "performance" to "at least medium," thus leaving out all variants that cannot satisfy this performance requirement.

The rationale for defining constraints in the strategies is that a strategy typically addresses the needs of a specific category of users—a market segment—and constraints effectively represent the (nonfunctional) requirements of those users.

3.1.4 Domain modeling

Domain modeling describes the domain as it emerges from the analysis of its products. For each product, this phase builds a product model formed by a use case model and an analysis model. The use case model describes the behavior of the product from the perspectives of users. The analysis model provides an object-oriented representation of the structure of the product.

In parallel with the construction of models for the individual products, domain modeling builds a model representing the whole domain. The domain model factors the commonality of all the products in the domain and points out, in a set of variation points, where peculiarities of the individual products can be plugged in.

The modeling process is iterative and aims at a broad understanding of the domain—starting from the domain's core products, the analysis grows to incorporate other products. The choice of the products to consider is an input from domain characterization.

3.1.5 Domain framework development

Domain framework development produces an object-oriented framework that can be used to build products within the domain. The framework comprises a set of reusable components. Combinations, extensions, and integration of the components generate the various behaviors that the domain requires. The framework also includes the following:

- Definition of the nature of the framework;
- Architecture of the framework;
- Documentation of the components in the framework;
- Catalog of the components in the framework;
- Guidelines to develop products using the framework.

The definition of the nature of the framework describes how the framework interacts with its context. The context is the environment with which the framework is integrated to build a product. Both the framework and its context make assumptions, which should not clash. Due to the variety of possible contexts, considering the assumptions and their consequences is a design priority.

The architecture is the "why" and "how" of the framework. The architecture has several projections, each describing the design of the framework from a different perspective. The projections cover the static and dynamic relations underlying the framework. All products developed using the framework need to comply with the architecture.

The documentation is a necessary part of any software. Domain framework development requires it to explicitly point out the relevance of documentation in reusable software.

The catalog of the components is a natural integration of the documentation that makes retrieval and reuse of the components easy.

The guidelines to develop products using the framework are the link between a potentially useful and a practically used framework. The guidelines give instructions and practical examples of how to build products through combination, extension, and integration of the components in the framework. Building a few sample products shows how reuse works and what kind of products can be expected from the framework.

3.2 Deliverables

So far we have presented Sherlock as a collection of phases. To develop a sound DA&E project, we also need to define its concrete and tangible output, that is, the *deliverables*. The deliverables are also instrumental to sound project coordination. Table 3.2 summarizes the deliverables of Sherlock.

The deliverables are discussed in the following chapters, along with the detailed presentation of the phases. The deliverables are also the substance of the examples and case studies in later chapters.

Table 3.2
Sherlock's Deliverables

Domain definition	DD1: Domain vocabulary	DD1 records the domain-specific terms and the nondomain-specific terms that might have ambiguous meaning. Acronyms, symbols, and any graphics used in the domain are included.
	DD2: Classified information on the domain	DD2 gathers classified information on the domain in a report according to a standard format.
	DD3: Definitions of feasible domain, strategic domain, and current domain	DD3 defines the feasible, strategic, and current domains. It also classifies available products into these domains.
	DD4: Feasibility analysis	DD4 shows whether it is profitable and useful to go on with DA&E. The document reports also the rationale of this decision.

Table 3.2 (continued)

Domain characterization	DC1: Diagrams of values (one for each real or potential product owned by the firm in the current domain)	DC1 identifies qualitatively for each product the value perceived by the users.
	DC2: Description of the installed bases	DC2 summarizes information on the installed base of the products: current number of users, sales, sales trends, etc.
	DC3: Tables of compatibility	DC3 evidences compatibility relations between products and with standards.
	DC4: User flows	DC4 shows how, in a context of alternative and complementary products, users can adopt and abandon the products. It also shows how and why these movements of users can take place.
	DC5: Market segments and pricing policy	DC5 divides the users into market segments and defines the pricing policy for each market segment.
	DC6: Plan of development of new products	DC6 schedules a plan for developing new products, as a result of the strategies analyzed in domain characterization and domain scoping.
Domain scoping	DS1: The variability space, the attributes of the products in the domain, and the related constraints	DS1 summarizes the variation points and the associated variants. It also defines attributes and constraints applicable to the strategies defined on the variability space.
	DS2: Definition of product strategies	DS2 presents the strategies as sets of variants selected for implementation.
	DS3: Identification of the product strategies to develop in the future	DS3 schedules the development of the strategies for the future.
Domain modeling	DM1: Product use case models	DM1 describes a use case model for each product in the domain. Use cases represent requirements in textual form.
	DM2: Product analysis models	DM2 describes an analysis model for each product in the domain. Analysis models are object-oriented representations of use cases.
	DM3: Domain use case model	DM3 describes a common use case model for the whole domain.
	DM4: Domain analysis model	DM4 describes a common domain analysis model for the whole domain.
	DM5: Traces between use cases and analysis classes	DM5 provides traceability links between use cases and analysis classes.

Table 3.2 (continued)

Domain framework development	DF1: Definition of the nature of the domain framework	DF1 defines if the framework is active or passive.
	DF2: Architecture of the domain framework	DF2 defines the architecture of the framework through a set of projections. The main projections are the package, class, and object projections. Other projections are possible. The architecture applies to all the products developed using the framework.
	DF3: Documentation of the components in the domain framework	DF3 documents the components in the framework.
	DF4: Browsable and searchable catalog of the components in the domain framework	DF4 provides means to classify the components in the framework for easy retrieval at a later stage.
	DF5: Guidelines to develop products using the framework	DF5 shows how products can be built from reuse, customization, and extension of the framework.

We cannot stress enough the value of a standard format for the deliverables. A standard format is fundamental for the coordination of many people. This includes the definition of the assignments and the monitoring of the work's progress.

3.3 The Webmetrics example

The following chapters discuss the phases of Sherlock. Several small examples accompany the theory. These examples usually illustrate specific concepts presented in the sections they belong to and are not carried out through the chapters. In addition to these, a major, homogeneous example is provided that spans all the chapters. This example evolves incrementally, following the guidelines of the theory.

The example originates from a software project developed by the authors. The project's name is *Webmetrics*. Webmetrics is a framework for software metrics measurement over the Internet. The core idea of Webmetrics is (1) to provide automatic measurement of software metrics and (2) to create a client–server architecture where the client does the actual metric measurements and the server collects and stores the measured data.

Webmetrics belongs to the domain of tools for software metric measurement. This domain is the fulcrum of the example.

3.4 Reading paths

Different people have different views of DA&E. The views reflect what each person does with DA&E and what problems he or she addresses with it. Generally, people working in different roles in software development have different views of DA&E.

Although generalizations are difficult, it is reasonable to assume that managers and developers will have different expectations from Sherlock. The book gives answers to the problems of both managers and developers. To make access to these answers easier, we propose two reading paths: Managers should focus on domain definition, characterization, and scoping, and developers should focus on domain scoping, modeling, and framework development. These reading paths apply to the theory as well as the included examples and case studies.

It is interesting to note that domain scoping—the "variability central" of Sherlock—is the point at which managers and developers meet. The connection is possible because most decision problems experienced by both managers and developers can be expressed in terms of variation points. This connection underlines the fact that there is a common language that any DA&E practitioner can speak.

The scope of this book is not limited to the concerns of software practitioners in the industry. Academic readers can also benefit from it. Sections of the book have actually been used as textbooks for a number of graduate and undergraduate courses. Here are a few suggestions: an undergraduate course on operations management in software engineering (with an emphasis on domain scoping), an undergraduate course on object-oriented analysis and design (with an emphasis on domain modeling and domain framework development), and a graduate course on software engineering economics (with an emphasis on domain characterization and domain scoping).

CHAPTER

4

Contents

Domain definition

Domain definition is like organizing a trip—we need to decide where we are going, what places we will visit, and how long the trip will take. We also need to put useful things into a suitcase, in case the trip requires them. These are all preliminary steps to ensure that we do not get lost during the trip.

Domain definition collects information from several sources. The sources can be documents, contributions from market and domain experts, and so on. Then, domain definition generates a vocabulary of the terms used within the domain, a systematization of the collected information, and the definition of the boundaries of the domain.

Domain definition addresses the risks of a DA&E trip. DA&E involves observation, planning, and implementation of the plan. The risks are that once we have implemented the plan we may discover that the conclusions of observation and planning are wrong. In other words, we may realize that things do not work after we have already done them. Sometimes things do not work because external, unforeseeable events occur. Other times there is a problem with the observation and planning at the early stages.

This kind of risk is nothing new to software engineers, who face the risks of undefined, blurred, or changing requirements every day. Fixing this can be extremely expensive. As many software engineers suggest, it is worthwhile to spend the time and money to do things right up front, so that you do not have to redo work later. Domain definition reduces the risk of starting with wrong, incomplete, or unreliable information. Domain definition digs into and systematizes information, so that later phases can use it with confidence. If errors are made in later phases, they are less likely to have come from bad information acquired in domain definition.

Software engineers sometimes also object that not everything can be determined up front, and it is necessary to check things over and over as we implement them. The iteration of Sherlock's phases and their application to the many products developed over a long time address this issue.

In domain definition we also decide whether to go on with DA&E. DA&E may terminate if we realize that it won't deliver its expected advantages. This can happen, for instance, if the domain is extremely unstable or the DA&E practitioner is uncertain about his or her business goals, or if the cost of reuse happens to be higher than the advantages. Letting DA&E determine whether or not it should terminate is not contradictory. Starting DA&E means only that we consider DA&E interesting and possibly useful. This is like saying that we like traveling. Nevertheless, we may not like this specific trip or we may discover that it is not the best time to start it. In this sense, domain definition is the feasibility analysis stage of DA&E.

Altogether, the goals of domain definition are (1) the identification and arrangement of useful information and (2) the decision of whether to go on with DA&E. This is reflected in the deliverables in greater detail and achieved through the following steps:

- *DD1:* Domain vocabulary;
- *DD2:* Classified information on the domain;
- *DD3:* Definitions of feasible domain, strategic domain, and current domain;
- *DD4:* Feasibility analysis.

The following sections discuss these topics in detail. The last section applies the presented concepts to the Webmetrics example.

4.1 Preparation of the domain vocabulary

The domain vocabulary includes the list of all significant terms and their definitions used in DA&E. The vocabulary helps the discussion between people who share information and participate in DA&E. The vocabulary is the first deliverable (DD1) of the domain definition phase.

The domain vocabulary is built incrementally during domain definition. The vocabulary usually gets started when a domain expert presents an overview of the domain. This is a good point at which to start tracking the terms and pinning down their exact meaning. Later, other people may enhance the dictionary with new entries and corrections. We cannot expect the initial vocabulary to be totally consistent, because the information that generated it is most likely inconsistent. Yet, through refinement, it is possible to obtain a consistent vocabulary while DA&E proceeds. At the end of domain definition, the vocabulary should be stable enough to be considered a reference document. As such, it is usually placed as the first document in the domain definition.

As the vocabulary is updated, the documents that use the terms of the vocabulary should also be updated to maintain consistency. This is not always easy or feasible, however—particularly for documents archived in paper format or documents from external sources (e.g., documents from standardization organizations).

The format of the vocabulary can be as simple as a definition list written as a stand-alone document or as complex as a database with cross references and version control. For complex domains, the vocabulary should definitely be in electronic form. Moreover, some editors and CASE (computer-aided software engineering) tools allow automatic checking of their documents against a given vocabulary.

4.2 Collection of information and identification of domain borders

Sound decisions come from good knowledge of the problem. The most valuable source of knowledge is the history of the firm—its products, its experience, and its strategic choices. People and written documents are the repository of this information. People know important information and can retrieve, adapt, and associate it in many different ways. Written documents are the long-term memory of the firm and survive despite personnel turnover. Altogether, it should be possible to retrieve information pertaining to the firm—history, mission, strategy, and so on—and pertaining to the projects—plans, reports, market studies, motivations, documentation, and so on.

Other sources of information may be inside or outside the firm and include the following:

- *Domain experts.* The domain expert has a global view of the domain in which the firm works and can identify and describe the products within the domain.
- *Market experts.* The market expert considers the domain from the business point of view. The market expert knows the position of the competing firms in the domain.

Domain definition collects information from all of these sources. During the collection, the scope of the analysis becomes clear. Eventually, it is possible to distinguish between what is and is not relevant.

Even within relevant information, some information is more relevant than others. To express this formally, we introduce three domains representing three levels of relevance—the feasible domain, the strategic domain, and the current domain. The domains are ordered according to a relationship of inclusion and increasing relevance, the feasible domain being the largest and least relevant and the current domain being the smallest and most relevant (Figure 4.1). Domain definition requires defining what information pertains to each domain. The deliverable that summarizes these definitions is DD3. Defining what is inside and what is outside each domain, we identify the borders of the domains. In our product-oriented approach, putting a product in a domain means putting all the information associated with that product in the domain.

The feasible domain comprises everything in which the DA&E practitioner might reasonably be interested. For software firms, the feasible domain could be the "software" domain, regardless of what kind of software the firm produces. If this is too general, the feasible domain can be restricted to some specific area of software, like "software for office automation." If this is too narrow it can be broadened to a larger domain, like

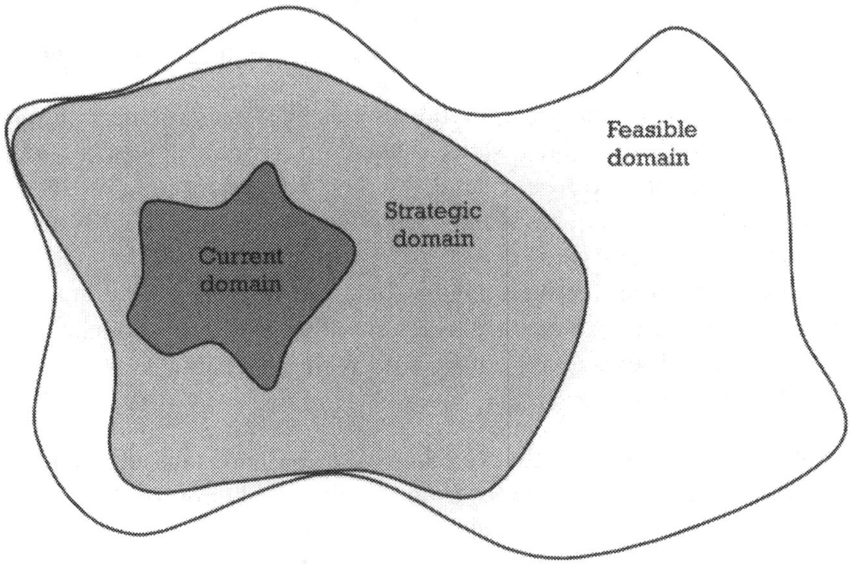

Figure 4.1 Feasible, strategic, and current domains.

"engineering systems." Generally the feasible domain is shrunk and stretched until it fits the firm's idea of what is feasible.

The strategic domain is the domain in which the firm is most interested. The firm's competitors and partners are also within this domain. The firm's definition of core business can define the strategic domain. For instance, the firm might state that it produces software for land mobile vehicles. The firm's current products are an easy way to exemplify the strategic domain. Yet, the firm's scope usually goes beyond the current products to consider future products. For instance, the firm might state that it is going to expand its business to software for underwater mobile vehicles. Hence, the strategic domain would also include these potential products.

The current domain comprises those products of the strategic domain that are more relevant at the time of analysis. These are usually the firm's current and under development products, and the direct competitors. A direct competitor is a product that competes with the firm's products on the same functionality; two WYSIWYG word processors, for example, would be direct competitors.

The strategic domain is a subset of the feasible domain. However, they look similar and are sometimes viewed as the same thing. Because a distinction between the two exists, we would like to spend a few minutes demonstrating that they are not the same by presenting two examples.

Example 1. Consider a large corporation producing telecommunication systems, satellites, automobiles, ships, consumer electronic appliances, and software. The software division is the reference firm performing DA&E. So far the software division has worked with the telecommunication systems and satellite divisions; these two areas are within its strategic domain. Yet because cooperation between divisions is possible, the software division includes the entire corporation's business within its feasible domain. For instance, the software division may work with the shipbuilding division. The shipbuilding area is feasible, though not strategic.

Example 2. Consider a firm that has changed its business radically over the years. The firm used to produce software for the specific area of office automation. At that time, the market was fast-growing and very competitive; now it is technologically and commercially stable. Restyling or innovating old products does not appear to be profitable, so the firm has changed its strategic domain to another area of software. The old strategic domain is still feasible, but it is not strategic at the present time.

This is not to say that old products cannot belong to the strategic domain. Old products can still be strategic—for example, because of their installed base, that is, their users. There are firms that do Y2K maintenance of old software, for example, which is considered nonstrategic even by its original producers.

Setting boundaries between the domains means leaving out some information. However, what is left out from an inner domain is not forgotten or removed from the analysis; it is merely moved to a less relevant domain. Relevance is not a true/false property, and this proves useful in the first stages of DA&E. This is the main justification for the introduction of the three domains: Domain practitioners more easily converge to a definition of three domains according to relevance.

The distinction between the three domains pertains only to domain definition. As a matter of fact, throughout this book the term *domain* refers only to the strategic domain, unless otherwise stated. The contribution of three domains is limited to this initial part of the DA&E, since the focus of the analysis is not known yet. The focus can be adjusted as a consequence of better observation. Later adjustments are actually frequent and need to be documented in the domain definition documents.

If the strategic domain is the focus of DA&E, the other two domains also play an important role. On one hand, the current domain shows where to start and where results from DA&E are most urgent. On the other hand, the feasible domain is not information we can forget about. It is a repository of information that reminds us what is feasible and may possibly become useful someday.

4.3 Classification of the collected information

Domain definition is the roots of the tree of DA&E. These roots get information from several sources and pass it on to the leaves—domain characterization, domain scoping, domain modeling, and domain framework development, as shown in Figure 4.2.

Because information is so important, it is worthwhile to organize it. The classification into three domains (feasible, strategic, and current) already worked in this direction. However, that classification was meant to rate the relevance of the information. We also need a classification that looks more at the content of the information. We do so in deliverable DD2.

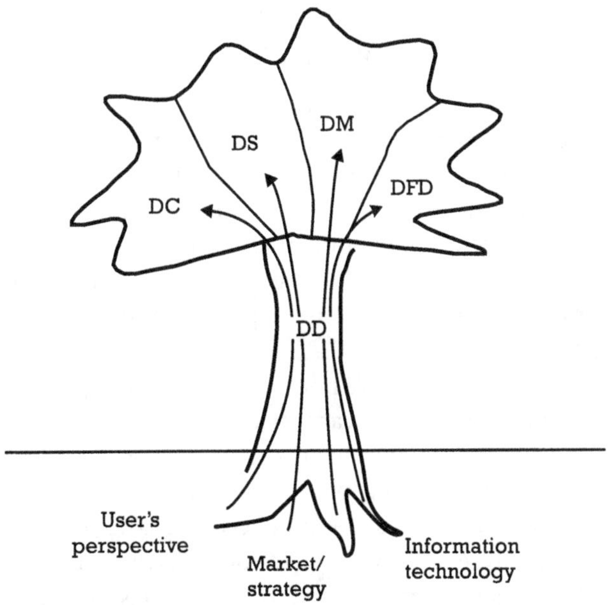

Figure 4.2 Domain definition feeding information to other phases.

Several classifications are possible and a simple classification by source of information could work. Here we propose a specific classification that may be useful as a guide for the DA&E practitioner to identify information for domain definition. Rather than searching blindly in all directions, the DA&E practitioner explores the categories of the chosen classification one by one and collects relevant information. This classification works as follows, according to three broad categories:

1. *User's perspective:* This category includes information on user demands and views of the domain.
2. *Market/strategy:* This category includes information regarding products, competitors, partners, alliances, shareholders, and so on.
3. *Information technology:* This category includes technical information that regards the software to be developed, under development, or planned.

DA&E practitioners should choose the most comfortable classification, and present the collected information according to it.

4.4 Why domain definition?

For a firm applying DA&E, domain definition incurs costs in terms of the effort required from staff and elapsed calendar time. It requires people with good experience and knowledge of the firm. Experienced managers are appropriate, because they know the firm's history and products. It requires people that know the domain and the market—the domain and market experts, who may be inside the firm or hired from the outside. It requires knowledgeable and responsible people to come up with the right decision.

DD4 is the feasibility analysis phase of DA&E. In this phase, we determine if the benefits of DA&E can offset its costs and decide whether DA&E should continue. While this is the last decision of domain definition, this delicate issue should pervade the whole phase. If the DA&E practitioner decides to invest some time to find a piece of information on the domain, to analyze a product, or to formalize a part of the terminology, then this time should be directed to the subjects that give better substance to the decisions of the feasibility analysis.

The described approach is meant to focus the DA&E practitioner on critical information. What "critical" means, however, depends on the specific situation. The DA&E practitioner may need a survey of the available products (e.g., to develop an alternative, innovative technology), in which case the criticality is in the broadness of the analysis. The DA&E practitioner may need a deep understanding of the competitors (e.g., to regain a leading position), in which case the criticality is in the depth of the analysis of competitors. Of course, other approaches to criticality exist. In this sense, finding the right focus for the feasibility analysis leads to finding the right focus for the whole DA&E.

Whatever the results of the feasibility analysis, domain definition has a value. If domain definition decides that DA&E should continue, its value is clear: Domain definition is a prerequisite of DA&E. DA&E improves the production of products, and products deliver value to the users and profits to the firm. That is, domain definition is the first step in a process that the firm has assessed to be profitable. Domain definition also has a value because it provides a sound and organized basis for a process—DA&E—which requires us to explore the complexity of a domain and can thus be hard to organize.

If domain definition decides that it is not worthwhile to go on with DA&E, then its value is that the firm has not wasted money and time in useless activities. The consequences are similar to a feasibility analysis in traditional product development when the response is negative. The firm gains a better knowledge of its domain, but does not undertake a domain-based approach to software development. The value of such knowledge is still reasonable outside the scope of DA&E. A typical benefit is that of reaping a deeper understanding of the competitors. This understanding is generally useful (e.g., for product positioning and marketing) even if DA&E is not adopted as the underlying approach to product development.

4.5 The Webmetrics example for domain definition

4.5.1 DD1: Domain vocabulary

The domain vocabulary is comprised of frequently used terms in the area of programming languages, compilation, and metrics analysis, plus some terms related to networking.

Backus-Naur form (BNF). Popular technique to formally specify languages, particularly programming languages.

Client. The client side of a client–server architecture.

Client–server architecture. A conceptual and physical scheme involving two entities—the client and the server—that perform different tasks. The client generates requests to the server, and the server generates responses to the requests. The server is permanently running and waiting for incoming requests.

Compilation. The execution of a compiler on source code.

Compiler. A program converting a source code into an executable code or into an intermediate code suitable for later conversion into an executable code. A parser is an important part of the compiler.

Executable code. Code that can be run on a hardware/software platform.

Executable file. See *executable code.* Refers specifically to the physical storage of executable code.

Integrated Development Environment. A tool that supports software development by offering the user a homogeneous and integrated interface.

Interpretation. The process that analyzes and executes a source file directly, without the intermediate production of executable code from the source file.

Metric. A numeric value representing some property of the subject to which the metric is applied. The term refers to both the specific value for a given subject and to the generic formula or algorithm to calculate that value.

Metric measurement. The application of a metric (in the sense of formula/algorithm) to a subject of measurement.

Parser. A program that performs parsing.

Parsing. The process of checking the compliance of a source code to a programming language. A parser may generate a data structure, such as a syntax tree, to illustrate the compliance and to allow further processing, for example, for the generation of executable code.

Programming language. A language used to instruct computers to perform operations. A programming language has a formal specification (usually in BNF) that shows how instructions must be stated.

Server. The server side of a client–server architecture.

Source code. A text written according to a programming language. Source code specifies the behavior of a piece of software. Source code usually requires compilation or interpretation to be executed.

Source file. See *source code.* Refers specifically to the physical storage of source code.

4.5.2 DD2: Classified information on the domain

A classification by source of information is adopted here. We discuss the history of the firm, the information from the domain experts, and the information from the market experts.

History of the firm

The reference firms for Webmetrics are the SERN lab and the LIPS lab.

Information on the SERN lab, ENEL, University of Calgary can be found at its Web site: http://www.sern.enel.ucalgary.ca. A brief description follows:

- *Current research projects:* Applying statistics to software engineering, comparative metrics in procedure-oriented and object-oriented programming, Pescarenico (an object-oriented tool set based on use cases and activity based on costs to model, improve, and reengineer the business process of a firm), process-based approach to solve the Y2K bug, programming real-time embedded applications, real-time digital process control for biomedical applications, Sherlock (a system to identify reusable components within an application domain), the design and development of the next-generation reuse libraries, development of empirical models for the impact of software reuse on quality and productivity, Webmetrics (a tool to collect software engineering data over the Internet).

Information on the LIPS lab, DIST, Università di Genova can be found at its Web site: http://lips.dist.unige.it/. A brief description follows:

- Research activity on the software production process (modeling, reengineering, performance, quality), software reuse (domain analysis, cost/benefit analysis, reuse-oriented production processes), software measurements (assessments, experimental protocols, post-measurement analysis), Internet for information sharing;

- Consulting on DA&E, on the development of software component libraries and of site-specific software metrics, and on technology transfer;
- Training and education on software engineering, computer architectures, operating systems, and computer networks;
- Development of parsers, remote metrics servers (Webmetrics), process modeling tools.

Information from domain experts

The domain experts have provided a list of popular programming languages and a list of metrics that can provide a good understanding of relevant attributes of software (especially regarding quality of software). This information comes from existing literature on software metrics, from existing software metrics tools, and from other tools for compilation and parsing.

The list of the languages is as follows: C, C++, Java, Cobol, RPG, Pascal, Lisp, BASIC, Smalltalk, Ada, and Fortran.

The list of the software metrics is as follows: lines of code, McCabe, Halstead, depth of inheritance, fan in, fan out, reuse level, reuse frequency, and reuse density.

The domain experts have also provided information on formal specification of programming languages through the BNF, as well as on techniques and tools that support them.

Information from market experts

The market experts have described the market history, current market trends, and the available products in the market.

The software market has a history of commercial applications mainly written in Cobol and RPG. These applications are legacy software programs still in use today. It is estimated that 70% of the code in use today is written in Cobol or RPG. The legacy code is maintained as new parts are added and old code is updated. Software metrics play an important role in this because they allow the quality of the code to be assessed at each stage of the maintenance.

The current market trends are in favor of object-oriented programming languages, tools, and methodologies. C++ and Java are widely used and are quickly evolving. C++ is the most popular object-oriented programming language at the industrial level. Years of experience and legacy libraries make this language a safe choice for software projects. Java is gaining significant momentum due to the commitment and support of several firms. Where object-oriented technologies are not possible (typically in embedded systems where restrictions on memory size and CPU power are strong), the C language is the standard solution. Many software firms using C++ and Java also use software metrics to assess the quality of their products.

The available products include the following (fake names are used for all products but Webmetrics):

- *Webmetrics:* the metrics system under development and discussed in this DA&E project;
- *FortranMetric:* software metrics tool for Fortran;
- *PascalMetric:* software metrics tool for Pascal;
- *CMetric:* software metrics tool for C;
- *MetricBuilder:* a tool that allows to define and apply custom metrics;
- *MeasureX:* software metrics tool for C, C++;
- *MeasureJava:* tool applying traditional and object-oriented metrics to Java.

FortranMetric, PascalMetric, and CMetric make up a homogeneous suite of products. They are also made by the same firm. All other products are made by different firms.

The products focus mainly on modern programming languages—specifically object-oriented programming languages—in accordance with the current market trends. Still, due to the large installed base of Cobol and RPG programs, software metrics tools for these languages address the needs of a large market and thus appear to be potentially profitable.

Firm's strategy

The SERN lab and the LIPS lab constitute the reference firm for which the strategy is considered.

On the industrial side, the strategy considers as crucial the production of tools that are useful to real software firms. In the case under analysis, these tools mean tools for software metrics measurement.

On the research side, the strategy aims at the identification of the correlation between the several attributes involved in the software production process, such as size, productivity, quality, and so on. The correlation would allow predicting some unknown attributes (especially quality) from other known attributes. The use of software metrics extracts those attributes that are measurable directly from the source code. The research strategy also serves the goal of the industrial strategy.

4.5.3 DD3: Definition of feasible domain, strategic domain, and current domain

Figure 4.3 shows the domains for Webmetrics. The feasible domain comprises all CASE tools, whereas the strategic domain comprises tools for software metrics measurement. All of Webmetrics' competitors are in this domain.

The current domain comprises the tools for software metrics measurement over the Internet. Webmetrics and its possible evolutions are within this domain. None of the competitors are currently in this domain since they do not support transfer of metrics over the Internet. If Webmetrics achieves a significant momentum, it is expected that other products will follow its approach.

4.5.4 DD4: Feasibility analysis

The Webmetrics project is envisioned as a modular, expandable system. The development of a prototype has demonstrated the technical

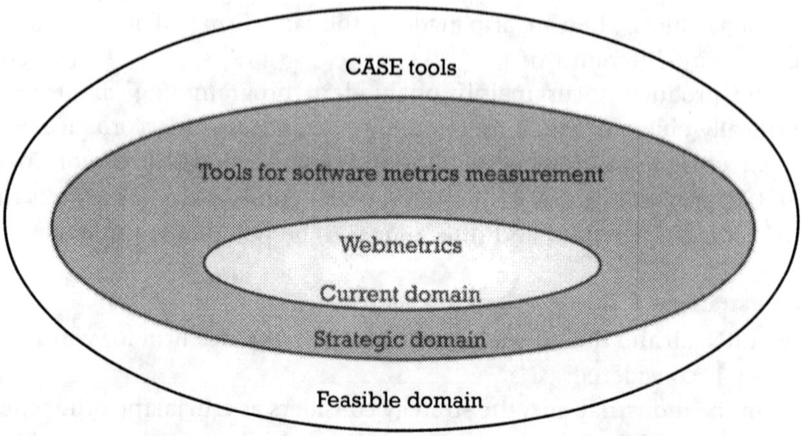

Figure 4.3 Feasible, strategic, and current domains for the Webmetrics DA&E project.

feasibility of a metrics system based on a client–server architecture. The market analysis suggests that Webmetrics would be an innovative product.

Webmetrics' modules are similar in structure: The parsers and the metrics extractors have a common base. Some common parts are widely documented in traditional computer science literature. Exploiting commonalities is a strong requisite for the successful development of the project. DA&E effectively achieves exploitation of commonalities. As a result, the feasibility analysis has assessed that DA&E should continue and pervade the entire Webmetrics development process.

4.5.5 Logging the evolution of domain definition

Table 4.1 summarizes the development efforts for this phase.

Table 4.1
The Evolution of Domain Definition

Author	Date	Action	Effort
Sherlock's authors	1998-1-21/22/23	Technical analysis of the products, definition of terms	20 man-hours
Sherlock's authors	1998-1-21	Market analysis of the products, definition of terms	12 man-hours
Sherlock's authors	1998-12-17/18/19	Revision of the market analysis, revision of the vocabulary	7 man-hours
Sherlock's authors	1999-7-26	Revision of the domain vocabulary	3 man-hours

CHAPTER

5

Contents

Domain characterization

Domain characterization is the observation of a domain and the planning of a strategy for the development of products within that domain. The observation is done with regard to the analysis of the products and firms in the domain, the pools of users, and the competitive or coordinating relations between these. The planning refers to the definition of a strategy that will produce profitable products. The goal can be to establish, take over, or maintain a market position in the domain. Any firm can benefit from domain characterization, but those that develop numerous products within DA&E have more variables to control, and can thus achieve better results.

5.1 Product value

In software markets characterized by mass production and competition, one hard task faced by software firms is to gain and maintain clients and users.

The software market exhibits low marginal costs of production: The production of an additional copy of a piece of software is practically null. Printing a CD and a manual is inexpensive, and distributing software through the Internet is even less expensive. In any case, the marginal costs of production are negligible with respect to sale prices. Price competition is possible. However, rather than offering low prices, software firms prefer to offer high value through newer, better products. This attitude is compliant with the rapid growth of the software market, which offers room for innovation, pervades new application areas, and constantly attracts new users.

Sherlock considers value to be the basis of domain characterization. The reason for this is that conceptual tools are available that understand the mechanisms of the market that derive from value. Once these mechanisms are known, the possibilities for manipulation are extremely generous. In Sherlock, the relevance of price competition is small. However, a section on pricing policies is included.

Sherlock breaks down the value of products at different levels (Figure 5.1). At the highest level, value is decomposed into internal and external types of value.

The internal value is what a user would perceive using the product on its own, regardless of other users, products, or environments. The internal value depends on the features and quality of the product. Features express "what" the product can do; quality expresses "how" the product performs, in terms of quality attributes to which the users are sensitive. For instance, the features of a word processor are the ability to

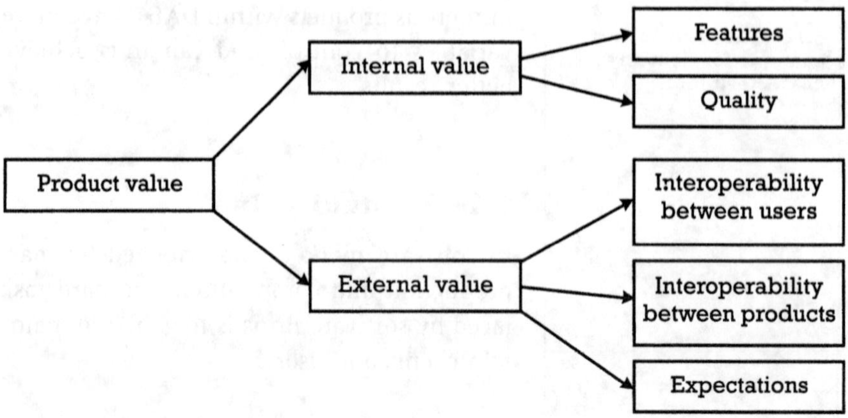

Figure 5.1 Value breakdown.

handle text, graphics, and styles, to employ different layouts, and to manage document versions. Its quality is, for instance, its user-friendliness, speed, and reliability.

The external value is what a user perceives from interacting with other users, products, and environments through the use of the considered product. The external value of a word processor is, for instance, the user's capability to share documents with other users. The external value is further decomposable into three aspects:

1. *Interoperability between users.* Users need to exchange information. They attribute higher value to products that allow them to do so easily. For instance, if the sales department of a manufacturing firm has an order in its database, the order has more value if it is passed on to the manufacturing department than if it just stays in the sales department for invoicing purposes. Generally, interoperability involves exchange or sharing of information. Users appreciate exchanging information generated through the use of the product. Also, users appreciate sharing information with other users when they learn to use the product. New users attribute higher value to products used by expert users. Existing knowledge makes the learning process more gradual and appealing to new users.

2. *Interoperability between products.* Products interoperate with each other exchanging information through data files, networks, APIs, and so on. In many cases, interoperability between products is simply a technical means to achieve interoperability between users. For instance, two users who have the same kind of word processor on their computers can interoperate because the word processors interoperate at file level. In other cases, interoperability between products generates a value of its own. This is the case for products that, through interaction, produce more complex "aggregate" products—or systems—that have a higher value to the users. For instance, spreadsheets interacting with statistical analysis tools produce a higher value than the individual products alone. The same holds for the various kinds of plug-ins and add-ons that can be integrated into a given software product. Generally, interoperability between products is an appreciated feature of modular and scalable software systems.

3. *Expectations about the future of the product.* Expectations reflect how users perceive the future of a product. A favorable perception makes the product more appealing. Expectations include the types of value we have discussed (internal value and interoperability), but they are considered in a future perspective. At a product level, users would not buy a product that is likely to be dismissed in a short time and, on the contrary, may be interested in a product for which the producing firm has made a strong commitment. At a market level, users also consider how the market will evolve—either as a monopoly or as a competing market—and adjust the value of products according to their feelings and preferences.

The distinction between internal and external value is not sharp. There is a gray area between the two. For instance, the localization of products for different languages affects both internal and external value. On one hand, it improves the usability (internal value) of the product, because the user does not need a dictionary to use the product. On the other hand, it increases the interoperability opportunities (external value) between international users.

Sometimes the external value of a product is dominant over the internal one. As a matter of fact, many products exist only because of their external value. All the telecommunication products fit this description, because their main purpose is to provide interoperability.

The value analysis proposed in this section is based on a hierarchical decomposition. This decomposition is also the base of the hedonic approach. The hedonic approach manages multivariable attributes or attributes decomposable into elementary attributes, much like in the presented discussion. There are remarkable examples of applications of the hedonic models, also in the software field, for the analysis of costs [1] and prices [2, 3]. References [1–3] give in-depth reviews of the approach.

5.2 Installed bases and network externalities

As mentioned in the discussion about external value, users are concerned about other users using the same products as they. For them, more users means more chances of interoperability. Software manufacturers are very interested in designing their products so that users' perception of value works to their advantage. There are mechanisms, based on compatibility and coordination, that do the job. Before introducing them, we turn our focus again to the principles of external value by presenting two concepts: installed base and network externalities.

The installed base of a product is the pool of users using the product. For instance, the pool of users who use Netscape Communicator is the installed base of Netscape Communicator. The installed base can be considered to be a formal definition of the popularity of a product. Sometimes the term *installed base* refers to the size of such a pool, rather than to the pool of users. In this case, the installed base counts the number of users.

Users are usually aware of the popularity of a product through surveys published in technical literature or through direct communication with other users. Products with large installed bases give users the perspective of higher interoperability. As we discussed in the product value section, users assign a higher external value to products that offer higher interoperability.

Network externalities is the term used to express the increased value of a product as a result of its installed base. The *network* is the effect achieved when the users of an installed based are able to interoperate. Network externalities are the underlying principle of the external value. Network externalities work as a positive feedback to the sales of a product. The rationale for this is explained in the following scenario: A product has a given installed base; the installed base improves the external value of the product; users perceive this value and become more prone to purchase the product; purchases mean new users; the new users combine with the previous ones; the resulting situation is similar to the initial one, but the installed base has increased; as a consequence, the process continues to occur over and over again. With each iteration the number of new users gradually decreases and, in the end, the installed base stabilizes, reaching saturation.

Even at this early stage of discussion, it is clear that the installed bases of products within a given domain must be considered together. The motivation is that the installed base of a product is not absolute; rather it is relative to the installed bases of the other products. Moreover, interoperability between products in a domain is possible and very likely. All of the previous definitions, such as "users consider the installed base of a product," should be restated in a relative, domain-based form, such as "users consider the installed base of a product with respect to the installed base of the other products in the domain." Also, network externalities cross the installed bases of several products and hold steady at the domain level.

Installed bases and network externalities pose new questions and uncover a complexity of domains that was not evident before. Installed bases and network externalities set the path for a good characterization of the domain from a market perspective. For now, we will take advantage of the discussion on installed bases: We propose to use a table to summarize the information on the installed bases in the domain under analysis. The table should show the installed base for each product within the domain. Since expectations about the future are also important, future installed bases should also be estimated. The estimation may require information about current sales and sales trend.

Table 5.1 exemplifies the proposed table. It shows a case with four products, namely, A, B, C, and D. The considered data are installed base, current sales, sales trend, and expected total sales at a certain time line in the future. This table alone is a good basis for debate. Assuming that the four products are competitors, from the installed base data, we can infer that B is the market leader, while the others are followers. Moreover, one of the followers, A, is the leader in current sales, boasting a current sales figure 20 times higher than the market leader's. An analysis on the expected total sale shows that eventually A and B will be competing for the leading position.

Variations on Table 5.1 could include more details, like the sales per geographic area or per distribution channel. Instead of the sales trend, a whole database could be built to hold historic data and to extrapolate future data. Specialized companies do surveys and keep updated databases containing information like this. When necessary, the information can be obtained from these companies.

Although this will be justified later, we strongly recommend considering different versions of a product as separate products.

Table 5.1
Sample Description of Installed Bases and Sales

	Installed Base	Current Sales	Sales Trend	Expected Total Sales
A	100,000	2,000/week	Increasing	800,000
B	700,000	100/week	Stable	800,000
C	0	100/week	Increasing	400,000
D	100,000	0/week	Stable	100,000

When analyzing sales data, keep in mind that "buying" and "owning" a product do not necessarily mean "using" it. Users may dismiss products when they are no longer useful or when there is a better replacement for them. Unlike purchases, data on dismissals are hardly available. When sales are not a trustworthy indicator, the installed bases should be measured or estimated by other means. A survey with the users might work. For some products it is possible to inquire about the products directly, without bothering the user. This is the case, for instance, with Web servers, which provide their identity in reply to a specific request. Another way is to prompt users to voluntarily signal that they are still using a product. Offering free benefits related to the product (such as mailing lists, free updates, new documentation) can work. A user using the benefit is probably still using the product.

5.3 Compatibility

The installed bases of products within a domain are connected. Conceptually, the users of all domain products make up a community with similar interests, goals, and needs. Practically, there is a technical device that explicitly connects the installed bases of different products: compatibility. Compatibility is the means through which interoperability between users and products is possible.

Compatibility is manifold and users can perceive of products as being compatible in many ways. Some examples of compatibility follow:

- *Compatibility of data formats.* Data formats are the specifications of the real data that programs read, write, and manipulate. For instance, HTML is the data format for HTML documents. Data are usually stored on physical memory devices or sent through networks.
- *Compatibility of APIs and of protocols.* APIs and protocols are agreements for communication between programs or parts of programs. For instance, programs that are extended with new features at runtime or through compilation offer APIs to specify how these extensions should be written. This is the case for plug-ins for Netscape Communicator, for modules for the Perl language and the Apache Web server, and for OLE objects in Microsoft applications. Protocols are much like APIs but are usually related to communication

through distinctly running entities, possibly at the peer level. For instance, network communication occurs though protocols. APIs and protocols involve actions—execution of code—by the participants, but may also involve the exchange of data specified according to some data format.

- *Compatibility of user interfaces (UIs).* UIs involve the interaction between a program and a user. The UIs of two programs are compatible if a user interacts with them in the same way. For instance, a new version of a product is UI compatible with an older version if a user can use the new one with the same kind of interaction that was possible with the old one. Compatibility of UIs is especially relevant for users who learn to use a new product. In this sense, the skills to use a product are assets, much like data. User interfaces are complex entities. An effective way to analyze them is to break them down into simpler elements such as the keyboard commands, the menu organization, the navigational paths through the documents, and so on. Simple UI elements include the keyboard sequences to cut, copy, and paste selected items, or the basic navigational buttons in a Web browser.

This list of compatibility categories is just a snapshot of what could happen in real domains. DA&E practitioners should determine whether there are other categories within their domain or if there is the need to organize the ones given above differently.

A compatibility element is an instance of one of the compatibility categories. For instance, a compatibility element is a specific data format, API, protocol, UI element, and so on. Programs usually have several compatibility elements for each of the categories.

Two entities are responsible for specifying compatibility elements: firms and standards organizations. Firms usually propose their own compatibility elements and have, from a technological and market viewpoint, full control over them. Sometimes firms coordinate with other firms with which they share control of the compatibility elements. Standards organizations are independent institutions, sometimes supported by federal governments or at the international level. Examples are ANSI, IEEE, and so on. Standards organizations may also originate as consortia between firms.

The Word document format, the OLE API, and the look-and-feel of Windows are examples of compatibility elements specified by a firm.

HTML, Common Object Request Broker Architecture (CORBA), and Common Desktop Environment are examples of compatibility elements specified by standardization organizations.

A product's native data format is a data format that is explicitly designed to be used with the product. Firms design and release products and their native data formats together. For example, Microsoft PowerPoint's native data format is the "ppt" format. The use of a product's native data format is not limited to that product: Other products can use it, although the format is not native for them. Similar definitions exist for native APIs, native protocols, and native UIs.

5.4 Connecting installed bases

Installed bases look simple. However, they can be tricky to manage. To explain this, let us consider the installed base of the phone system. The installed base includes all the users of regular phones. This definition is safe because all users of regular phones form a homogeneous network and are able to call each other and obtain the same service. Now we add a level of complexity by adding users of cellular phones to the installed base. Cellular phone users can call regular phones and can call other cell phones but enjoy different services and have limitations, such as geographical and roaming limitations, on the access to the phone network. The installed base can also be extended to fax users, although it is not clear if a fax is the same as a phone or a complementary product. To make the picture even fuzzier, the installed bases of ISDN, ATM, and voice communication systems through the Internet can join the considered installed base.

Limiting the analysis to regular phones keeps the example simple. However, even in this case, a manufacturer of a specific phone model may argue that the installed base of all the phones in the world is not very useful; it would be better to consider the installed base of the specific market segment or geographic area where the manufacturer operates.

Installed bases are connectable. If we have the installed bases of the single products, we can connect them to define more complex installed bases, such as bases for categories and aggregations of products. Thus, by connecting the installed bases of the various phone models, we obtain the installed bases of the product line of phones for a certain manufacturer, of the phones in a certain geographic area, of a specific market segment of phones, of all the phones in the world, and so on.

Sherlock's analysis focuses on the finest detail: installed bases at the level of individual products. Then, when necessary, the analysis can move to aggregates of installed bases, like the installed base of a category of products.

Interoperability between installed bases is possible through compatibility elements. For example, the installed base of word processor A can communicate with the installed base of word processor B because both products access a common data format X. Generally a multitude of products and compatibility elements are present in a domain. To make the analysis systematic and manageable, we put products and compatibility elements in a table and match them against each other.

As an example, we consider a domain containing four products: A, B, C, and D. The products are databases and store data on storage memory according to some data formats. The data formats are the following: Format1, Format2, Format3, Format4, and FormatStd. Format1 is A's native data format, Format2 is B's native data format, Format3 is C's native data format, and Format4 is D's native data format. FormatStd is a standard data format, defined, for example, by a standards organization.

We build the table incrementally. Table 5.2 shows the relationship between the products and their native formats. We put "I/O" at the intersections of products and data formats. I/O means "input and output;" that is, reading and writing of data are possible. The intersection, for instance, between A and Format1 specifies that A can read and write data written according to Format1. In the domain of databases it is reasonable for each product to read and write data in its own native data format. When needed, "I" specifies that only reading is possible, and "O" specifies that only writing is possible. Often software products refer to "input" and "output" as "import" and "export."

We can go forward in the analysis to determine the compatibility between a product and other products' native formats (Table 5.3). Focusing on one product at a time, we have the following situation:

Table 5.2
Products and Their Native Formats

	Format1	**Format2**	**Format3**	**Format4**	**FormatStd**
A	I/O	—	—	—	—
B	—	I/O	—	—	—
C	—	—	I/O	—	—
D	—	—	—	I/O	—

Table 5.3
Compatibility of Products With Other Products' Native Formats

	Format1	Format2	Format3	Format4	FormatStd
A	I/O	I	—	—	—
B	—	I/O	—	—	—
C	I/O	I/O	I/O	I/O	—
D	—	I	O	I/O	—

- Product A accepts Format2 as input, as shown by the "I" at the intersection of the product and the data format.
- Product B does not handle any native data format of other products.
- Product C can read and write any native data format of the other products, as shown by the "I/O" at C's intersections with all the data formats.

Product D can read Format2 and can write data in Format3, as shown by the "I" at the intersection between D and Format2 and by the "O" at the intersection between D and Format 3.

To complete the example, we put compatibility relations between the products and FormatStd. All products are I/O compatible with this standard as shown in Table 5.4. We can move through this table to determine which products are interoperable. Using a product, a user usually stores data in one format but later, using another product, the user may need to move data to another format. Checking the compatibility table, it is possible to determine the compatibility paths between the products. In the depicted example, there is at least one way for all the products to communicate: through FormatStd. All products support FormatStd for both reading and writing, so this standard is a good candidate for storing data when high interoperability between products is necessary. On the other hand, compatibility paths through native formats can have better performance or exploit product-specific features.

We can construct other compatibility tables like the ones presented so far, considering other aspects of compatibility, such as APIs, protocols, and UIs. These tables are similar, yet not identical to the ones for compatibility of data format. Compatibility of data formats can be for reading, writing, or both. This may be meaningless, for instance, for compatibility of APIs. There is no natural concept of reading or writing in APIs—rather, there is a general idea of "compliance." For compatibility items other than data format, a simple "tick" mark at the product–compatibility element

Table 5.4
All Compatibility Relations, Including Compatibility With Standards

	Format1	Format2	Format3	Format4	FormatStd
A	I/O	I	—	—	I/O
B	—	I/O	—	—	I/O
C	I/O	I/O	I/O	I/O	I/O
D	—	I	O	I/O	I/O

intersection in the compatibility table may be sufficient. When needed, DA&E practitioners can create a notation that fits the needs of the situation at hand. For instance, analyzing compatibility with the HTTP protocol, we may want to emphasize the role—client or server— the product plays with respect to the protocol. For a scenario involving two servers and two clients, we can produce Table 5.5. Clearly, any two servers or any two clients are compatible as alternative products. On the other hand, servers and clients are compatible as complementary products.

The last issue about compatibility tables concerns management of multiple versions of compatibility elements. Suppose we have a text editor released in two versions: Editor 1.0 and Editor 2.0. The second version is more recent and has more features than the previous one. Data created using the text editor are stored according to a data format, which was initially released as version 1.0 and later released as version 2.0 to accommodate the new features. Table 5.6 depicts the relationship between the two versions of the product and the two versions of the data format.

Editor 1.0 is I/O compatible with Text 1.0 and Editor 2.0 is I/O compatible with Text 2.0. Editor 1.0 is not compatible with Text 2.0, because this format is more recent and contains features not supported in Editor 1.0. Editor 2.0 is "input" compatible with Text 1.0. This means that if we have a document created using Editor 1.0, we can load it from Editor 2.0, but we cannot save it in any format other than Text 2.0.

Table 5.5
Different Roles in Compatibility

	HTTP
AServer	Server
AnotherServer	Server
AClient	Client
AnotherClient	Client

Table 5.6
Compatibility Between Different Versions

	Text 1.0	Text 2.0
Editor 1.0	I/O	—
Editor 2.0	I	I/O

Sometimes the issue of version compatibility is very complicated. Interesting cases have surfaced with the different versions of the HTTP protocol. The definitions of the protocol apparently left an ambiguity as to how the version numbers should be interpreted and used. The ambiguity generated interoperability problems between products complying with the protocol. An Internet Request for Comment [4] eventually clarified the interpretation. This Request for Comment accounted for all the misinterpretations and problems that had occurred.

5.4.1 Object-oriented representation of compatibility

The tables used to describe compatibility can be represented through object-oriented diagrams. The information the diagrams convey is the same and many users prefer to see information in object-oriented form. Generally, the object-oriented representation is more compact, and possibly easier to read, than a table when the table is sparse—that is, contains many empty intersections.

We represent both products and compatibility elements as objects. The stereotype for product objects is *product*; the stereotype for compatibility elements reflects the type of the compatibility element (*data format, API, protocol, UI,* and so on). The intersections between products and compatibility elements in the table become links between objects in the diagram. For example, Table 5.4, presented in the previous section, is converted into the diagram shown in Figure 5.2.

The links in Figure 5.2 are arrows. The direction of an arrow shows in which direction—input or output—the compatibility holds. For instance, the arrow from Format2 to A shows that A can import Format2. On the other hand, the bidirectional arrow between A and Format1 shows an input/output relationship between A and Format1. Arrows are a suitable short notation to represent the input/output or import/export relationships. Note, however, that they may not be applicable to other kinds of compatibility elements. In these cases it is necessary to specify explicitly the compatibility relation each link represents. Figure 5.3 shows the object-oriented representation for Table 5.5 from the previous section.

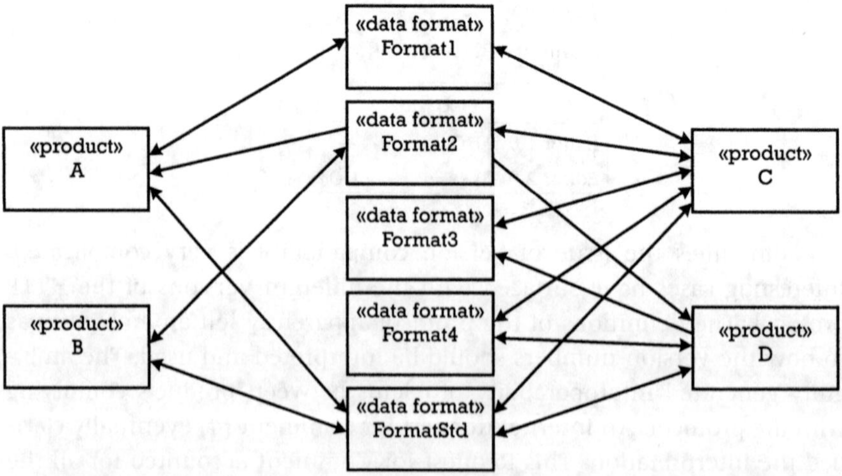

Figure 5.2 Object-oriented compatibility diagram.

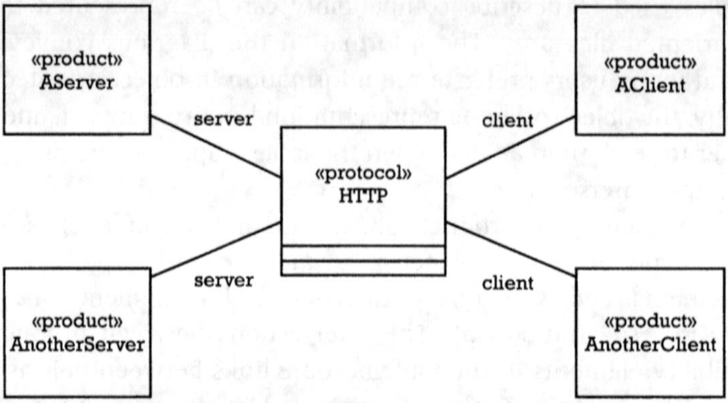

Figure 5.3 Explicit compatibility relations on links.

5.5 Standards

Standards are widely accepted compatibility elements. There are two kinds of standards:

1. De jure standards, which are compatibility elements defined by a standardization organization;

2. De facto standards, which are compatibility elements widely accepted by a large group of firms and users but not defined by a standardization organization.

Some firms introduce compatibility elements and promote them to become standards, as a consequence of a wide acceptance or of a recognition by a standardization organization. Being the promoter of a standard is a market and technology advantage. The process of getting a compatibility element widely accepted and of ultimately becoming a standard requires momentum to build among its users and other firms. It is likely that some of these firms are competitors.

Sometimes several competitors propose their compatibility elements and push to promote them as standards. In this situation, the competitors are in a symmetrical situation and everyone tries to overcome the others. The firms that can afford this competition are usually leaders, either commercially or technologically. In contrast, firms other than the leaders are not willing or able to promote a standard of their own. Despite their subordinate role, these firms can support compatibility elements made by others, and contribute significantly to the success of one of the compatibility elements. In the competition to promote a standard, the winner can be the firm that has the best compatibility element from a technological viewpoint. However, it is common for the compatibility elements proposed at the same time to all be state of the art technologically and, consequently, equivalent. In these cases, the winner is usually the firm that better exploits network externalities, possibly leveraging existing installed bases of previous products.

Subsidization is another way to raise network externalities, especially when an existing installed base is not available. A subsidizing firm promotes its compatibility element by licensing it (or the underlying technology) for free or even by paying competitors to adopt it. Economides [5] has discussed the subsidization of competitors for the diffusion of a technology. Although counterintuitive, this tactic is profitable. Subsidization boosts the installed base and the expectations of sale of the products it involves. This results in actual higher sales. Even sales prices can be higher due to the extra value of network externalities that users are willing to pay for. With this approach the subsidizer has economic advantages, as long as the network externalities are strong enough. Moreover, as another advantage, the subsidizer retains control—or at least part of it—over the compatibility element. Through subsidization, the subsidizer also shows its commitment to avoid a monopoly, which is often viewed by users as negative.

5.6 Converters

Converters are software tools that allow interoperability between products that originally were not designed to interoperate. Suppose that product A supports data format X and that product B supports data format Y and that none of the products supports the data format of the other product. In this situation, A and B cannot interoperate. Introducing a converter C that converts between X and Y, the two products can interoperate. Converter C reads data in format X generated using A and produces data in format Y readable by B. The process in the opposite direction—from data generated using B to data readable by A—may be possible too.

Converters are a special kind of product. They have a task to complete, conversion, and they comply with compatibility elements. As such, converters and their relations with compatibility elements can be handled with the compatibility tables discussed earlier. Table 5.7 exemplifies this for the previous example involving A, B, and converter C.

With object-oriented diagrams, the task of converters—namely, creating compatibility paths between products—becomes visually evident. Figure 5.4 shows converter C creating a compatibility path between data formats X and Y and, consequently, between products A and B.

Conversion of a data format is typically implemented as follows: First, the converter parses the input data, building an internal representation of the content. Then the converter transverses the internal representation, producing the output data. Sometimes, the conversion can be performed on the fly, without the internal representation.

Conversion of APIs and protocols is also possible. They are implemented through bridges and adapters, two widely used design patterns [6].

Table 5.7
Converter Allowing Interoperability Between Two Products

	X	**Y**
A	I/O	—
B	—	I/O
C	I/O	I/O

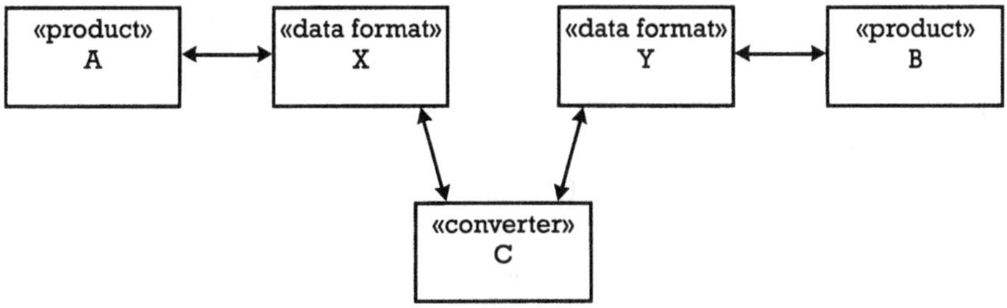

Figure 5.4 Diagram focusing on product B.

Converters can operate on large sets of compatibility elements. For instance, many converters can convert between almost any of the existing image formats. Sometimes conversion is possible in some directions but not in others. For instance, some converters convert from jpeg to PostScript but not the other way around. This can be due to technical difficulties, as in the case of conversion from PostScript to jpeg, which would require a complete PostScript interpreter, or due to an unwillingness to provide interoperability in some directions. Converters are powerful tools for connecting installed bases and for controlling user flows (see next section). Firms produce converters providing only those conversion capabilities that support their strategy.

Converters are a kind of product. Like products, they comply with compatibility elements and have their own internal features, which may go beyond simple conversion. For instance, converters of graphical formats frequently have some basic image processing features, like scaling, cropping, rotation, and so on. These features contribute to the internal value of the converters. They also give us the chance to create different and innovative converters, which otherwise would all be too similar. Distinguishing features are important for a converter as with any other product.

5.7 Timing effects

Demand-side economies of scale arise in compatible environments, where there is a dominant installed base referring to compatible products. In these environments there are real benefits for both users and firms in doing things the same way as others do. These benefits include interchangeability of complementary products, ease of communication among users in the same network, and cost savings, especially due to mass production and selling. In a situation of compatibility, important network externalities effects arise. As a consequence, a customer who wants to switch to a new product or technology bears a disproportionate share of transient incompatibility costs. This can create an excessive reluctance to adopt innovations, which is called *excess inertia.*

On the other hand, a new product can offer its first customers an important advantage. Therefore, users may adopt a new product as soon as it is released, without evaluating its real, long-term benefits. If this is the case, inefficient adoption of new products can arise, resulting in the disruption of any previous network of users. This inefficient adoption is called *excess momentum.*

Different aspects influence the transition dynamics toward innovative products: the size of the previous installed bases, how quickly the network externalities arise, the relative superiority of the new product, and the marketing strategy. Information and communication also play a central role; in the case of incomplete information, excess inertia is likely to occur. One of the possible coordination mechanisms that can arise in a market where different standards have been proposed is named *bandwagon*. If an important organization makes a unilateral public commitment to one standard, other firms know that if they follow that leader, they will be compatible at least with the first mover, and probably with the later movers [7]. In the bandwagon mechanism, the first leader to adopt a specific standard is followed by other firms that want to benefit from compatibility with the leader and to enter its network. Depending on the strength of the leader and on the market situation, the bandwagon mechanism can sometimes result in rapid and effective coordination, resulting in a common standard adoption by the market.

The earlier a firm joins the leader, the greater the benefits it can expect from its choice, mainly due to the experience and knowledge it manages to acquire before other firms join the network. In contrast, however, the earlier a firm joins the leader, the worse the damage if the network does not survive in the market.

5.8 User flows

This section summarizes how the discussed concepts—installed base, compatibility, converters—should practically be used in a domain-based software development. More specifically it shows how to create favorable user flows. A user flow is the flow of users adopting a given product, moving from other products, or approaching the domain for the first time. A user flow turns into a cash flow when we consider that the adoption of a product is related to the purchase of that product. A favorable user flow is the one that creates favorable sales for the products under analysis and for the firm producing them.

A critical point is the relationship between user flows and installed bases. Although both are related to sales, it is clear that the former are related to sales at a given time, while the latter are related to sales prior to a given time. If sales are the goal, then user flows should be the focus and installed bases are the mechanics that should be understood and managed to create favorable user flows. User flows are a useful abstraction that answers questions such as "Who are the users?" and "How can they be attracted?"

Large installed bases give real value to users. The interoperability between two users is readily available as long as the users own the same or compatible products. For instance, a user using Microsoft Access merely needs to give his or her files to another user of Access for them to be able to share the information contained in the files.

Large installed bases do not, per se, give any value to firms. For example, let us consider the scenario of a firm that has produced an excellent word processor. The internal value has helped the product gain an initial installed base of enthusiastic users. These users have told their friends how good the product is and the friends, who initially were not so enthusiastic about the product, have started buying it just because they wanted to exchange documents with the existing installed base. The installed base grew up quickly until the product took over the market and established a monopoly over it. Now the firm faces the following problem: The market is saturated because the installed base covers almost all potential users and very few new sales are possible. This happens even though the users happily interoperate among them and are satisfied with the product. The firm can address the problem by releasing a new version of the word processor with improved and new features. Yet, the installed base of the old product may turn out to be a burden, rather than an advantage.

A user flow is associated with users buying a product. Flows bring in cash. Installed bases do not bring in cash directly but heavily influence user flows. In the previous example the firm experienced good profits when users were flowing to its product. The flow was determined initially by the internal value and later by the existing installed base. When the market was saturated, the flow stopped, and so did the profits.

The previous example showed a stop of flow caused by the installed base. The problem is usually not in the installed base but in the complex way user flows work. Here we analyze user flows in detail. Figure 5.5 presents the user flows for ProductX, a sample reference product, depicted in the middle of the diagram. The arrows between the considered product and other elements are explained here:

- *New users:* ProductX attracts users that have never used any of the products represented in the picture.
- *Competitors:* The arrow from the competitors to ProductX represents users that switch from the competitors to ProductX. This flow is a subtraction flow as an increase in ProductX's installed base corresponds to a reduction in the competitors' installed bases. Sometimes users use more than one competing product at the same time. This case is not analyzed here.

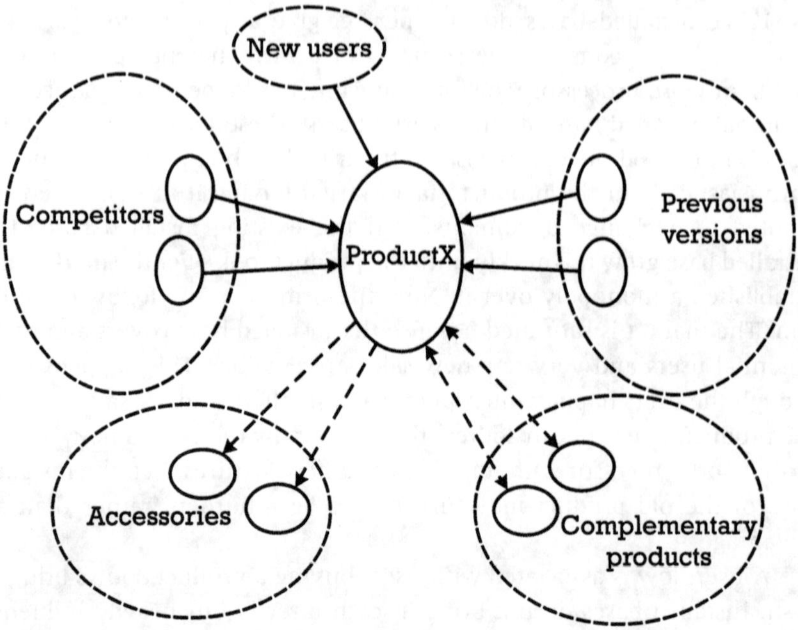

Figure 5.5 User flows for a reference product.

- *Previous versions:* Users of ProductX's previous versions upgrade their product by purchasing ProductX. This flow is subtractive as ProductX increases its installed base at its previous versions' expense. However, for the firm producing ProductX and its previous versions, there is no loss nor gain in the total number of customers.
- *Accessories:* Accessories are products that are usable only in conjunction with ProductX. Plug-ins are typical accessories. An arrow represents the user flow from ProductX to its accessory. This flow increases the accessories' installed bases without impairing ProductX's installed base. The arrow is dashed since accessories do not "predate" customers from ProductX.
- *Complementary products:* ProductX and complementary products affect each other's installed base. The user flow is bidirectional and is favorable for all the products involved. Complementary products are similar to accessories but can be used independently from ProductX. Many complementary products can be produced within the same strategy as ProductX: This allows the firm producing the products to have a higher control over the user flows between them. Also here, the arrow is dashed since complementary products do not "predate" customers from ProductX.

The analysis we have presented has been focused on one reference product and on the user flows that are favorable for it. The analysis can and should be extended focusing on the other products in the domain. This gives a global view of the interactions between the products and allows us to plan a strategy to affect those interactions.

Each flow has a unique motivation that explains why users move from one product to another. For example, let us consider a reference product called FancyFeatures. The following paragraph describes the scenario of the example and justifies each user flow, as required:

> The reference product is called FancyFeatures and is produced by OurFirm. It has a previous version called StandardFeatures and two competitors: OldAndRobust and RunAlone. There is also a complementary product called OtherStuff. FancyFeatures attracts users from OldAndRobust that does not have an important feature FancyFeatures has, yet the flow is low because OldAndRobust has a lower price. FancyFeatures attracts users from RunAlone and from StandardFeatures because it integrates better with OtherStuff. FancyFeatures does not attract more new

users than its previous version, StandardFeatures, did. FancyFeatures generates moderate flows to its accessories.

The products and user flows involved are depicted in Figure 5.6. From the example, we can infer the following:

- FancyFeatures is an augmented version of StandardFeatures with a new feature and better integration with OtherStuff.
- The new feature is not subtracting many users from OldAndRobust because of OldAndRobust's lower price. That is, if the new feature has been designed to attract OldAndRobust users, then the investment is not paying off.
- The integration with OtherStuff is effective to move the installed base of StandardFeatures to FancyFeatures and to subtract users from RunAlone.
- Accessories do not play an important role.

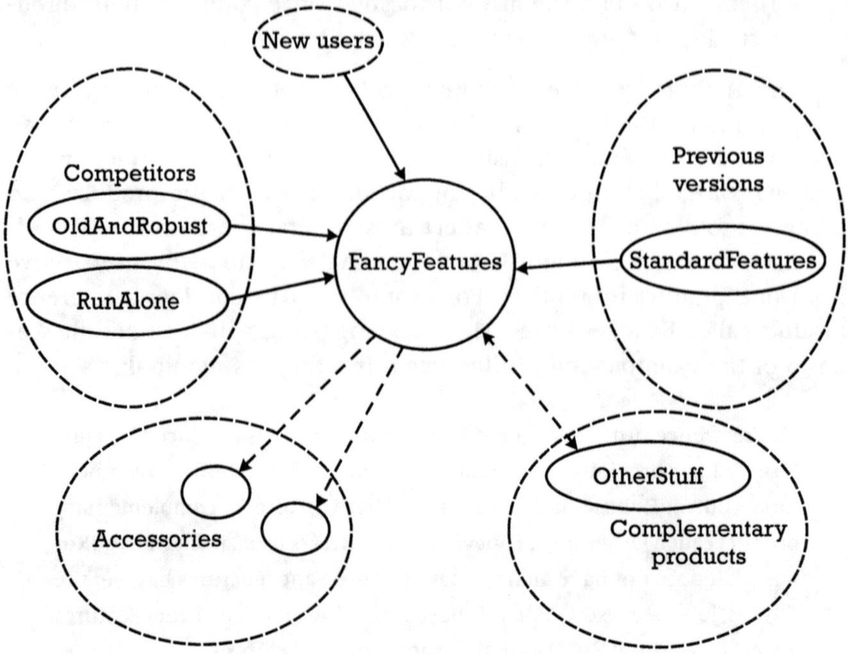

Figure 5.6 FancyFeatures's user flows.

With these assumptions, OurFirm may take the following actions:

- OurFirm may engage in price competition with OldAndRobust.
- OurFirm may enhance the interoperability, and consequently the network externalities, with OtherStuff. OurFirm can make an agreement with the firm producing OtherStuff so that interoperability between FancyFeatures and OtherStuff is easier and creates greater benefits to users. The agreement would also ensure that other products cannot interoperate with OtherStuff at all, or have higher interoperation costs.
- OurFirm may bundle OtherStuff and FancyFeatures together. This requires an agreement with the firm producing OtherStuff, too. Selling the bundle at good price—in any case, lower than the sum of the individual prices of FancyFeatures and OtherStuff—may have the same effect as launching a price competition against OldAndRobust. Bundling is easy and does not require interoperability to be improved between the bundled products.
- OurFirm may invest some time and money to investigate in depth the installed base of OldAndRobust to identify other products that those users use. For instance, if the users of OldAndRobust use also SomethingElse, then OurFirm may try to find some coordination of FancyFeatures with SomethingElse. This action might force a revision of the definition of the strategic domain to include SomethingElse if this was not included previously. SomethingElse can be totally unrelated to FancyFeatures. The interest in it is only strategic and aimed to affect OldAndRobust's installed base.

Sherlock requires each user flow to be described. Descriptions like the one presented in the example can be produced with the contribution of market experts. The descriptions depict a current situation, highlight problems, and spot possibilities for improvement. The DA&E practitioner should address each issue regarding user flows and take appropriate actions. Actions include changing the existing products, designing new products, or coordinating with other firms and products. Generally, internal and external value should both be taken care of, as any contribution to the internal and external value of the products has an impact on the user flows. Sometimes, however, some aspects of the external value are strictly necessary to make some user flows possible.

Note that it is not uncommon for the user flow analysis to be applied to future products. In this case, the analysis is part of the planning and design that is necessary before implementing the product and introducing it to the market.

5.9 Competing using prices

Software companies compete in the area of prices. Prices for software are strange because the marginal cost to produce an item of a product is almost null. Virtually, this would allow competitors to compete until the prices are also null. This is the reason why most software companies prefer to compete offering higher value, rather then low prices. However, price has some relevance too and, everything else being the same, users tend to buy the cheapest products.

Associated with each sale is an opportunity cost: If a user gets a free copy of a product, he or she is not likely to buy one. Before the free copy is donated, there is an opportunity for the firm to sell a copy of the product. After the donation, the opportunity disappears.

A market segment is a category of users in the market for a given product. Each market segment identifies a mode and/or a reason for acquiring a product, and a ceiling exists for the amount it is willing to pay for a product. Software producers differentiate the price product they sell according to market segments. If a user is not buying a product because he or she does not have enough money or because there is another product with similar functionality, then the opportunity cost for giving a free copy of the product to that user is almost null. We have already mentioned that the marginal cost is also negligible. However, the larger the installed base of a product, the larger its external value. A firm therefore has a strong incentive to provide the product to such a user for free or at a very high discount. This is practical and favorable also from a legal perspective, because users of a software product do not buy a product but a license to use the product without the right to resell such license.

Sherlock has pricing policy diagrams to represent market segment and company decisions on how to price products. Arrows link market segments to products; the label of an arrow is the price of the product for that market segment. The label may also indicate the mode of purchase (for instance, whether it is an upgrade or not). A user can belong to two or more market segments, for example, as a user at work and as a user at home.

Figure 5.7 shows FancyFeatures' pricing policy diagram. Four market segments—standard retail, academic, volume retail, and volume academic—can access FancyFeatures at different prices. Substantially cheaper access to FancyFeatures is available through upgrades from other products, made either by OurFirm or other firms.

5.10 Remarks on domain characterization

This chapter has discussed extensively a variety of market mechanisms. These mechanisms play a central role in determining which products succeed and which products fail. The focus on the market is coherent with DA&E because (1) *domain* is frequently used as a synonym for *market* and (2) the described network effects easily fit in a domain-based approach due to the close relations between products in a domain.

We believe that all DA&E practitioners should master the described mechanisms. One might think that these mechanisms are applicable only to large firms that control huge pools of users. This is not true. The concepts apply to both small and large businesses. Unfortunately, we often see software firms that ignore or do not apply them. Some firms cannot find a good balance between internal and external value; other firms, in a secondary market position, erroneously apply strategies that would be more adequate for a market leader; other firms are not able to capitalize

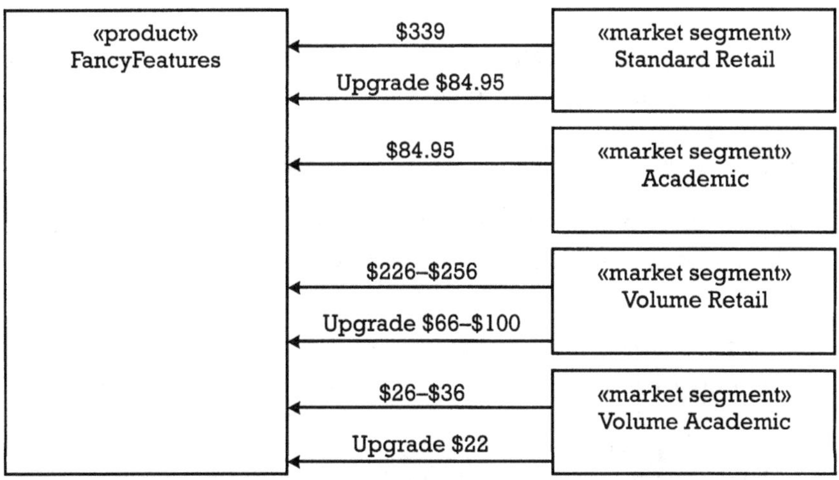

Figure 5.7 FancyFeatures' pricing policy diagram.

on their history of products. On the other hand, there are notable examples showing the validity and relevance of the presented concepts.

While the mechanisms are always valid, the true difference between firms is in the leverages of these mechanisms they can exploit. Some firms have large installed bases, others move fast, others are innovative, others have a good network of partners. Each leverage has benefits, but there are also tradeoffs between leverages and no firm can fully exploit all of them simultaneously. Domain characterization helps find the right role in the market given the firm's unique characteristics.

According to Sherlock, the "right" role is expressed in very practical terms, such as products, market positioning, and development plans. Of course, in some situations—such as when the market is saturated—few opportunities are possible and the right role hardly exists. Yet, domain characterization has the tools—for example, the analysis of the user flows—to make these situations evident and allow proper remedies to be applied.

5.11 Deliverables of domain definition

In Sherlock concepts boil down to deliverables. This provides a definite path toward the application of its concepts. The deliverables for this phase start from an understanding of the available data. They then move toward planning and decision-making. More specifically, the required deliverables are as follows:

- *DC1:* Diagrams of values. The diagrams describe the internal and external values of the products. A diagram should be built at least for each product made by the DA&E practitioner in the domain. For these products lots of information are likely to be available.
- *DC2:* Description of the installed bases. The description is a table that summarizes, for each product, the current and expected installed base.
- *DC3:* Tables of compatibility. These tables (or the equivalent object-oriented diagrams) show the compatibility relations in the domain.
- *DC4:* User flows diagrams. The diagrams show how users can move between products. The diagrams should emphasize the flows that

are favorable to the DA&E practitioner. A discussion attached to the diagrams should show the actions to be taken in order to create the favorable flows or to make them more effective.

- *DC5:* Market segments and pricing policy diagrams. The diagrams depict the costing strategy for the products and for each identified market segment.
- *DC6:* Plan of development of new products. The plan should list and motivate the new products that the DA&E practitioner is planning to introduce to the market. The motivations should be in the perspective of the marker characterization done so far.

These deliverables are exemplified, as usual, in the Webmetrics example.

5.12 The Webmetrics example for domain characterization

5.12.1 DC1: Diagrams of value

The products considered for this deliverable are those identified in DD2, namely, Webmetrics, FortranMetric, PascalMetric, CMetric, MetricBuilder, MeasureX, and MeasureJava. Their diagrams of value are shown in Tables 5.8 through 5.12. FortranMetric, PascalMetric, and CMetric are analyzed together as a single suite.

Table 5.8
Diagram of Value for Webmetrics

Internal	Features	Measurement of software metrics on source code.
		Support for several metrics and programming languages.
		Server supporting centralized collection of data.
		Clients performing local computation of metrics.
		Report generation.
		User authentication.

Table 5.8 (continued)

Internal	Quality	Ease of installation through network distribution of clients. Security of source code, which is never sent across the network. Portability, provided that a Java virtual machine is available for the platform.
External	Interoperability between users	Support for "software groups" and "software projects." Flow of information from the software developers to the project manager. Familiar, Internet-based UI, based on HTML pages and Java Applets.
	Interoperability between products	Interoperability with most Web browsers for the client side, and with some operating systems for the server side. Full interoperability across Webmetrics' parts.
	Expectations	Support for the most popular programming languages at industrial level. Interoperability with software development tools, such as compilers and CASE tools.

Table 5.9

Diagram of Value for FortranMetric, PascalMetric, and CMetric

Internal	Features	Measurement of software metrics on source code. Support for most metrics applicable to procedural programming languages (size, complexity, fanout). Support for Fortran, Pascal, and C. Report generation.
	Quality	Major features easily run automatically.
External	Interoperability between users	Metrics measurement at project level; good for software teams.
	Interoperability between products	Full interoperability between the parts of the suite. Aimed at Unix environments.
	Expectations	The suite is actively supported by the producer.

Table 5.10
Diagram of Value for MetricBuilder

Internal	Features	Support for C and Ada.
		Support for many procedural-oriented metrics.
		Customizable metrics and reports.
	Quality	Ease of customization.
		Ease of installation and good portability.
External	Interoperability between users	Support for software teams.
	Interoperability between products	Integration with compilers and editors.
	Expectations	The product has experienced very little evolution in the past years.

Table 5.11
Diagram of Value for MeasureX

Internal	Features	Support for C and C++.
		Mainly aimed at object-oriented metrics, but procedural-oriented metrics are also supported.
		Report generation.
	Quality	Availability of source code.
		Command line interface.
		Manual operations.
External	Interoperability between users	Little or no support for software teams.
	Interoperability between products	Simple interoperability with compilers.
	Expectations	The product has experienced very little evolution in the past years.

5.12.2 DC2: Description of installed bases

In this domain, almost no surveys exist on the usage of the products. The available public documents usually review one product at a time, occasionally providing comparisons with other products. More information can be obtained through direct inquiry to the producing firms. Despite the fact that these data are not homogeneous, a qualitative chart of the installed bases is possible and is given in Table 5.13.

Table 5.12
Diagram of Value for MeasureJava

Internal	Features	Support for Java.
		Support for object-oriented and traditional metrics.
		Report generation.
	Quality	Ease of use.
		Portability; written in Java.
External	Interoperability between users	Little or no support for software teams.
	Interoperability between products	Integration with IDEs.
	Expectations	The product has been actively supported by the producer and new releases are expected for the future.

Table 5.13
Installed Bases and Sales for Metric Measurement Products

	Installed Base	**Current Sales**	**Sales Trend**
Webmetrics	Low	Low	Increasing
FortranMetric	Average	Average	Stable
PascalMetric	Low	Unknown	Stable
CMetric	High	High	Stable
MetricBuilder	Average	Unknown, likely low	Unknown
MeasureX	Average	Unknown, likely low	Unknown
MeasureJava	High	High	Increasing

5.12.3 DC3: Tables of compatibility

The relevant compatibility elements are the user interface (UI) and the file format in which reports are produced.

The UI (Table 5.14) is important because software metric tools are auxiliary to software development products, such as compilers and editors. Software developers want auxiliary tools to be as easy to use as possible. Compatibility with IDEs refers to integration of the software metric tool within the IDEs. The latest trend is for compatibility with IDEs.

Table 5.14
UI Compatibility for Metric Measurement Products

UI	Unix-Like Command Line Interface	WWW-Like Graphical UI	IDEs
Webmetrics	—	v	—
FortranMetric	v	—	—
PascalMetric	v	—	—
CMetric	v	—	—
MetricBuilder	v	—	—
MeasureX	v	—	—
MeasureJava	v	—	v

All the considered products generate reports in some format (Table 5.15). Text and HTML reports allow immediate use of the reports, whereas reports stored in databases or spreadsheets are used for later, historical processing.

5.12.4 DC4: User flows

Webmetrics was originally designed to serve the needs of Cobol and RPG developers. No other product supports Cobol and RPG. As a result, Cobol and RPG developers adopting Webmetrics would be new users for the domain.

With the Cobol and RPG parsers already in place, Webmetrics can extend its coverage to other popular languages, thus becoming a direct competitor of other products in the domain. Webmetrics' advantage in this competition is its client–server architecture. This should attract other

Table 5.15
Report File Format Compatibility for Metric Measurement Products

Report File Format	Text	HTML	Database or Spreadsheet
Webmetrics	—	O	I/O
FortranMetric	O	O	—
PascalMetric	O	O	—
CMetric	O	O	—
MetricBuilder	O	—	O
MeasureX	—	O	—
MeasureJava	—	O	I/O

products' users who work in distributed environments and need a coordinated control of software metrics. It is estimated that switching to a client–server architecture would be an expensive move for the other products.

Finally, integration with complementary software development tools allows Webmetrics to benefit from the network externalities with those tools. This integration is still under development.

Figure 5.8 depicts the favorable user flows for Webmetrics. For simplicity, software development tools are considered to be a product category, without providing details about the actual products considered.

5.12.5 DC5: Market segments and pricing policy

As shown in Figure 5.9, Webmetrics has two market segments: retail and academic sites. The retail market segment represents regular, industrial clients. The price is $250 per user. The Webmetrics server controls the licenses and, consequently, the enabled users. The academic site market segment can purchase Webmetrics for $200 and has no limitation on the number of users. This market segment and pricing policy aims at the diffusion of Webmetrics among future software practitioners.

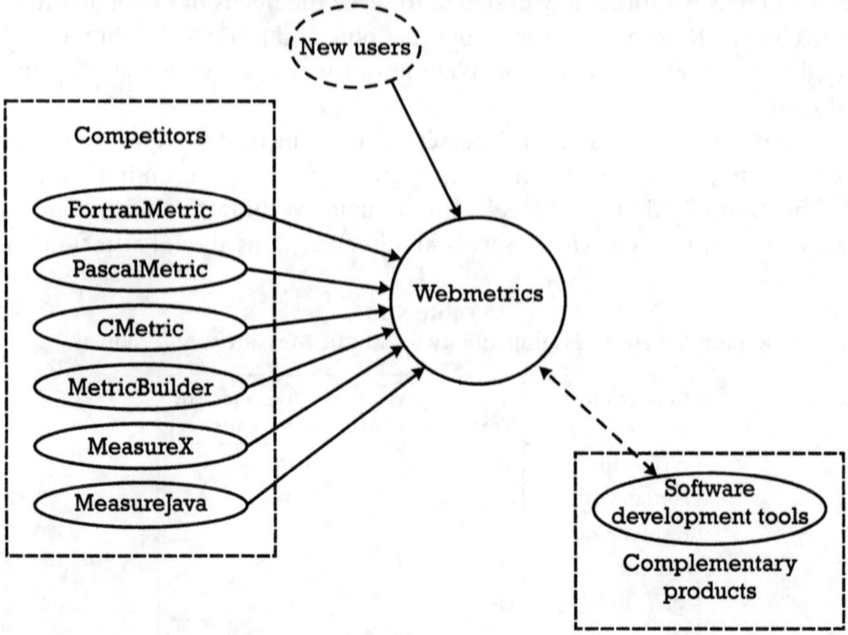

Figure 5.8 User flows for Webmetrics.

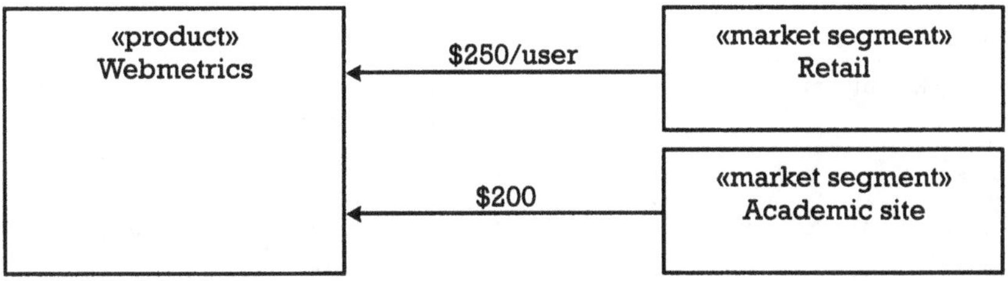

Figure 5.9 Market segments and pricing policy for Webmetrics.

5.12.6 DC6: Plan for development of new products

The baseline for the plan is the currently available version of Webmetrics. This version has parsers for Cobol, RPG, C, C++, and Java. It also implements size, complexity, and reuse metrics. Some of the parsers and metrics are still in prototypal form.

The plan covers 3 years, starting from mid-1999. The plan is also divided in 1-year periods.

The first year will be devoted to the stabilization of the current features of Webmetrics, producing a version that is easily installable and usable in an industrial setting. Integration with the most popular existing IDEs will also begin.

The second year will support more programming languages and more metrics. Smalltalk and Ada are good candidates because of their relatively large diffusion. Most existing object-oriented metrics will be implemented. The integration with IDEs will be enhanced.

The third year will focus on design metrics. The necessary parsers will be developed along with the integration of Webmetrics with software design tools.

5.12.7 Logging the evolution of domain characterization

Table 5.16 summarizes the development efforts for this phase.

Table 5.16
Evolution of Domain Characterization

Author	Date	Action	Effort
Sherlock's authors	1998-12-17/18/19	Analysis of product value.	20 man-hours
Sherlock's authors	1998-12-19	Analysis of compatibility and of the user flows.	7 man-hours
Sherlock's authors	1999-7-10	Review of product value.	5 man-hours

Table 5.16 (continued)

Sherlock's authors	1999-7-10/11/12	Planning of the development of new products and definition of the pricing policy.	18 man-hours
Sherlock's authors	1999-7-12	Review of the definition of the user flows.	4 man-hours

References

[1] Baumol, W. J., J. C. Panzar, and R. D. Willig, *Contestable Markets and the Theory of Industrial Structure*, New York: Harcourt Brace Jovanovich, 1982.

[2] Gandal, N., "Hedonic Price Indexes for Spreadsheets and an Empirical Test of the Network Externalities Hypothesis," *RAND Journal of Economics*, Vol. 25, No. 1, 1994.

[3] Brynjolfsson, E., and C. F. Kemerer, "Network Externalities in Microcomputer Software: An Econometric Analysis of the Spreadsheet Market," *Management Science*, Vol. 42, No. 12, 1996, pp. 1627–1647.

[4] Mogul, J. C., et al., "Use and Interpretation of HTTP Version Numbers," Internet Request for Comment 2145, May 1997.

[5] Economides, N., "A Monopolist's Incentive To Invite Competitors to Enter in Telecommunications Services," pp. 227–239 in *Global Telecommunications Strategies and Technological Changes*, G. Pogorel, Ed., New York: Elsevier, 1993.

[6] Gamma, E., et al., *Design Patterns: Elements of Reusable Object-Oriented Software*, Reading, MA: Addison-Wesley, 1995.

[7] Farrell, J., and G. Saloner, "Coordination Through Committees and Markets," *RAND Journal of Economics*, Vol. 19, No. 2, 1988, pp. 235–252.

CHAPTER

6

Contents

Domain scoping

Domain scoping is the analysis of variability within the domain. From the previous phase (domain characterization), domain scoping obtains the list of the products within the domain and proceeds to deal with the commonalities and differences between those products. Commonalities are the common parts of the products. Differences are the parts that make the products distinct from one another.

The commonalities need to be general enough to accommodate all the products. However, to be general, commonalities must leave some aspects unspecified. For instance, if the products generate output in plain text, RTF, and HTML, then the common part should only specify that output is produced according to some format, without specifying the actual formats. As a result, the common part contains a variation point. A *variation point* is a not fully specified feature in the common part that can be implemented in different ways in specific products.

A *variant* is a specific implementation of a variation point. For instance, "RTF" is a variant of the "output format" variation point. Variants may not be present in all the products; hence, they belong to the differences. Figure 6.1 shows how variation points and variants are the result of the identification of the commonalities and differences in the domain. The picture shows the abstraction of commonalities and differences from actual products. The inverse process is also possible: A product is synthesized from the commonalities plus an appropriate choice of variants.

Domain scoping performs an analysis of variability based on variation points and their variants. The combination of the variants makes a variability space. The variability space is a flexible tool for visualizing possible choices and analyzing them. On this space products can be positioned. The variability space is multidimensional and generally very large. Domain scoping includes techniques to slice the space into small subsets, thus reducing complexity to a manageable level.

6.1 Identification of variation points and variants: interaction with domain characterization and domain modeling

Variation points come from variable parts of the products in the domain. Products can vary in many ways:

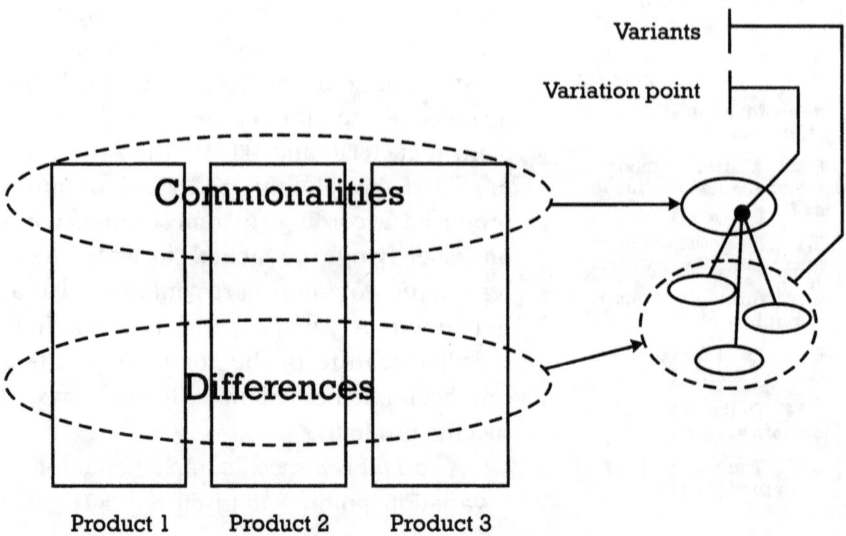

Figure 6.1 Commonalities and differences.

- Several products share the same feature but implement it in different ways. For instance, "vi" and "emacs" provide the same text editing functionality but require the user to type different key combinations and sequences to activate the editing commands. "Keyboard user interface" is the resulting variation point.
- One product implements a feature in several ways and offers the user a choice between them. For instance, a *daemon* (a program that normally sleeps unless a certain event occurs and needs to be processed) can run as a single process, as a combination of many processes, or as a combination of many threads within a single process. "Daemon mode" is the resulting variation point.
- One or more products implement a feature in the same way but it is foreseeable that, in future products, the feature will be implemented in different ways. For instance, word processors currently allow users to type text using the keyboard; in the future, they might allow users to dictate text through a microphone (maybe this variant is already a reality, but a few years ago it was only foreseeable).

The three cases presented show that variability can be identified in several products, in a single product, or in future products. A thorough identification of variability usually involves all of these cases.

Despite the focus on variability, domain scoping does not search variation points and variants directly. Rather, it relies on domain characterization and domain modeling for this search. Here is the contribution of these phases:

- Domain characterization identifies the products in the market and produces a summary of their value. Domain characterization does not look deep into the details about those products; however, its analysis is quite thorough from the viewpoint of compatibility. Compatibility elements happen to be sources of variability. For instance, "output format" is a variation point and its variants can be "plain text," "HTML," "RTF," and so on. Other sources of variability in domain characterization may come from characteristics of the market. It is quite common for the country in which the products are sold to be a variation point, due to the need for product localization. Also, sometimes, different market segmentation addresses users with different skills, which results in another variability the product should be able to handle.

- Domain modeling will be presented in the next chapter. We can anticipate that it describes product features, looking into the details that domain characterization omitted. Domain modeling spots technical variation points and variants. These represent the technical variability that arises from the many different ways in which a product can be implemented. For instance, in a domain of databases, "database reference model" could be a variation point, with "relational model," "hierarchical model," and "network model" as its variants.

Domain scoping is the "variability central" that controls domain characterization and domain modeling: Its task is to coordinate and organize the search for variability. It collects information from domain characterization and domain modeling, builds and analyzes the variability space, and returns the results to the mentioned phases, starting a new cycle of analysis. In this process, the DA&E practitioner can build a set of strategies in terms of the identified variants and make a strategic plan based on those strategies.

The interaction between domain characterization, domain scoping, and domain modeling resembles the quest for gold. When we look for gold in a given area, first we identify (domain characterization) a few spots (the products) that look interesting. Then we start digging in those spots (domain modeling). Some spots have gold, others do not, but we do not know which are which until we dig. Incrementally we build (in domain scoping) a good map (the variability space) of the area, which shows the spots with gold. Then we use the map to identify, with a higher confidence, new spots to dig. When we have enough confidence, we dig only in those spots where larger quantities of gold (the new products to develop) are likely to be found.

6.2 Variation points and variants: the variability space

A variation point is a conceptually common feature that can be implemented in different ways. A variant is a specific implementation of a variation point. Any domain comprises several variation points, each of which has several associated variants. Let VP_i be the *i*th variation point of the domain and $V_{i,j}$ be the *j*th variant for VP_i. Let V_i be the set of variants for VP_i, that is, V_i is the set $\{V_{i,1}, V_{i,2}, \ldots, V_{i,m}\}$ where *m* is the number of variants available for VP_i. Assuming that the domain has *n* variation points, the variability space for the domain is defined as $V_1 * V_2 * \ldots * V_i * \ldots * V_n$. An element in this space is an *n*-tuple. In a four-dimensional variability space (*n* is four) an element may be the following: $V_{1,3}$, $V_{2,1}$, $V_{3,3}$, $V_{4,2}$. Such a tuple would represent the element resulting from picking the third variant ($V_{1,3}$) for VP_1, the first variant ($V_{2,1}$) for VP_2, the third variant ($V_{3,3}$) for VP_3, and the second variant ($V_{4,2}$) for VP_4.

Let us consider the domain of products for calculating software metrics on source code. The common part of the products can be described as follows:

The product reads a set of files specified by the user. Each file is a source code file written in some programming language. The product parses the files. The product performs some software metrics on the parsed files. The software metrics produce numeric results. The results are stored according to some format.

The common description contains not fully specified parts. These are underlined in the text. Each of the parts is a variation point, summarized as follows: VP_1, programming language; VP_2, parsing technique; VP_3, software metric; VP_4, results storing; and VP_5, output format.

Table 6.1 shows the variants for the variation points. This is a simplified version of the Webmetrics example.

According to our definitions, V_1 is the set {C, C++, Java, Cobol, RPG}, V_2 is the set {custom parser, YACC, PCCTS, JavaCC}, V_3 is the set {LOC, Halstead, depth of inheritance}, V_4 is the set {local, remote}, and V_5 is the set {comma-separated text, MS Access table, HTML table}. The variability space is $V_1 * V_2 * V_3 * V_4 * V_5$.

Each variation point represents a choice. When building a product, a choice needs to be made for each variation point. Multiple choices can be made for a single variation point: for instance, we can choose both $V_{1,1}$ and $V_{1,2}$ for the first variation point.

6.3 External and internal variation points

Variation points can be external or internal. External variation points have external factors influencing their choices. External factors are, for

Table 6.1
Variation Points and Variants

VP_1: Parsed Programming Language
$V_{1,1}$: C
$V_{1,2}$: C++
$V_{1,3}$: Java
$V_{1,4}$: Cobol
$V_{1,5}$: RPG
VP_2: Parsing Technique
$V_{2,1}$: custom parser
$V_{2,2}$: YACC
$V_{2,3}$: PCCTS
$V_{2,4}$: JavaCC
VP_3: Software Metric
$V_{3,1}$: LOC
$V_{3,2}$: Halstead
$V_{3,3}$: depth of inheritance
VP_4: Results Storing
$V_{4,1}$: local
$V_{4,2}$: remote
VP_5: Output Format
$V_{5,1}$: comma-separated text
$V_{5,2}$: MS Access table
$V_{5,3}$: HTML table

instance, customer or market requirements. Internal variation points are determined by internal decisions, often related to technological factors.

In the example considered, VP_1, VP_3, VP_4, and VP_5 are external variation points: User requirements directly influence them. VP_2 is an internal variation point in that a user usually does not know and does not care about the parsing technique used. Some internal variation points are related indirectly to external factors. For example, an internal variation point may serve for a better implementation of an external variation point.

The distinction between external and internal is meant to focus the DA&E practitioner's attention on who determines the choice for a variation point. Choices may change over time and it is useful to know who, externally or internally, can cause the change.

6.4 Representation and projections of the variability space

Variability spaces grow exponentially with the number of variation points. Assuming *n* variation points and *m* variants per variation point, the variability space has m^n elements. For instance, if *n* is five and *m* is four, the variability space has 1,024 elements. The major problem is *n*, which makes the variability space grow enormously. For nontrivial values of *n*, a one-by-one analysis of the elements in the space is simply unfeasible.

So far, we have not represented the variability space in any graphical representation. This representation does not reduce the complexity of the problem; that is, the number of elements in the space is not decreased. However, a graphical representation makes the problem more manageable. Many complex problems in mathematics, physics, and computer science benefit from a graphical representation, even if the problems are not originally graphical: Just consider how many problems have a graph-based representation.

Figure 6.2 shows two representations of a three-dimensional variability space comprising variation points VP_1, VP_2, and VP_3. Each variation point is assumed to have three variants. We will use representation (b) because it is inherently bidimensional and because it can theoretically handle any number of variation points. Representation (a) is possible when supported by an automatic tool, but is hardly scalable to

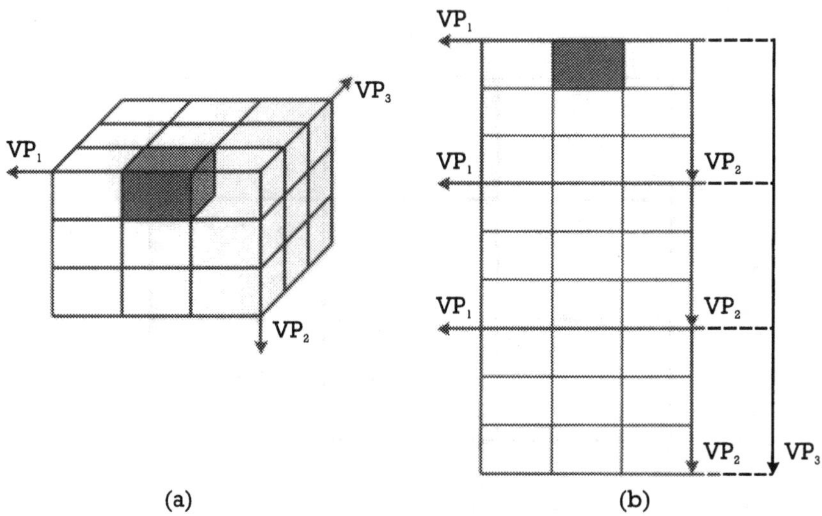

Figure 6.2 Graphical representations of a three-dimensional variability space.

dimensions higher than three. Representation (b) is similar to Karnough maps in the way it approaches the problem of multidimensionality.

Each cell in the representation identifies a unique choice of variants. For instance, the gray cells in Figure 6.2 represent, for both representations, the choice of variant $V_{1,2}$ for variation point VP_1, of variant $V_{2,1}$ for variation point VP_2, and of variant $V_{3,1}$ for variation point VP_3.

A projection of the variability space is the variability space resulting from considering only a subset of the variation points and ignoring the others. For example, let us consider a domain that has three variation points—VP_1, VP_2, and VP_3—and has a variability space defined as $V_1 * V_2 * V_3$. Considering, for instance, the variation point subset {VP_1, VP_3}, its projection of the variability space is defined as $V_1 * V_3$. The same representation for variability spaces holds for projections, too. Figure 6.3 shows the representation of $V_1 * V_3$.

The graphical representation of the whole variability space is easy and effective only when the number of variation points is not high. Limiting the number of variation points a priori, just to make the representation easy, would be an unacceptable constraint on the analysis. Fortunately, this is not necessary. Rather, DA&E follows a "divide and conquer" approach: It splits the variation points into subsets, each of which contains only a few variation points. Each subset is analyzed independently from the others. Each subset also generates a projection of the variability space. As a result of the divide and conquer approach, the

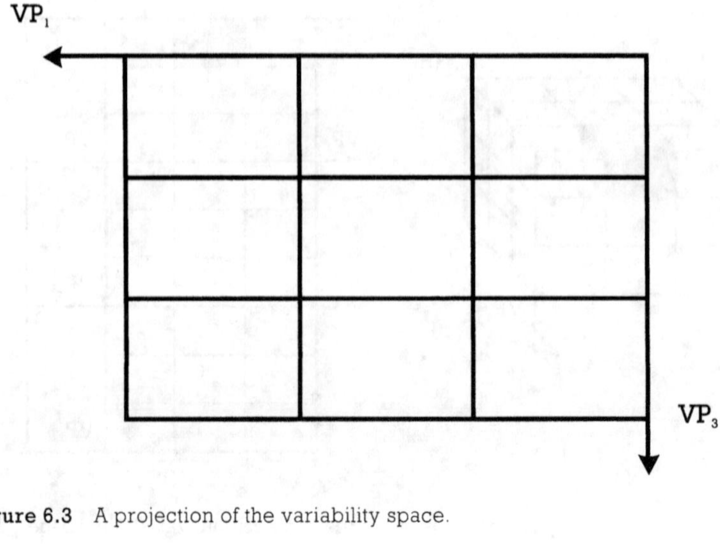

Figure 6.3 A projection of the variability space.

focus of the analysis is not on the variability space as a whole, but on the projections resulting from the subsets.

The major problem is the choice of the subsets or "Why should a variation point stay in one subset rather than in another?" For now, we can only give a generic rule. Any subset should contain only correlated variation points. Variation points are correlated if the choice of the variants for one variation point affects the choice of the variants for the other variation points. Correlation expresses our need to make choices that are good not only at a single variation point level, but at a more general level.

Variation points can be correlated in pairs, triples, and any other grouping. We can expect that some variation points may not be correlated to any other variation points: The analysis of these variation points is "local" in the sense that choices can be made without considering any other variation point.

Several subsets can exist in a domain and usually DA&E practitioners find a few of them by applying the rule of correlation. However, this approach can miss some occurrences of correlation. The section on attributes will discuss a technique for a more reliable identification of the subsets and of the variation points that belong to them.

6.5 Variability space as a container of products

The variability space represents the possible choices allowed by variation points and variants. From the perspective of variability, the choice of the variants for a product is the most distinguishing aspect of the product. Consequently, the variability space is the best way to describe—or "contain"—products.

Each cell in the variability space represents a unique choice of variants for each variation point. A product that implements exactly one variant per variation point occupies one cell of the variability space. Products usually implement more than one variant per variation point and thus span more than one cell. Visually, products appear as blotches covering a certain amount of cells in the variability space. The positioning of products on the variability space displays the different choices each product represents and allows an easier comparison between them.

To clarify this concept, suppose we have a product, Product1, in the previous software metrics domain. We could assume that Product1 implements the following variants:

$V_{1,1}$ (C), $V_{1,2}$ (C++) for VP_1 (parsed programming language);

$V_{2,2}$ (YACC) for VP_2 (parsing technique);

$V_{3,1}$ (LOC), $V_{3,2}$ (Halstead) for VP_3 (software metric);

$V_{4,1}$ (local) for VP_4 (result storing);

$V_{5,1}$ (comma-separated text) for VP_5 (output format).

To summarize, Product1 is the result of the choice of the following variants: $V_{1,1}$, $V_{1,2}$, $V_{2,2}$, $V_{3,1}$, $V_{3,2}$, $V_{4,1}$, and $V_{5,1}$. We can also notice that it implements two variants for VP_1 and VP_3, while it implements only one variant for each of the other variation points. Product1 occupies four cells in the variability space: $V_{1,1}$, $V_{2,2}$, $V_{3,1}$, $V_{4,1}$, $V_{5,1}$, $V_{1,2}$, $V_{2,2}$, $V_{3,1}$, $V_{4,1}$, $V_{5,1}$, $V_{1,1}$, $V_{2,2}$, $V_{3,2}$, $V_{4,1}$, $V_{5,1}$, and $V_{1,2}$, $V_{2,2}$, $V_{3,2}$, $V_{4,1}$, $V_{5,1}$. Figure 6.4 presents the variability space for the domain. The open circles mark the four cells occupied by Product1.

To complete the example, it is interesting to compare Product1 with some other products, say, Product2 and Product3. Their differences are in the variants they implement.

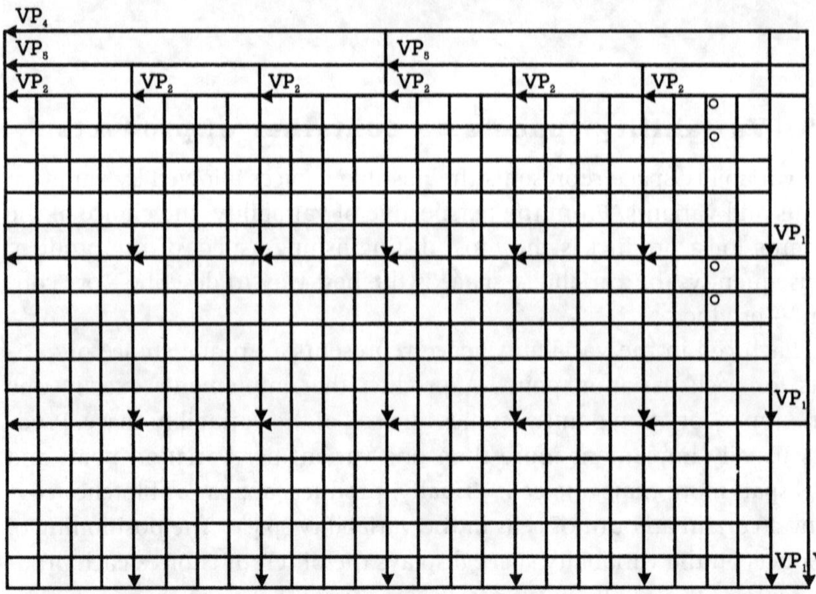

Figure 6.4 Positioning a product on the variability space.

We assume that Product2 implements $V_{1,1}$, $V_{1,2}$, $V_{1,3}$, $V_{1,4}$, $V_{1,5}$, $V_{2,2}$, $V_{3,1}$, $V_{3,2}$, $V_{4,1}$, $V_{5,1}$, and $V_{5,3}$. This means five variants for VP_1, two variants for VP_3, and one variant for each of the other variation points. The result is 10 cells: $V_{1,1}$, $V_{2,2}$, $V_{3,1}$, $V_{4,1}$, $V_{5,1}$, $V_{1,2}$, $V_{2,2}$, $V_{3,1}$, $V_{4,1}$, $V_{5,1}$, $V_{1,3}$, $V_{2,2}$, $V_{3,1}$, $V_{4,1}$, $V_{5,1}$, $V_{1,4}$, $V_{2,2}$, $V_{3,1}$, $V_{4,1}$, $V_{5,1}$, $V_{1,5}$, $V_{2,2}$, $V_{3,1}$, $V_{4,1}$, $V_{5,1}$, $V_{1,1}$, $V_{2,2}$, $V_{3,2}$, $V_{4,1}$, $V_{5,1}$, $V_{1,2}$, $V_{2,2}$, $V_{3,2}$, $V_{4,1}$, $V_{5,1}$, $V_{1,3}$, $V_{2,2}$, $V_{3,2}$, $V_{4,1}$, $V_{5,1}$, $V_{1,4}$, $V_{2,2}$, $V_{3,2}$, $V_{4,1}$, $V_{5,1}$, $V_{1,5}$, $V_{2,2}$, $V_{3,2}$, $V_{4,1}$, $V_{5,1}$.

We also assume that Product3 implements $V_{1,1}$, $V_{2,2}$, $V_{3,1}$, $V_{3,2}$, $V_{4,1}$, $V_{5,1}$, and $V_{5,3}$. This means two variants for VP_3 and VP_5, and one variant for the others. Consequently the product occupies four cells: $V_{1,1}$, $V_{2,2}$, $V_{3,1}$, $V_{4,1}$, $V_{5,1}$, $V_{1,1}$, $V_{2,2}$, $V_{3,2}$, $V_{4,1}$, $V_{5,1}$, $V_{1,1}$, $V_{2,2}$, $V_{3,1}$, $V_{4,1}$, $V_{5,3}$, $V_{1,1}$, $V_{2,2}$, $V_{3,2}$, $V_{4,1}$, $V_{5,3}$.

Figure 6.5 depicts Product1, Product2, and Product3 on the variability space.

An examination of the depicted products reveals that Product2 implements a superset of Product1's variants, while Product3 implements a partially overlapping set of Product1's variants. These speculations usually have a strategic interpretation. For instance, Product2 may be trying

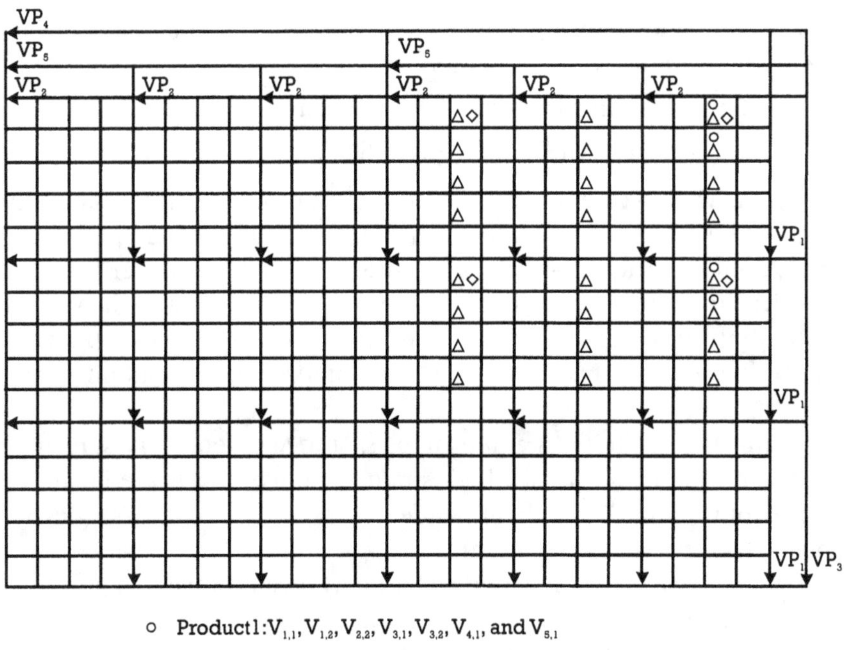

○ **Product1: $V_{1,1}$, $V_{1,2}$, $V_{2,2}$, $V_{3,1}$, $V_{3,2}$, $V_{4,1}$, and $V_{5,1}$**

△ **Product2: $V_{1,1}$, $V_{1,2}$, $V_{1,3}$, $V_{1,4}$, $V_{1,5}$, $V_{2,2}$, $V_{3,1}$, $V_{3,2}$, $V_{4,1}$, $V_{5,1}$, and $V_{5,3}$**

◇ **Product3: $V_{1,1}$, $V_{2,2}$, $V_{3,1}$, $V_{3,2}$, $V_{4,1}$, $V_{5,1}$, and $V_{5,3}$**

Figure 6.5 Positioning several products on the variability space.

to overcome Product1 by offering the same features as Product1 plus some others. On the other hand, Product3 may be trying to be different from Product1, while still retaining some common features with it.

6.6 Variability space as a container of strategies

A strategy is the idea or motivation behind the development of a product. Suppose that we are designing a new car and that we have identified two variation points, along with their associated variants:

VP_1: Heating system

$V_{1,1}$: Fan

$V_{1,2}$: Computerized air conditioning

VP_2: Parking support

$V_{2,1}$: Radar

We can produce two strategies for this example: one addressing the needs of low-income people, the other addressing the needs of billionaires. The identified strategies are S_1 and S_2, as follows:

S_1—Compact: compact design for low-income people;

S_2—Luxurious: luxurious design for billionaires.

The market segments suggested these strategies. Strategies are fully specified by a set of variants. In the example, $\{V_{1,1}\}$ specifies S_1 and $\{V_{1,2}, V_{2,1}\}$ specifies S_2. The variant of a strategy S, V(S), is the set of variants that specifies the strategy. In the car example, $V(S_1) = \{V_{1,1}\}$, that is, the variant of the strategy "compact" is "fan," and $V(S_2) = \{V_{1,2}, V_{2,1}\}$, that is, the variants of the strategy "luxurious" are "computerized air conditioning" and "radar."

With these definitions and examples, strategies look very similar to products. As a matter of fact, both strategies and products are identified by a set of variants. There are also differences, though. First, strategies are conceptual, whereas products are concrete entities of the market. Second, a strategy may be the rationale for many, even competing, products. Third, strategies can be defined on projections of the variability space. This means that strategies focus on some variation points, for which they implement certain variants, and ignore the others. Different strategies may focus on different variation points. In the car example, the domain could contain more variation points than just VP_1 and VP_2; nevertheless, defining strategies only on these two variation points is a legal approach. This is not possible for products, which need to specify the variants for all the variation points.

To summarize, we may think of strategies as the conceptual building blocks of products. A "building block" refers to how strategies are assembled by cumulating their variants. Any assembly of strategies is a strategy set. A strategy set groups all the variants of the strategies it contains. A strategy set makes its variants available to produce many products. Any of these products uses some variants of the strategy set. Considered together, the products consume all the variants of the strategy set. However, no single product usually uses all variants of a strategy set.

Even if many strategies can be devised theoretically, the number of meaningful strategies is much smaller than the number of possible combinations of variants.

In the car example, the two devised strategies were unrelated, that is, they shared no common variants. This is not true for all strategies. As a matter of fact, many strategies found in real domains share common variants. To prove this we can introduce S_3, a "midrange" strategy in the car example, comprising $V_{1,2}$ (the computerized air-conditioning system) and no variant for the parking support. This strategy is partially overlapping—in terms of variants—with the previously defined strategies.

6.7 Attributes and conditions of attributes

Attributes are observable properties of products and strategies. Examples of attributes are performance, reliability, and safety. Nonfunctional requirements are typically valid attributes. There can be several attributes and they are sequentially identified with a subscript: A_1, A_2, A_3, and so on. Products and strategies fulfill attributes at a certain degree. For instance, product X can have "high" performance, but "average" reliability. More formally, we can say that products give attributes a value. In the previous example, for product X, the value of performance is "high" and the value of reliability is "average."

An attribute can take values from ordered sets, such as {low, medium, high}, or from real numbers. In the latter case, the attribute should define the scale on which its values are measured. For instance, "performance" could define its scale as the "average transaction time in seconds." In this case, a valid value for attribute performance could be "1.5 seconds."

A problem that arises frequently is in the definition of attributes as observable properties. The problem is that many observable features may also look like attributes. More specifically, there is sometimes confusion between variation points and attributes. Both are observable and both have values (if we consider variants as the values of variation points). For example, in an application of Sherlock, the DA&E practitioner found that an important, observable feature was the fact that the product was made in the DA&E practitioner's country. This first led to the definition of an attribute that measured the percentage of the product made in the country. Later this was changed to the definition of the variation "place of production" point, which appeared to be more appropriate. (The justification is that a national product was considered more reliable. So reliability, as an attribute, was the real concern, while the place of production was one of the many variation points affecting reliability.) Attributes and variation points are somehow similar, but variation points subsume discrete alternatives while attributes represent different levels of a quality. Attributes have two purposes, as discussed next.

The first purpose is that attributes help find the sets of correlated variation points. The value of an attribute for a given product depends on the variants the product implements: If the variants are different, the value of the attribute should be expected to be different too. However, not all variants affect all attributes. For instance, if some variant in the UI of a product changes, the performance attribute may not be affected at all. More formally, we reason at the level of variation points. A variation point affects an attribute if different choices of its variants affect the value of the attribute.

If we gather together all the variation points that affect an attribute, we obtain a set of correlated variation points. The variation points in a set are worth studying together because they affect the same attribute: The choice of the variants for one variation point affects the choice of the variants for another variation point, which was our definition of correlated variation points. The importance of the sets of correlated variation points was pointed out when we discussed the need to break down the variability space into smaller, more manageable projections.

Note that a variation point can belong to more than one set of correlated variables. For instance, let us suppose that variation points VP_1 and VP_2 affect attribute "performance," and that variation points VP_2 and VP_3

affect attribute "reliability." Clearly, VP_2 affects two attributes and thus belongs to two sets. A consequence is that VP_1 and VP_3 are transitively correlated: VP_1 affects VP_2, which affects VP_3, so VP_1 affects VP_3. Apparently, this leads us to consider all the variation points as correlated and impairs our attempt to break the variability space in separate parts. To solve this problem, we suggest a two-step approach: First, study the attributes individually, ignoring transitive correlation; then consider the results of the first step and make sure they do not generate conflicts. So, in the first step, if VP_1 does not affect attribute reliability, then it should not be considered when studying reliability, and if VP_3 does not affect attribute performance, then it should not be considered when studying performance. In the second step, "reliability" and "performance" are checked together to ensure that they are in agreement. If there is a conflict (for example, high reliability impairs performance and vice versa), it is possible to go back to step 1 and find less restrictive values of attributes that avoid conflicts.

The second purpose is that attributes define the many perspectives from which we can judge which strategies or products are better. In this way, we can say, for example, that product X is better than product Y as far as performance is concerned. In addition to this, attributes can be compared against given threshold values. This kind of comparison is a condition on the attributes. A *condition* is a restriction on an attribute.

Conditions are formally stated in a form like "the value of attribute A_n must be at least X," "the value of attribute A_n must be at most Y," "the value of attribute A_n must be between W and Z," and the like. A natural way to organize attributes is to name them in this way: $C_{n,m}$ is the *m*th condition on attribute A_n. For instance, if performance (measured as the average transaction time) is attribute A_1, then two possible conditions can be the following:

$C_{1,1}$: "Fast," average transaction time below 1 second;

$C_{1,2}$: "Fair," average transaction time below 10 seconds.

A default condition exists for any attribute: "don't care." This condition means that no restriction is posed on the attribute.

The rationale for introducing conditions is that conditions naturally arise in many situations. A quality standard, an environment constraint, and an explicit customer request for certain attributes are typical sources of conditions. Once the conditions are identified, strategies and products are checked against them. Some strategies or products may not fulfill the conditions. For instance, if the variants of a strategy imply the choice of low-performance components, the strategy probably does not fulfill some tight conditions on performance.

Strategies and products that do not fulfill a condition should be discarded. However conditions are not absolute: They hold according to the situation at hand. For example, a condition required for a professional market segment may not be required for a consumer market segment. Accordingly, in the former case the condition discards any strategy or product that does not fulfill it; in the latter case the condition has no effect.

6.8 Strategy cost, conditional cost, and value

The cost of strategy S, C(S), is the cost needed to implement S in a product. In other words, C(S) is the cost to build a product that is specified by the variants of S. This is an absolute cost that assumes no strategy has been implemented before S. Cost C(S) is the cost of development for the firm performing DA&E. Other firms may have other development costs. If other firms implement S at a lower cost and sell the implementation of S, the DA&E practitioner can decide to purchase that implementation. In this case C(S) is the cost of purchasing S.

Cost C(S) is a good point at which to start thinking about the costs of implementing strategies. However, this cost is of little use, because its assumption holds very rarely. Strategies are not implemented from scratch; rather, each firm has a history of implemented strategies that influences the cost to develop a new strategy. The history represents experience, an extremely valuable asset of any firm. To express this concept, we introduce the conditional cost of strategy S given strategies $Z_1, \ldots, Z_n$, which is expressed as $C(S|Z_1, \ldots, Z_n)$. The conditional cost is the cost to develop S having already developed the $Z_1, \ldots, Z_n$. Strategies $Z_1, \ldots, Z_n$ represent the firm's history and S represents the new strategy to implement. Trivially, the cost of S is the conditional cost of S, given no previous strategy: $C(S) = C(S|\varnothing)$.

The conditional cost is a way to introduce the effects of time in domain scoping. A first consequence is that experience is relevant in the development of any strategy. Generally we can assume that the cost of implementing a strategy S_1 given some experience is lower than or equal to the cost of implementing S_1 from scratch. Formally, this is written as $C(S_1|S_2) \leq C(S_1)$.

Another consequence is that the order in which strategies are implemented affects the total cost of development. Suppose we want to develop S_1 and S_2. We can develop S_1 first and then S_2, or S_2 first and then S_1. In the former case the total cost is $C(S_1) + C(S_2|S_1)$; in the latter case the total cost is $C(S_2) + C(S_1|S_2)$. Which approach is better depends on many factors. Moreover, existing constraints—such as a restriction on the initial cost that can be paid—can affect the choice severely.

The value of a strategy S, R(S), is the value of the product resulting from S. Value R(S) is usually more practical if referred to the value of a single copy of the product, as perceived by the user. From domain characterization, the value of a product is the sum of an internal value and of an external value. For strategies, R(S) is the sum of an internal value, IR(S), and of an external value, ER(S). Because products are frequently the combination of several strategies, it is natural to extend the previous definitions also to sets of strategies, by introducing $R(S_1, \ldots, S_n)$, $IR(S_1, \ldots, S_n)$, and $ER(S_1, \ldots, S_n)$.

6.9 More remarks on strategies

The internal part of a strategy, I(S), is the set of variants that refers to internal variation points. The external part of a strategy, E(S), is the set of variants that refers to external variation points.

When software is developed for a specific customer, the customer can fix E(S). In this case the software producer's choices determine only I(S).

The observable part of a strategy, O(S), is the set of variants and attributes that influences the observable behavior of the resulting product. The hidden part of a strategy, H(S), is the part of a strategy that can be altered without affecting the observable behavior of the resulting product.

Note that a domain can have several products based on strategies with the same observable part O(S). The difference between the products is in their hidden part. Although hidden, H(S) can contribute to the success of a product. First, the hidden part can be less expensive to produce or can accommodate changes better. Second, some hidden parts can become observable in the future: Users can see and exploit them. If a firm has implemented a hidden part that outperforms competitors, it can strive to make it observable, so users can attach greater value to it.

6.10 A brief summary of the concepts introduced so far

Before proceeding with the discussion on the choice of the strategies to implement, we would like to summarize the concepts introduced so far:

Variation point. A variation point is a not-fully-specified feature within the domain that can be implemented in different ways for specific products.

Variant. A variant is a specific implementation of a variation point.

Variability space. A variability space is the multidimensional space identified by a given set of variation points.

Projection of the variability space. This is the variability space resulting from a subset of the variation point within the domain.

Strategy. A strategy is the underlying idea or motivation for the development of one or more products.

Variants of a strategy. The variants of a strategy S, V(S), are the set of variants associated with the strategy.

Strategy set. A set containing several strategies. The set is characterized by the union of the variants V(S), for any strategy S in the set.

Cost of the strategy. The cost of a strategy S, C(S), is the cost needed to develop the product identified by V(S).

Conditional cost of a strategy. The conditional cost of strategy S given $Z_1, \ldots, Z_n$, $C(S|Z_1, \ldots, Z_n)$ is the cost needed to develop S1 when strategies $Z_1, \ldots, Z_n$ have already been developed.

Value of a strategy. The value of strategy S, R(S), is the value of the product resulting from the implementation of S.

Internal value of a strategy. The internal value—as defined in domain characterization—of a strategy.

External value of a strategy. The external value—as defined in domain characterization—of a strategy.

Attribute. An attribute is an observable property of products and strategies.

Attribute value. An attribute value is the value of an attribute.

Condition. A condition is a restriction on an attribute.

Internal part of a strategy. The internal part of a strategy, I(S), is the set of the variants referring to internal variation points.

External part of a strategy. The external part of a strategy, E(S), is the set of the variants referring to external variation points.

Observable part of a strategy. The observable part of a strategy, O(S), is the set of variants and attributes that influence the observable behavior of the resulting product.

Hidden part of a strategy. The hidden part of a strategy, H(S), is the part of a strategy that can be altered without affecting the observable behavior of the resulting product.

6.11 Strategic choices: formalizing the problem

The problem of making the right strategic choices can be stated as follows: "Find the sequence of strategy sets Σ_0, Σ_1, Σ_2, ..., Σ_n that, applied in a sequence of time steps t_0, t_1, t_2, . . . t_n, generates the maximum profit for the firm."

The definition assumes a discrete time approach, as opposed to a continuous time approach; this makes the problem similar to many typical problems of dynamic programming. The time steps are equally distributed over time, usually one per week, per month, or per year. Time step t_0 represents the first point in time to consider in the analysis. This may coincide with the beginning of the DA&E practice, although it may also represent a moment in the past, such as the point at which the firm began being in business. Time step t_n is a moment after t_0 and represents the time horizon of the analysis. Beyond t_n planning of strategies becomes difficult or useless, because t_{n+1} is too far in the future to make predictions on it.

DA&E is an ongoing process. In any moment, some time step t_k represents the present time. Steps t_0 through t_{k-1} represent the past. Steps t_{k+1} through t_n represent the future. At t_k it is possible to plan and implement decisions only for the future or, at most, for the present and the future. As DA&E goes on, the time horizon can move forward from t_n to some time step t_{n+d} further in the future.

The variables under the DA&E practitioner's control are the strategy sets implemented at each time step. If t_k is the current time step, Σ_k is the set of strategies currently implemented and Σ_{k+1} is the set of strategies implemented at the next time step. Σ_{k+1} is typically a superset of Σ_k because it contains all strategies of Σ_k plus all the new strategies implemented in t_k. As a consequence, the set of implemented strategies grows with time by adding the new strategies implemented at each time step. This is equivalent to saying that, as time goes on, more variants are implemented. These variants contribute either to build new products or to improve old ones. The exception to the growth of the strategy set is when the DA&E practitioner discards an old strategy from the strategy set. This happens, for instance, when a previously used technology is dropped to adopt a new one.

Maximization of profits first requires defining the profit as a function of the strategy sets. Let us assume that P is the total profit from t_0 to t_n. Profit P is defined as follows:

$$P = \sum_{i=0}^{n-1} P_i$$

Where P_i is the discounted profit gained from t_i to t_{i+1}. Profit P_i depends on XX_i but also on the history of the strategy sets developed previously, namely, Σ_0 through Σ_{i-1}.

$$P_i = g_i(\Sigma_0, \Sigma_1, \ldots, \Sigma_i)$$

These definitions considered the strategies of the firm as the only factor that determines the profit. This is a partial view of reality: external events—competitors' strategies, random factors, and so on—affect the profit as well. Let us assume that ε_i summarizes all these external events for time step t_i. A definition of P_i that includes ε_i follows:

$$P_i = g_i(\Sigma_0, \Sigma_1, \ldots, \Sigma_i, \varepsilon_0, \varepsilon_1, \ldots, \varepsilon_i)$$

Function g_i is usually nonlinear and very complex.

With the introduction of external events, the decision process has to cope with two sets of variables: the firm's strategy sets and the external events. The strategy sets are controllable, whereas the external events are not controllable. The decision process uses the controllable variables to maximize the profit, while handling the uncontrollable variables according to some criterion. Different criteria reflect different pessimistic or optimistic approaches to decision-making. Some popular criteria are maximax, maximin, and minimax regret [1]. Mathematically, these criteria look like the following formula:

$$\max_{\Sigma_0, \ldots, \Sigma_n} \max_{\varepsilon_0, \ldots, \varepsilon_n} P(\Sigma_0, \Sigma_1, \ldots, \Sigma_n, \varepsilon_0, \varepsilon_1, \ldots, \varepsilon_n)$$

The formula represents the maximax criterion. It uses the controllable variables, Σ_0 through Σ_n, to maximize the profit. It assumes the best conditions on the uncontrollable variables, as shown by the maximization over ε_0 through ε_n.

The decision under uncertainty can benefit from the knowledge of the probabilities of the uncertain variable. A criterion that exploits probabilities is the maximum of the expected value, formalized as follows:

$$\max_{\Sigma_0, \ldots, \Sigma_n} E_{\varepsilon_0, \ldots, \varepsilon_n} \left(P(\Sigma_0, \ldots, \Sigma_n, \varepsilon_0, \varepsilon_1, \ldots, \varepsilon_n) \right)$$

The difference with respect to the maximax is that it assumes average conditions on the uncontrollable variables. The maximax, maximin, and minimax regret can also be revisited to exploit information on probabilities. Abranovic [1] provides all details required to do so.

Uncontrollable variables reflect external factors. Considering probabilities for the uncontrollable variables means that we assume the external factors are random. Some external factors have such complex and uncontrollable causes that it is easier to consider them as random. However, the competitors' strategies, a significant part of the external factors, cannot be considered to be random. As a matter of fact, competitor strategies definitely depend on our decisions, much like our decisions depend on what the competitors do. Game theory [2] discusses cases like this. In our analysis, external factors are usually not observable, and the decision criteria the competitors use are not known. These factors contribute to the complexity of the study.

To summarize, the formal approach has the following advantages:

- It is defined in a mathematical form.
- It relies on existing theories: dynamic programming, game theory.
- Optimal decisions can be expected.

The formal approach also has the following drawbacks:

- Functions g_i are extremely complex to define.
- Random external factors are difficult to model and observe.
- Competitors use unknown decision criteria.

The drawbacks make the formal approach hardly applicable in practice. Missing or incorrect information can make the results of the formal approach meaningless.

In the next section we present an approach based on heuristics. Even when there is little information, decisions can be made. The approach is less mathematical and relies more on domain-specific knowledge.

6.12 Strategic choices: our approach

Assuming that the formal approach is too difficult to put in practice, we propose an alternative approach based on heuristics. Practical experimentation and experience are the basis of heuristics. The goal of our approach to strategic choices is the same as the goal of the formal approach—finding a sequence of strategy sets Σ_0, Σ_1, Σ_2, ..., Σ_n that, applied within a sequence of time steps t_0, t_1, t_2, ..., t_n, generates the maximum profit for the firm.

We have identified seven heuristics and divided them into two groups. The first group contains four heuristics focused on determining the worth of strategies in terms of cost and value. The second group contains three heuristics focused on the competitive relationship between the DA&E practitioner and the competitors.

The proposed heuristics are quite general. However, they are not as rigorous as the formal approach and work better in some situations than in others. Generally the DA&E practitioner is free to use the heuristics that best fit his or her needs. When possible, we also illustrate the situations in which a heuristic typically works best. Because experience plays an important role in heuristics, it is very likely that the DA&E practitioner will want to include his or her own experience in the decision process. Formalizing and generalizing this experience, new heuristics may arise.

6.12.1 The first group

The first group of heuristics is described here. They all assume that we are at time step t_k, that Σ_k is the current strategy set, and that we need to decide how Σ_{k+1} should look. All the heuristics build Σ_{k+1} by augmenting Σ_k with some new strategies. The new strategies are usually named S, Z, and so on, and are representative of the larger pool of identified candidate strategies. Thus, the goal of the heuristics is to pick the best new strategy under certain hypotheses and criteria.

Heuristic 1

Given two strategies S and Z, the choice between them should consider their cost and value. If, say, S has lower cost and higher value than Z has, then S is clearly better and should be implemented. This is formalized as follows: $C(S) < C(Z)$ and $R(S) > R(Z)$.

The previous case occurs rarely. Usually, there is a tradeoff between cost and value, which gives one strategy a lower cost and the other strategy a higher value: for example, $C(S) < C(Z)$ and $R(Z) > R(S)$. In this case no strategy is better than the other from all viewpoints. As mentioned, there is a tradeoff. The heuristic suggests two alternative approaches:

1. Set a maximum cost that can be paid and pick the strategy with the highest value and with a cost lower than the maximum cost. If none of the strategies complies with the requirement on the maximum cost, then set a higher maximum cost that is still acceptable and repeat the selection.
2. Set a minimum value that should be achieved and pick the strategy with the lowest cost and with a value higher than the minimum value. If none of the strategies complies with the requirement on the minimum value, then set a lower minimum value that is still acceptable and repeat the selection.

This strategy assumes that there is a strategy set Σ_k as a baseline for the decision. So the problem should be restated as "choose the strategy—S or Z—that should be added to the existing strategy set Σ_k." Also, the costs of the strategies should be considered as the conditional cost of the strategies given Σ_k.

Heuristic 2

Given Σ_k and two candidate strategies S and Z, we assume that the absolute cost of S is the same as the absolute cost of Z, that is, $C(S) = C(Z)$. These costs can be obtained, for example, through an estimation of the development effort. A typical case in which S and Z cost the same is when their development generates the same number of lines of code.

Under these assumptions, we want to determine the relative cost of S and Z given Σ_k. The heuristic states that the strategy that shares more variants with *k* has a lower relative cost given Σ_k. For example, suppose S shares 50% of its variants with Σ_k, whereas Z shares only 20% of its variants with Σ_k. The conclusion of the heuristics is that $C(S|\Sigma_k) < C(Z|\Sigma_k)$.

Heuristic 3

Let us assume that Σ_k is the strategy set at the current time step t_k and that Σ_{k+m} is the strategy set that should be implemented at time step t_{k+m} in the future. Time steps t_k and t_{k+m} are not necessarily consecutive.

Suppose we have four strategies—R, S, T, and Z—that can be implemented at t_k. Moreover suppose that the four strategies are related to Σ_k and Σ_{k+m} as follows:

R shares variants with both Σ_k and Σ_{k+m}.

S shares variants with Σ_k but not with Σ_{k+m}.

T shares variants with Σ_{k+m} but not with Σ_k.

Z shares variants neither with Σ_k nor with Σ_{k+m}.

Note that the implementation of R, S, T, or Z at t_k determines Σ_{k+1} directly and Σ_{k+m} only indirectly. (All the strategies implemented between t_{k+1} and t_{k+m-1} should also be considered to determine Σ_{k+m}.)

Assuming no preference is given to any strategy for cost or value reasons, the heuristic states that R is the best strategy to implement and Z is the worst. Strategy R is the best because it stays with what is available at t_k but also sets the path toward Σ_{k+m} in the future. Strategy Z is the worst for the opposite reason.

Strategies S and T are better than Z and worse than R. However, a comparison between S and T does not yield a unique answer. Strategy S is more conservative, because it stays with the past; T is more risky and forward looking. The final choice usually depends on the timing effects that occur in the implementation of strategies. Sometimes it is better to move quickly to the future perspective, sometimes it is better to wait and see how the situation evolves.

Heuristic 4

In the absence of exact information on cost and value of strategies, extrapolations from the past of correlated data can replace the missing figures.

6.12.2 The second group

The second group of heuristics suggests specific behaviors with respect to competitors. The heuristics have names—Move, Bridge, and Push—that resemble these behaviors. These heuristics are more complex and their application may span several time steps.

Move

The Move heuristic suggests that the strategy set be changed by small variations. Each small variation augments the strategy set with a few new strategies. These strategies typically share some variants with the strategy set. The new strategies do not subvert the previous history. Rather, they make small adjustments to accommodate small changes in the market/domain.

This heuristic is conservative. The new implemented strategies make small movements and are likely to have a low relative cost given the current strategy set. In the variability space, the heuristic is a movement from a current strategy set to the neighboring cells. Figure 6.6 represents the concept of *neighboring* as "physically neighboring on the variability space"; keep in mind that this is just a visual interpretation of the neighboring concept.

A firm using the Move heuristic usually implements a homogeneous development plan. The Move heuristic supports competition through evolution of the products, rather than through risky, aggressive actions.

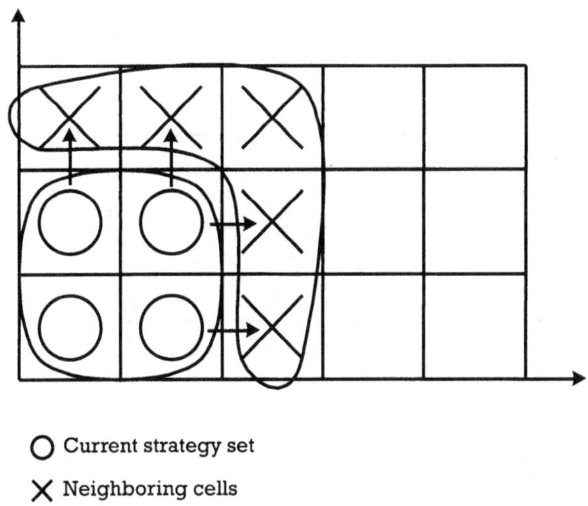

Figure 6.6 The Move heuristic.

The heuristic can be profitable for a market leader in a domain with little evolution. Small movements allow the leader to keep up with the evolution while maintaining its leading position.

Bridge

The Bridge heuristic requires the developer to implement strategies that differ significantly from the current set of strategies. Such an action is expensive because the new strategy cannot rely much on previous history and experience.

On the variability space, the heuristic extends the current set of strategies to a remote area. Figure 6.7 depicts this visually.

The purpose of such a move is usually to invade an area occupied by a competitor. Another goal can be to be the forerunner of a new technology. In any case, the Bridge heuristic promotes an aggressive approach. Its adoption should be the result of a good balance between benefits, costs, and risks.

Push

The Push heuristic suggests that no new strategies be implemented. This heuristic is applicable when the DA&E practitioner is a market leader and can leverage a large installed base. The heuristic exploits network externalities and works as shown in the following scenario.

Suppose a competitor has a product that implements different strategies from those of the DA&E practitioner. Let us analyze first what happens if the Push heuristic is not applied: The DA&E practitioner could Move or Bridge to those strategies, thus putting its product in direct

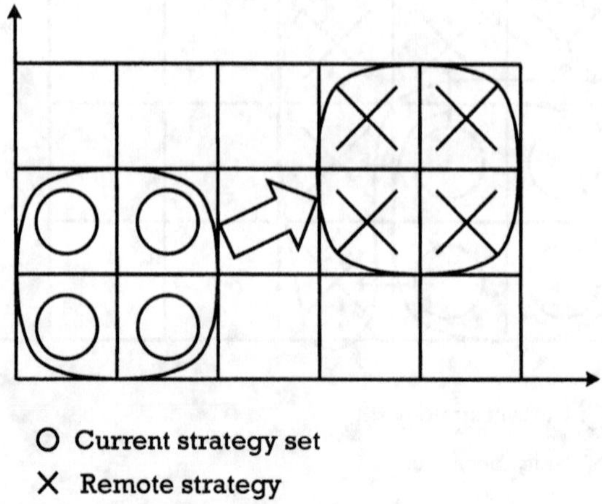

Figure 6.7 The Bridge heuristic.

competition with the competitor's. This would also make the two products—the DA&E practitioner's and the competitor's—more similar. Similarity, under certain hypotheses of compatibility, leads to interoperability and to network externalities between the two products. More precisely, network externalities occur between the DA&E practitioner's large installed base and the competitor's smaller installed base. It may happen that network externalities are more favorable to the competitor, who gains access to a large installed base, than to the DA&E practitioner, who already owns one.

In cases for which the Push heuristic is applied, the scenario works differently: The DA&E practitioner does not implement the competitor's strategies. This cuts the network externalities between the products, which has a negative impact, mainly on the competitor. If the competitor is not able to reach a significant momentum, the users of its product may eventually migrate to the DA&E practitioner's product because of its large installed base. The Push heuristic does not take any actions on the strategies; rather, it "pushes" the users to adopt the existing product with the largest installed base (Figure 6.8).

Applications of this heuristic are typical in the adoption of new technologies. If a competitor comes up with a new technology, adopting it is a way to recognize it as a candidate to become a standard. The competitor, as the promoter of the technology, has the first mover advantage. In this case, the success of the technology depends mainly on its ability to start the bandwagon.

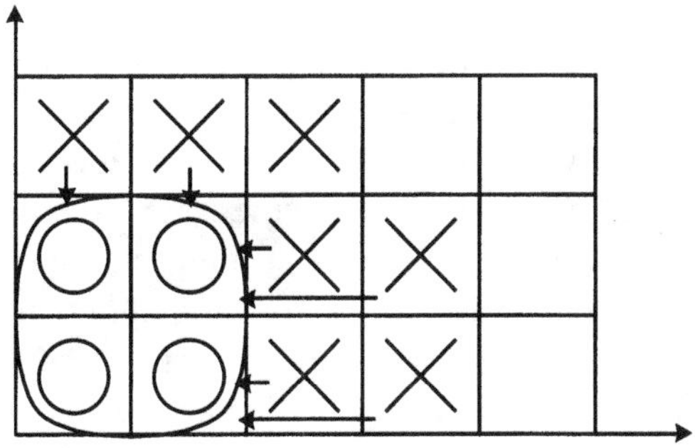

O Current strategy set
X Strategies implemented by the competitor
← Migrating users

Figure 6.8 The Push heuristic.

6.12.3 Comments on strategic planning

As a general note, strategic planning is done to achieve long-term objectives. These objectives can be, for example, to conquer a market segment, to adopt a technology, or to achieve a certain quality of production. The objectives are compliant with the general goal set at the beginning of the discussion: maximizing the profit over a certain period of time. This means that if the objectives are met, the profit is maximized. Sherlock's step-by-step approach fills the gap between the planning of long-term objectives and their implementation in practice. More specifically, this task is assigned to the heuristics, which take into account both short-term needs—the "what to do next?" problem—and longer term objectives.

Another note is that oftentimes predictions are wrong and planned results are not achieved. This is unavoidable, so it is necessary to be ready to take the appropriate countermeasures. As a result, the actions taken at any time step are a mix of implementing previously planned strategies, determining whether previous goals have been met, and replanning if necessary.

6.13 Final remarks on domain scoping

Domain scoping is frequently compared to version management. Both deal with variability. Domain scoping can be seen as a particular kind of version management that manages versions in terms of variation points and variants. This and other similarities actually exist. However, domain scoping goes beyond version management. The first difference is that domain scoping focuses on planning. Domain scoping plans future strategies and products and is not a simple log of changes. With domain scoping, we can say that a certain future version of a product will implement certain variants. With version management, we generally cannot do so.

Even if we augment version management with planning—like many currently available tools do—domain scoping still has an advantage. Domain scoping is based on the concept of variability space. On this space any product can be visualized. Past, current, future, and competing products are all handled in the same way. The variability space is extremely valuable in the comparison of products. When we explicitly know that two or more products differ by certain variants, we can know which one is better and why, and what actions can be taken to improve any of them.

Domain scoping recognizes that variability is essential in software development. It also recognizes that there are practical problems—such as cost and complexity—in implementing variability. There is a clear distinction between the first part of domain scoping, which seeks possible variability, and the second part of domain scoping, which decides which variabilities can be implemented. In the possible variability, we do not want surprises, so we study all the possible sources of variability. We also have the tools for a thorough elicitation of variability through the interaction with domain characterization and domain modeling. On the other hand, in the implementing of variability, we find the forms of variability that, with our limited resources, we can implement and that allow our products to evolve with an acceptable risk of changes.

Finally, domain scoping is the basis of product lines: A whole series of products can be built from a common core and a pool of variants. This is the same conceptual basis of software reuse. The value of domain scoping is that it puts reuse under a new perspective: Planned reuse now means planned variability. Domain scoping breaks the problem of reuse into small, accessible problems and puts reuse into the broad context of domain-based software production.

6.14 Deliverables of domain scoping

Domain scoping generates the following deliverables:

- DS1: The variability space, the attributes of the products within the domain, and the related constraints.
- DS2: Definition of product strategies.
- DS3: Identification of the product strategies to develop in the future.

DS1 gathers and organizes all information on variability, in terms of variation points, variants and attributes, and constraints. This deliverable should also specify what projections of the variability space are interesting for the analysis.

DS2 is a preparation for DS3. It identifies feasible strategies but it does not decide which ones should actually be implemented. The strategies come from observation of existing products and from domain and market experts.

DS3 is the strategic planning. It defines a plan in terms of time steps and strategies implemented at each time step.

6.15 The Webmetrics example for domain scoping

6.15.1 DS1: Variability space, attributes of the products in the domain, and related constraints

Table 6.2 summarizes the variation points and the variants in the domain. These define the variability space.

VP_1 and VP_3 were identified in the domain definition. VP_2 is a technical feature identified in domain modeling; it can also be found, with many details, in the literature of compiler and parser building. VP_4 cannot be found from the analysis of the existing products in the market because all products implement the same variant, so apparently there is no variability in "results storing." VP_4 exists because it is the novelty of Webmetrics, which is the only one to implement the "remote" variant. VP_5 and VP_6 were identified in domain characterization from the analysis of compatibility.

The relevant attributes of the domain are as follows:

A_1: Performance of parsing, measured as the number of LOCs processed per second;

A_2: Performance of result generation, processing and retrieval, measured on the ordered set {low, medium, high};

A_3: Ease of use, measured as the time required to learn the usage of the product.

The domain puts few constraints on the attributes. It is desirable for products to have good values for the attribute, but a poor value usually does not impair the usefulness of the products. The only exception is a condition on A_1:

$C_{1,1}$: Performance of parsing should be comparable with the performance of existing commercial compilers.

The condition is necessary because users expect the same performance from compilers and software metric tools. For all the other attributes the default "don't care" condition applies.

A_1 affects most strategies because almost any product feature has a certain influence on performance. However, conditions $C_{1,0}$ and $C_{1,1}$ do not seem to be difficult to satisfy for any of the proposed strategies. On the other hand, $C_{1,2}$ can be a problem for strategy S_{203}, because parsers based on JavaCC can be slow, and for strategy S_{301}, because storing data remotely can add significant overhead for accessing a remote computer through a network. None of the constraints regarding A_1 rule out any of

Table 6.2
Variation Points and Variants for Webmetrics

VP_1: Parsed Programming Language
$V_{1,1}$: C
$V_{1,2}$: C++
$V_{1,3}$: Java
$V_{1,4}$: Cobol
$V_{1,5}$: RPG
$V_{1,6}$: Pascal
$V_{1,7}$: Lisp
$V_{1,8}$: BASIC
$V_{1,9}$: Smalltalk
$V_{1,10}$: Ada
$V_{1,11}$: Fortran
VP_2: Parsing Technique
$V_{2,1}$: Custom parser
$V_{2,2}$: YACC
$V_{2,3}$: PCCTS
$V_{2,4}$: JavaCC
VP_3: Software Metric
$V_{3,1}$: LOC
$V_{3,2}$: Halstead
$V_{3,3}$: McCabe
$V_{3,4}$: Depth of inheritance
$V_{3,5}$: Fan-in/fan-out
$V_{3,6}$: Reuse metrics: reuse level, reuse frequency, and reuse density
VP_4: Results Storing
$V_{4,1}$: Local
$V_{4,2}$: Remote
VP_5: Output Format
$V_{5,1}$: Comma-separated text
$V_{5,2}$: HTML
$V_{5,3}$: Database/spreadsheet
VP_6: User Interface
$V_{6,1}$: Unix-like command line interface
$V_{6,2}$: WWW-like graphical UI
$V_{6,3}$: IDEs

the strategies altogether. Rather, the chosen combination of strategies for a specific product should be validated against any posed constraints.

A_2 affects strategies S_{300} and S_{301}. Learning how to store results locally (S_{300}) is easier than learning how to store results remotely (S_{301}). While S_{300} satisfies any constraints, S_{301} can hardly satisfy $C_{2,1}$. As a result, if constraint $C_{2,1}$ is imposed on the product, S_{301} should not be considered.

A_3 affects strategies S_{200}, S_{201}, S_{202}, and S_{202}. Due to its simpler and less flexible design, the custom parser strategy (S_{200}) is contradictory with constraint $C_{3,2}$.

6.15.2 Definition of product strategies

Strategies are defined on projections of the variability space. To avoid name clashes between strategies defined for different projections, we adopt the convention of starting the numbering of strategies for a projection from a multiple of 100: S_{100}, S_{200}, S_{300}, and so on.

Strategies on the VP_1 (Parsed Programming Language)–VP_3 (Software Metric) Projection

The VP_1–VP_3 projection intersects programming languages and software metrics. Strategies on this projection should be technically sound and functionally useful to the user. According to our numbering convention, the strategies will start from S_{100}. We propose the following strategies:

- S_{100}: C strategy which considers the metrics that are applicable to $V_{1,1}$ (C language); that is, $V_{3,1}$, $V_{3,2}$, $V_{3,3}$, $V_{3,5}$, $V_{3,6}$. The strategy extends the metrics to $V_{1,2}$ (C++), the language that derives directly from the C language.
- S_{101}: Pure object-oriented strategy for all object-oriented languages ($V_{1,2}$, $V_{1,3}$, $V_{1,9}$,$V_{1,10}$) that implements the only object-oriented metric, namely, $V_{3,4}$.
- S_{102}: Pure procedural strategy that implements the procedural metrics ($V_{3,1}$, $V_{3,2}$, $V_{3,3}$, $V_{3,5}$, $V_{3,6}$) and applies them only to pure procedural languages ($V_{1,1}$, $V_{1,4}$, $V_{1,5}$, $V_{1,6}$, $V_{1,8}$, $V_{1,11}$).
- S_{103}: Legacy strategy that implements the procedural metrics ($V_{3,1}$, $V_{3,2}$, $V_{3,3}$, $V_{3,5}$, $V_{3,6}$) and applies them to Cobol ($V_{1,4}$) and RPG ($V_{1,4}$), the most popular languages of legacy systems.

Strategies on the VP_2 (Parsing Technique)–VP_4 (Results Storing)–VP_6 (User Interface) Projection

The projection focuses on the overall technical soundness of the product. The choice for VP_2 sets the general framework of the strategy. The choices for VP_4 and VP_6 should be coherent with that framework. The strategies are as follows:

S_{200}: Custom parser strategy that implements $V_{2,1}$, $V_{4,1}$, and $V_{6,1}$. It is appropriate for a small product or as a prototype.

S_{201}: YACC strategy that implements $V_{2,2}$, $V_{4,1}$, and $V_{6,1}$. The strategy is similar to S_{200} but is adequate for larger products.

S_{202}: PCCTS strategy that implements $V_{2,3}$, $V_{4,1}$, $V_{6,1}$, and $V_{6,3}$. The use of a complex modern tool like PCCTS allows more flexibility on the user interface.

S_{203}: JavaCC strategy that implements $V_{2,4}$, $V_{4,2}$, and $V_{6,2}$. The choice of Java dominates the features provided in the strategy.

S_{204}: Extended JavaCC strategy that implements $V_{2,4}$, $V_{4,2}$, $V_{6,2}$, and $V_{6,3}$. The strategy extends S_{203} by also implementing $V_{6,3}$.

Strategies on the VP_2 (Parsing Technique) Projection

This projection is a consequence of the A_1—performance of parsing—attribute. A_1 may also affect VP_3, but experiments show that the computation on software metrics results in just minor overhead compared to the complexity of parsing. These are the strategies:

S_{300}: Custom parser strategy that implements $V_{2,1}$;

S_{301}: YACC strategy that implements $V_{2,2}$;

S_{302}: PCCTS strategy that implements $V_{2,3}$;

S_{303}: JavaCC strategy that implements $V_{2,4}$.

Only S_{303} has low performance. However, it still satisfies condition $C_{1,1}$.

Strategies on the VP_4 (Results Storing)–VP_5 (Output Format) Projection

Variation points VP_4 and VP_5 affect attribute A_2 (performance of result generation, processing, and retrieval). The strategies are as follows:

S_{400}: Local strategy that implements $V_{4,1}$, $V_{5,1}$, and $V_{5,2}$. Simplicity is the rationale of this strategy.

S_{401}: Remote strategy that implements $V_{4,2}$, and $V_{5,3}$. Flexibility is the rationale of this strategy.

Clearly, S_{400} has higher performance than S_{401}.

Strategies on the VP_4 (Results Storing)–VP_6 (User Interface) Projection

Variation points VP_4 and VP_6 affect attribute A_3 (ease of use). The strategies are as follows:

S_{500}: Traditional UI strategy that implements $V_{4,1}$, and $V_{6,1}$. Most traditional Unix tools implement this strategy.

S_{501}: Web UI strategy that implements $V_{4,2}$, and $V_{6,2}$. Java applets and some client–server applications implement this strategy.

S_{502}: IDE UI strategy that implements $V_{4,1}$, and $V_{6,3}$. Most plug-ins for IDEs implement this strategy.

All three strategies provide a good level of ease of use. This is possible because each strategy represents a popular user interface. Users can leverage their previous experience with these UIs.

6.15.3 DS3: Identification of the product strategies to develop in the future

In terms of strategies, the competitors are basically characterized by implementation of the following strategies: C strategy (S_{100}), pure object-oriented strategy (S_{101}), local strategy (S_{400}), traditional UI strategy (S_{500}), and IDE UI strategy (S_{501}). Considering these strategies, we can infer that the competitors support C and object-oriented developers and ensure high performance and ease of use.

Competing with these competitors is a hard task. Having the C strategy in place, the competitors benefit from a good competitive position. From that position they can exploit almost any of the proposed strategic heuristics against a new entrant. To analyze these issues, we discuss two situations and propose a solution, which summarizes the decisions made and the strategies implemented for Webmetrics.

Situation 1: If Webmetrics implements the C strategy, it enters into competition with the same strategy as the competitors. The competitors, who already have an installed base, can adopt a "push" approach, attracting the few users of Webmetrics.

Situation 2: Webmetrics can implement the legacy strategy, which is not overlapping with the C strategy. This would differentiate Webmetrics from the competitors. This approach has the drawback that the competitors can regain leadership with a simple move from the C strategy to the legacy strategy.

Our solution is as follows. The differentiation approach taken in situation 2 was promising although applied in the wrong context. It is evident that the C strategy is a very good baseline from which the competitors can easily move to any other strategy on the VP_1–VP_3 projection. Regardless of where Webmetrics attacks the competitors, they still have a privileged position. The solution is to differentiate from another perspective: on the VP_4–VP_5 projection. On this partition, all the competitors implement the local strategy, so Webmetrics can differentiate implementing the remote strategy. Having the local strategy in place provides little advantage when implementing the remote strategy, whereas having the remote strategy in place provides the local strategy almost for free. An objection can be made that the remote strategy is more expensive and provides lower performance. An analysis of the competitors shows that moving from the local strategy to the remote strategy would actually be a very expensive bridge. Moreover, despite any competitors' actions, Webmetrics would have the first mover advantage on the remote strategy.

As a result of these considerations, Webmetrics should be designed according to the following criteria:

- Competition should be based on the local versus remote strategy discussion.
- Webmetrics can implement the C strategy and the legacy strategy right away, exploiting the fact that its real competitive advantage will be in the remote strategy.
- Webmetrics should pursue network externalities with tools for networking and cooperation. Webmetrics should be open to integration.
- Webmetrics should use Java as the underlying technology. This fulfills all of the above-mentioned interoperability requirements. Moreover this allows Webmetrics to be deployed as a Java applet, which is also a powerful distribution channel.

The development plan for Webmetrics is shown in Table 6.3.

6.15.4 Logging the evolution of domain scoping

Table 6.4 summarizes the development efforts for this phase.

Table 6.3
Development Plan for Webmetrics

Year	Strategy Sets Implemented
First year	$1 = \{S_{100}, S_{103}, S_{203}, S_{303}, S_{401}, S_{501}\}$
Second year	$2 = \{S_{100}, S_{101}, S_{103}, S_{203}, S_{303}, S_{401}, S_{501}\}$
Third year	$3 = \{S_{100}, S_{101}, S_{103}, S_{203}, S_{303}, S_{401}, S_{501}, S_{502}\}$

Table 6.4
Evolution of Domain Scoping

Author	Date	Action	Effort
Sherlock's authors	1998-1-26/27/28/29	Formalization of variation points	30 man-hours
Sherlock's authors	1998-2-2	Formalization of new variation points	4 man-hours
Sherlock's authors	1998-2-2	Definition of early strategies	2 man-hours
Sherlock's authors	1998-2-23	Definition of strategies	3 man-hours
Sherlock's authors	1998-10-1/2/3	Review of variation points and strategies	18 man-hours
Sherlock's authors	1999-7-27/28	Review of variation points and strategies	14 man-hours

References

[1] Abranovic, W. A., *Statistical Thinking and Data Analysis for Managers*, Reading, MA: Addison-Wesley, 1997.

[2] Zaninotto, E., *Decisioni, Giochi, Management (Decision, games, and management)*, Cafoscariana, 1992.

CHAPTER

7

Contents

Domain modeling

Domain modeling produces a model of the domain and a model for each product within the domain. A *product model* is a description of one of the products in the domain. The domain model is meant to represent all products, so it is a synthesis of all product models. The domain model is very similar, in terms of tools and description style, to a product model. It is built from the product models through factorization of commonality and identification of variability. A domain model typically looks like the description of a very generic product.

Any model—of either the products or the domain—comprises a use case model and an analysis model in UML. A use case defines a "case of use" from the user's perspective, that is, one of the features provided to the user [1]. An analysis model describes the core objects and their structure. Domain modeling closely resembles requirement acquisition and analysis in a traditional software life cycle.

The use case model and the analysis model are strictly related. The use case model [1] provides a high-level representation of the functionality a system offers. From this model an analysis model is derived to show how the objects in the use case work. Feedback from the analysis model to the use case model is possible (Figure 7.1).

While the domain model is conceptually the result of the product models, it is not necessarily built after all the product models are ready. Usually, the domain model grows in parallel with the product models and the rest of the analysis. Domain modeling fulfills the following type of request: "Incorporate product X into the model." To serve the request, domain modeling builds a product model for product X and revises the domain model to make it representative of product X (in addition to any other products formerly analyzed). If product X is different from the previously analyzed products, the domain model must represent this variability. Domain modeling expresses variability in terms of variation points and variants. Figure 7.2 illustrates how the product models and the domain model proceed in parallel and subsume the construction of use case and analysis models.

As was done with previous phases, domain modeling is developed in iterations. The incremental study of the products provides the basis for the iteration.

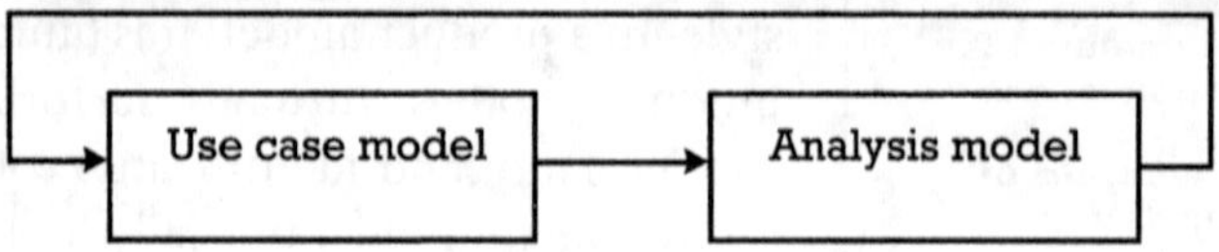

Figure 7.1 Use case model and analysis model.

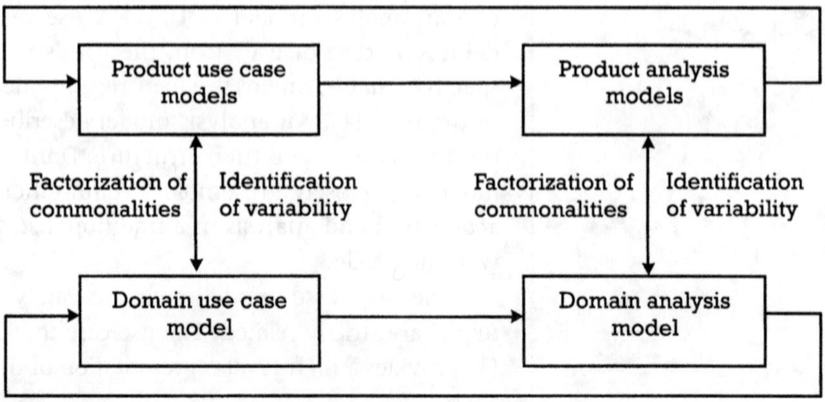

Figure 7.2 Products and domain models: comparison and relationship.

7.1 Product use case model

The use case model presents the functionality and the responsibilities allocated to the user and to the product. Figure 7.3 contains a sample use case model describing the interaction between the user and a system that makes cappuccino beverages. The figure includes the textual description of the use case.

More complex use case models may include more actors and more cases of use of the system. A textual description is often attached to each use case diagram, to detail the expected interaction between the actor(s) and the system.

Let us consider the example of a firm that manufactures mechanical components, Reusable Solutions S.p.A. The firm has a software engineering department. The firm wants to build an information system to support its manufacturing business. Reusable Solutions S.p.A. is also considering selling its information system to other firms that run similar businesses. Because not all the firms are the same, Reusable Solutions S.p.A. performs DA&E to produce software that is flexible enough to accommodate different requirements. Reusable Solutions S.p.A. starts domain modeling from one product. This product is the information system to support its manufacturing business. The information system is based on the firm's business. A basic description of the business is presented in Figure 7.4.

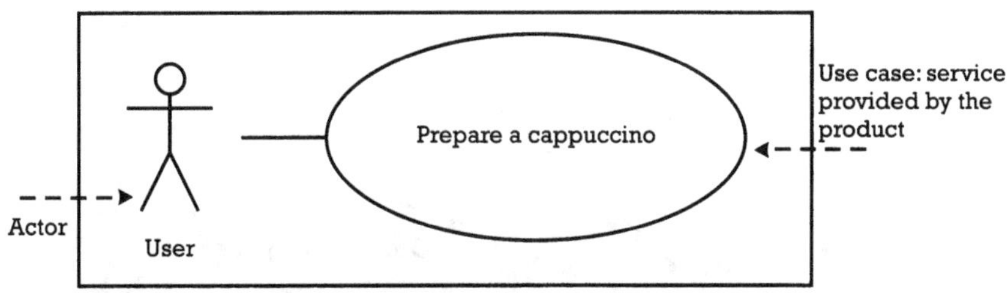

Description: The user accesses the system and requests a cappuccino. The system asks the user his/her preferences for size, blend, and milk. The user supplies the requested information. After a while the system informs the user that the cappuccino is ready and asks the sweetening preference—honey, white sugar, or raw sugar—and the amount of sweetener. The user supplies the requested information. The system adds the sweetener, stirs the beverage, and puts on the outer shelf the cup ready to drink. The user gets the cup.

Figure 7.3 Sample use case model.

Through interviews and deeper analysis of the business, a high-level description of the system is derived (Figure 7.5). Figure 7.6 presents the textual description of the identified use cases.

The model built so far can be improved by highlighting interesting relations between the use cases. For instance, a first improvement would be to point out that "order management" and "just-in-time supply" require access to the firm's catalog, through the "catalog browsing" use case. A "uses" relationship shows this; see the example in Figure 7.7.

Another improvement would be to show that "order management" and "just-in-time supply" have commonalities. Both cases deliver a product to the customer and utilize "catalog browsing." If two or more product use cases share a feature, we put that feature in a new use case. This use case represents commonalities, so we call it a *common use case.* It also belongs to a product model, so its complete definition is *common product*

"The firm's clients can order batches of components asking for either a standard delivery or a just-in-time delivery. Anybody who uses the components is a user. The firm has a catalog so users can access it to see what components are available. A user who places an order becomes a customer."

Figure 7.4 Basic business description.

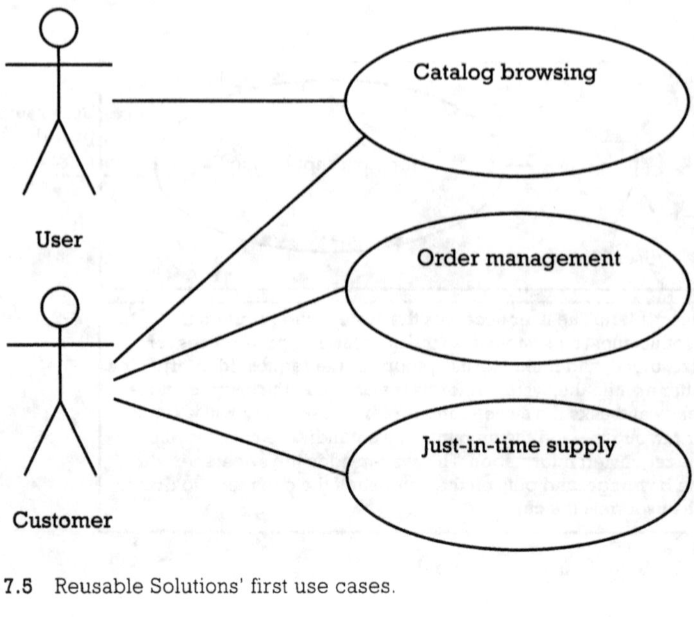

Figure 7.5 Reusable Solutions' first use cases.

Product use case:
Catalog browsing
Description:
The client requires information from the firm's catalog. The catalog allows access to its data through a set of operations. The operations are "access through indexes" and "unconstrained search." There is an access policy that provides confidentiality levels and ensures that the clients have access only to authorized data. The result of the search can be printed, exported to a file, or discarded.

Product use case:
Order management
Description:
The client requires a firm's product. The product must be in the firm's catalog. If the product is in the catalog but is not currently available, then an order is issued to the production department. The client's order is also processed according to the accounting procedure. The ordered product is delivered to the client. The client pays according to the payment procedure and the invoice is issued.

Product use case:
Just-in-time supply
Description:
The client requires a firm's product. The product must be in the firm's catalog. A special production and delivery plan is generated to ensure the availability of the product according to the client's requirements. The client's order is also processed according to the accounting procedure. The firm produces and delivers the ordered product as specified in the production and delivery plan. The client pays according to the payment procedure and the invoice is issued.

Figure 7.6 Reusable Solutions' use case descriptions.

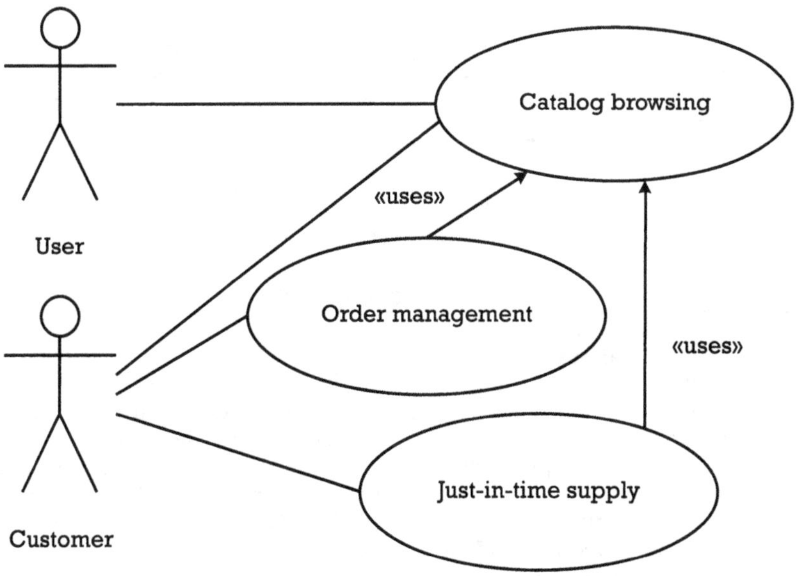

Figure 7.7 "Uses" relationship.

use case. The common product use case is connected to the use cases it generalizes through an "extends" relationship (Figure 7.8). Figure 7.9 provides the textual description of the common product use case.

Use of the "uses" and "extends" relationship reveals that factorization was sought in the development of the product use case model. This may come as a surprise because factorization seems more adequate for domain models. However, an individual product can also contain variability, so factorization might be required also here. A product model deals with commonality and variability inside a product. The domain model deals with commonality and variability inside products and between products.

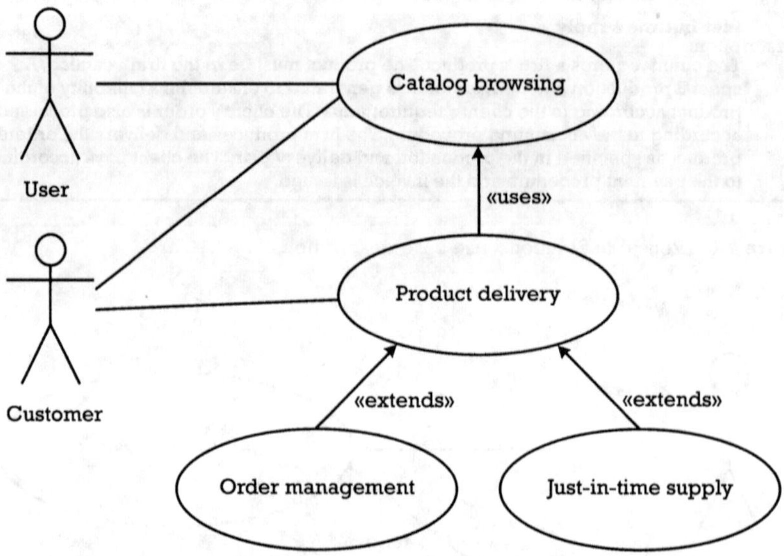

Figure 7.8 Common product use case and "extends" relationship.

> **Common product use case:**
> **Product delivery**
> **Description:**
> **The client requires a firm's product. The product must be in the firm's catalog. The production department is involved in the order handling according to the production policy. The client's order is also processed according to the accounting procedure. The product is delivered to the client according to a delivery policy. The client pays according to the payment procedure and the invoice is issued.**

Figure 7.9 Textual description of the common product use case.

7.2 Product analysis model

Once the product use case model has provided us with a global view of the functionality of the product, we can focus on how the use cases are implemented in terms of objects. The product analysis model serves this purpose.

The first issue that we face is identification of the objects. The starting point is the textual descriptions of the use cases. We look for nouns that are good candidates to become objects. Figure 7.10 presents the results of the analysis for the "catalog browsing" use case. The identified objects are marked in bold.

Once we have the objects, we look for actions and relations between them. The result is a product analysis model like the one shown in Figure 7.11 (for simplicity, only "catalog browsing" is considered).

A simple way to represent traceability is through *trace relations*, as shown in Figure 7.12.

7.3 Domain use case model

Once some of the product models are in place, the domain model—or at least a first version of it—can be built. The first part of the domain model

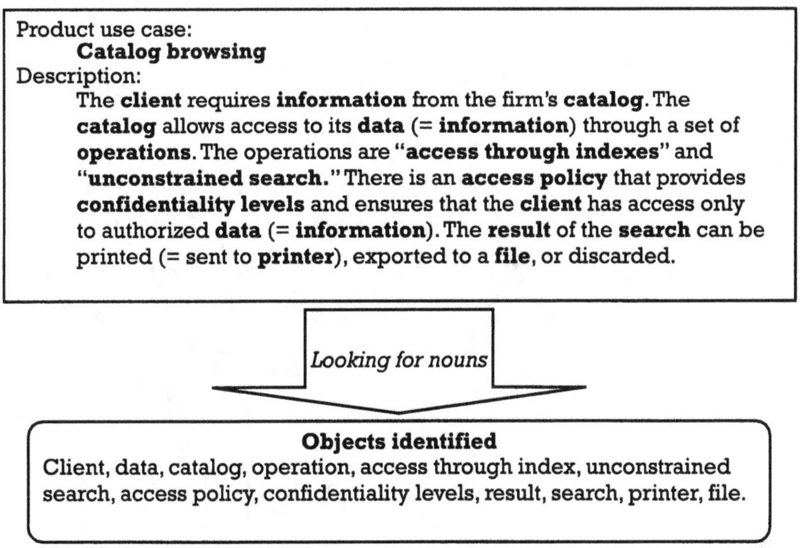

Figure 7.10 Identification of objects in the use case.

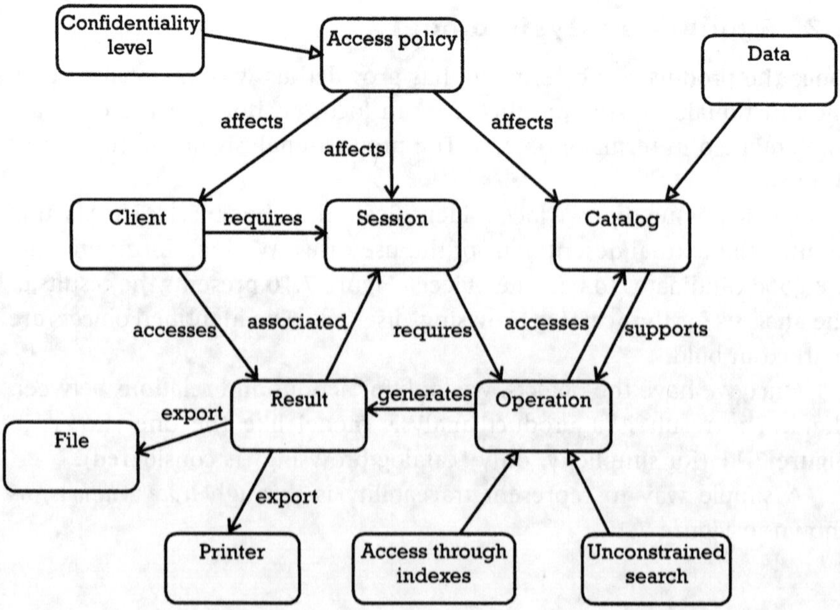

Figure 7.11 Product analysis model.

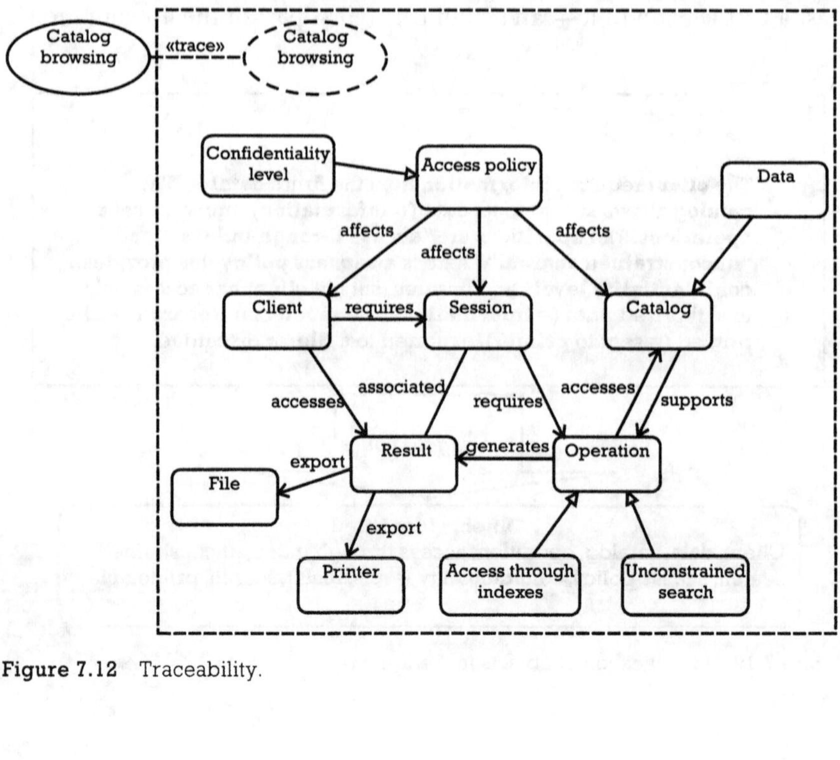

Figure 7.12 Traceability.

is the domain use case model, which factorizes commonalities between the product use case models (Figure 7.13).

So far, the Reusable Solutions S.p.A. example has considered only one product: the one based on the firm's own business. The product has variability inside, as shown by the fact that we were able to factorize a common product use case from two use cases of the same product. However, more variability can be expected from the analysis of other products in the same domain.

So, Reusable Solutions S.p.A. starts considering other products, that is, information systems based on the needs of other businesses. From the manufacturing business, Reusable Solutions S.p.A. moves to the analysis of consulting services. The result is a new use case, named "service delivery" and described in Figure 7.14.

The new product use case resembles some of the previously identified use cases. Moreover, it seems to match the previous common product use case. However, the match is not perfect, as shown by the following facts:

- The "service delivery" use case deals with delivery of services; the common use case deals with delivery of products.

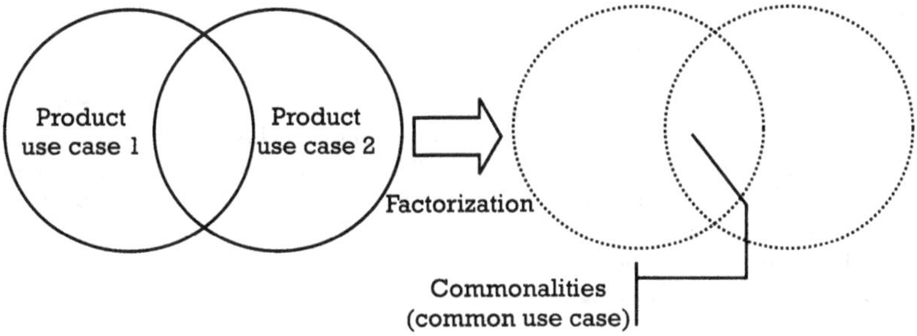

Figure 7.13 Identification of commonalities.

Product use case:
Service delivery
Description:
The client requires a firm's service. The service must be in the firm's catalog. People in the firm are recruited to provide the service. The client's request is also processed according to the accounting procedure. The required service is delivered to the client. The client pays according to the payment procedure and the invoice is issued.

Figure 7.14 "Service delivery" use case.

- The production department is not mentioned in the "service delivery" use case.

The mismatching is minimal, though, and can be overcome by defining a more general use case. This use case would belong to the domain model because it generalized use cases belonging to different products. Such a use case is called a *domain use case* and is meant to capture commonality across products. In the example, the domain use case can be described as shown in Figure 7.15.

Clearly, the "product delivery" domain use case belongs to the domain use case model. However, other use cases are necessary to give a complete view of the domain. For instance, the domain model needs a "catalog browsing" use case. Such a use case is already available in the product models. We also assume that "catalog browsing" is exactly the same in all the product models. In this case, the domain use case can be the same as the product use case. So, in the example, we introduce a "catalog browsing" domain use case that is identical to product use case "catalog browsing" (Figure 7.16).

> Domain use case:
> **Product delivery**
> Description:
> **The client requires a firm's product. The product must be in the firm's catalog. The firm allocates resources to handle the order according to a resource management policy. The client's order is also processed according to the accounting procedure. The product is delivered to the client according to a delivery policy. The client pays according to the payment procedure and the invoice is issued.**

Figure 7.15 "Product delivery" domain use case.

> Domain use case:
> **Catalog browsing**
> Description:
> **The client requires information from the firm's catalog. The catalog allows access to its data through a set of operations. The operations are "access through indexes" and "unconstrained search." There is an access policy that provides confidentiality levels and ensures that the client has access only to authorized data. The result of the search can be printed, exported to a file, or discarded.**

Figure 7.16 "Catalog browsing" domain use case.

Factorization of product use case models should proceed until the domain use case model covers all the features of the domain. Domain use cases should represent nonoverlapping functionalities. This requirement emphasizes the need for use cases that are as general as possible. If two domain use cases overlap, a third use case probably exists that can encapsulate the overlapping, common part. As a reminder, the tools to handle factorization inside a model are the "uses" and "extends" relation. These work in domain use case models exactly like they work for product use case models.

7.4 Identification of variation points and variants

When we identify the commonalities in several product use cases, we leave out the details specific to product use cases. The factorization gives a unifying general view of the domain, but loses much of the information concerning single products. A domain model with commonalities alone is not sufficient; we need to represent differences as well.

We use variation points in the common part as a means of inserting differences. For instance, the "product delivery" domain use case has many unspecified details:

- The term *product* can refer to either a physical product or a service.
- The resource management policy is not specified.
- The accounting procedure is not specified.
- The delivery policy is not specified.
- The payment procedure is not specified.

Figure 7.17 shows in bold type the variation points of the domain use case. Variation points are usually shown in either bold type or delimited by curly braces.

We represent the presence of the unspecified details by putting a "variation point" for each of them in the use case diagram (Figure 7.18).

There are several alternative ways (variants) to implement the variation points. We look for variants in the product use cases already presented in Figure 7.9 and Figure 7.14. Finally, we summarize the variation points and the variants in a variation point table (Figure 7.19).

Domain use case:
Product delivery
Description:
The client of the use case requires a firm's **product**. The **product** must be in the firm's catalog. The firm allocates resources to handle the order according to a **resource management policy**. The client's order is also processed according to the **accounting procedure**. The **product** is delivered to the client according to a **delivery policy.** The client pays according to the **payment procedure** and the invoice is issued.

Figure 7.17 Variation points in the common use case.

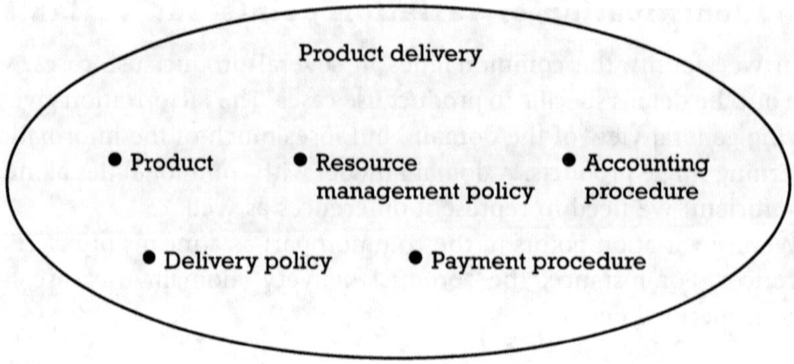

Figure 7.18 Variation points in use case diagram.

We can organize the information from this table with a use case diagram (Figure 7.20). A use case balloon is shown for each domain use case and for each variant. Each variation point can have incoming arrows from other use cases that specify a variant. The arrows have an "extends" label to show that the specification of a variation point is a form of extension.

7.5 Domain analysis model

The analysis model captures analysis objects in the domain. Commonality is expressed (1) through a set of objects and relations that are common to all the products, and (2) through a generic/default behavior associated

Variation point V1: Product Variants: • V1.1: physical product • V1.2: service
Variation point V2: Resource management policy Variants: • V2.1: if product is not available then an order is issued to the production department • V2.2: a production plan is generated • V2.3: recruitment of people
Variation point V3: Accounting procedure Variants: • V3.1: standard procedure
Variation point V4: Delivery procedure Variants • V4.1: simple delivery • V4.2: just-in-time delivery
Variation point V5: Payment procedure Variants • V5.1: standard procedure

Figure 7.19 Variation point table.

with the objects. Variability is expressed through (1) extension of the set of objects and relations, and (2) specialization or extension of the generic/default behavior.

Let us consider again the product analysis model shown in Figure 7.11. The model contains variability according to technique (2): "operation" represents a generic behavior; "access through indexes" and "unconstrained search" are specializations of "operation."

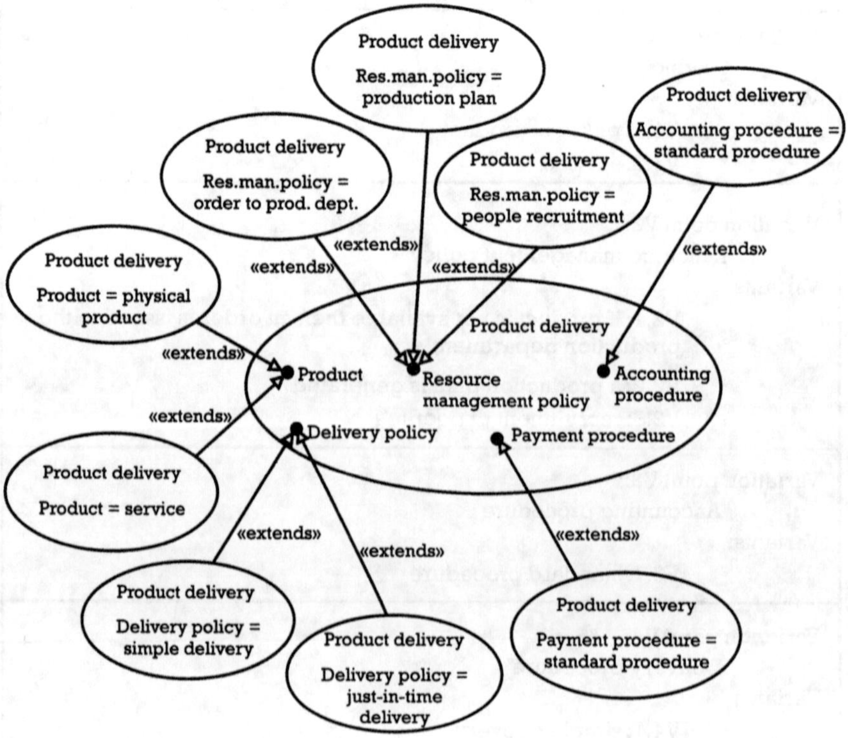

Figure 7.20 Variation points and variants in use case diagram.

From other product use cases not analyzed here, we could identify other specializations of "operation." For instance, in an airport information system product, the catalog of products would contain the list of flights and an operation on it could be "fixed page view." As a result, we generate the domain analysis model shown in Figure 7.21.

Technique (1) is used for objects that may or may not be present. For instance, some products may export the results to an external database, while the products considered thus far do not. We add "external DB" to the analysis model and mark it as an optional object (Figure 7.22).

During the analysis of the product we can discover that some objects previously considered as common actually belong only to some of the products. In this case we should mark those objects as optional. For example, "confidentiality level" and "file" could be considered optional objects (Figure 7.23).

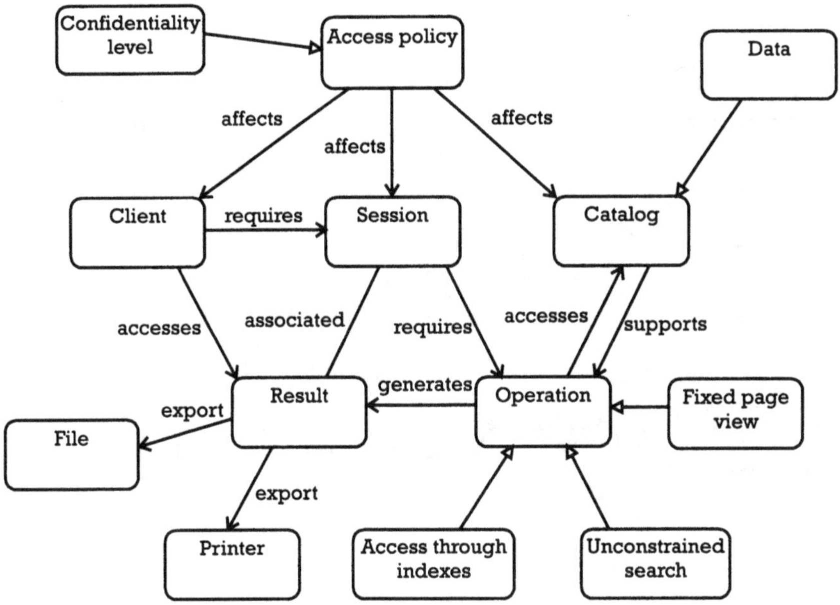

Figure 7.21 Domain analysis model.

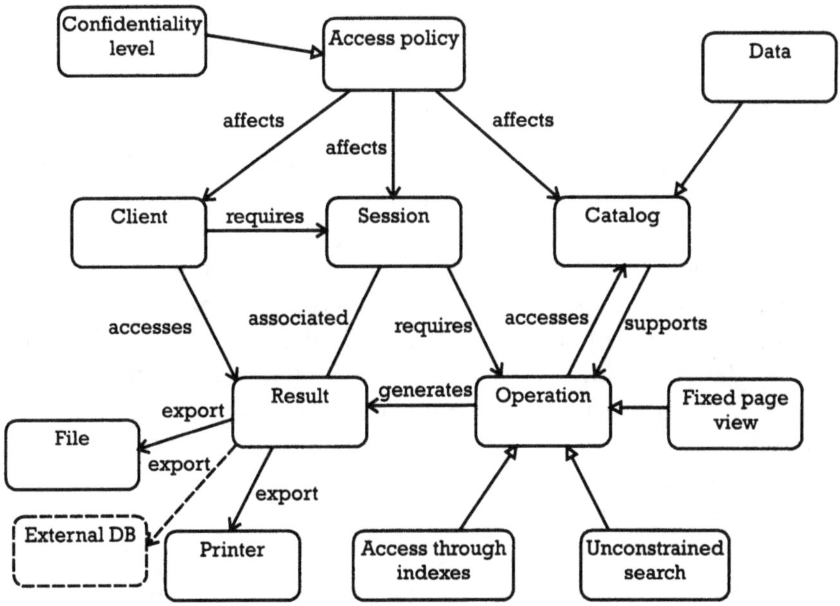

Figure 7.22 Adding optional objects to the domain analysis model.

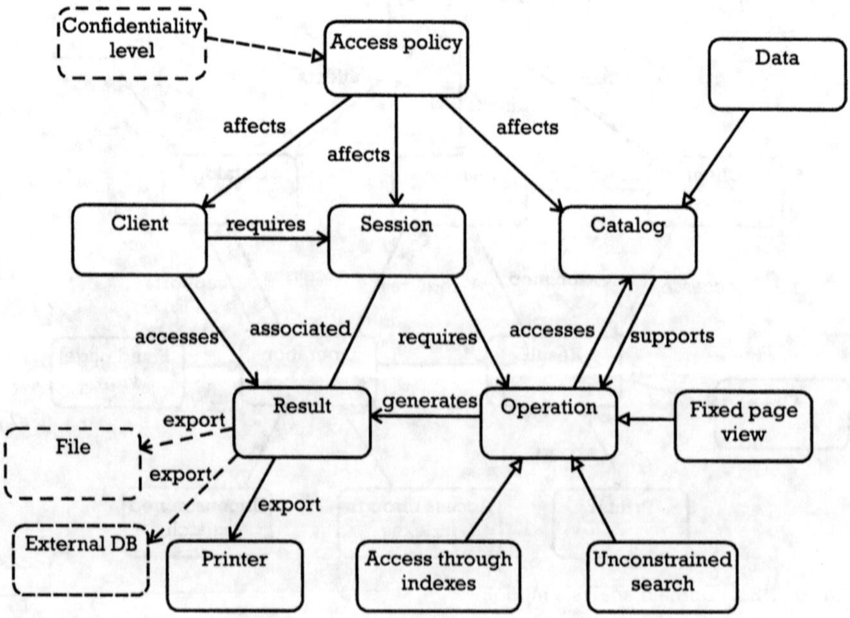

Figure 7.23 Marking optional objects.

7.6 Implementing the variation points

Here we give a short description of the software techniques used to implement variation points. The techniques are as follows: use of parameters, method overloading, inheritance, virtual methods, interfaces, multiple inheritance, templates, aggregation, and delegation.

The final choice of which implementation technique to use is not possible during domain modeling because the domain framework has not yet been designed. However, an early guess at the means used to implement variation points is useful to estimate the framework of the development effort.

Let us consider the implementation of the variation points in the Reusable Solution S.p.A. example:

- **Product** can be implemented through a taxonomy of classes. An *interface* can specify the common operation on the products.

Concrete classes can implement the variants, overriding the methods of the interface.

- **Delivery policy** and **resource management policy** can be implemented through *delegation*. These variation points require great flexibility and dynamic configurability, so it is handy to create separate *delegate objects* that are responsible for the required actions. The delegate objects could exploit network resources for connection to the production information systems and to the resource manager's information system.
- **Accounting procedure** and **payment procedure** can be implemented through *inheritance* and *virtual methods*. A careful analysis of these variation points shows that there is only one variant representing the standard procedure for each variation point. This suggests implementing the variation points as virtual methods with a default implementation in an "order" object, allowing further specialization in subclasses.

7.7 Deliverables of domain modeling

The deliverables for this phase are as follows:

- *DM1:* Product use case models
- *DM2:* Product analysis models
- *DM3:* Domain use case model
- *DM4:* Domain analysis model
- *DM5:* Traces between use cases and analysis classes

DM1 through DM4 work as described in this chapter. DM5 is a reminder to provide explicit traceability links between the use case models and the analysis models.

7.8 The Webmetrics example for domain modeling

As a reminder, the products in the domain are FortranMetric, PascalMetric, CMetric, MetricBuilder, MeasureX, MeasureJava, and Webmetrics. The product models are based on this list.

7.8.1 DM1: Product use case models

Tables 7.1 through 7.5 list the use cases for the seven products of concern.

7.8.2 DM2: Product analysis models

The use cases for FortranMetric, PascalMetric, and CMetric define the following analysis classes: user, file, parser, metric, report, result, report format, file system, automation tool, and Unix-like UI. Some of these classes have derived classes: procedural-oriented metric, C parser, Fortran parser, and Pascal parser. Figure 7.24 shows the analysis model for these products.

FortranMetric, PascalMetric, and CMetric are representative of many features also present in the other products. The analysis model for FortranMetric, PascalMetric, and CMetric will be our baseline. For the other products, we focus mainly on the parts that diverge from the baseline.

The analysis model for MetricBuilder has the potential to define custom metrics, to parse C and Ada, and to store reports on a database (Figure 7.25).

The analysis model for MeasureX has the potential to parse C and C+ +, and to apply both procedural-oriented and object-oriented metrics. This product provides no support for automation of metrics measurement (Figure 7.26).

The analysis model for MeasureJava has the potential to parse Java and to integrate the product in IDEs (Figure 7.27).

Table 7.1
Use Cases for FortranMetric, PascalMetric, and CMetric

Use Case	Description
Metrics measurement	The product reads a set of files specified by the user. Each file is a source code file written in Fortran, Pascal, or C. The product parses the files. The product performs size, complexity, and fan- out metrics on the parsed files. The software metrics produce numeric results. The results are stored on the file system as plain text or in HTML.
Report examination	The user views any of the reports stored on the file system.
Automation of metrics measurement	The user automates the metrics measurement using the tools of a Unix-like command line interface. This use case "extends" the metrics measurement use case.

Table 7.2
Use Cases for MetricBuilder

Use Case	Description
Metrics measurement	The product reads a set of files specified by the user. Each file is a source code file written in C or Ada. The product parses the files. The product performs procedural-oriented metrics on the parsed files. The software metrics produce numeric results. The results are stored as plain text on the file system or on a database. This use case "uses" the metric customization and report customization use cases.
Report examination	The user views any of the reports stored on the file system or on the database.
Automation of metrics measurement	The user automates the metrics measurement using the tools of a Unix-like command line interface. This use case "extends" the metrics measurement use case.
Metric customization	The user defines the custom metrics according to a metric definition language. This language is proprietary to MetricBuilder.

Table 7.3
Use Cases for MeasureX

Use Case	Description
Metrics measurement	The product reads a set of files specified by the user. Each file is a source code file written in C or C++. The product parses the files. The product performs object-oriented and procedural-oriented metrics on the parsed files. The software metrics produce numeric results. The results are stored on the file system as HTML files.
Report examination	The user views any of the reports stored on the file system. This use case "uses" the metrics measurement use case.

The analysis model for Webmetrics introduces all objects that support remote storage of data, server administration, and user authentication. A core object is "server" (Figure 7.28).

Table 7.4
Use Cases for MeasureJava

Use Case	Description
Metrics measurement	The product reads a set of files specified by the user. Each file is a source code file written in Java. The product parses the files. The product performs procedural-oriented and object-oriented metrics on the parsed files. The software metrics produce numeric results. The results are stored as HTML on the file system or on a database.
Report examination	The user views any of the reports stored on the file system or on the database.
Automation of metrics measurement	The user automates the metrics measurement through direct integration of the product with IDEs. This use case "extends" the metrics measurement use case.

Table 7.5
Use Cases for Webmetrics

Use Case	Description
Metrics measurement	The product reads a set of files specified by the user. Each file is a source code file written in procedural-oriented or object-oriented languages. The product parses the files. The product performs procedural-oriented metrics on the parsed files. The software metrics produce numeric results. The results are sent to a remote server for storage.
Report examination	The user views any of the reports stored on the server.
Server access	The user accesses the server through a network connection. The user must be authenticated. The user provides a request, the server provides a response. The server stores and retrieves information from a database. This use case "uses" the user authentication use case.
Server administration	The administrator sets up and configures the server, and defines the user access policies.
User authentication	The user provides a username and password to prove his or her identity.

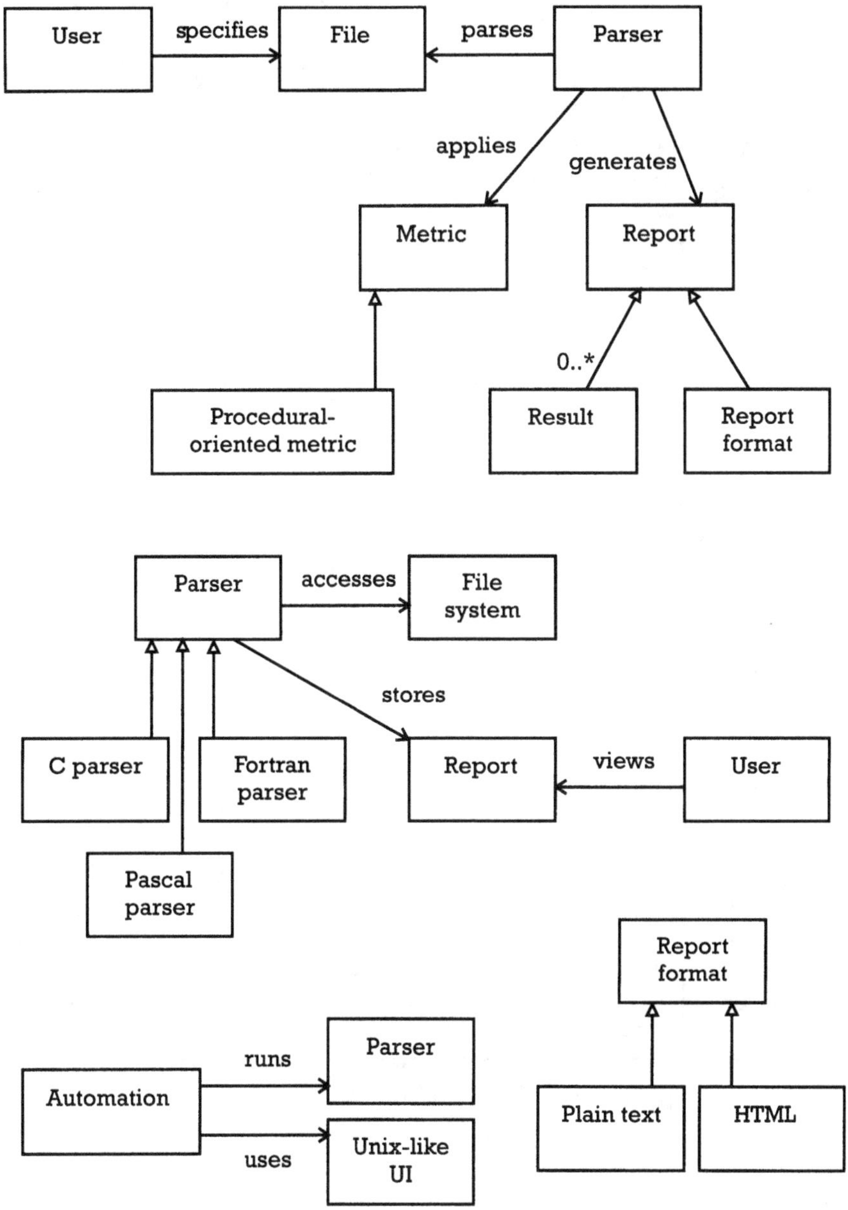

Figure 7.24 Product analysis model for FortranMetric, PascalMetric, and CMetric.

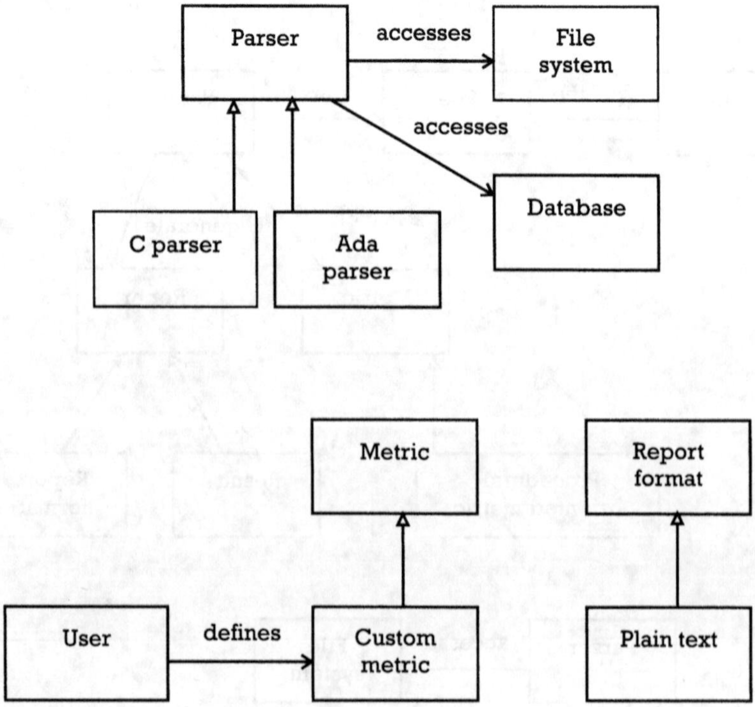

Figure 7.25 Product analysis model for MetricBuilder.

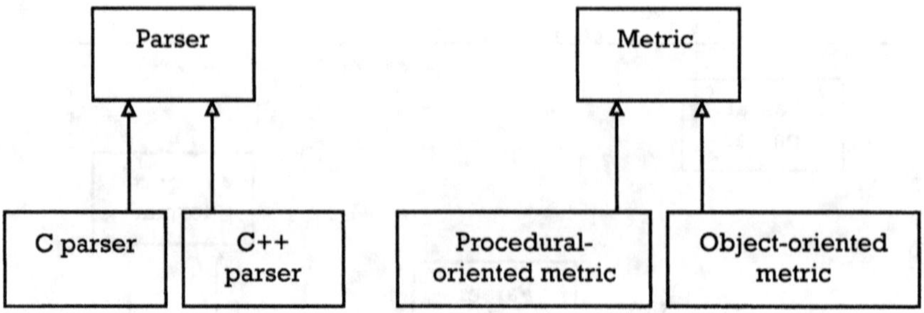

Figure 7.26 Product analysis model for MeasureX.

7.8.3 DM3: Domain use case model

The use case model for the domain is shown in Table 7.6. The italicized terms represent sources of variability, and are candidate variation points. These contribute to define the variation point table presented in domain

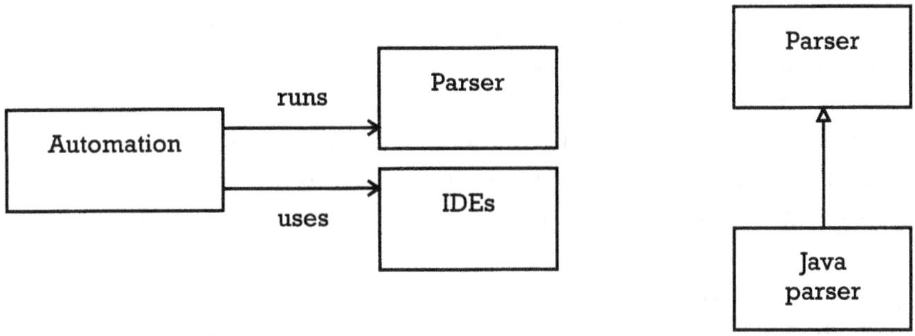

Figure 7.27 Product analysis model for MeasureJava.

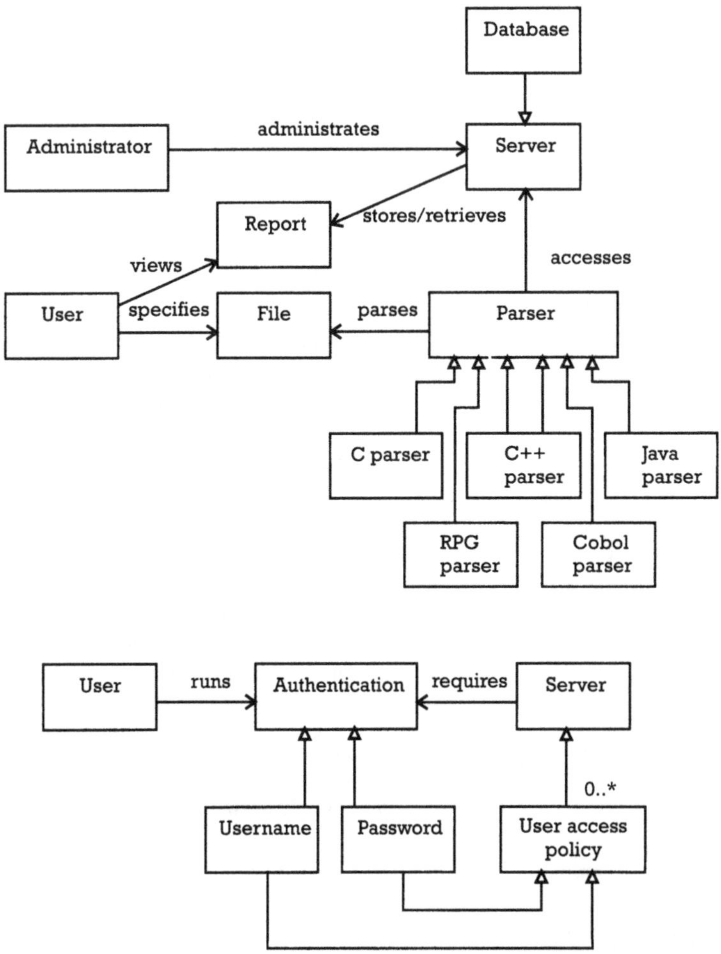

Figure 7.28 Product analysis model for Webmetrics.

scoping (Table 7.2). For each term, a note in parentheses specifies which variation points the term contributes to.

7.8.4 DM4: Domain analysis models

Figures 7.29 and 7.30 present the domain analysis model. The illustrations summarize all of the features, in terms of classes and relations, present in the domain.

7.8.5 DM5: Traces between use cases and analysis classes

Table 7.7 summarizes the traces between the use cases and the analysis classes. An intersection between a use case and a class represents a trace between the two elements.

Table 7.6
Domain Use Cases

Use Case	Description
1: Metrics measurement	The product reads a set of files specified by the user. Each file is a source code file written in some programming language (VP_1). The product parses (VP_2) the files. The product performs some software metrics (VP_3) on the parsed files. The software metrics produce numeric results. The results are stored (VP_4) according to some format (VP_5).
2: Report examination	The user views any of the stored (VP_4, VP_5) reports.
3: Automation of metrics measurement	The user automates the metrics measurement through the mechanisms allowed by the user interface (VP_6). This use case "extends" the metrics measurement use case.
4: Metric customization	The user defines the custom metrics according to a metric definition language (VP_3).
5: Server access	The user accesses the server through a network connection. The user must be authenticated. The user provides a request, the server provides an response. The server stores and retrieves information from a database. This use case "uses" the user authentication use case.
6: Server administration	The administrator sets up and configures the server, and defines the user access policies.
7: User authentication	The user provides a username and password to prove his or her identity.

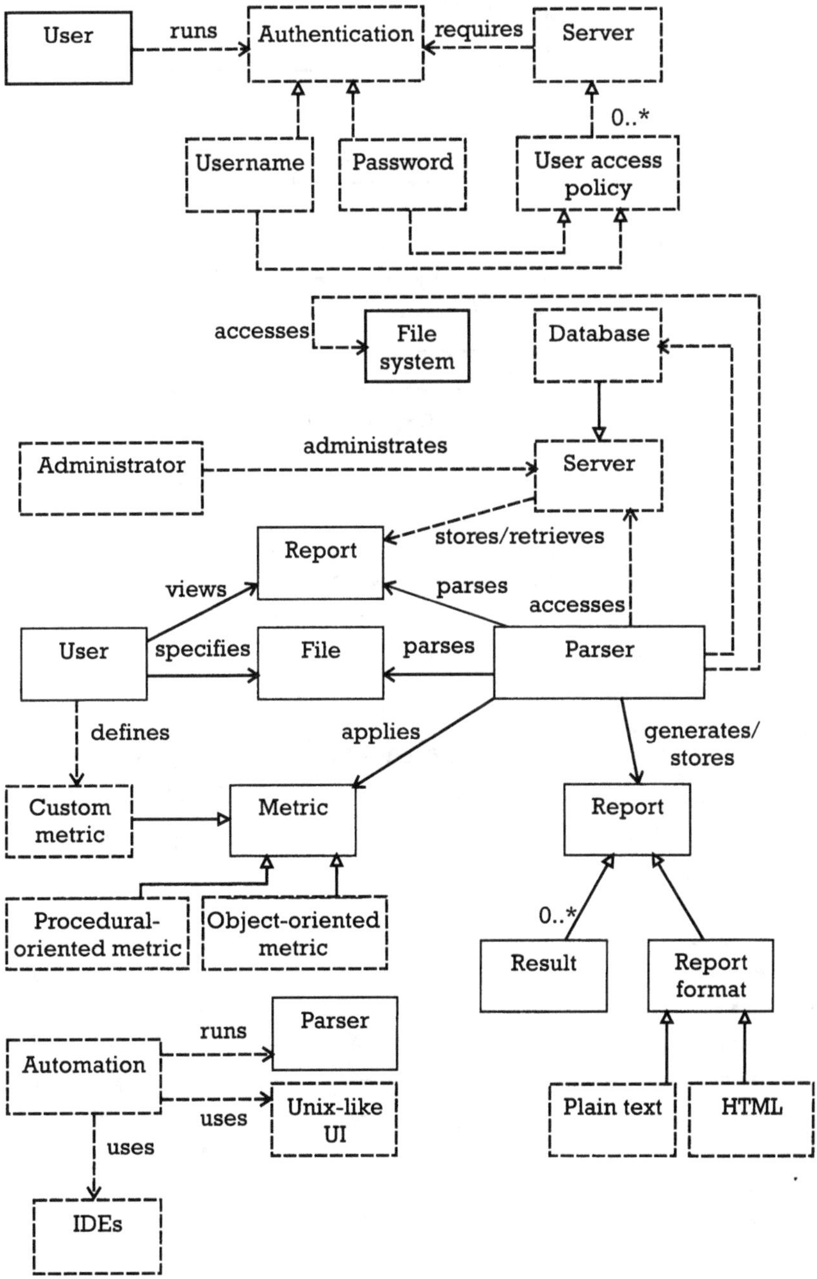

Figure 7.29 Domain analysis model, part 1.

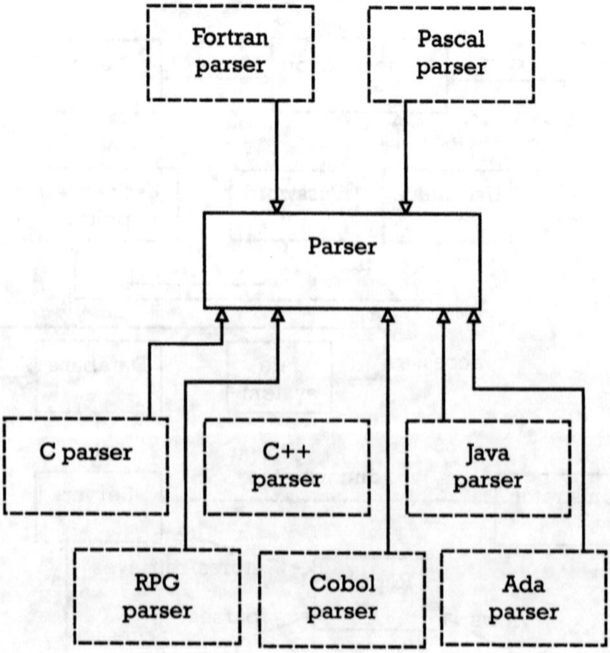

Figure 7.30 Domain analysis model, part 2.

Table 7.7
Traceability Table

	Use case 1	Use case 2	Use case 3	Use case 4	Use case 5	Use case 6	Use case 7
User	√	√	√	√	√	—	√
Authentication	—	—	—	—	√	√	√
Server	√	√	—	—	√	√	√
Username	—	—	—	—	—	—	√
Password	—	—	—	—	—	—	√
User access policy	—	—	—	—	√	√	√
File system	√	√	—	—	—	—	—
Database	√	√	—	—	√	—	—
Administrator	—	—	—	—	—	√	—
Report	√	√	—	—	—	—	—
File	√	√	—	—	—	—	—
Parser	√	—	√	—	—	—	—
Custom metric	—	—	—	√	—	—	—

Table 7.7 (continued)

	Use case 1	Use case 2	Use case 3	Use case 4	Use case 5	Use case 6	Use case 7
Metric	√	√	√	√	—	—	—
Procedural-oriented metric	√	—	—	—	—	—	—
Object-oriented metric	√	—	—	—	—	—	—
Results	√	√	√	—	—	—	—
Report format	√	√	—	—	—	—	—
Plain text	√	√	—	—	—	—	—
HTML	√	√	—	—	—	—	—
Automation	—	—	√	—	—	—	—
Unix-like UI	—	—	√	—	—	—	—
IDEs	—	—	√	—	—	—	—
Fortran parser	√	—	—	—	—	—	—
Pascal parser	√	—	—	—	—	—	—
C parser	√	—	—	—	—	—	—
C++ parser	√	—	—	—	—	—	—
RPG parser	√	—	—	—	—	—	—
Cobol parser	√	—	—	—	—	—	—
Ada parser	√	—	—	—	—	—	—

7.8.6 Logging the evolution of domain modeling

Table 7.8 summarizes the development efforts for this phase.

Table 7.8
Evolution of Domain Modeling

Author	Date	Action	Effort
Sherlock's authors	1997-11-17/18/19/20	Analysis of FortranMetric, PascalMetric, and CMetric	14 man-hours
Sherlock's authors	1997-11-30 1997-12-1	Early analysis of Webmetrics	5 man-hours
Sherlock's authors	1998-1-5	Analysis of MetricBuilder and MeasureX	8 man-hours
Sherlock's authors	1998-1-6	Analysis of MeasureJava	4 man-hours
Sherlock's authors	1998-1-6	Revision of Webmetrics analysis and identification of variation points	4 man-hours

Table 7.8 (continued)

Author	Date	Action	Effort
Sherlock's authors	1998-1-27/28	Revision of product analysis and of variation points	13 man-hours
Sherlock's authors	1998-2-4/5	Formalization of use cases	10 man-hours
Sherlock's authors	1998-2-6/7	Formalization of analysis models and traceability	16 man-hours
Sherlock's authors	1998-9-29/30 1998-10-1/2/3	Revision of models; revision of variation points	15 man-hours
Sherlock's authors	1999-7-10	Revision of models; revision of variation points	3 man-hours

Reference

[1] Jacobson, I., M. Griss, and P. Jonsson, *Software Reuse: Architecture Process and Organization for Business Success*, Reading, MA: Addison-Wesley, 1997.

CHAPTER

8

Contents

Domain framework development

A domain framework is an organized set of software components and an architecture designed to build applications within the domain. A *component* is a piece of software that provides a functionality and can be deployed individually. An *architecture* is a description of the structure of the domain's software. An architecture is made up of several *projections.* Each projection shows the structure of the software from a different perspective. Several projections are needed because no single perspective suffices to describe the whole architecture.

The presence of components demonstrates that domain frameworks are concrete software entities that can be used to develop products. The presence of an architecture demonstrates that those products will be developed with a thoughtful design supporting them. The framework allows products to be built within the domain. Products use the components and share the framework architecture. Ideally, the framework should allow all products in the domain to be built with maximum ease. In reality, the characteristics of a real framework determine to what extent the framework covers the products in the domain and the effort required to build the products.

A domain framework is not a collection of products. It is not possible to build a product just by picking it out of the framework. To build a product, we need to integrate the framework with a product-specific part.

The framework and the product-specific part work side by side: The framework provides the components, and the product-specific part establishes the relations among those components and also provides components of its own.

The union of the framework with a product-specific part generates a product. By changing the product-specific part, other products can be generated. Figures 8.1(a) and (b) show two products—Product 1 and Product 2—built using the domain framework and different product-specific parts. These products are deployed to the user. The user sees the product as a single entity and does not perceive its internal division in framework plus product-specific part.

A framework can also be deployed as a stand-alone product [Figure 8.1(c)]. In this case the term *product* refers to a sellable item, rather than to a running and usable application. In this case the user knows what the framework is and how to use it to generate products.

8.1 Relationship between the framework and the product-specific part

The cooperation of the framework with the product-specific parts generates the products. There are several kinds of cooperation:

- The framework works as a box of components. The product-specific part picks the right components and puts them together in the most appropriate way for the particular product.
- The framework provides the skeleton of a product. The product-specific part provides the components. The resulting product has the shape of the skeleton with the substance of the product-specific components.
- The framework provides the skeleton and the components of a product. The product-specific part attaches the components to the skeleton. In this process, the product-specific part has a certain

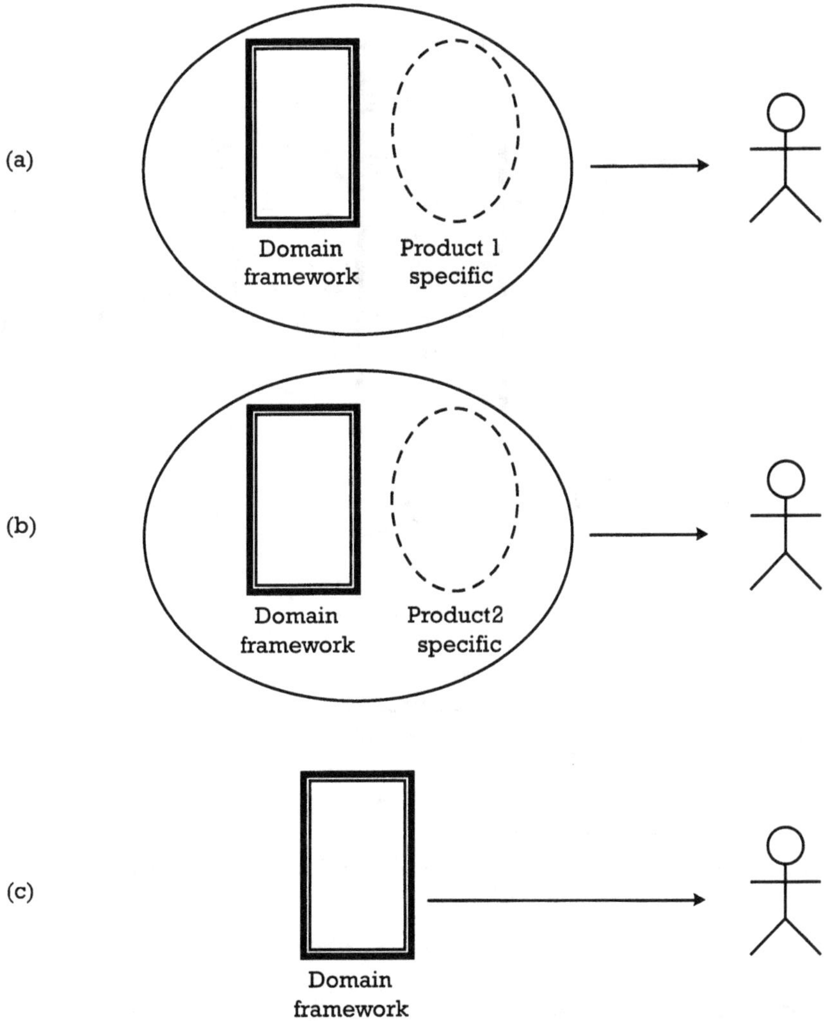

Figure 8.1 Deployment of a framework within products and as stand-alone products.

degree of choice because some components in the framework are interchangeable.

The features of the framework (Figure 8.2) are offered either as components—a, b, c, d, e, and f—or as hooks available for attaching behaviors—x, y, and w. This holds also for the product-specific part. In Figure 8.2, the

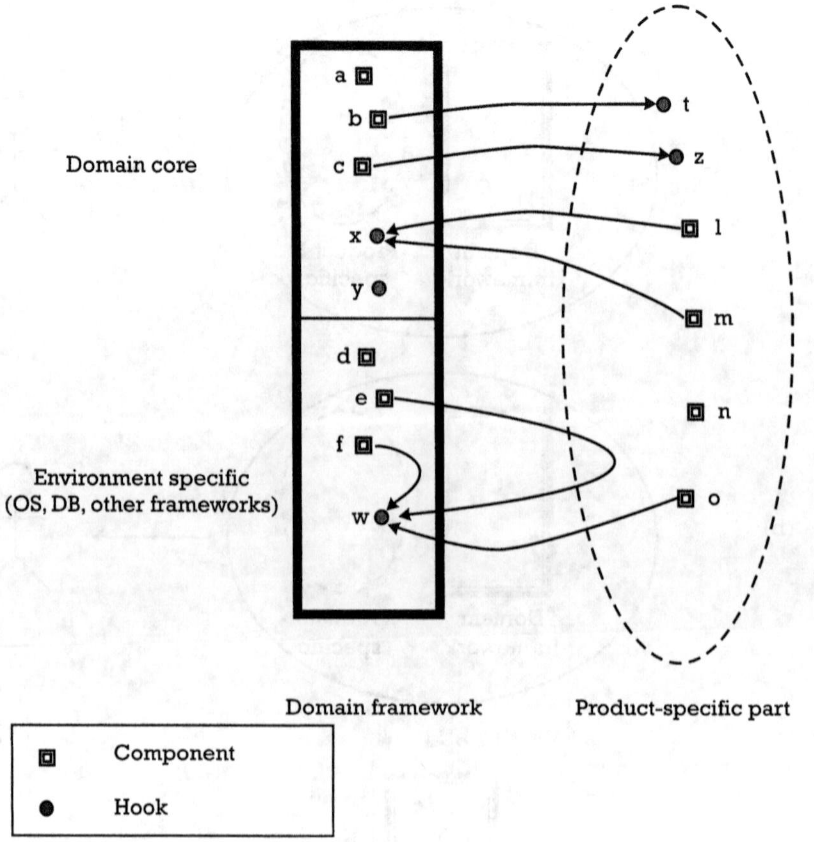

Figure 8.2 Interaction between the domain framework and the product-specific part.

framework and the product-specific part fill each other's hooks with components: *b* fills *t*, *c* fills *z*, *l* fills *x*, *m* fills *x*, *e* fills *w*, *f* fills *w*, and *o* fills *w*.

A hook can be of different kinds, including the following:

- An interface or abstract class to which the implementation needs to be provided;
- A concrete class that developers can subclass to better fit their needs;
- A pointer to a function that can be associated with a real function by a developer; this real function can be either defined by the system or by the developer.

Generally, the links between components and hooks belong to the product-specific part; the product-specific part sets the *patch cords* between the components. This is obvious when the product-specific part sets a link involving either a product-specific hook or a product-specific component. This is also true when the product-specific part sets a link between a component and a hook both belonging to the framework. The link between *e* and *w* in Figure 8.2 is an example of this. In contrast, some links belong to the framework. These links involve a component and a hook both belonging to the framework (link between *f* and *w* in Figure 8.2) and represent a default link set in the framework.

Figure 8.2 shows that the domain framework is organized in two layers: (1) a layer specific to the environment and (2) a layer specific to the core, environment-independent functionality of the domain. The environment typically comprises the operating system, possible databases, and other frameworks that are used by the target domain framework.

8.2 Callbacks and callback loops

A callback occurs when the developer specifies the body of a function that is then called by the system. Callbacks often occur in a framework designed to react to events calling functions that are specified by developers, like GUIs. Consider the case in which we want the function popUpMenu() to be called in response to a mouse click. In certain frameworks, one way to achieve this goal is with a call like assign (MOUSE_CLICK, popUpMenu), where "assign" is a framework function that assigns a function to an event, MOUSE_CLICK is the event that signals the click of a mouse button, and popUpMenu is the developer function to call in response to the event of clicking the mouse. The name "callback" comes from the fact that usually the developer calls framework functions directly, whereas in this case the framework calls a developer function.

Some frameworks require the developers to specify only the functions to call "back" in response to events. This is common in frameworks for GUI, such as Motif. When the application built on the framework is run, a system-defined main function is called. Such a function simply loops, waiting for events to occur. When an event occurs, the appropriate developer-defined function is called. These frameworks are said to be based on the callback loop.

In principle, a single application can be developed using multiple frameworks. However, each framework may pose requirements on the structure of the applications using them. For instance, the presence of two frameworks based on callback loops poses the difficult problem of having the same application reside in two callback loops at the same time.

This has been called the problem of *architectural mismatch* and researchers have considered it one of the major inhibitors to reuse. Therefore, frameworks should be designed wisely, trying to limit as much as possible the assumptions they make on the applications that will use them.

8.3 Passive and reactive frameworks

We have already mentioned that a framework can have a very diverse structure. We identify two opposite situations:

1. A *passive* framework, which is a library with no callbacks;
2. A *reactive* framework organized on the basis of a callback loop.

Table 8.1 shows these opposing situations for the selection of frameworks.

Passive frameworks are the best choice when the products in the domain use a large set of loosely coupled components in very different ways and do not share a "dominant" control flow. Libraries are well-known examples of passive frameworks. Passive frameworks are also appropriate for products spanning multiple domains, since they pose few constraints on the design of the products.

Reactive frameworks are the best choice when the products in the domain can be organized around the same event-driven metaphor. Some programming languages and development environments are tailored specifically to this approach. An example is Component Pascal with its associated framework, BlackBox.

Table 8.1
Selecting the Nature of the Framework

Situation	Framework Type
Several entities are loosely coupled and the product-specific parts have fairly different control structures.	Passive
The applications in the domain can be organized as reactive systems using a single event-driven metaphor.	Reactive

Attaching behavior is not very common in traditional libraries, but it is still present. In Unix/C, the signal function is used by programmers to instruct the system to execute the function they want to run when a given exception is raised. Attaching behavior is more common in reactive, event-driven systems, such as graphic environments—for example, Motif—or database applications.

Real domains and products often require a combination of the passive and reactive approaches. Reactive frameworks provide for the control of operations. Passive frameworks provide the bulk of the components. Links provide the match between the frameworks' hooks and components.

8.4 Frameworks in Sherlock

The key ingredients of a domain framework in Sherlock are as follows:

1. The definition of the nature of the domain framework to develop, that is, whether the framework is mainly reactive or passive;
2. The architecture of the domain framework, which outlines the logical structure of applications in the domain;
3. The documentation of the components in the domain framework;
4. A browsable and searchable catalog of the components in the domain framework;
5. Guidelines to develop applications using the components. These guidelines may be in the form of design patterns.

Domain framework development is an incremental activity. Items 1 through 5 in the preceding list are not produced in one shot. They are developed with an incremental and iterative approach until a satisfactory framework has been designed.

The decision on the nature of the domain framework is based on the study of the core entities of the domain, as they come from domain modeling, and on the similarity of the real and potential applications in the core domain.

We develop frameworks for applications not yet developed. We want the design of the framework to influence the design of the applications and we use architectures for this purpose.

Throughout this book we have assumed and used an object-oriented paradigm for software development. Objects provide the functionalities of systems. In a running application, only objects exist and the behavior of the system is always determined by the state of its objects. However, we design classes of objects. Class definitions express the behavior of objects implicitly, before the application is run. The number of classes is determined at compile time. The number of objects is not known a priori and can vary at run time.

A framework provides classes, not objects; objects belong to running applications. Yet, a framework influences the objects and this influence must be clearly stated and enforced.

When we refer to objects we refer both to the real objects in a running application and to the classes to which they belong. When we refer to classes, we refer only to the static behavior of the system.

8.5 Architecture of the domain framework and of the derived products

An architecture is a model that organizes components and their relations in a logical way. Sherlock requires an architecture to show how the framework is organized and how products derived from the framework should be organized.

An architecture is described by several architectural projections. An architectural projection is a particular perspective under which the system is described.

Sherlock requires the presence of three projections: the package, the class, and the object dynamics projection. These are closely related to components and to compositional reuse; moreover, significant examples of frameworks—Java Foundation Classes, BlackBox Component Framework—exist where these projections are dominant.

In addition, there can be other projections depending on the requirement of the application domain. In particular, the object interaction projection, the functional projection, the process projection, and the component projection are often present.

A projection can be represented in one or more UML diagrams. If there are multiple diagrams, each diagram should contain a cohesive subset of the projection; however, a diagram does not need to provide a complete description of the elements in it. The description can be distributed across all diagrams. This makes it easier to understand the diagrams, letting developers hide the unnecessary details.

The following sections describe the three major projections and other projections, emphasizing how they support variability in the domain.

8.5.1 Package projection

The package projection describes how the design documents and the source code have been divided to ease the task of developers. A package is a cohesive set of design documents or of pieces of source code. A package may contain other packages, like directories that include other directories; cycles are forbidden. A design document, a piece of source code, and a package can belong to only one package.

The package projection also describes the reference relations existing between packages. A package may refer to other packages. Therefore, references are allowed across packages. Reference relations can be circular.

Packages are usually divided into work packages and assigned to people. This has a management implication. Early assignments of people can change but at high cost: Developers moved to work on a new package have to experience a learning curve before they become productive. The hardest variability to handle in package projection therefore is the variability of the assignment of people to work packages.

8.5.2 Class projection

The class projection describes the classes of the objects in the system using relations of association, aggregation, composition, generalization, and so on. UML's class diagrams are the tool used to represent the class projection.

Class projection is directly related to the analysis model built during domain modeling. However, mapping between the analysis classes of domain modeling and the design and implementation classes of the class projection is not one to one. Analysis classes are closer to requirements and speak the language of the user; classes in this projection are closer to implementation and speak the language of the software developer.

Variability in the class projection allows practically any definition and combination of classes. The class projection implies decomposition of functionality at a fine level of detail.

The constraints of the class projection are similar to those of the functional projection but at a finer detail. The class projection is flexible enough to offer different solutions for the same problem. However, each solution makes some assumptions and poses some constraints.

8.5.3 Object projections

So far we have only considered classes of objects. While developing the architecture of the domain framework, we consider two separate projections: the class projection focusing on classes and the object projection focusing on objects.

Although similar to a class projection, the object projections are (1) conceptually different, because they represent objects (that is, active entities), and not classes; and (2) practically different, because there can be several separate objects for a single class. The object projections show the objects in the domain and the interactions between the objects. Objects belong to classes. Each class can have several objects. The object projections grasp data and control flow of running applications. The possible configurations a program can reach are (almost) infinite and describing them all is not feasible. The object projections focus on patterns and typical scenarios that are representative of the run-time behavior of the products.

To develop the object projections, we first decompose the application into subparts that interact frequently through data and control flow. This can be done by looking at the class and other projections. Then we study the interaction between the parts. Run-time issues such as synchronization, locking, and priority should be taken into account.

Sherlock has two object projections: the object dynamics projection, which is required, and the object interaction projection, which is optional.

The object dynamics projection represents the flow of message exchanges between objects without taking into consideration time. The object interaction projection also represents the timing of the messages exchanges. Figure 8.3 presents the high-level object dynamics projection of a programming language compiler.

There can be several diagrams for the object dynamics projection. A description in plain English can be added to each diagram.

The object interaction projection for the compiler example is shown in Figure 8.4. The information that is conveyed by the interaction dynamic projection includes that of the object dynamics projection. The object dynamics projection is an essential portion of the framework, since it provides a synthetic view of how the objects in the domain interact. The object interaction projection is required when timing is a crucial

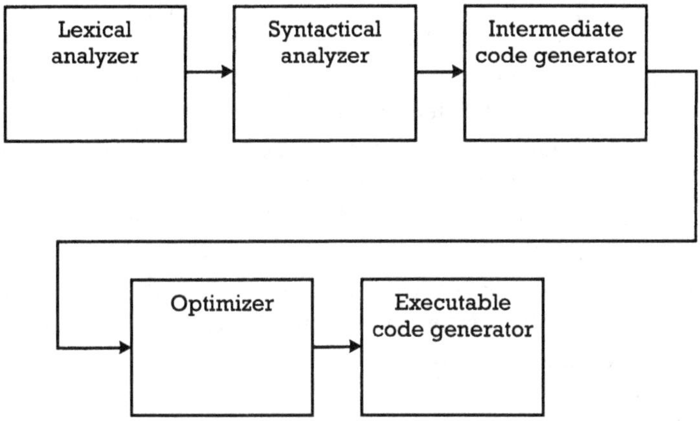

Figure 8.3 Sample object dynamics projection.

aspect of the system that cannot be inferred by the object dynamics projection and the associated documentation.

The supported variability of the object projection derives from the infinite possible ways of instantiating and combining objects at run time.

The imposed constraints are a consequence of the constraints of the class projection.

8.5.4 Functional projection

The functional projection decomposes the system into functional parts, that is, parts that perform clearly visible, distinct functions. The

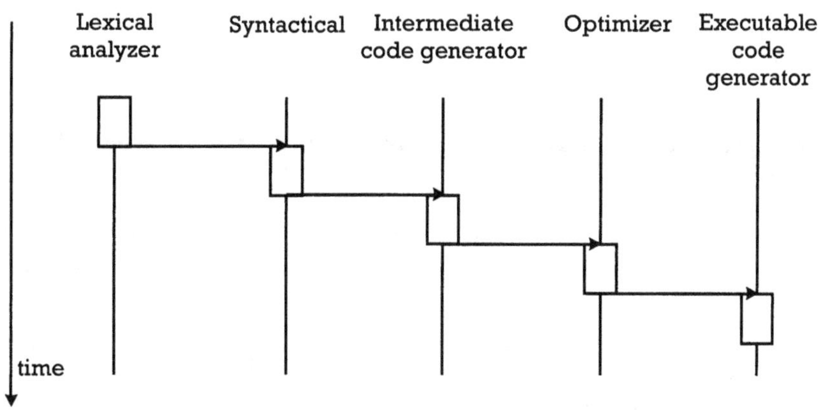

Figure 8.4 Sample object interaction projection.

functional projection also describes the connections between the parts in terms of exchanged and shared data.

The functional projection can be used to relate the functionality of the framework to the features of the domain use cases.

The supported variability is in the combination of elementary functional parts to create a variety of aggregated, or macro, functions.

The imposed constraints are in the definition of the functions. The boundaries of the functions are usually flexible but, once set, are hard to change. This can be a problem when the system interacts with and uses functions of other systems where the functional decomposition has been done according to other choices.

8.5.5 Process projection

The process projection describes the processes running in the system and how functionalities are mapped on the processes and from processes to processors.

The supported variability is in the freedom to assign functionalities to processes. This freedom is a consequence of the fact that many functionalities can run independently and concurrently.

The imposed constraints are concerned with the limits on the parallelism of the process: Processes need synchronization and sequencing.

8.5.6 Component projection

The component projection describes the major components in the framework. It can be used to describe the interaction between running subsystems, and how subsystems are mapped to physical nodes.

It can also be used to package complex distributed documentations or source files.

8.6 Documentation of components in the domain framework

Sherlock requires that each component in the framework have a suitable documentation. The documentation should include at least the following items:

- The full identification of the component in the package projection. In C++ this can be the path for the header file (for example, mylib/foo.h), the path for the source file (for example, mylib/foo.c) and the path for the compiled library (for example, mylib.a). In Java this can be the full class name (for example, mylib.Foo). These simple examples reflect the natural module/package projection of some languages but can be extended to handle multiple versions and distributed storage of components. The full identification allows efficient retrieval of the components.

- A brief description of the functionality of the component. This allows the user to determine at a quick glance whether the component is what he or she needs.
- A detailed description of the component. This includes excerpts from and references to the architecture documents related to the component. Examples of how to reuse the component improve the description.

8.7 Browsable and searchable catalog of components

The catalog helps the user locate the desired components in the framework. There are two main ways to locate components: by browsing the catalog or searching the catalog.

If the domain is fairly simple, the catalog can be as simple as an alphabetically sorted list of the components with a few keywords per component. The more components there are in the framework, the more powerful the catalog should be. For any query, the catalog should return the least number of components, without missing any suitable component.

Two widely used techniques to support browsing and searching of complex catalogs are hierarchical organization and faceted classification [1].

Hierarchical organization splits the whole set of components into categories; then it splits the categories into subcategories and so on. This splitting process stops when an *n*th level category contains a suitable number of strictly related components. The hierarchical organization is the basis of the Dewey classification scheme of books. Browsing the hierarchically organized catalog is like a tree search: The user starts from the root of the hierarchy, chooses the category where the component he or she is looking for fits best (thus restricting the search), does other choices, and finally obtains a small set of components. If the search is successful, the required component is in the final set. The search is interactive because it allows browsing of the tree until the required component is found.

Faceted classification relies on the fact that components hardly fit in a single, possibly hierarchical, classification. For instance, a component could fit in two or more categories of a hierarchical classification. The source of the problem is that a component may fit in one part of the hierarchy for one aspect and in another part of the hierarchy for another aspect.

Faceted classification considers all aspects separately. Aspects are called *facets*. The user can specify how the component he or she is looking for is related to each facet. For example, let us assume that the framework contains GUI components and that they are classified according to the following facets: information direction, content type, and editability. We are looking for a component that displays and handles a button widget. The search is shown in Figure 8.5. Ending up with only two components (ButtonWidget and MenuWidget), it is easy to pick the right one by just reading their documentation.

Faceted classification, although powerful, is more complex than hierarchical classification. Moreover, faceted classification requires complex infrastructures (a search engine) and a lot of initial work (setting up the classification), whereas hierarchical classification can be effectively implemented through a static set of web pages (without any engine but the browser). Yet, for large frameworks, powerful searching capabilities are necessary. A compromise solution is to replace faceted classification with full-text indexing on the documentation of the components. Full-text indexing provides a kind of lexicographic classification but does not attach any semantics to the indexed words.

8.8 Guidelines for developing applications using the framework

The last ingredient in the framework is a set of guidelines on how to use the framework to create new products. These guidelines are examples of how product developers can use the classes (components) of the framework to produce working products. In general, the guidelines are not prescriptive; they are meant to be as general as possible to fit many real situations.

The steps to develop the guidelines follow:

Searched component:
A component to display and handle a button widget.

Facets:

- Information direction: input
- Content type: text/graphics
- Editability: no

Result of search:
Button Widget, Menu Widget.

Figure 8.5 Search with faceted classification.

1. Identify the main kinds of potential applications that can be developed using the framework. The list of products in the current domain is a good starting point for this task.
2. Provide examples of how to combine classes and objects to create such products. This refers to a form of reuse often called *black-box reuse* or *reuse as is*.
3. Discuss how to create new product-specific components based on the framework's components when simple composition of existing components is not sufficient. This refers to a form of reuse often called *white-box reuse* or *reuse with change*.

8.9 Commonality and variability: implementation issues

Throughout the book we have discussed how, at different stages, we can manage commonality and variability. The last step is to manage these two concepts during code implementation. The following is a list of techniques specifically designed and commonly used to manage commonality and variability:

- Parameters

- Method overloading
- Inheritance
- Virtual methods
- Interfaces
- Multiple inheritance
- Generics
- Aggregation

Parameters are placeholders used to generate sets of functions, classes, methods, files, and so on. Typical examples of parameters are the arguments, or formal parameters, of methods. Parameters can also be expressed as file constants, class constants, object constants, and flags to distinguish among different configurations—for example, the #ifdef statements in C and C++.

A method of a class is fully identified by its name and its argument list. Several programming languages allow multiple methods with the same name, as long as the argument list is different in length and in the sequence of argument types. This language feature is called overloading and supports variability in method invocation.

Inheritance and virtual methods are already widely discussed in the literature, so we do not see the need to present them here.

Interfaces are contracts to specify commonality of behavior without defining how such behavior is implemented.

Multiple inheritance means that a class has two or more superclasses; that is, two or more different and possibly not overlapping behaviors are inherited. Multiple inheritance is a way to specify that a class belongs to several taxonomies or that there are multiple "views" of the same class, one per superclass.

Generics are means to parameterize types or constants for functions, classes, interfaces, and methods. Generics support variability because a single definition of a generic entity (for example, a class or a function) defines implicitly a whole set of entities that differ in the type they can handle. The generic entity is the common part, the "formal" type is a variation point, and the "actual" type is a variant.

Aggregation is the inclusion of objects in one object. There are usually a primary object and some auxiliary objects. Variability is obtained through dynamic binding of any auxiliary object to any primary object.

Several other techniques are available for handling commonality and variability, such as global variables, higher order functions, variant data structures, type relaxation, and so on. Readers interested in the subject can consult a good book on the design of programming languages, such as the one by Sethi [2].

8.10 Coding the framework: language-specific issues

"Should we use C++ or Java?" "How can we code the framework if we use C?" "What about Visual Basic?" We are asked questions like this every day. Although we cannot give absolute answers to these questions, we want to share a few considerations:

- Using an object-oriented language such as C++, Smalltalk, or Java can make the development of the framework simpler.
- In some circumstances, Java and some other object-oriented programming languages are not appropriate for reasons related to the environment in which the framework is developed or used. These can be performance or reliability issues, lack of experience, of documentation, of compilers and other tools, and so on.

"Normal" procedural languages, such as Pascal, nonobject-oriented Fortran, and Visual Basic, are suitable for implementing object-oriented (OO) systems, even if the lack of inheritance, virtual functions, polymorphism, and other features of OO languages make OO programming difficult.

C is somehow in the middle between procedural and OO languages, because experienced C programmers can simulate OO features using advanced C constructs, such as the # and the ## operators in macros, functions with variable numbers of arguments, void pointers, and so on.

Table 8.2 illustrates how C++, Java, Smalltalk, and C support the commonality and variability mechanisms mentioned in the previous section.

As is evident from Table 8.2, the three object-oriented languages listed provide different supports and there is no clear winner, even though the number of "No support" entries varies: one for C++, two for Java, and three for Smalltalk. It is interesting to notice that C, commonly

Table 8.2
Variability Support in Current Programming Languages

	C++	Java	Smalltalk	C
Parameters	Full support	Full support	Full support	Full support
Method overloading	Full support	Full support	Full support	No support
Inheritance	Full support	Full support	Full support	No support
Virtual methods	Full support	Full support	Full support	With some effort using void pointers
Interfaces	No support	Full support	No support	No support
Multiple inheritance	Full support	No support	No support	No support
Generics	With templates	No support	No support	With some effort using the # and ## operators
Aggregation and delegation	Full support	Full support	Full support	Full support

considered an "old" programming language, is not very far from Smalltalk, with only four "No support" entries.

8.11 The Webmetrics example for domain framework development

Webmetrics parses source code files and applies to them a set of metrics measurements. The results of the measurements are stored in a database, which allows later retrieval of data. Statistical analysis can be performed on the data in the database.

Using the framework as a basis, several products can be built according to specific customer needs.

The following sections present the details of the application of Sherlock. Here we show a brief summary of the most relevant features:

- There are two main entities: the client and the server. These entities perform different functionalities and are mapped on different processes and, possibly, on different hardware.
- The client runs in response to a user's request and performs the metrics measurement on source code specified by the user.

- The server runs unattended, collecting data coming from the client and storing the data in a database.
- There is usually one server and several clients. Clients and server communicate through a network.
- A special kind of client retrieves data from the server and performs the statistical analyses. In this case the server provides, rather than collects, the data from the database.
- Authentication and user management are supported.

The interfaces, protocols, and APIs that allow communication between the various components of the framework are made visible to the product developer so that he or she can develop new products by combining the framework's components with custom-developed components.

8.11.1 DF1: Definition of the nature of the domain framework

The client side of the framework is passive. The client is a Java program activated by a user request. When the client is not activated, it does not even exist as a process.

The client can also be incorporated in another program. In this case the execution of the client is bound to the execution of the hosting program. Also in this case the client is passive because its execution is triggered by a request from the hosting program.

The server side of the framework is active. The server continuously waits for connections from the clients. In this process, the server keeps the control of execution.

The server components provide full support to manage the control of execution. Product developers using the framework are not required, nor recommended, to extend this part. Product developers can extend the server's features regarding database access, logging, user management, and so on. These are noncore features that can be plugged into the server's core through the provided APIs.

8.11.2 DF2: Architecture of the domain framework

The architecture comprises the three core projections: module, class, and object dynamics. The functional projection is added to ensure that all the major functionalities of the system have been taken care of.

Package projection

Figure 8.6 contains the package projection. The associated description follows:

- *webmetrics:* This package contains classes common to the whole system and is concerned with the communication between the client and the server. Concepts such as request, response, user, payload, metric, and data are handled here.
- *webmetrics.server:* This package contains server-specific classes to manage client connections, database connections, logging, resources, and interaction with the underlying operating system.
- *webmetrics.client:* This package contains the interface that clients must implement and a class to provide a description of the clients.
- *webmetrics.tools:* This package should contain classes specific to all the tools in the framework. Currently there are no classes in the package. The package only creates a group of subpackages.
- *webmetrics.tools.administration:* This package contains classes for server administration.
- *webmetrics.tools.parser:* This package groups the subpackages that implement the various source code parsers and analyzers.

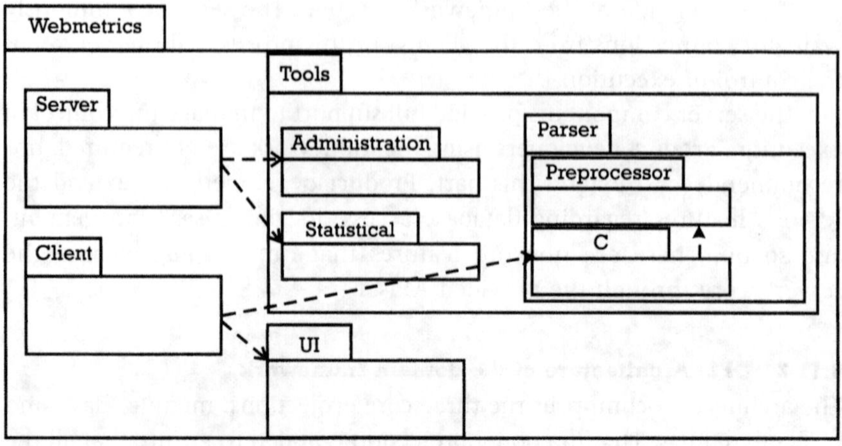

Figure 8.6 The package projection for the framework.

- *webmetrics.tools.parser.c:* This package contains the C parser and analyzer.
- *webmetrics.tools.parser.preprocessor:* This package contains a preprocessor for C-like languages.
- *webmetrics.tools.statistical:* This package contains classes to perform statistical analyses on generic data.
- *webmetrics.ui:* This package contains classes to build a graphical user interface for the server and the client.

In Sherlock, packages are then mapped into workpackages, that is, units of work assigned to groups of developers:

- Workpackage 1 includes webmetrics, webmetrics.server, and webmetrics.client.
- Workpackage 2 includes webmetrics.tools.administration.
- Workpackage 3 includes the packages rooted in webmetrics.tools.parser.
- Workpackage 4 includes webmetrics.tools.statistical.
- Workpackage 5 includes webmetrics.ui.

Class projection

The domain is fairly large. In this case it is advisable to break down Sherlock's class projection into several class diagrams, as discussed in the following sections.

Class diagram for the server side

Figure 8.7 shows the classes the framework provides to build a server under Windows NT. This set of classes is self-sufficient and does not need any additional classes to make a running server. However, additional classes can be added to provide custom features not provided by the framework.

The diagram includes classes belonging to the webmetrics and webmetrics.server packages.

The upper part and the lower part of the diagram describe distinct functionalities.

The upper part comprises the following classes: DataPayload, Payload, Packet, MetricPayload, Metric, Response, Token, Request, and WebmetricsServerThread. This part is related to the communication between the server and the client.

The lower part comprises the following classes: dBase, WebmetricsServerThread, Manager, AuthenticationServer, Log, WebmetricsServer, NTservice, DataTableModel. This part describes the back-office activities of the server: waiting for connections, logging, accessing the database, and authenticating users. The NTservice class provides the functionality of starting the server on a Windows NT platform.

The upper and lower parts share the WebmetricsServerThread class, which works as a connection between the communication activities and the server back-office activities. It is useful to notice that most classes in the upper part belong to the webmetrics package and are shared with the clients, while most classes in the lower part belong to the webmetrics. server package and are specific to the server only.

To build a running server, the product developer needs to do the following:

- If the server is to run on a Windows NT platform, the developer should install the class NTservice as an NT service as specified in the documentation.
- If the server is to run on other platforms, the developer should create a platform-specific class and instruct the platform to run the server (on Unix, this means creating and registering a daemon). This is an extension of the framework, which, by default, supports only Windows NT.

To extend the server, the product developer can do the following:

- Subclass dBase to provide access to databases not supported by the framework (by default, the framework supports Microsoft Access);
- Subclass AuthenticationServer to manage users and authentication according to custom techniques;
- Subclass Log to log server activities in a custom way.

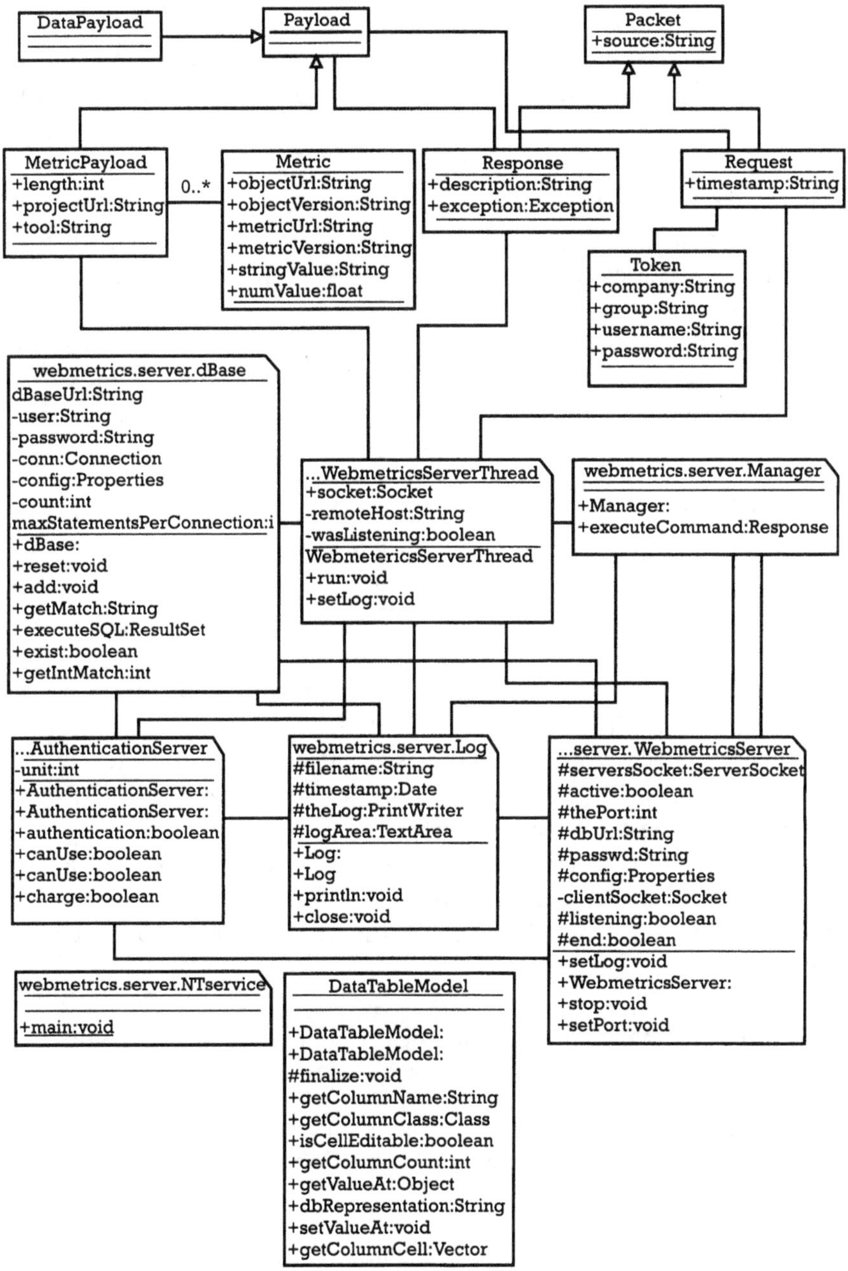

Figure 8.7 Class projection of the server side.

Other extensions of the framework are possible but have a higher cost and are not explicitly supported nor documented in the framework.

Minor details of the server class projection, such as pooling of resources and database connections, have been omitted from this discussion.

Class diagram for the client side

The diagram in Figure 8.8 shows the classes the framework provides to build a client. These classes belong to the webmetrics and webmetrics.client packages.

Packet, Payload, DataPayload, Response, Token, Request, MetricPayload, and Metric belong to the webmetrics package and provide a communication between the server and the client. On the other hand, WebmetricsClient, RemoteDatabaseInterface, and ClientInfo represent concepts specific to the client.

WebmetricsClient is the class that product developers need to extend to create a running client. WebmetricsClient provides only the basic functionality to interact with the server. Webmetrics can establish a communication channel with the server but does not know what to send through that channel.

ClientInfo provides information about the client and is used for the authentication of the client.

RemoteDatabaseInterface is a class that wraps database access. Clients can use this class to access the database on the server side without knowing that the database is remote.

The webmetrics.client package is not self-sufficient, because it does not provide a client that can be run out of the box. Product developers who want to create a client using the framework need to do the following:

- Subclass WebmetricsClient and provide information about user authentication.
- Attach a parser. A C parser is available in the webmetrics.tools.parser.c package. The developer is responsible for creating custom parsers for other languages.
- Attach a user interface from webmetrics.ui.
- Pass the metrics data coming from the parser to the server through the RemoteDatabaseInterface.

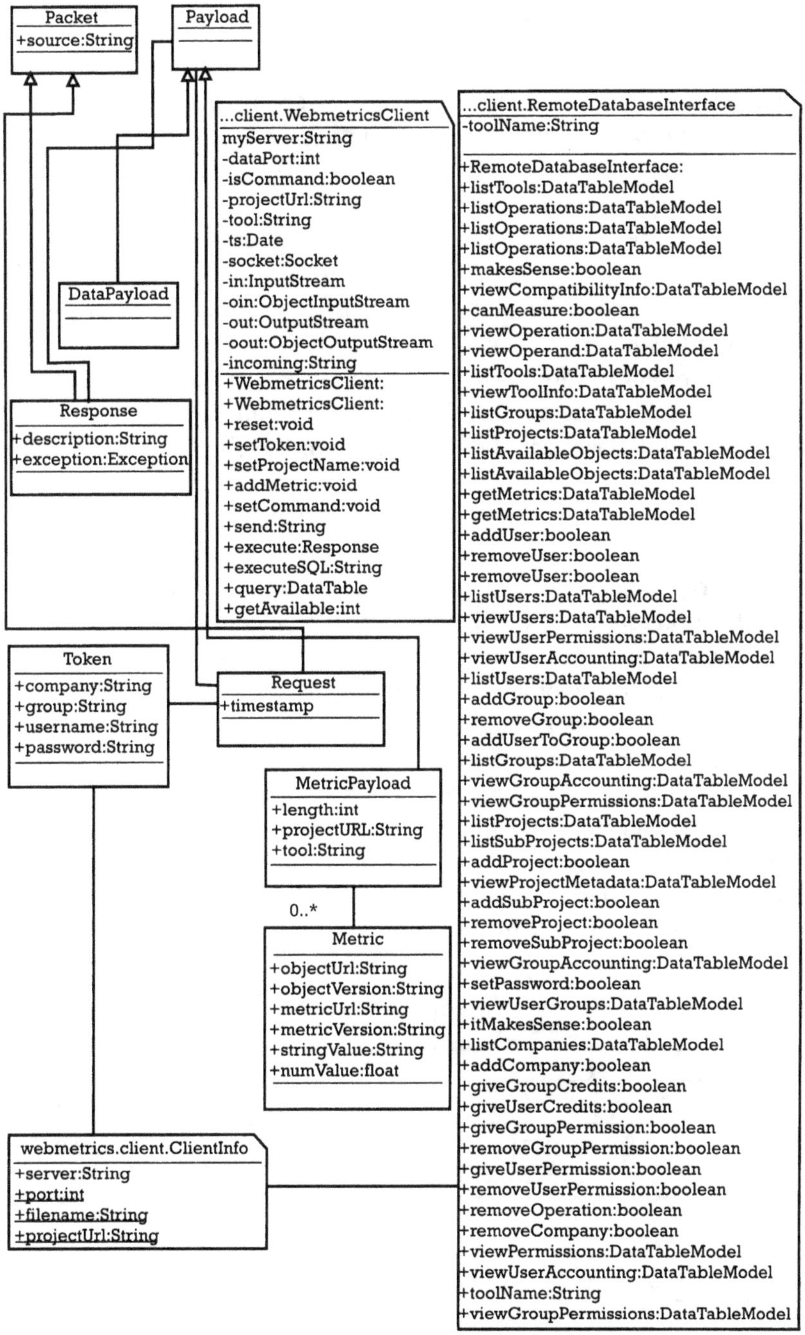

Figure 8.8 Class diagram for the client side.

Class projection of other functionalities

Webmetrics provides support for other functionalities, such as server and database administration and statistical analysis of data. For space constraints these class diagrams are not included here.

Object dynamics projection

In most cases the classes presented in the class projection run in single instances; that is, there is only one object for each class. As a result, the object dynamics projection reflects the class projection for many aspects. There are a few cases, however, in which this is not true and the object projection provides more information. Because there are no severe timing issues requiring detailed specifications beyond the object dynamics projection and the associated documentation, the object interaction projection is omitted.

A significant case is the connection of clients to the server. Let us assume that there is only one server and one client running. The server side has running instances of WebmetricsServer, dBase, Log, and AuthenticationServer. The control flow is in WebmetricsServer, which continuously waits for connections from clients. The client side has a running instance of WebmetricsClient, possibly subclassed by the product developer to provide some useful behavior.

When the client attempts to connect to the server the situation is the one depicted in the object diagram shown in Figure 8.9. WebmetricsServer does not handle the connection directly. It spawns a WebmetricsServerThread to handle the connection. After that, WebmetricsServer enters its wait-for-another-connection state, while WebmetricsServerThread runs in a separate thread.

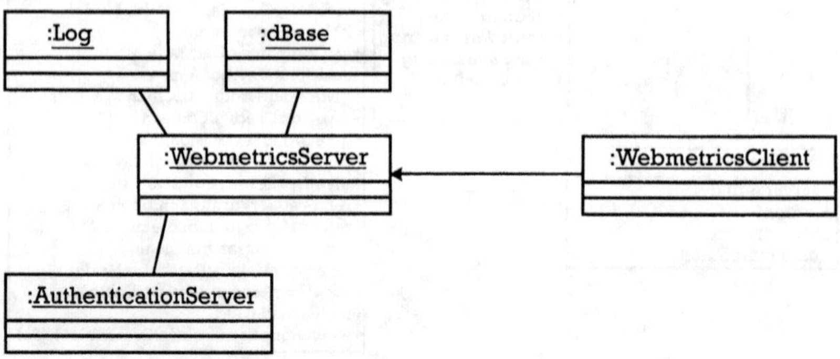

Figure 8.9 Connection to the server.

WebmetricsServerThread shares the same Log, dBase, and AuthenticationServer objects as WebmetricsServer. The situation after the generation of the WebmetricsServerThread is shown in Figure 8.10.

A typical scenario is the one in which one server is serving multiple clients at the same time. Figure 8.11 represents the typical scenario. Details are omitted. We do not provide the details of the object interaction projection, because the timing of the interactions is not difficult to understand from the preceding discussion.

Functional projection

The functional parts of the framework are as follows:

- Parsing of source code
- Metrics measurement on source code
- Client to server connection management
- User authentication
- Database access
- Logging
- Statistical analysis of data
- Server and database administration

Figure 8.12 shows the data communication and sharing between the functional parts.

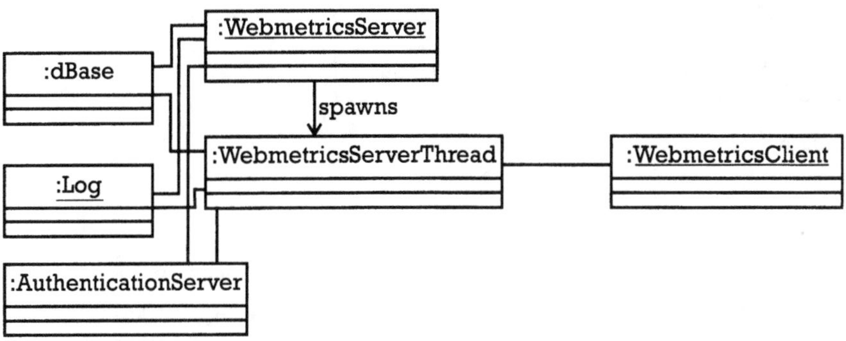

Figure 8.10 Situation after the generation of the WebmetricsServerThread.

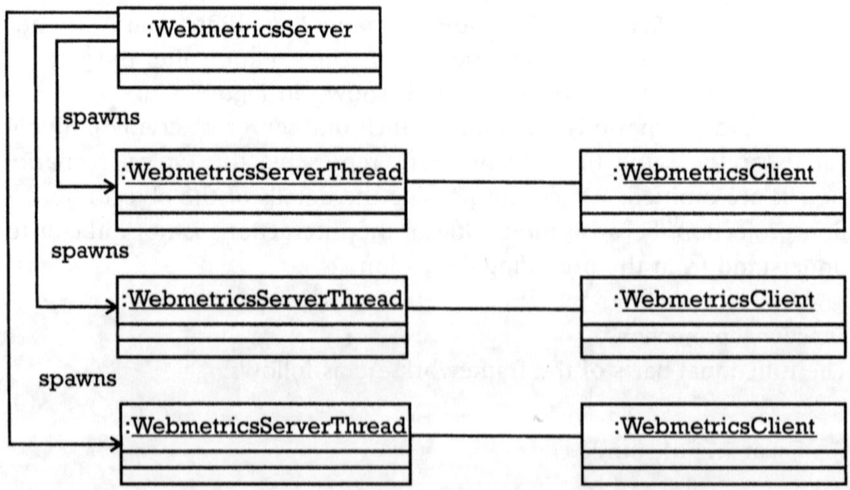

Figure 8.11 Typical working scenario.

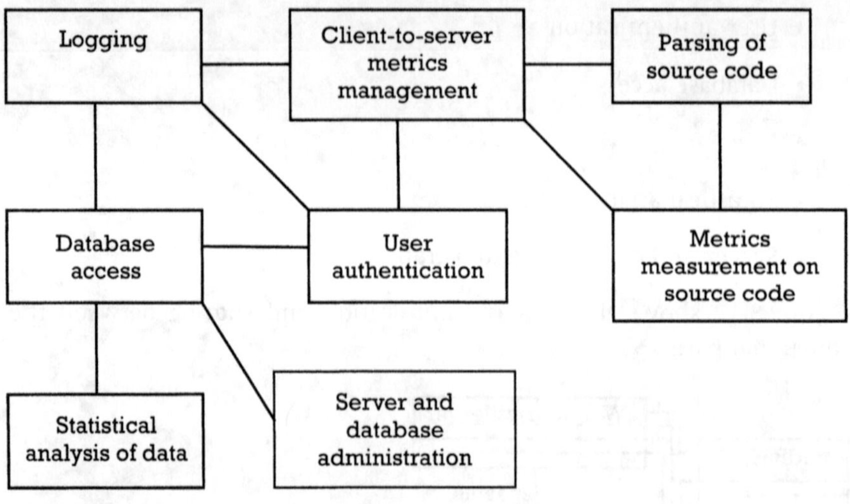

Figure 8.12 Functional projection.

The functional projection is completed by two traces: one from functional parts and domain use cases, to ensure complete traceability with the domain model, and one from functional parts to object diagrams, to verify that the system is effectively doing what it is supposed to.

8.11.3 DF3: Documentation of components in the domain framework

In this case, the framework is completely written in Java, a language that supports an advanced technique for generating documentation: Javadoc. It seems natural to use Javadoc to create the Sherlock documentation of components.

For each component/class, Javadoc automatically extracts information regarding (1) the package to which the component belongs, (2) the class hierarchy of the component, and (3) the relationship to other components. Moreover, Javadoc reports information in natural language written by the authors of the component. Javadoc allows two levels of detail in the documentation: summary and detailed. Figure 8.13 presents an example of Javadoc documentation in summary form for the webmetrics.client package.

In the considered framework, the documentation quotes relevant parts of the analysis and design documents.

Additional examples and use scenarios are also given in the documentation.

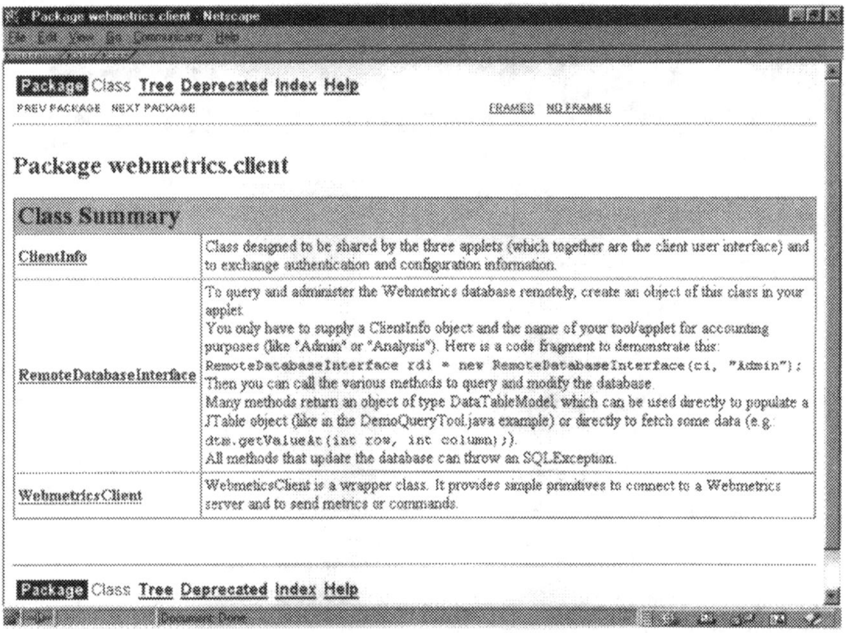

Figure 8.13 Example of Javadoc documentation summary.

8.11.4 DF4: Browsable and searchable catalog of components in the domain framework

The documentation of the framework is written in Javadoc, as discussed in the previous section. Javadoc generates a collection of HTML files organized hierarchically according to the package projection of the framework. Javadoc exploits the hypertext capabilities of HTML to create a browsable catalog of components.

Figure 8.14 shows access to the catalog through a standard Web browser. The two frames on the left allow the packages and the classes within a package to be browsed. The frame on the right displays documentation for a specific class.

Javadoc does not allow faceted classification but instead supports a form of indexing of keywords. Keywords include class, method, and variable names. Full-text indexing can be built on top of Javadoc using one of the available tools for HTML pages indexing. Figure 8.15 shows the standard keyword indexing facility provided by Javadoc.

8.11.5 DF5: Guidelines for developing applications using the framework

The last step in Sherlock is to write guidelines for developing applications using the components. The Webmetrics framework can be used to

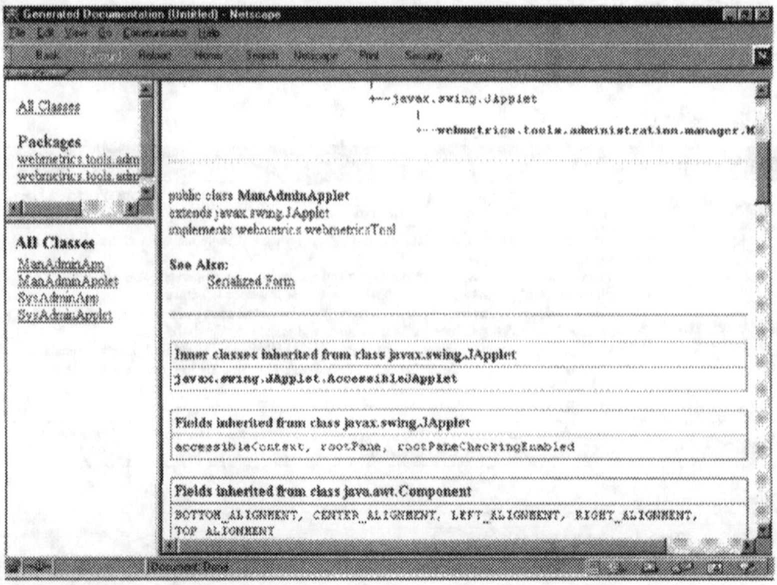

Figure 8.14 Access to the catalog.

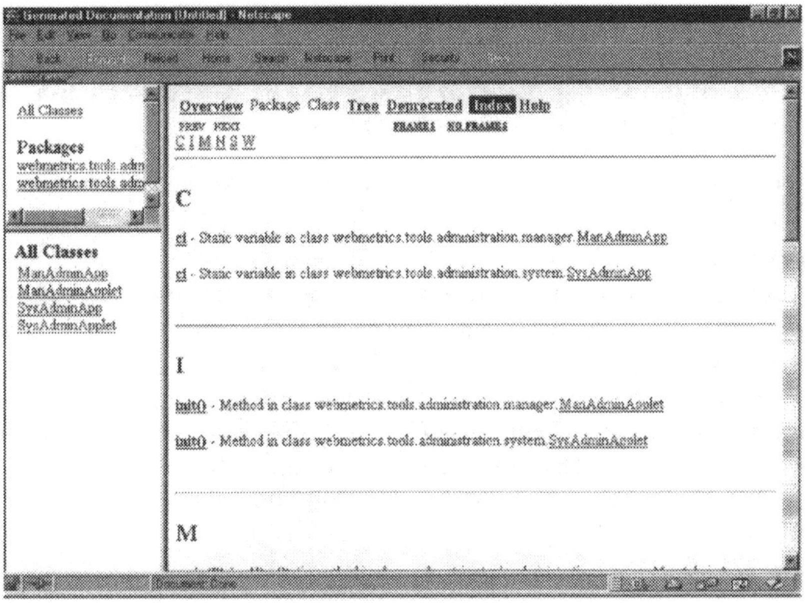

Figure 8.15 Indexing facility in Javadoc.

generate a variety of products. A complete product should comprise a server and a set of clients. One server can handle any number of clients. Several clients are usually necessary to handle various programming languages and metrics.

We present two examples showing how complete products can be built. The first example requires little customization of the framework and is based on "reuse as is." The second example requires more customization and code writing and is based on "reuse with change."

Example 1

The requirements are to build a product for software metrics measurement on source code written in C. The metrics are the standard ones applicable to C. The server is supposed to work on an NT platform relying on Microsoft Access as the underlying database.

The steps for a product developer to build the required system are as follows:

- Keep the server classes as they are. The default behavior of these components (platform, database) exactly fits the requirement.

- Build a client as specified in the class projection. Basic support for clients and for managing parsing and metrics measurement in C is provided in the framework. What needs to be done is to provide the "glue" between the required components.
- Install the server and the clients on the appropriate machines.

Example 2

The requirements are to build a product for software metrics measurement on source code written in C and Cobol. The metrics are the standard ones applicable to C and Cobol. The server is supposed to work on a Unix environment relying on Oracle as the underlying database. Moreover, the user authentication technique is required to be integrated with the standard Unix technique based on /etc/passwd.

The steps for a product developer to build the required system are as follows:

- Create a class that can be used to start up the server on a Unix platform. The class can be created modifying the existing one for Windows NT platforms. It may also be necessary to register the product as a service on the Unix system.
- Extend or replace the dBase class as discussed in the class projection to support access to Oracle, since this database is not supported in the framework.
- Create a client for parsing C source code as discussed in example 1.
- Create a parser and a metrics analyzer for Cobol. Integrate these pieces with the standard classes available in the framework to manage the clients (WebmetricsClient, ClientInfo, RemoteDatabaseInterface).
- Extend or replace the class AuthenticationServer so that it can refer to the /etc/passwd file for authentication on Unix platforms.
- Install the server on a Unix machine and C/Cobol clients where required according to the languages in use.

8.11.6 Logging the evolution of domain framework development

Table 8.3 summarizes the development efforts for this phase.

Table 8.3
Evolution of Domain Framework Development

Author	Date	Action	Effort
Sherlock's authors	1997	Early prototyping	100 man-hours
Sherlock's authors	1998	Framework development	1,000 man-hours
Sherlock's authors	1999	Framework development	700 man-hours

References

[1] Prieto-Diaz, R., "Implementing Faceted Classification for Software Reuse," *Communications of the ACM*, Vol. 35, No. 5, 1991.

[2] Sethi, R., *Programming Languages: Concepts and Constructs*, Reading, MA: Addison-Wesley, 1996.

CHAPTER

9

Contents

Case study 1: Sherlock applied to WaveRider Communications, Inc.[1]

9.1 Background

This chapter describes the experience of the application of Sherlock at WaveRider Communications, Inc., a firm that produces wireless "Last Mile Solutions®" for the Internet. Last Mile Solutions® are those technologies related to connecting the end Internet user to a base station, which is then connected to the usual Internet service provider. WaveRider's core business is producing a product line of wireless last mile solutions.

Reductions and changes have been made from the original documents to preserve confidential information and to focus on the explanatory goal of this chapter. Specifically, the description of competitors in the domain characterization phase and the overall domain scoping phase have been completely altered to avoid any form of

1. This chapter was coauthored by Mr. Walter Simbriski of WaveRider Communications, Inc.

interference with the strategic directions of WaveRider. All names but that of WaveRider are fictitious; prices are expressed using "Luis," the pre–French Revolution French currency; details on compatibility are not given; and the domain modeling and domain framework development phases have been significantly reduced in size, focusing only on a few major functionalities of the target domain.

It is our belief that the documents presented here are self-explanatory in nature. Therefore, we will just present them one after the other with limited comments.

9.2 Domain definition

9.2.1 Classified information on the domain

WaveRider and its history

The following excerpt was taken from the WaveRider Web site:

> WaveRider Communications, Inc. was created in response to an existing and growing market need. Early in 1996, Mr. Richard Antoine approached Mr. Stephen Grant of JetStream Internet Services with a proposition to supply Internet bandwidth to educational institutions. The school board's demand for high Internet bandwidth led Antoine and Grant to research alternate sources of data transmission, including wireless solutions. They purchased and tested an existing wireless bridge. This product was expensive and did not meet their bandwidth and routing requirements [1].

Mission statement and values

> *Our Mission.* To be the leader in the global wireless data communications industry by developing, selling and supporting customer driven products.
>
> *Our Values.* At WaveRider we believe in improving the economic well being and quality of life of all our stakeholders. We value:
>
> Accountability, responsibility and goal achievement through dedication, speed and accuracy.
>
> Open and honest communication; our foundation is formed on integrity and respect.

Initiative, creativity and flexibility in problem solving and personal interaction.

Growth—in our company, our industry and in our employees.

Excitement, enjoyment and self-fulfillment in our daily work.

Our Stakeholders. Customers, Employees, Shareholders, Business Partners, & Suppliers [2].

Basic technical beliefs

WaveRider expresses its basic philosophy as follows:

> WaveRider wireless Internet products are significantly faster and easier to implement than traditional "hard-wired" communications networks. Our first product, the NCL135, will target businesses needing point to multi-point, LAN-to-Internet connectivity. Once released, it will be upgradeable to WaveRider's flagship product, the LMS 270, designed to wirelessly link thousands of end users to the Internet.

The systems combine an advanced form of spread spectrum radio transmission with Digital Signal Processing (DSP), in order to provide wireless data services around a centralized Network Access Point (NAP). Several low-cost Cellular Access Points (CAPs) are deployed within each cell of the Wireless Internet Network, giving the system a strong and identifiable signal in any topographical area.

In terms of benefits, the technology enables Internet service providers (ISPs) to increase the number of end users on a network and enhance the level of service by installing additional CAPs in any particular cell. It is a scalable system able to meet the needs of foreign and domestic markets. WaveRider's spread spectrum technology will give ISPs the flexibility to offer their customers a variable cost projection on a variety of Internet access speeds—from 33.6 through 135 Kbps (ISDN speed) in the LMS 270 and up to 512 Kbps in a future update. Overall, ISPs will be able to deploy a flexible network rapidly, while significantly reducing operating costs [3].

WaveRider's products

WaveRider's products include the following:

- *NCL 135:* This is a wireless bridge and router, operating in the 2.4-GHz ISM band(s). See description at URL: http://www.waverider.com/products/downloads/NCL135.pdf.
- *LMS 170:* This is a system providing a wireless ISDN link. See WaveRider's LMS 170 Tailoring Plan (Item identification: APTP-LM000).
- *LMS 270:* This is a system that provides IP last mile connectivity in the 900-MHz ISM band. See description at URL: http://www.waverider.com/products/downloads/LMS270.pdf.

Table 9.1 lists NCL 135 R and NCL 135 B as two different products. The source of this information explains the difference between the two products. For the purpose of DA&E, they will be considered a single product.

Carleton University maintains a Web site (http://hydra.carleton.ca) that contains information on equipment that is available for wireless telecommunications. The information comprises technical descriptions, prices, and links to the manufacturers' Web sites. Some pages, like the wireless LAN/MAN modem product directory, have been updated recently; others have not been updated since 1997 or before.

Information from domain experts

Domain experts have developed a comparison of products in the domain. For each product the comparison provides a series of technical data:

Table 9.1
List of Competitors

Vendor	Product
WaveRider	NCL 135 R
	NCL 135 B
FreeNet	Eagle
NetRider	NetNet
URLSolutions	Jump
WaveNet	Tornado
ZZZ	Silent
	Laud

Source: "Competitive Products," internal reports, version 3, October 22, 1998

vendor, product, type, receiver threshold, data rate sync/async, range, channels, data interface, network interface, output power ERIP 100 mW, O/S upgrade via flash ROM, transport MAC, SNMP manageable, data encryption, telnet/console configurable, integrated router, routing protocol used, price, and other additional information [4].

Information from market experts

Since September 21, 1998, WaveRider has been issuing a market intelligence report every 1 to 2 weeks. The reports contain mainly press excerpts from the Internet. Each excerpt contains a brief summary and a reference to the source. Depending on the availability of information, the reports may contain the following sections:

- Competitor announcements and news
- Internet market developments
- New items in the clipping file
- Alternative last mile technologies and providers
- Regulatory announcements and approvals
- Information resources
- Mergers and acquisitions
- Other news

WaveRider's strategy

WaveRider describes its position in the market as follows:

> WaveRider Communications, Inc. is recognized as becoming an international industry leader in wireless data communications through the introduction of high-speed, low-cost alternatives to traditional "hard-wired" Internet service. With an executive team experienced in directing and managing rapid growth and leading-edge R&D developers and designers with a track record in achieving technological excellence, WaveRider has an outstanding foundation for its new Last Mile Solution® wireless products. As an innovator in wireless data communications, WaveRider is developing Wireless Internet Network systems that will provide the telecommunications industry with solutions that will connect end users and, in turn, fulfill the promise of the new digital age—to provide corporations and consumers alike with high-speed worldwide connectivity [5].

WaveRider's long-term plan is to become the market leader in wireless last mile technologies. To achieve this, it is developing a Last Mile Solution system. Several products are being developed to implement the system: NCL 135, LMS 170, LMS 270, and LMS 540. The products differ in complexity and functionality, and are to be developed and released in subsequent steps. The Last Mile Solution is WaveRider's competing edge in the wireless Internet connectivity market.

The LMS has two kinds of clients: Internet service providers (ISPs) and end users. The ISPs run and administrate the LMS; the end users buy and use the EUMs on their premises. The ISPs buy the whole system and distribute the EUMs to the end users.

The value added for the ISPs is the capability to deploy easily and at low cost a wireless network for Internet connectivity. The ISPs' business is to provide Internet connectivity. It is likely that the wireless solution the LMS offers will attract users that have not used Internet connectivity before, which is profitable for the ISPs. To address the competition of other, possibly wired, Internet connectivity solutions, WaveRider is developing a suite of software tools that will allow ISPs to manage the network more efficiently than other solutions allow.

The value added for end users is the capability to connect to the Internet through an inexpensive EUM. The advantage of the wireless technology over the wired technology is the mobility of the end user. WaveRider is developing a set of services (for example, automatic e-mail notification and delivery) that will create further value added to the end user.

The development of the LMS technology takes time. Moreover, the market may not be ready to accept it immediately. To address this, WaveRider plans to release three products in a scheduled time sequence: the NCL 135, the LMS 170, and then the LMS 270. The NCL 135 is a wireless bridge and was originally designed to be part of the LMS 270. Through the NCL 135, WaveRider is getting visibility and good reputation in the market. The LMS 170 is a wireless ISDN replacement. The introduction of the LMS 170 is also a stepping stone for the introduction of the more complex LMS 270. WaveRider is educating its clients to deal with wireless technologies, thus preparing them for more complex technologies. Dealing with existing clients will make the introduction of new products easier and more profitable.

From the introduction of the LMS 270, WaveRider is planning to gain a strong enough position in the market to become a leader in wireless Internet connectivity. From that point, WaveRider will introduce and manage new, more complex products (LMS 540). WaveRider is also interested in establishing a domain-based approach to the production of its software.

9.2.2 Definition of feasible, strategic, and current domains

Table 9.2 summarizes WaveRider's product development plan. The tentative feasible, strategic, and current domains are shown in Figure 9.1.

The feasible domain contains hardware and software products for Internet connectivity. Because of the huge number of products related to internetworking available in the market, it is convenient to limit this domain to the products providing some overlapping functionality with WaveRider's present and future products. Bridges, routers, modems, hubs, network administration tools, and e-mail delivery systems belong to the feasible domain and, for some aspects, are competing or auxiliary with WaveRider's products.

The strategic domain contains hardware and software products for wireless Internet connectivity. The WaveRider NCL 135 and most competitors of WaveRider's products are in this domain.

The current domain contains the WaveRider LMS 170 and the LMS 270. These products are in the current domain because their development is strategically important.

9.2.3 Feasibility analysis

WaveRider became interested in domain analysis and engineering because it desires to manage its product line effectively. This interest is motivated by several factors:

- *WaveRider is a new firm.* WaveRider needs to define a suitable development process. A process definition based on domain analysis and engineering at an early stage of the firm's history would allow proper management of the product line from the very beginning.

Table 9.2
WaveRider's Development Plan

Year	Product
1998	NCL 135
1999	LMS 170
2000	LMS 270

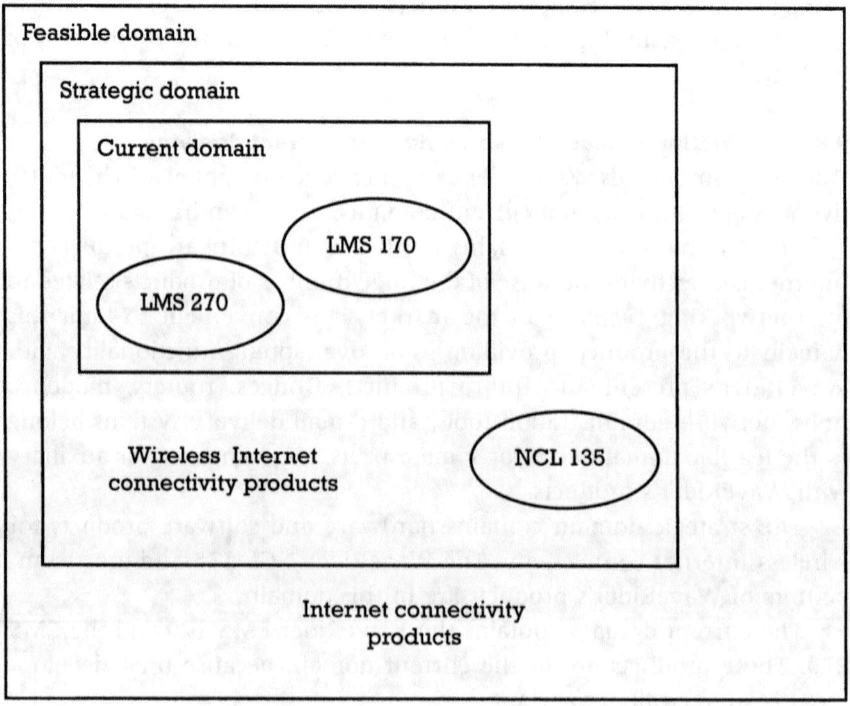

Figure 9.1 Feasible, strategic, and current domains for WaveRider at the beginning of the analysis.

- *WaveRider is hiring new employees.* Understanding what the firm does and in which direction it is going in the future will allow WaveRider to hire people that best fit the firm's needs. Having the development process defined would also introduce quickly the new employees to the firm's history, philosophy, needs, plans, and way of working.

- *WaveRider is developing a product line.* Managing the product line properly is important to introduce new products in the market: Existing products support new ones and all products cooperate to achieve a higher impact than single products alone would allow. Domain analysis and engineering allow all products to be coordinated so that they are focused on one goal. WaveRider is currently managing its product line through a development plan that will be implemented in the coming years. Technically, domain analysis and engineering foster development of products with reuse in mind, thus allowing faster development of new, high-quality products in the future.

- *WaveRider is strongly motivated.* WaveRider is motivated to maintain a high-quality decision-making process, based on high-quality information, analysis, generation of alternatives, evaluation of activity, choices, and implementations.

The products that are most relevant for WaveRider currently are the LMS 170 and the LMS 270. These two products have a strategic importance because they provide WaveRider with its competing edge over the competition.

The result of the feasibility analysis is for WaveRider to continue with the domain analysis and engineering process. To that end, WaveRider is planning the following:

1. Apply domain analysis and engineering immediately to the development of the LMS 170 and the LMS 270.

2. Position the other products correctly, both from the internal and external market perspectives, and consequently apply domain analysis and engineering to them.

3. Define a software development process based on domain analysis and engineering and deploy the process in the firm's environment.

The feasibility analysis has determined the economic soundness of domain analysis based on the short-term return on investment that is foreseen for the deployment of the LMS 170 and the LMS 270.

9.2.4 Domain vocabulary

The following terms have been defined:

Availability. A measure of a system's performance expressed as a percentage of hours the system is functional over a defined period of time—years, months, and so on.

Bit error rate (BER). The number of bits received in error. For example, if 1,000 bits are transmitted and 1 bit is in error then the BER is 1/1,000. It is usually expressed as a power of 10. In the example given, the BER would be 10 to the negative 3. In a radio environment the BER will increase with distance or it will vary inversely with signal strength.

Capacity. The number of users/connections that can be carried or supported by the system.

Cellular access port (CAP). Interface providing concentration between EUM and NAP in a cellular architecture. Cellular base station used in the LMS architecture.

Cellular base station. Connects EUMs to an NAP and provides concentration and distribution.

Cellular-like architecture. A distributed area coverage system based on similar repeating regions and frequency reuse.

Connection. The physical and logical infrastructures that enable the exchange of data between two or more points in a network.

Connectivity. (1) The possibility of a point being connected to a given network; (2) the possibility of a point of a network being connected to another point in the network.

Data processing. Manipulation of information.

Data rate. The speed at which data move on a channel of a network. The data rate is usually specified in terms of multiples of bits per second, for instance, Kbps, Mbps, Gbps, or frames per second. The term *data* can refer to different concepts, such as user data, raw channel data, recovered user data, monodirectional data, bidirectional data, and so on. Therefore, in addition to the numeric value, the following should be provided to specify the data rate: measurement unit, type of data, type of channel and its capacity, whether it refers to a monodirectional or bidirectional channel, and whether it is inclusive of the protocol overhead or not (if it is not inclusive of the protocol overhead, then the protocol overhead must be specified).

Examples of complete definitions of data rate figures follow. Uplink data rate of 10K user bps, net of protocol overhead. Downlink data rate of 100K raw bps, gross of protocol overhead. Bidirectional NAP to CAP data rate of 1 Mbps in each way, net of protocol overhead.

The additional information can be omitted if it is uniquely inferable from the context (for example, comparison with other figures) or if it has been specified previously. Data rate figures can be measured by the NMS or equivalent test platform.

Note that the data rate by itself is not a full specification of the performances of a channel. On a given data rate it may be relevant to consider the data rate versus distance from the source, the data rate versus signal level, data rate versus bit error rate, and so on [4].

End user modem (EUM). Provides interface between end user computer and network. Access device on the subscriber's premises in the LMS architecture.

Engineering support services (ESS). An independent United States government agency, charged with regulating interstate and international communications by radio, television, wire, satellite and cable[6].

Ergonomics. Collection of product attributes that are apparent to the user of the product, or element thereof. Includes mechanical size, shape, color, user interface.

Ethernet connector. A connector capable of connecting to a network supporting the Ethernet Protocol.

Federal Communication Commission (FCC). An independent United States government agency, charged with regulating interstate and international communications by radio, television, wire, satellite and cable.

Fix mobility. Definition of state of mobility where a wireless user of a system is not permitted to move.

Frequency reuse. A technique to provide higher system capacity by allowing physically separated transmitters to operate on the same frequency with acceptable interference.

High-speed mobility. Provision of service at high data rates to nonstationary or nonfixed subscribers.

Integrated Services Digital Network (ISDN). A set of communication standards allowing a single wire or optical fiber to carry voice, video, and network services.

Interference. Confusion on a received signal due to the presence of either a noise coming from the environment (atmospheric, traffic, and so on) or of one or more other signals.

Internet. An electronic communications network that (1) connects computer networks and organizational computer facilities around the world and (2) supports the provision of services through itself.

Internet service provider. An organization that sells access to the Internet.

Interoperability. Ability of a product or of an element of a product to interface to a third-party product.

Latency. The time taken to transmit and receive a response between two points in a network.

Last Mile Solution® (LMS). WaveRider's proprietary name for its family of products offering high-speed wireless connections to the Internet.

LMS 170. A system providing a wireless ISDN link. The LSM 170 is meant to provide a replacement to wired ISDN links.

LMS 270. A system that provides IP last mile connectivity in the 900-MHz ISM band. It is a cellular-like architecture designed to deliver at most 134 Kbps to each end user.

LMS family. A family of products providing a last mile data network connectivity.

Mobility. The ability of a product to operate while moving either within or across multiple networks.

Mobility of EUM. Refers to geographic relocation of EUM. May be within cells, intercell, fast/slow.

Modulation. A way of manipulating radio waves to improve network capacity, reliability, and so on.

NAP to CAP link (NCL). A device originally designed to provide remote connectivity between the NAP and the CAP in the LMS 270 system.

NCL 135. A wireless bridge and router, operating in the 2.4-GHz ISM band(s), providing high data rate interconnections.

Network access point (NAP). The connection to an ISP's network.

Network management protocol. A network protocol that allows remote devices to be configured or managed (statistics) from a central location.

Network management system (NMS). The tool used to control and manage the LMS or any network product. Allows the network provider to maintain a reliable, accessible, and usable system.

Noninterfering orthogonal frequency hopping. A technique to optimize the access to the same network for different technologies, thus enabling easy upgrading of systems.

Performance. A subjective statement based on the customers ranking of key product attributes such as data rate, range, availability, price, and so on.

Product Line Management (PLM). An independent United States government agency, charged with regulating interstate and international communications by radio, television, wire, satellite and cable [6].

Protocol. Collection of messages and procedures that allow communications to be established between two points.

Remote Authentication Dial-In User Service (RADIUS). A protocol for carrying authentication, authorization, and configuration information between a network access server, which wants to authenticate its links, and a shared authentication server [7].

Reliability. A metric for describing how error-free a service is.

Roaming. The ability of subscribers to use their subscriber devices (EUMs) on a network operated by an entity with whom they have no direct relationship.

Simple Network Management Protocol (SNMP). A network management system.

Spread spectrum. Radio transmission method spreading power across the band.

Usability. The requirement of a product to be practical and useful. This is typically seen as "How easy is the product to use in practical situations?"

Various protocols. Schema defining interface at various levels between two pieces of hardware and software. Includes framing, synchronization, control information, error recovery, data transmission, and parameterization.

Wireless. Not hard-wired, specifically radio in wireless applications.

9.3 Domain characterization

9.3.1 Diagrams of value

Diagram of value for LMS 170

Internal values

Let's start with a look at the diagram of internal values for the LMS 170. The LMS 170 is a wireless ISDN replacement providing point-to-point connectivity. The quality constraints for the LMS 170 follow:

- *Reliability:* MTTF above 100,000 hr.
- *Usability:* Untrained people should be able to install the LMS 170. Basic skills in ISDN networking should suffice to operate the LMS 170. This implies a level 1 of ease of use, according to the internal WaveRider standards for ease of use of products (WR-TR-980971).
- *Performance:* As required by ISDN.
- *Cost:* If possible, cheaper than other ISDN-equivalent products.

There is a tradeoff between the quality attributes. Advanced users and operators may prefer high reliability and performance to low cost. Unskilled users may prefer high usability and low cost to high reliability. Different preferences and requirements will define different market segments.

External values

The LMS 170 will provide the same interoperability as existing ISDN links. Moreover, it will offer the interoperability advantages of wireless links. The LMS will also interoperate with existing ISDN hardware and software. Interoperability with PCs is planned only for PC/Windows platforms. The LMS 170 will also interoperate with the LMS 270.

Expectations. The LMS 170 is a new product still under development. The LMS 170 is expected to create a distribution channel for the LMS 270 and will benefit from the network externalities with the LMS 270.

Diagrams of value for LMS 270

There are two users for which the LMS 270 creates value: the ISPs and the end users. The ISPs purchase the LMS 270 from WaveRider and sell

EUMs and subscriptions to the end users. Added value for the end user is relevant because it makes the ISPs see the LMS 270 as a more profitable solution.

In regions where no wired networks exist, the LMS 270 would have no existing competitors and would offer the only connectivity solution. In regions where a wired network already exists, the LMS 270 should offer some extra value to the basic connectivity. The LMS 270 should also have a competitive price compared to existing wired solutions.

Internal value

The LMS 270 provides wireless access to the Internet through a cellular-like architecture. The LMS 270 specifically creates value for those end users who cannot use or do not like wired solutions.

Other features are still to be determined through an analysis of ISPs to determine exactly what the users want. Some of these features have already been identified: subscriber management, billing, configuration management, maintenance management, troubleshooting management, and inventory management.

Quality features specific to ISPs include ease of deployment and ease of management, according to the internal WaveRider standards for ease of use of products (WR-TR-980971).

Quality features specific to end users include ease of installation and ease of use. Any user with basic PC skills should be able to operate an EUM out of the box.

The LMS 270's reliability is the same as that of the LMS 170.

External value

Interoperability Between Users:

- *ISPs as users:* Interoperability between the various administrator roles;
- *End users:* Some interoperability as provided by the Internet; increased capability to interoperate through mobility.

Interoperability Between Products:

- Interoperability with other network devices at NAP and EUM level;
- Interoperability with network management tools in use by ISPs;

- Interoperability with LMS 170 and NCL 135.

Expectations. The LMS 270 is still under development. Potential customers know the LMS 270 through WaveRider's Web site and other information channels.

WaveRider will use the NCL 135 and the LMS 170 to create positive expectations about the LMS 270. The expectations will drive the sales of the LMS 270. The NCL 135 and the LMS 170 will also give users a suitable technical background to use the LMS 270.

9.3.2 Description of the installed base

Installed base for LMS 170

The product is still under development and has no installed base. The following information is relevant for estimating the potential sales:

- There are already many ISDN providers.
- Seventy-five percent of the ISPs offer ISDN services.
- The ISPs are expanding and new users are getting Internet connections.

Other manufacturers provide 900-MHz wireless services at ISDN speed. The Web site at Carleton University (http://hydra.carleton.ca) provides an updated list of them.

Installed base for LMS 270

The product is still under development and has no installed base. The following information is relevant for estimating the potential sales:

- There are 4,700 ISPs in North America.
- Twelve percent of the ISPs in Canada provide some wireless services.
- The ISPs are expanding and new users are getting Internet connections.

Installed base for NCL 135

The installed base for the NCL 135 is given in Table 9.3 as a reference for the other WaveRider products. The term *testers* in Table 9.3 refers to users

Table 9.3
Installed Base for the NCL 135

NCL 135	Installed Base		Current Sales	Sales Trend	Expected Total Sales at the End of 1999
	Number of units	Number of clients			
Testers	20	10	0/month	Stopped	20
Users	290	35	80/month	Positive	1,000

who are using the NCL 135 at no cost for test purposes. WaveRider has contacted the testers through direct marketing.

9.3.3 Tables of compatibility

The following is a list of compatibility groups for the system (Table 9.4):

- *ISDN:* Compatibility with ISDN hardware and software.
- *Administration tools in use by ISPs:* The list of tools and the compatibility elements they use should be identified. Once available, the tools should be placed as products, that is, as rows in Table 9.4, while the compatibility elements should be placed as columns in the table.
- *PC/Windows platform:* Hardware and software compatibility elements related to PC/Windows platforms. If other platforms are to be supported, they should be analyzed, too.

Table 9.4
Table of Compatibilities

	ISDN	Administration Tools in Use by ISPs	PC/Windows Platform	RF Emission Regulations	RADIUS
LMS 170	√	√	√	√	
LMS 270		√	√	√	√
NCL 135			√	√	

- *RF emission regulations:* Compatibility element depending on the specific countries' regulations.
- *RADIUS:* A protocol for carrying authentication, authorization, and configuration information between a network access server, which desires to authenticate its links, and a shared authentication server [7]. RADIUS is a candidate compatibility element but can also be a group of finer grain compatibility elements.

9.3.4 User flows

The user flows for the LMS 170 are (Figure 9.2):

- *Flow from new users:* The LMS 170 will attract users who are willing to use a wireless ISDN link and who are not satisfied with other wired ISDN products.
- *Flow from other wired ISDN products:* The LMS 170 will exploit its wireless advantage and attract users of existing wired ISDN products. There could possibly be price competition.

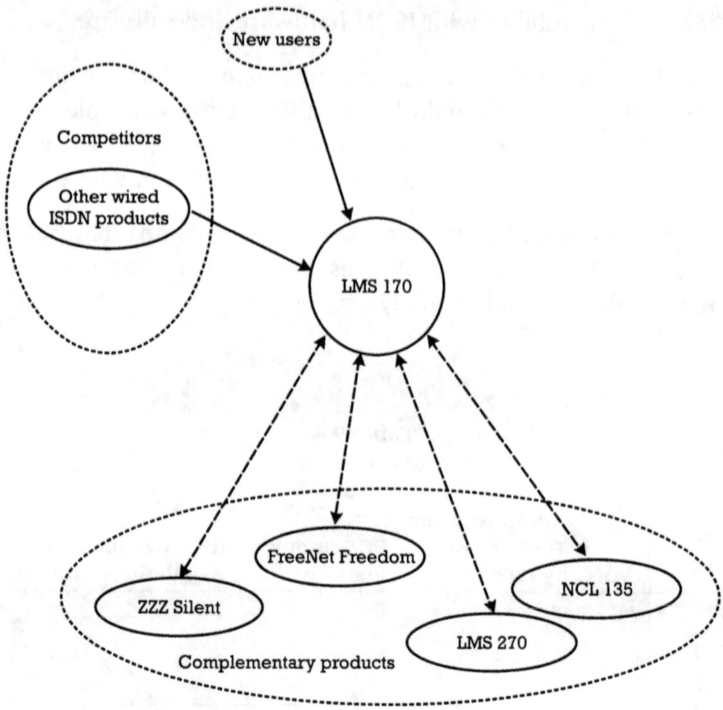

Figure 9.2 User flows for the LMS 170.

- *Flows from ZZZ Silent and FreeNet Freedom:* These products are made by other manufacturers and can operate side by side with the LMS 170. Neither competition nor substitutability with these products exists. Network externalities will move users between these products and the LMS 170.
- *Flows from NCL 135 and LMS 270:* The LMS 170 will create a distribution channel for the LMS 270, with which it is supposed to share a significant part of the installed base. The NCL 135 will also contribute to the network externalities of the LMS 170.

The user flows for the LMS 270 are (Figure 9.3):

- *Flow from new users:* The LMS 270 will attract users who are willing to access the Internet through a wireless technology and who are not satisfied with existing wired Internet technologies.
- *Flow from wired Internet technologies:* The LMS 270 will attract users of wired Internet technologies offering wireless mobility, low cost, ease of installation and use.

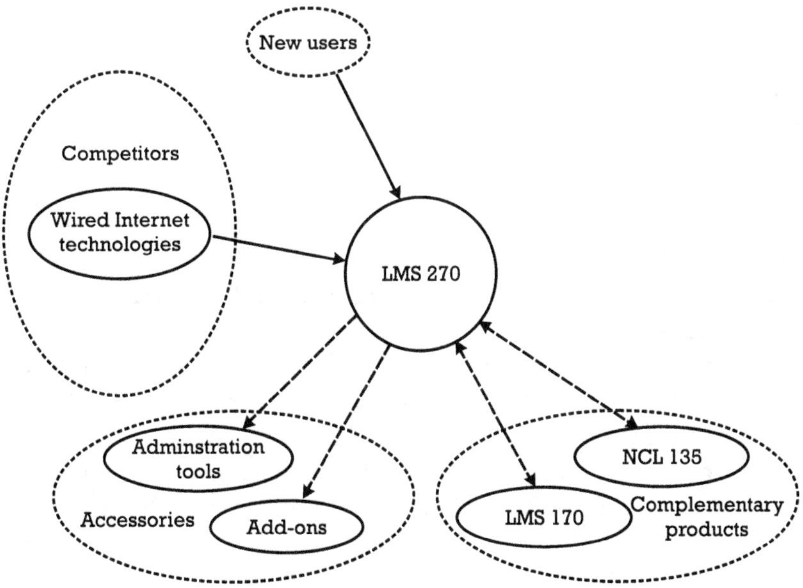

Figure 9.3 User flows for the LMS 270.

- *Flows to administration tools and add-ons:* The LMS 270 will create a market for accessory tools that will be distributed according to the specific requirements of the customers.
- *Flows from NCL 135 and LMS 170:* The LMS 270 will exploit the network externalities of the NCL 135 and the LMS 270. It will also exploit the distribution channel created by the LMS 170.

9.3.5 Market segments and pricing policy

WaveRider has identified the following market segments:

- *Testers:* Users testing new products;
- *ISPs:* WaveRider direct customers;
- *End users:* ISPs' customers;
- *Users:* Regular users where the distinction between ISPs and end users is not applicable.

Other market segments may become evident from further fragmentation of the proposed ones. Users have different requirements in terms of quality. An analysis of the requirements will define finer market segments.

The pricing policy is shown in Figure 9.4.

9.3.6 Plan for development of new products

Table 9.5 summarizes WaveRider's product development plan.

9.4 Domain scoping

9.4.1 Variability space, attributes of product in the domain, and related constraints

The variation points are organized in three sections focused on individual products—LMS 170 and LMS 270—and on the whole product line. The section on the LMS 270 is further divided in subsections on the individual components of the LMS 270: the NAP, the CAP, and the EUM. Duplication of variation points in different sections is provided for ease of reading.

This organization is temporary and is meant for refinement and validation.

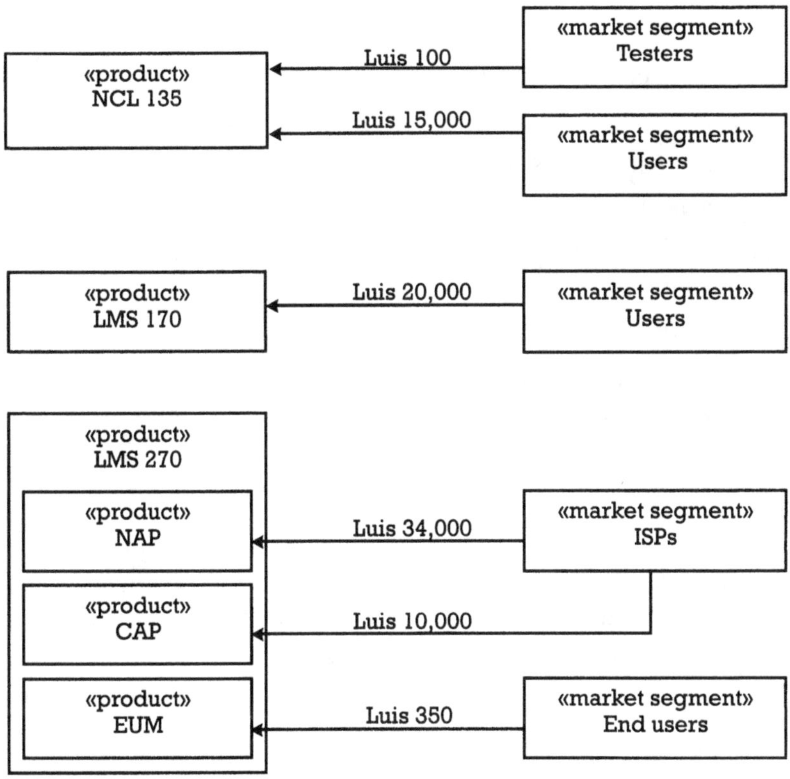

Figure 9.4 Pricing policy.

Table 9.5
Product Development Plan

Year	Product
1998	NCL 135
1999	LMS 170
2000	LMS 270

The list of variation points in the domain scoping document is a superset of the variation points in the domain modeling document. Interaction between stable and validated DS and DM documents will fill the gap.

Variation points and variants related to the LMS 170

VP_1: Interface to PC

$V_{1,1}$: RS 232

VP_2: Connection management

$V_{2,1}$: Permanent connection

VP_3: System administration

$V_{3,1}$: SNMP

VP_4: RF emission regulations for point-to-point wireless architecture

$V_{4,1}$: North American regulations

$V_{4,2}$: European regulations

VP_5: Physical channel control

$V_{5,1}$: Adaptive

$V_{5,2}$: Static

Variation points and variants related to the LMS 270

Variation Points and Variants Related to NAP:

VP_1: Interface to Internet/Intranet

$V_{1,1}$: LAN

$V_{1,2}$: ATM

$V_{1,3}$: T1

VP_2: Interface to CAP

$V_{2,1}$: Wired

$V_{2,2}$: Wireless through NCL 135

VP_3: Connection management

$V_{3,1}$: Permanent connection

$V_{3,2}$: Volatile connection

VP_4: Accounting procedure

$V_{4,1}$: RADIUS-based

$V_{4,2}$: Custom

VP_5: System administration

$V_{5,1}$: SNMP

$V_{5,2}$: Through administration tools in use by ISPs

Variation Points and Variants Related to CAP:

VP_1: Interface to NAP

$V_{1,1}$: Wired

$V_{1,2}$: Wireless through NCL 135

VP_2: RF emission regulations for cell-like architecture

$V_{2,1}$: North American regulation

$V_{2,2}$: European regulation

VP_3: Modulation technique

$V_{3,1}$: Frequency hopping spread spectrum modulation

VP_4: Cell distribution

$V_{4,1}$: *x* cell distribution (details omitted)

$V_{4,2}$: *y* cell distribution (details omitted)

$V_{4,3}$: *z* cell distribution (details omitted)

VP_5: Physical channel control

$V_{5,1}$: Adaptive

$V_{5,2}$: Static

VP_6: Connection management

$V_{6,1}$: Permanent connection

$V_{6,2}$: Volatile connection

VP_7: Accounting procedure

$V_{7,1}$: RADIUS-based

$V_{7,2}$: Custom

VP_8: Roaming

$V_{8,1}$: Not allowed

$V_{8,2}$: Allowed—limited to predefined cells

$V_{8,3}$: Allowed—unconstrained

Variation Points and Variants Related to EUM:

VP_1: Interface to PC

$V_{1,1}$: Serial port

VP_2: RF emission regulations for cell-like architecture

$V_{2,1}$: North America

$V_{2,2}$: Europe

VP_3: Modulation technique

$V_{3,1}$: Frequency hopping spread spectrum modulation

VP_4: Physical channel control

$V_{4,1}$: Adaptive

$V_{4,2}$: Static

VP_5: Connection management

$V_{5,1}$: Permanent connection

$V_{5,2}$: Volatile connection

VP_6: Accounting procedure

$V_{6,1}$: RADIUS-based

$V_{6,2}$: Custom

VP_7: Roaming

$V_{7,1}$: Not allowed

$V_{7,2}$: Allowed—limited to predefined cells

$V_{7,3}$: Allowed—unconstrained

Variation points and variants related to the product line

VP_1: Interface with network administration tools

$V_{1,1}$: Full interface with existing standards

$V_{1,2}$: Nothing

$V_{1,3}$: Built-in network administration tool

VP_2: Platform for EUM

$V_{2,1}$: PC/Windows

$V_{2,2}$: Unix/Linux

VP_3: Frequency

$V_{3,1}$: 900 MHz

$V_{3,2}$: 2.4 GHz

$V_{3,3}$: 5.7 GHz

$V_{3,4}$: License band

VP_4: Processor selection

$V_{4,1}$: M850/860

VP_5: OS for embedded processor

$V_{5,1}$: VX

$V_{5,2}$: PSOS

VP_6: Protocol for air interface

$V_{6,1}$: 802.11

$V_{6,2}$: Proprietary

$V_{6,3}$: Edge/3G

VP_8: Network management and administration

VP_9: HW configuration

VP_{10}: Troubleshooting

VP_{11}: Subscriber support

VP_{12}: Commercial DB to manage the information for network administration

$V_{12,1}$: Oracle

VP_{13}: Number of end points

$V_{13,1}$: Two

$V_{13,2}$: Any

VP_{14}: Kind of end point

$V_{14,1}$: EUM

VP_{15}: Destination of the connection

$V_{15,1}$: EUM

$V_{15,2}$: Single IP wireless network

$V_{15,3}$: Internet

VP_{16}: Speed of the connection

$V_{16,1}$: Fixed

$V_{16,2}$: Variable

VP_{17}: Deployment site

$V_{17,1}$: Site of end user

$V_{17,2}$: Site of ISP

Attributes

A_1: Reliability measured as the mean time to failure

A_2: Usability measured on an ordinal scale (trivial, easy, medium, hard, very hard)

A_3: Capacity measured as the raw baud rate

A_4: Distance of wireless link measured as the distance in feet or meters between the two antennas of a link

9.4.2 Definition of product strategies

Three strategies have been identified so far:

S_1: Bare-bone LMS. This strategy delivers the basic connectivity functionality of the LMS systems. Administration tools are provided with the system but implement only one administrative solution.

S_2: LMS customized to user needs. This strategy extends the number of variants regarding network administration and product customization to address specific needs of WaveRider's customers.

S_3: Network administration tool market. This strategy further extends the number of variants regarding network administration and aims at achieving a leading position in the market of administration tools for wireless networks.

A small subset of the variation points is likely to give the most significant characterization of the strategies from the market perspective. This subset is extracted from the list given earlier of variation points and variants related to the product line and includes the following:

VP_1: Interface with network administration tools

VP_8: Network management and administration

VP_9: Hardware configuration

VP_{10}: Troubleshooting

VP_{12}: Commercial DB to manage the information for network administration

These variation points are all related to network administration and product customization. Other variation points (to be identified) may integrate the definition of the strategies from a more technical viewpoint.

9.4.3 Selection of product strategies to develop in the future

All the strategies will be implemented. The planned order is S_1, S_2, S_3.

Strategy S_1 is the initial strategy and also represents the core of the subsequent strategies. Each strategy is a superset of the previous ones. The strategies are ordered according to increasing complexity. The reason for not implementing S_3, the most complex, right away is its high cost and the long time to develop, which would delay the entry of WaveRider's products into the market.

Due to the incremental definition of the strategies, there is no big leap between the strategies. Therefore, it is foreseen that the strategies will be implemented with a Move approach as seen in Figure 9.4a.

These strategies map onto WaveRider's products proposed in the *plan of development of new products* in domain characterization. A tentative mapping is given in Table 9.6. So far, there is no one-to-one mapping between products and strategies.

9.5 Domain modeling

9.5.1 Product use case models for LMS 170

The use case diagram for the LMS 170 is shown in Figure 9.5. These use cases are discussed next.

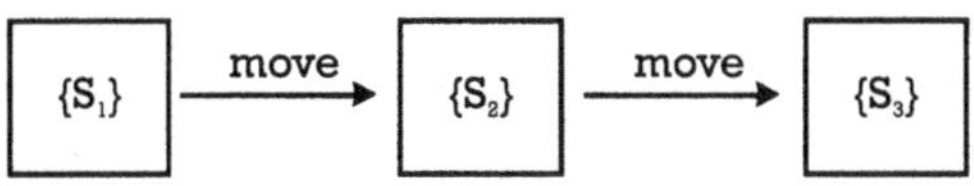

Figure 9.4a The Move approach.

Table 9.6
Tentative Map of WaveRider's Strategies and Products

Strategy	Product
S_1	NCL 135 LMS 170 LMS 270
S_2	LMS 270 with more customization features
S_3	LMS 270 with administration support tools

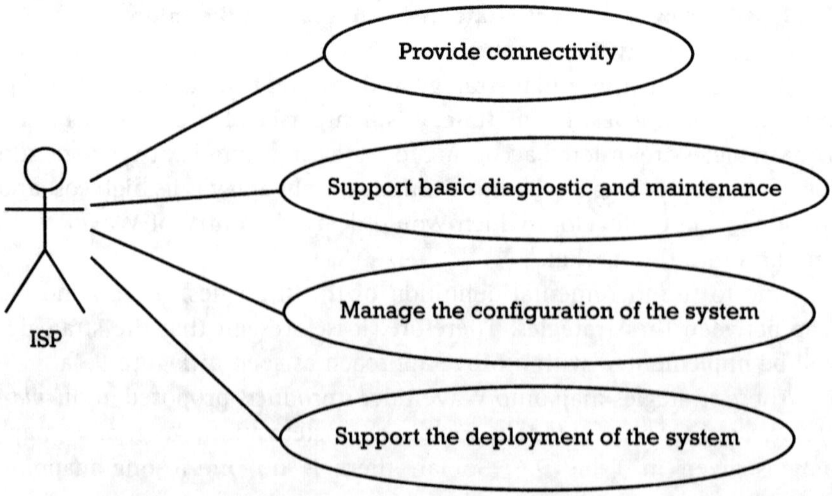

Figure 9.5 Use case diagram for the LMS 170.

Use Cases:

- *Provide connectivity:* The system connects two EUMs at a given speed through an RS232 network interface.
- *Support basic diagnostics and maintenance:* The system records the status of the 170 providing basic diagnostics to the ISP, advising the ISP when maintenance operations are required, and providing intelligent support for such operations.
- *Manage the configuration of the system:* The system supports the management of its configuration at the end user site.
- *Support the deployment of the system:* The system supports the deployment of a new connection based on the LMS 170 at an end user's site.

List of Actors:

- *ISP:* The Internet service provider.

9.5.2 Product use case models for LMS 270

The use case diagram for the LMS 270 is shown in Figure 9.6. These use cases are discussed next.

Use Cases:

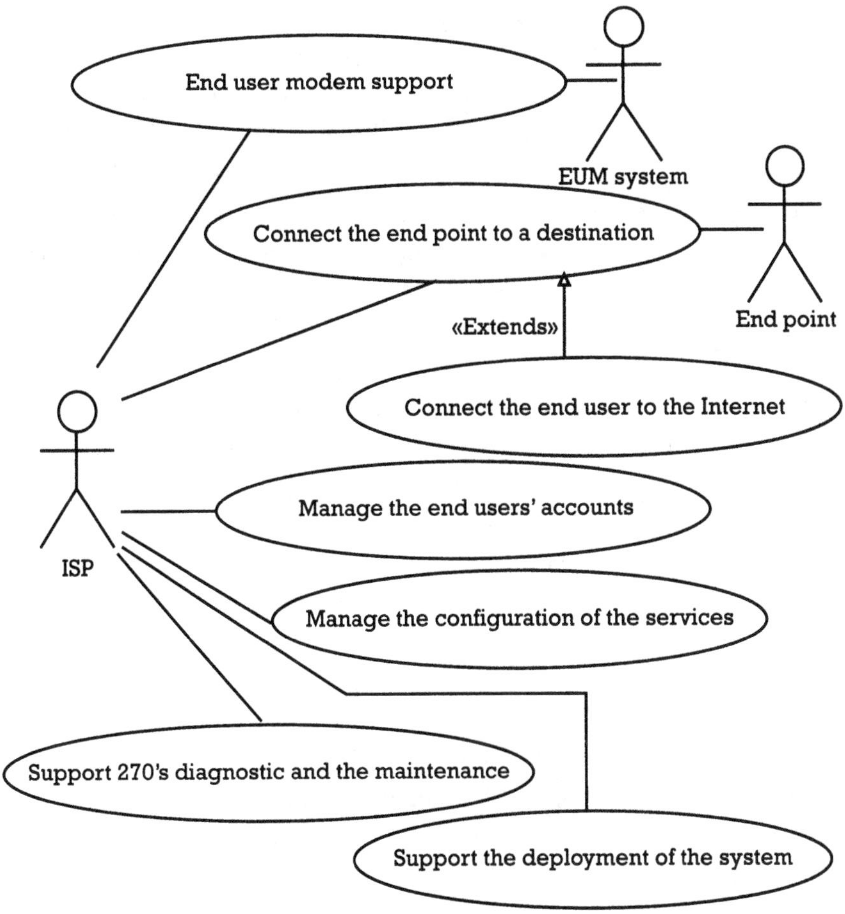

Figure 9.6 Use case diagram for the LMS 270.

- *End user modem support:* The system connects the ISP to the end user modem system.
- *Connect the end point to a destination:* The system connects multiple end points to a destination at a given speed through a network interface.
- *Manage the configuration of the services:* The system supports the configuration of the LMS 270 system. The system manages the configuration of the services. The configuration includes the optimization of the configuration of the IP, the users' connections, the resources, and so on.

- *Manage the end users' accounts:* The system manages the end users' accounts, keeping track of used resources. End users' accounts have privileges to access resources. The accounting system has an accounting application interface and uses an accounting procedure.
- *Support diagnostics and maintenance:* The system records the status of the LMS 270 system in a diagnosis and maintenance database. This provides diagnostics to the ISP, advising the ISP when maintenance operations are required, and providing intelligent support for such operations.
- *Connect the end user to the Internet:* The system connects multiple end points to the Internet at a given speed through a network interface.
- *Support the deployment of the system:* The system supports the deployment and the installation of an LMS 270 system at the ISP and end users' sites. Information on deployed systems is stored in a database of knowledge on deployment for ease in later deployments.

List of Actors:

ISP: Internet service provider;

End point: An end point in the overall Internet network;

EUM system: The end user modem system.

9.5.3 Product domain models for LMS 170

The LMS 170 product model is organized in the following diagrams:

- Configuration subsystem
- Deployment support subsystem
- Maintenance support subsystem
- Connectivity subsystem
- Diagram configuration subsystem

Configuration System Diagram. A database of configurations holds a set of existing configurations of the system (Figure 9.7). Each configuration refers to an arbitrary number of items—in this case products, which can be connected to one another.

Diagram Deployment Support Subsystem. A generic deployment support class is specialized for the needs of the LMS 170 (Figure 9.8). It refers to a given deployment site, which for the LMS 170 is the site of the end user. The knowledge for deployment is stored in a database of knowledge.

Diagram Maintenance Support Subsystem. A generic maintenance support subsystem is specialized to the need of the LMS 170 (Figure 9.9). It receives data from one or more sensors. The sensors are also specialized to the needs of the LMS 170.

Diagram Connectivity Subsystem. A connection links two or more end points to a destination (Figure 9.10). In the case for the LMS 170 the destination is not restricted, and the end points are end user modems. A connection requires a network interface; for the LMS 270 the network interface is an RS232 for the LMS 170.

9.5.4 Product domain models for LMS 270

The LMS170 product model is organized in the following diagrams:

- System core
- Maintenance support subsystem

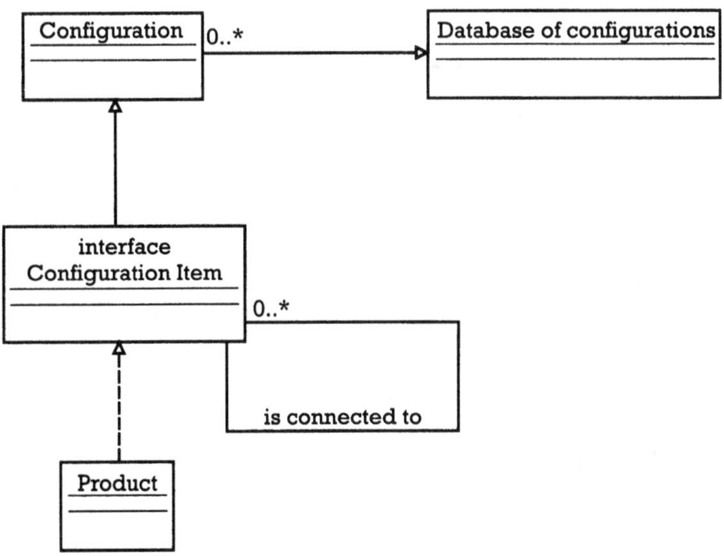

Figure 9.7 LMS 170 analysis diagram for the configuration system.

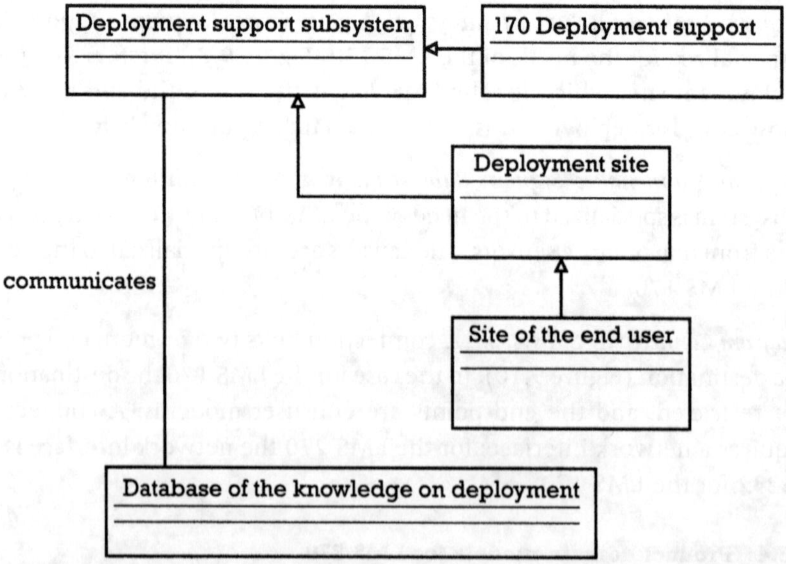

Figure 9.8 LMS 170 analysis diagram for the deployment support subsystem.

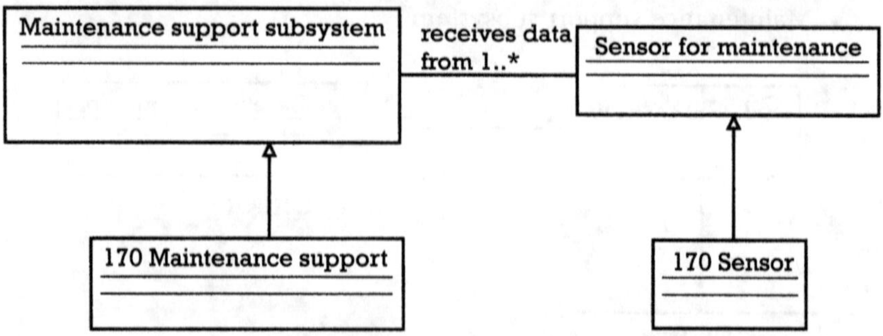

Figure 9.9 LMS 170 analysis diagram for the maintenance support subsystem.

- Deployment support subsystem
- Accounting subsystem
- Configuration subsystem
- Connectivity subsystem

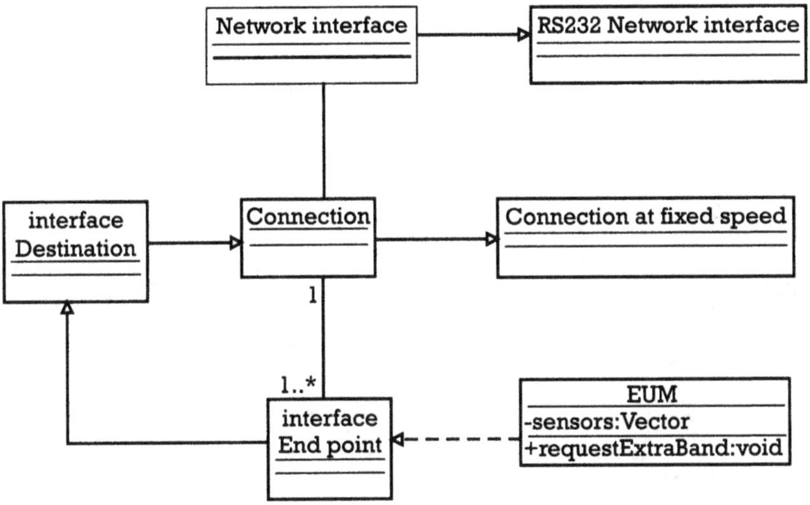

Figure 9.10 LMS 170 analysis diagram for the connectivity subsystem.

Analysis Diagram System Core. The core of an LMS 270 is formed by the actual LMS 270 system, which belongs to the LMS family (Figure 9.11). It provides LMS 270 services, refers to an LMS 270 network, and has one or more LMS 270 sensors.

Analysis Diagram Maintenance Support Subsystem. A generic maintenance support subsystem is specialized to the needs of the LMS 270 (Figure 9.12). It receives data from one or more sensors. Also the sensors are specialized to the needs of the LMS 270.

Analysis Diagram Deployment Support Subsystem. A generic deployment support class is specialized for the needs of the 270 (Figure 9.13). It refers to a given deployment site, which for the 270 is either the site of the end user or the site of the Internet service provider. The knowledge for deployment is stored in a database of knowledge.

Analysis Diagram Accounting Subsystem. An accounting subsystem manages user privileges to access resources (Figure 9.14). Resources can be services, such as end user roaming, e-mail notification, or network bandwidth. Resources are assigned to users upon a request from a user. An accounting subsystem defines its own application interface and follows accounting procedures, which can comply with the RADIUS standard.

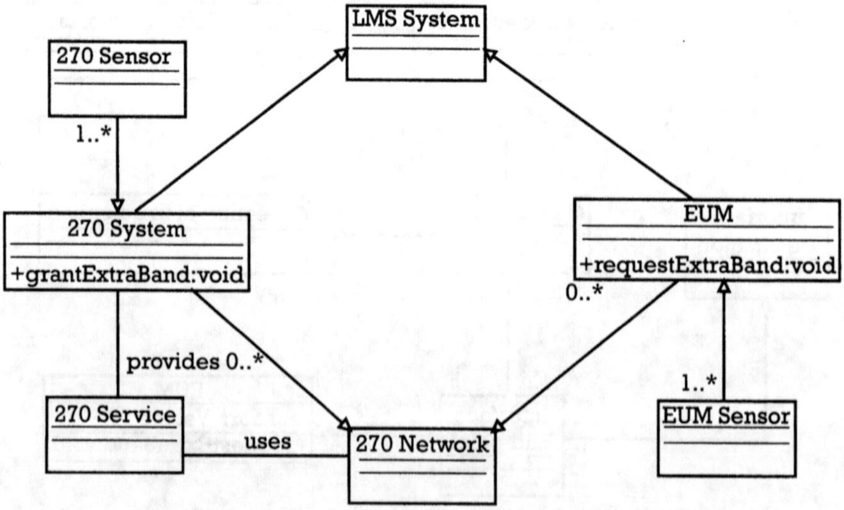

Figure 9.11 LMS 270 analysis diagram for the system core.

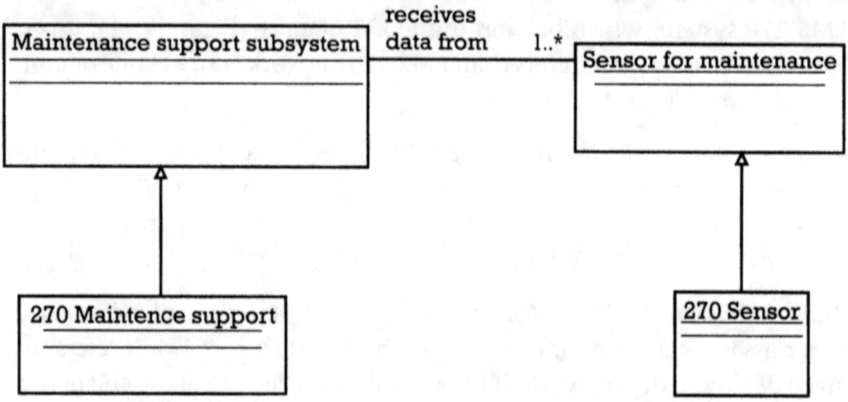

Figure 9.12 LMS 270 analysis diagram for the maintenance support subsystem.

Analysis Diagram Configuration Subsystem. A database of configurations holds a set of existing configurations of the system (Figure 9.15). Each configuration refers to an arbitrary number of items—in this case, either products or services, which can be connected to one another.

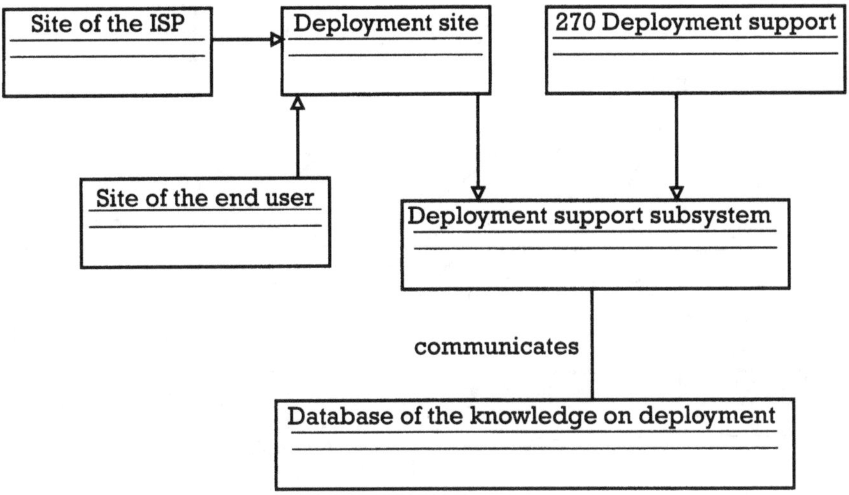

Figure 9.13 LMS 270 analysis diagram for the deployment support subsystem.

Analysis Diagram Connectivity Subsystem. A connection links two or more end points to a destination (Figure 9.16). In the case for the LMS 270, the destination is a single IP wireless network, and the end points are end user modems. A connection requires a network interface, which is an RS232 for the LMS 270. A connection can be either at fixed speed or at variable speed.

9.5.5 Domain use case model

A list of the use case diagrams follows:

- Connectivity
- Manage the configuration
- Manage end users' accounts
- Request extra bandwidth
- Support deployment
- Support diagnostics and maintenance

Use Case Diagram for Connectivity. See Figure 9.17.

Use Case:

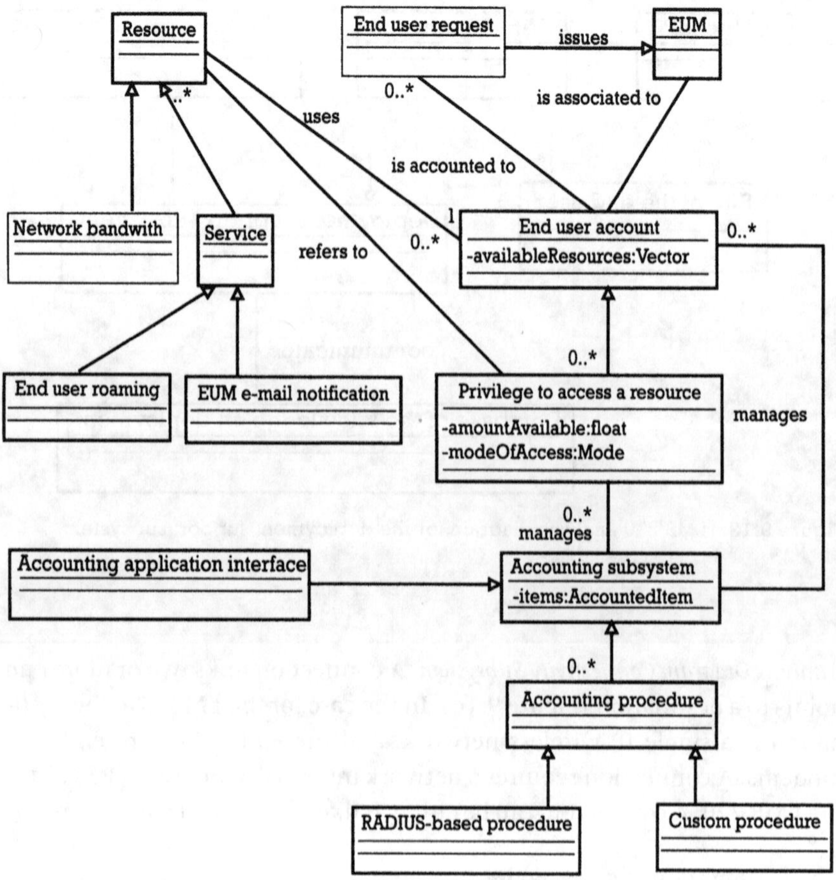

Figure 9.14 LMS 270 analysis diagram for the accounting subsystem.

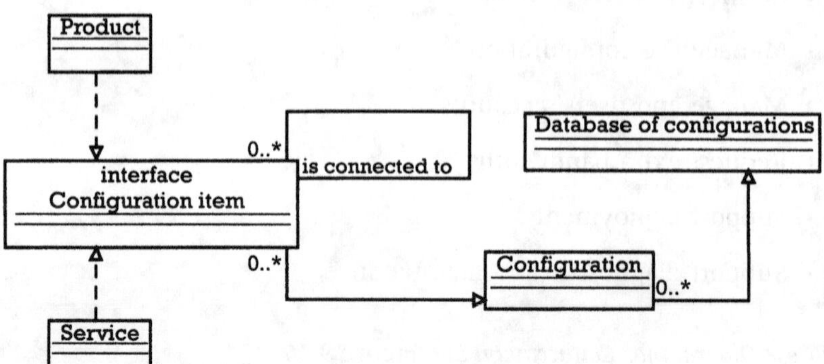

Figure 9.15 LMS 270 analysis diagram for the configuration subsystem.

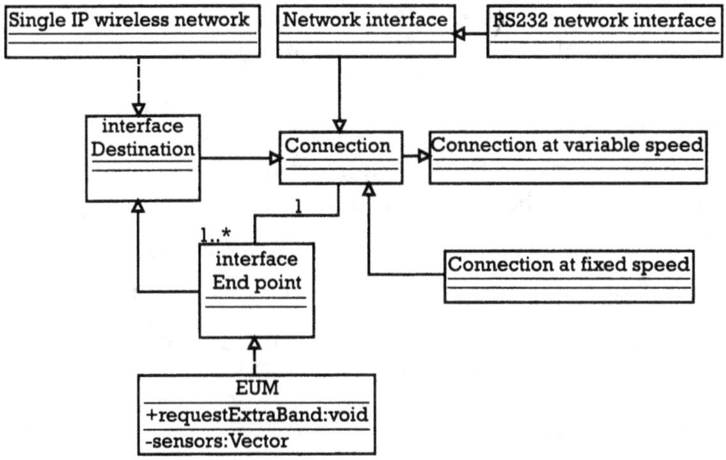

Figure 9.16 LMS 270 analysis diagram for the connectivity subsystem.

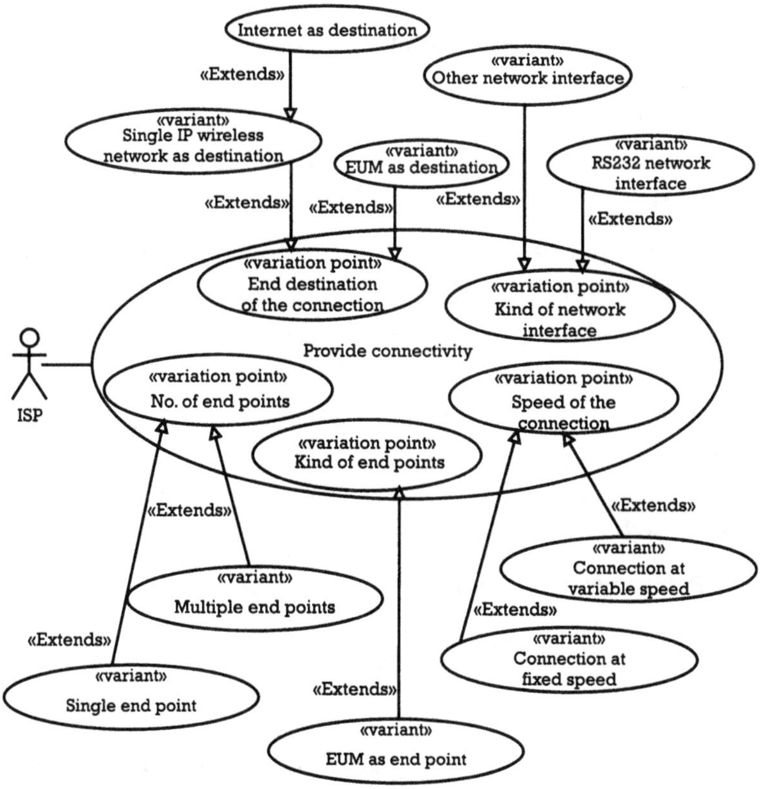

Figure 9.17 Domain use case diagram for connectivity.

- *Provide connectivity:* The system connects a number of end points to a destination at a given speed through a network interface.

Variants:

- *Multiple end points:* There is no fixed number of end points in the system; this is the case of the 270.
- *Single end point:* There is only one end point connected to the destination within the connection. This is the case for the LMS 170.
- *EUM as end point:* An EUM is the end point in the connection. Applicable to LMS 170 and LMS 270.
- *Single IP wireless network as destination:* The destination may be a single IP wireless network; this is the case of the EUM270.
- *EUM as destination:* A destination can be a single EUM. This is the case of the 270.
- *Internet as destination:* A special case of single IP wireless network is as a destination when the destination network is connected to the Internet.
- *Connection at variable speed:* The system supports multiple speeds of connections. This is the case for the 270.
- *Connection at a fixed speed:* The system supports only one speed of connection. This is the case for the 170.
- *Other network interface:* Another network interface is acceptable to the system. This is the case for the LMS 270.
- *RS232 network interface:* The only network interface acceptable is the RS232; this is the case for the LMS 170.

List of Actors:

- *ISP:* Internet service provider.

Use Case Diagram for Manage the Configuration. See Figure 9.18.

Use Case:

- *Manage the configuration:* The ISP is supported in the configuration of a configuration item.

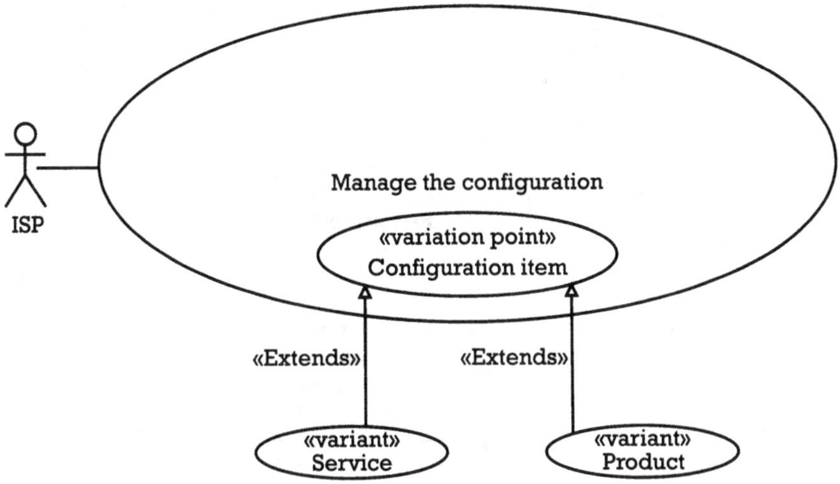

Figure 9.18 Domain use case diagram for manage the configuration.

Variants:

- *Product:* The configuration item is a 270 network.
- *Service:* The configuration item is a service.

List of Actors:

- *ISP:* Internet service provider.

Use Case Diagram for Manage End User Accounts. See Figure 9.19.

Use Case:

- *Manage end user accounts:* The system manages the end user accounts, keeping track of used resources. End user accounts have privileges to access resources. The accounting system has an accounting application interface and uses an accounting procedure.

Variants:

- *RADIUS-based procedure:* The system exchanges data with other accounting systems using RADIUS.
- *Custom procedure:* In-house procedure for accounting.

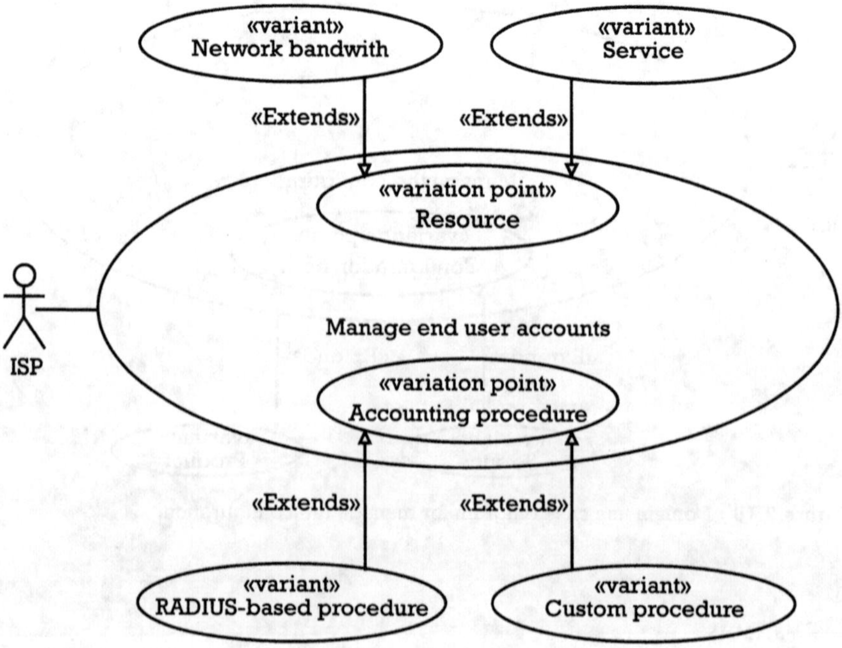

Figure 9.19 Use case diagram for manage end user accounts.

- *Network bandwidth:* Network bandwidth as resource.
- *Service:* Service as resource.

List of Actors:

- *ISP:* Internet service provider.

Use Case Diagram for Request Extra Bandwidth. See Figure 9.20.

Use Case:

- *Request extra bandwidth:* The end user may ask the system to provide extra bandwidth for a given period of time to perform some

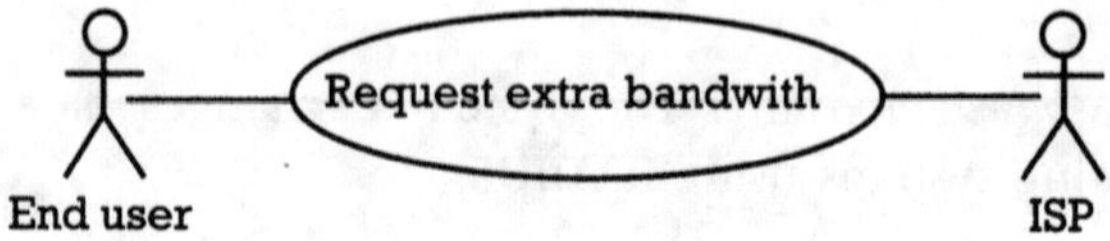

Figure 9.20 Use case diagram for request extra bandwidth.

bandwidth-intensive application. The request is forwarded to the ISP, which then notifies the user about the response to the request. See the use case on connectivity for management of connectivity at variable speed. See the use case on managing end user accounts for information about accounting for the end user's request for extra resources.

List of Actors:

- *End user:* the end user of the system;
- *ISP:* Internet service provider.

Use Case Diagram for Support Deployment. See Figure 9.21.

Use Case:

- *Support the deployment of a wireless system:* The system supports the deployment and the installation of a deployed system at a deployment site. Information on deployed systems is stored in a database of knowledge on deployment for ease in later deployments.

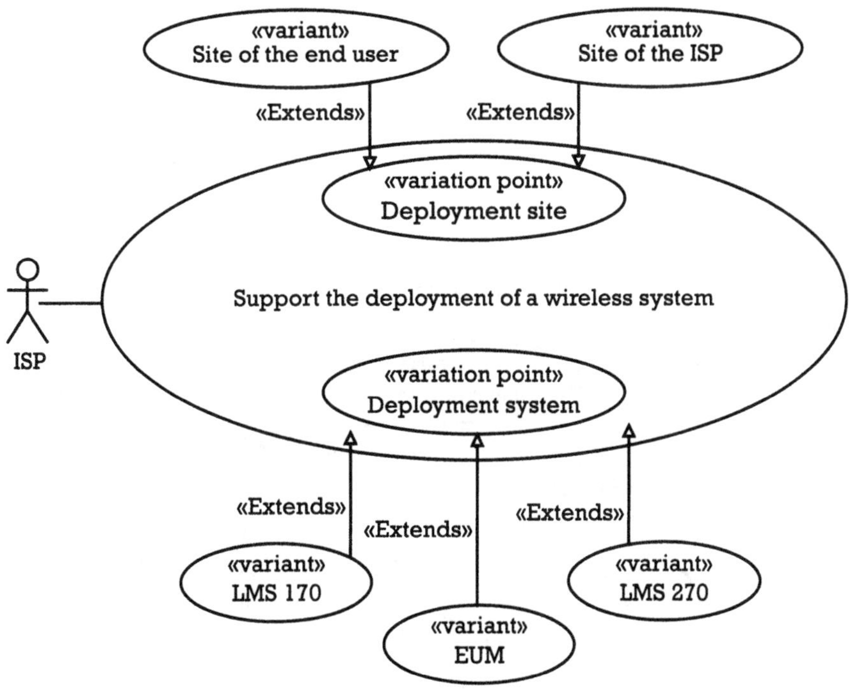

Figure 9.21 Use case diagram for support deployment.

Variants:

- *EUM:* The wireless system being deployed is an EUM.
- *LMS 170:* The wireless system being deployed is an LMS 170.
- *LMS 270:* The wireless system being deployed is an LMS 270.
- *Site of the end user:* The wireless system is deployed at the end user location.
- *Site of the ISP:* The wireless system is deployed at the location of the Internet service provider.

List of Actors:

- *ISP:* Internet service provider.

Use Case Diagram for Support Diagnostics and Maintenance. See Figure 9.22.

Use Case:

- *Support diagnostics and maintenance:* The system records the status of the diagnostics and maintenance system in a diagnosis and maintenance database. This provides diagnostic to the ISP, advising the

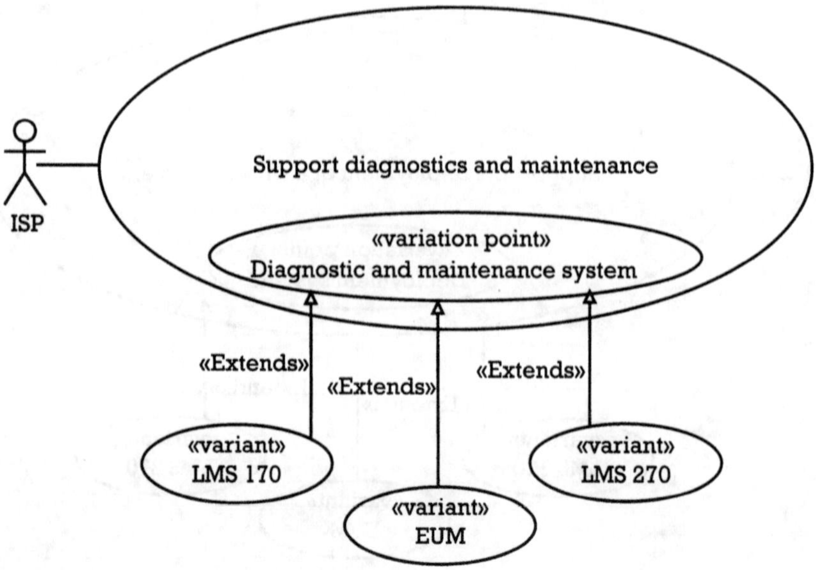

Figure 9.22 Use case diagram for support diagnostics and maintenance.

ISP when maintenance operations are required and providing intelligent support for such operations.

Variants:

- *LMS 170:* The target system whose diagnostic and maintenance to support is an LMS 170.
- *LMS 270:* The target system whose diagnostic and maintenance to support is an LMS 270.
- *EUM:* The target system whose diagnostic and maintenance to support is an EUM.

List of Actors:

- *ISP:* Internet service provider.

9.5.6 Domain analysis model

The following diagrams are used in the domain analysis model:

- Diagram system core
- Diagram accounting subsystem
- Diagram configuration subsystem
- Diagram connectivity subsystem
- Diagram deployment support subsystem
- Diagram maintenance support subsystem

Domain Analysis Diagram for the System Core. The core of an LMS system is formed by the actual LMS system—either an EUM, a 170, or a 270 (Figure 9.23). The LMS 270 provides LMS 270 services, refers to an LMS 270 network, and has one or more LMS 270 sensors. LMS 170 sensors and EUM sensors are attached to the LMS 170 and the EUM, respectively.

Domain Analysis Diagram for the Accounting Subsystem. An accounting subsystem is part of an LMS system (Figure 9.24). It manages users' privileges to access resources. Resources can be services, such as end user roaming or e-mail notification, or network bandwidth. Resources are assigned to users after users' requests. An accounting subsystem defines its own application

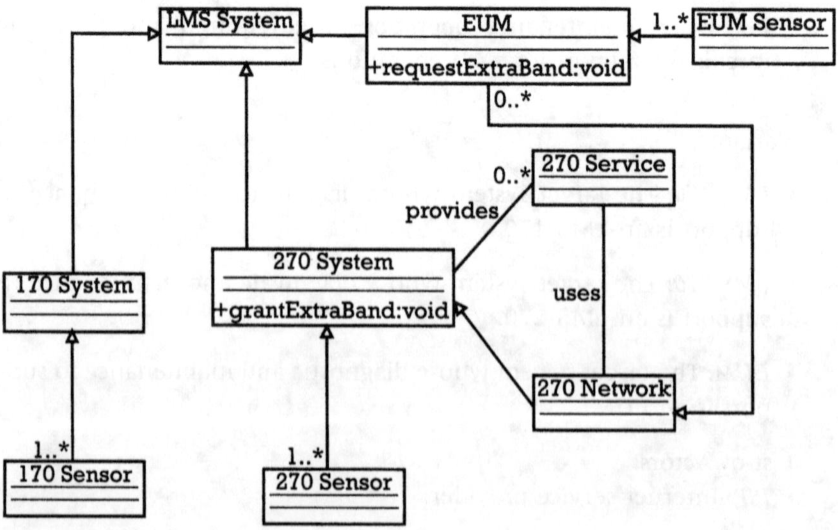

Figure 9.23 Domain analysis diagram for the system core.

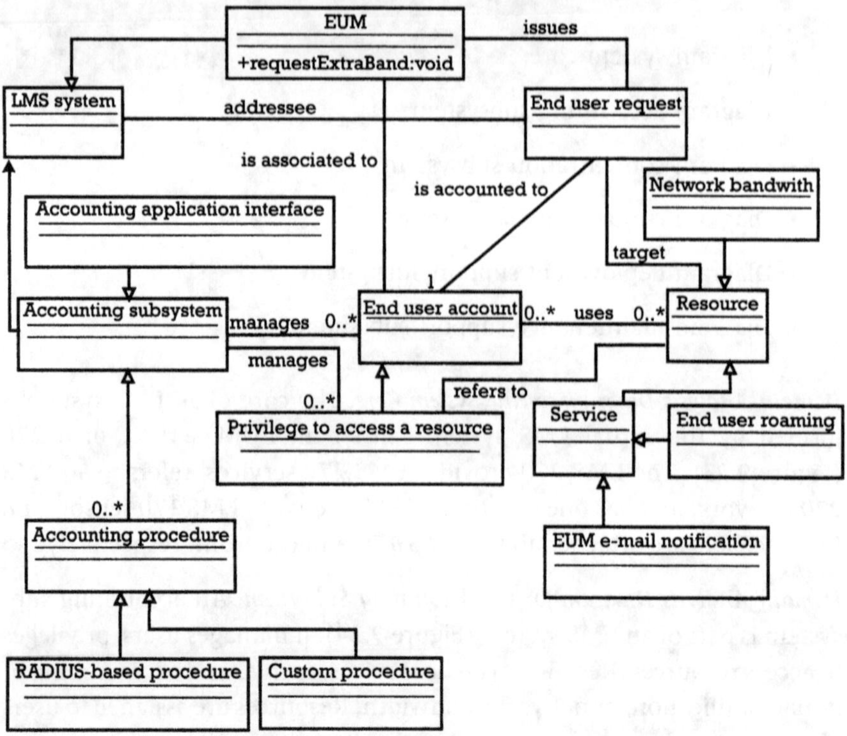

Figure 9.24 Domain analysis diagram for the accounting subsystem.

interface and follows accounting procedures, which can comply with the RADIUS standard.

Domain Analysis Diagram for the Configuration Subsystem. A database of configurations holds a set of existing configurations of the system (Figure 9.25). Each configuration refers to an arbitrary number of items—in this case, either products or services, which can be connected to one another.

Domain Analysis Diagram for the Connectivity Subsystem. A connection links two or more end points to a destination (Figure 9.26). A destination can be a single IP wireless network, and the end points are end user modems. A connection requires a network interface, which can be a RS232. A connection can be either at fixed speed or at variable speed.

Domain Analysis Diagram for the Deployment Support Subsystem. A generic deployment support class is specialized for the needs of the 170, the 270, or the end user modem (Figure 9.27). It refers to a given deployment site, which is either the site of the end user or the site of the Internet service provider. The knowledge for deployment is stored in a database of knowledge.

Domain Analysis Diagram for the Maintenance Support Subsystem. A generic maintenance support subsystem is specialized to the needs of the 170, the 270, or the end user modem (Figure 9.28). It receives data from one or more sensors. Also, the sensors are specialized to the needs of the three LMS products.

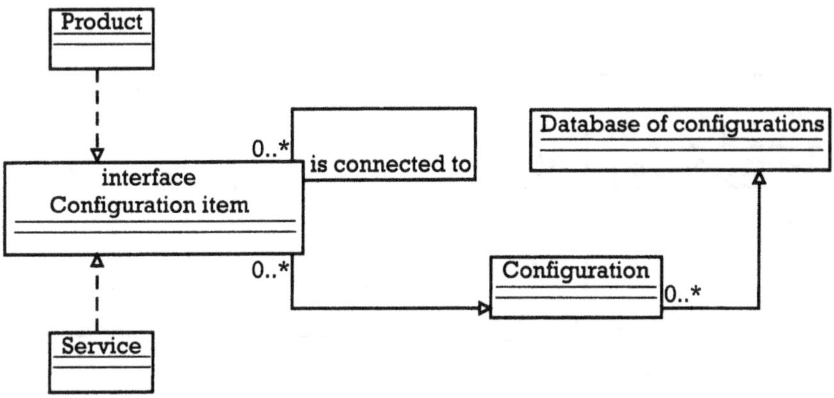

Figure 9.25 Domain analysis diagram for the configuration subsystem.

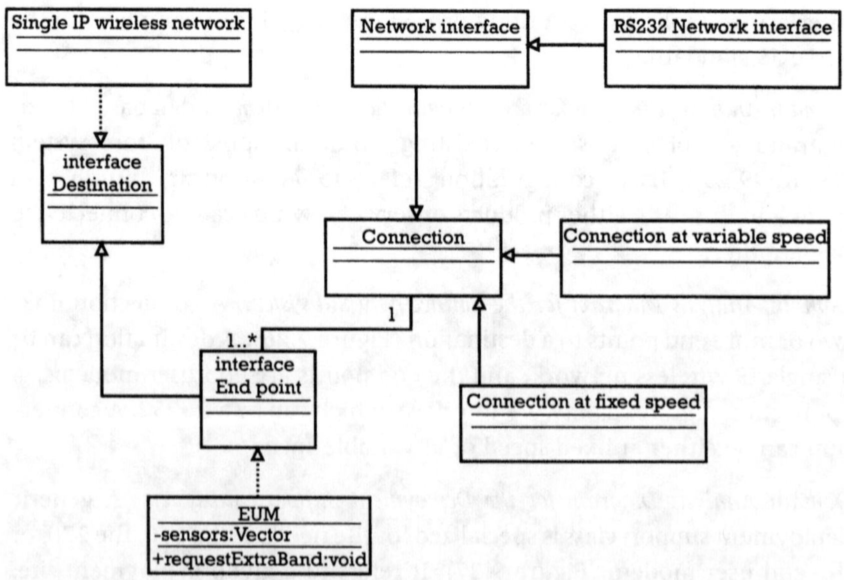

Figure 9.26 Domain analysis diagram for the connectivity subsystem.

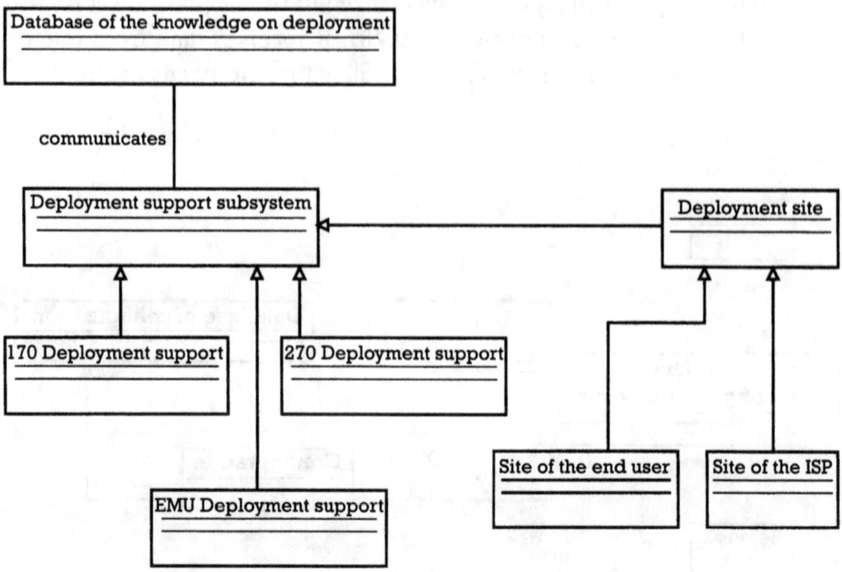

Figure 9.27 Domain analysis diagram for the deployment support subsystem.

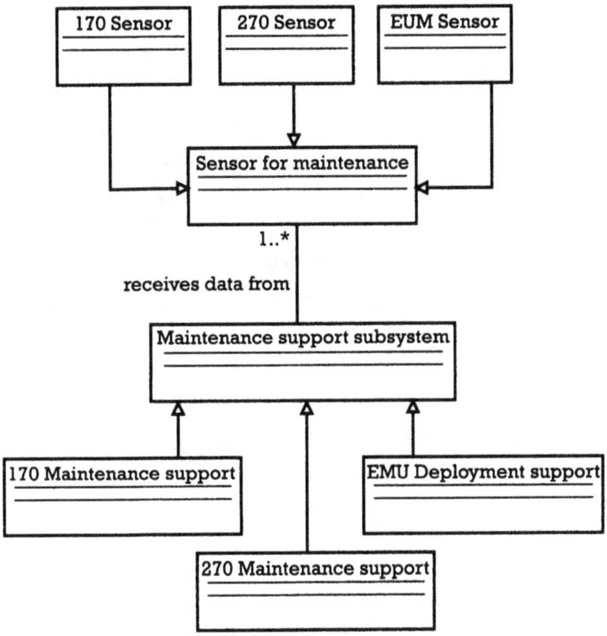

Figure 9.28 Domain analysis diagram for the maintenance support subsystem.

9.6 Domain framework development

This section does not cover all parts of the domain framework development phase because of space restrictions.

9.6.1 Definition of the nature of the domain framework

The framework has reactive and passive parts. The reactive part sets up and runs an LMS system made of several hardware elements and software services. This part is reactive because it manages the main control, allowing the framework's user to add elements and services seamlessly to the system. The passive part provides utility components that can work as a library in different contexts. The hardware drivers for the various hardware components of the system are the core of the passive parts.

At the level of a single network element (for example, NAP, CAP, or EUM), the framework works as an operating system. It allows plug-in capability for different types of hardware, which is detected automatically at power-up, and software. Software can be plugged in at start-up or later, providing maximum flexibility.

At the network level, the framework is meant to support the activities of connectivity and a service provider. Connectivity can be seen as an elementary service. However, the framework is aimed at more advanced services that have a higher value. The services can refer either to the service provider—in which case they focus on network, user, account, and service management—or to the end users connected through the EUMs.

9.6.2 Architecture of the domain framework

The architecture comprises three core projections: package, class, and object dynamics.

Package projection

The framework is written in C and C++. The package projection for these languages is reflected in the directory hierarchy where the framework is stored. Figure 9.29 provides an overview of the package projection.

The following list details the package projection of the framework:

- lms: root of the hierarchy.
- lms/control: common procedures for system control.
- lms/defs: common definitions of the framework.
- lms/eum: EUM-specific features.
- lms/eum/cell: cell management for EUM. Includes procedures for the identification of the cell, initialization in a cell-like network, and roaming. Also includes data structures for the description of the cell characteristics that can be transmitted to the CAP or passed to the user for installation or maintenance purposes.
- lms/eum/services: includes classes for the registration of services at EUM level. This is a small reactive framework where services can be registered and then activated upon arrival of a specific event or message. This framework is analyzed in greater detail later.
- lms/eum/services/email: EUM service for automatic notification of e-mail arrival. Includes also management of e-mail protocols.
- lms/eum/services/messages: EUM service for visualization of messages on EUM's built-in display. Supports messages generated internally in the EUM or received from the NAP.

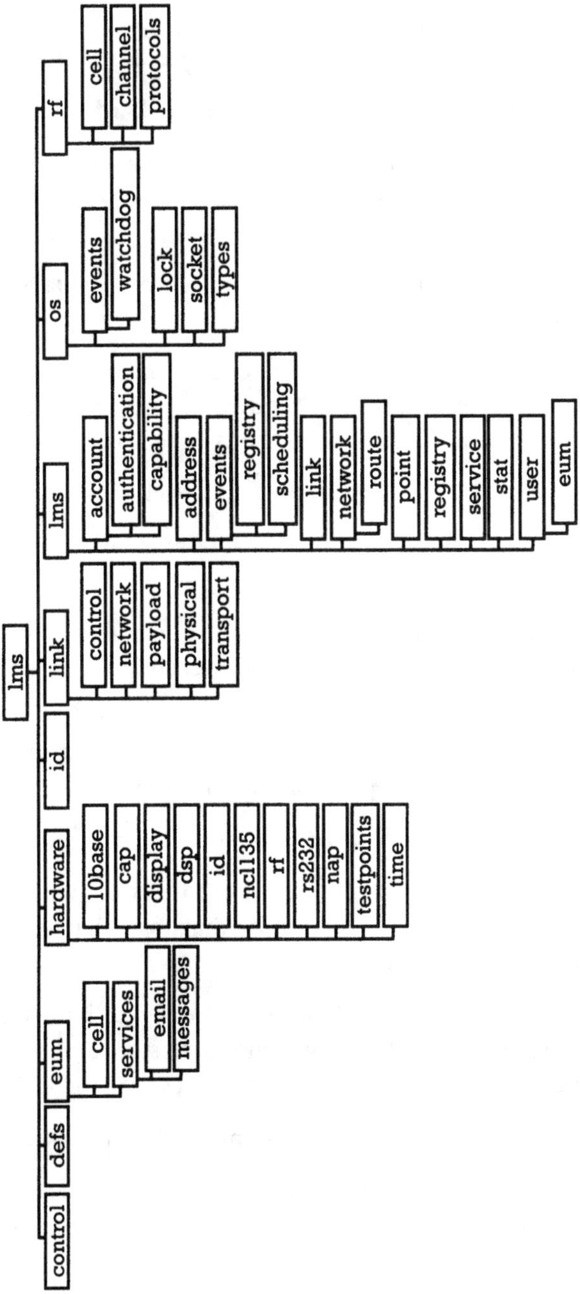

Figure 9.29 Overview of the package projection.

- lms/hardware: package providing support for various hardware on the system.
- lms/hardware/10base: support for 10base Ethernet hardware.
- lms/hardware/cap: support for CAP-specific hardware.
- lms/hardware/display: support for LCD display on EUM. Contains procedures for initialization, refresh, and visualization of messages on the display.
- lms/hardware/dsp: support for different types of digital signal processing hardware.
- lms/hardware/id: procedures and data structures for automatic detection and identification of hardware. The procedures retrieve and store the identification codes hard-wired on LMS hardware.
- lms/hardware/ncl135: support for NCL-specific hardware.
- lms/hardware/eproms: support for erasable and programmable ROMs.
- lms/hardware/rf: support for digitally controlled RF hardware. Includes procedures for selection of receiving and transmitting bands, frequency and output power. Also includes procedures for hardware start-up and diagnosis.
- lms/hardware/rs232: support for communication on RS232.
- lms/hardware/nap: support for NAP-specific hardware.
- lms/hardware/testpoints: contains procedures for maintenance of hardware. Makes hardware generate diagnosis signals that can be checked at specific test points.
- lms/hardware/time: support for several types of hardware timers. Provides procedures that manage timers and store timer information (timestamps) in appropriate data structures.
- lms/id: identification of elements in an LMS network.
- lms/link: support for point-to-point links. This package defines the framework for setting up a layered architecture like the OSI stack.
- lms/link/control: support for transmission of control messages through the layered architecture and across the link.

- lms/link/network: network layer in the layered architecture.
- lms/link/payload: infrastructure for defining the payload for different protocols. No specific payload or protocol is defined here.
- lms/link/physical: physical layer in the layered architecture. This package relies on other packages for the identification and configuration of the proper hardware to use.
- lms/link/transport: transport layer in the layered architecture.
- lms/lms: root for subpackages that manage the LMS network and its elements. Most of the files contained here are C++ classes.
- lms/lms/account: class definition for account definition, storing, and management.
- lms/lms/account/authentication: procedures for authenticating users and binding them to an account.
- lms/lms/account/capability: interfaces and classes for managing the capabilities of an account. Capabilities can be set on the short or long term. A set of procedures scans the capability lists, checking consistency and generating reports. Concrete classes for capabilities define, for instance, the allocated bandwidth and the access to services.
- lms/lms/addresses: support for addresses in an LMS network. Includes also address mapping and address caching.
- lms/lms/events: support for events generated in an element of an LMS system.
- lms/lms/events/registry: support for registering events.
- lms/lms/events/scheduling: a class for scheduling events. Internally contains an event registry.
- lms/lms/link: support for point-to-point links in an LMS network. This package provides classes for managing and exchanging information on links at LMS network level. This package relies on the "lms/link" package for the actual operations of the links.
- lms/lms/network: LMS network and network element identification.
- lms/lms/network/route: support for routing.

- lms/lms/point: interfaces and default classes for the description of network elements.
- lms/lms/registry: general support for loggable and archivable registries. This package provides a system for registering entities that need to be retrieved—for example, through a name—or notified of certain events.
- lms/lms/service: provides interfaces and default implementation for service handlers.
- lms/lms/stat: contains interfaces and default implementation for defining data structures that represent statistics. The default implementation provides support for a simple "measurement" of data on an LMS element.
- lms/lms/user: class definition for users.
- lms/lms/user/eum: class definition for binding users to EUMs.
- lms/os: common features of the operating system running of the LMS elements.
- lms/os/events: support for events.
- lms/os/watchdog: support for watchdogs.
- lms/os/lock: procedures and data structures for semaphores and management of locks.
- lms/os/socket: Unix-like socket implementation.
- lms/os/types: definition of common types in the system.
- lms/rf: this package provides support for RF and cell management. The hardware-related part is delegated to "lms/hardware/rf."
- lms/rf/cell: procedures and data structures to manage a cell.
- lms/rf/channel: procedures and data structure to manage a channel in a cell.
- lms/rf/protocols: procedures to manage different RF protocols. The procedures are meant for control and diagnosis purposes.

The package projection has been used as the basis for the division of work among groups of developers. There are three groups of developers:

1. The NCL 135 group is responsible for the development of the embedded software on the NCL 135.

2. The EUM group is responsible for the development of the embedded software on the EUM.

3. The LMS group is responsible for the development of the embedded software on the NAP and SAP, and of the infrastructure software that makes the LMS run as a coherent system.

A major part, rooted in "lms/lms" and written in C++, has been assigned to the LMS group. This part manages the LMS network, the users and their accounts, and the advanced services. This part offers great extensibility to accommodate the different user needs that may arise. Extension is foreseen especially in the direction of new services.

Other packages have a deeper relation to hardware and run as embedded software. Subpackages of these packages can be traced directly to specific hardware components. These packages have been developed mainly in C. They are rooted in "lms/eum," "lms/hardware," and "lms/id" and were assigned to the NCL 135, EUM, and LMS groups.

The NCL 135 and EUM groups have also developed a set of packages ("lms/control," "lms/defs," "lms/link," "lms/os," and "lms/rf") that work as a common operating system for all the hardware components.

Class projection

Because of space restrictions, this section describes only a small, reactive part of the framework: the management of services on the EUM.

The EUM's basic purpose is to work as a wireless modem attached to a personal computer or workstation. The EUM receives and transmits packets on the wireless network. The packets are mainly passed to or received from the computer. The EUM's advanced purpose is to host a set of intelligent services that live in parallel with the normal modem activity of the EUM.

The EUM contains a sub-framework for the management of services that allows us to add any number of services to the EUM. As of 2000, two services were available on an EUM: e-mail arrival notification and visualization of messages on the LCD display.

Any service must follow a registration mechanism to notify the framework that the service exists. Once registered, a service is put in a state that does nothing but wait for activation. The activation of a service happens when an event occurs, such as a time-out or a message arrival directed at the service. Each service specifies its activation mechanism during the registration process.

When a service receives an event, the service can handle the event or pass it to another service. This other service can handle or pass the event in a similar way. The mechanism of handling an event locally in one service or passing it to another service implements a chain of responsibility. The default implementation of the services supports the chain of responsibility. This is useful when the registry cannot determine which service is the target of an event, so it passes the event to the first service in the chain and expects each service to determine whether to consume the event or not. The chain of responsibility also allows a service to receive a message, process it partially, and then pass it to the next service in the chain for further processing.

The registration of services, the activation, and the chain of responsibility mechanisms involve the following C++ classes:

- *Registry.* This class implements a general-purpose registry. Registry can register any number of generic RegistryEntry.
- *RegistryEntry.* Any class that needs to be handled by Registry must extend RegistryEntry. RegistryEntry is an abstract class. We have used an abstract class because C++ does not support interfaces.
- *EUMRegistry.* This class keeps track of the registered services. Its implementation is based on the superclass Registry. EUMRegistry is a Registry that handles only EUM services. EUMRegistry also provides a namespace for the services.
- *EUMService.* This class is a subclass of RegistryEntry. It contains the basic, default implementation of a service. Real services inherit from EUMService and provide a more specialized behavior. EUMService contains the class methods to implement a chain of responsibility in event handling. The "has a" relationship connecting EUMService to itself is the means by which EUMServices are connected in a chain.
- *EmailNotification and MessageVisualization.* These classes specialize EUMService and provide support for notifying users of new e-mail arrivals and for visualizing messages on the EUM's built-in display.
- *PropertySet.* This class can contain a set of Property for a service. PropertySet does not attach any semantics to the properties it contains.

This class usually contains the configuration parameters of a service. It also contains some properties that the registry interprets as modes to activate, deactivate, and interrupt services.

- *Property.* A Property is a key-value pair.

Figure 9.30 summarizes the classes and relationships of the class projection.

The activation and chain of responsibility mechanisms reveal that the nature of the framework is reactive. The framework provides the registry and the event management infrastructure; the user provides any number of services. The main control flow is under control of the framework. The services gain control only through the described mechanisms.

Object dynamics projection

The object dynamics projection divides the considered framework into a front end and a back end.

The front end is concerned with the management of events between the registry and the services. As far as the services are concerned, the registry is the only source of events. This simplifies the system because the services interact only with the registry. This also makes the system more reliable because erroneous behaviors of the services are not propagated beyond the registry, which works as a barrier between the services and the rest of the system.

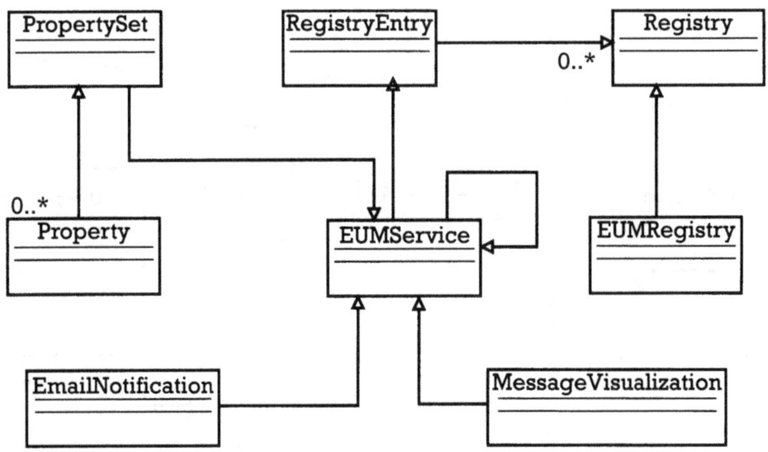

Figure 9.30 EUM framework class projection.

The back end is concerned with the management of the events between the registry and the event sources. The registry is not a source of event: It relies on the event sources for the generation of the events. Event sources include the following:

- Timers that trigger an event at a programmed time;
- Hardware managers that signal problems or special events at the hardware level;
- Packet manager. Services have a namespace and are addressable from the external world. A packet that is directed to a service is first passed to the registry and then dispatched to the proper service.

An abstract class, EventSource, works as the common interface to all the event sources.

The registry processes the events one at a time, fetching the next event to process from an event queue. The event sources write in the queue regardless of the registry's activities. For simplicity, the following discussion does not consider the queue mechanism between the event source and the registry.

Figure 9.31 depicts the objects involved in the front end and in the back end. In both the front end and back end there is a variant of the "publisher-subscriber" (also known as "observer") design pattern. The

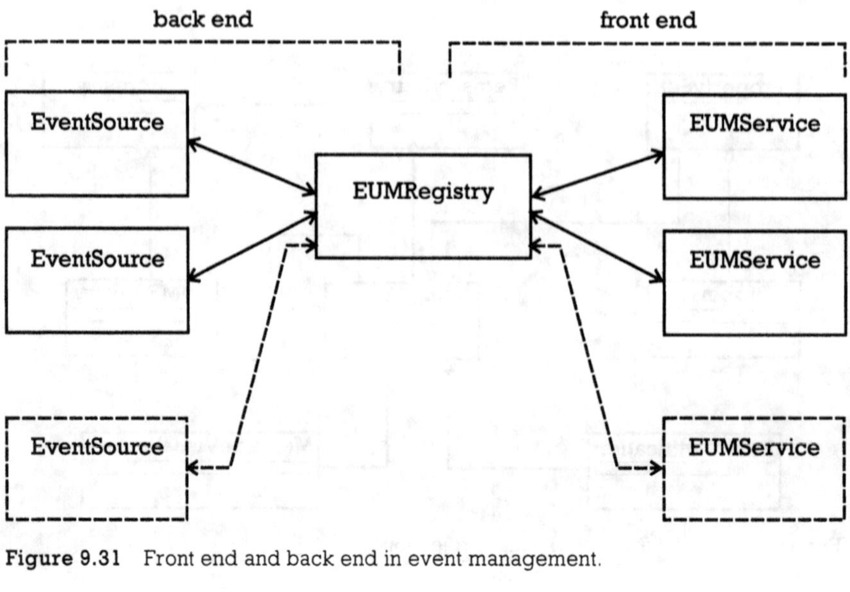

Figure 9.31 Front end and back end in event management.

publisher is the sender of the event (EventSource in the back end and EUMRegistry in the front end), while the subscriber is the receiver of the event (EUMRegistry in the back end and EUMService in the front end).

The object interaction projection describes a typical scenario: an EventSource triggering an event that is consumed by two services. We assume that the two services are named "service1" and "service2." Two cases are possible.

In the first case, "service1" and "service2" are known to be the targets of the events. The activation of the services works as follows:

- An EventSource triggers the event, which is passed to the EUMRegistry.
- The registry determines that two services—"service1" and "service2"—require to consume the event.
- The registry passes the event to "service1" through the activate() method.
- The registry waits for termination of the "service1" processing.
- The registry passes the event to "service2" through the activate() method.
- The registry waits for termination of the "service2" processing.

Figure 9.32 depicts the steps of this case.

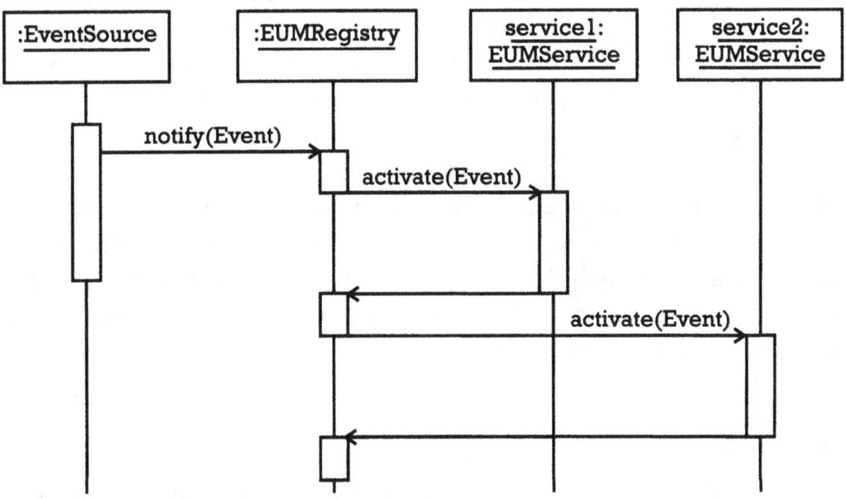

Figure 9.32 Event path with the activation mechanism.

In the second case, the target of the event is not known, so the event is passed to the services according to the chain of responsibility technique. The propagation of the event works as follows:

- An EventSource triggers the event, which is passed to the EUMRegistry.
- The registry determines the first service in the chain of responsibility. Let us assume this is "service1."
- The registry passes the event to "service1" through the chain() method.
- "Service1" processes the event.
- "Service1" determines that the event can also be processed by others, so it passes the event to the next service in the chain—"service2"—through the chain() method.
- "Service2" processes the event.
- "Service2" determines that the event can also be processed also by others but also determines that there are no more services in the chain. As a result it returns control to the EUMRegistry.

Figure 9.33 depicts the steps of this scenario.

Alternatively to this scenario, "service1" could process the event and determine that the event is consumed and does not need any more processing by others. Here, "service1" returns the control to the EUMRegistry without passing the event to "service2." This terminates the chain at the first step (Figure 9.34).

9.6.3 Documentation of components in the domain framework

Each component has documentation built into the code. This documentation is concerned mainly with the use and integration of the component. When a larger view of the system is required to understand the component, the documentation of the component contains references to design documents.

The documentation of the components follows a standard format adopted in WaveRider for maximum consistency and readability.

The documentation of the components is not presented here because of space restrictions.

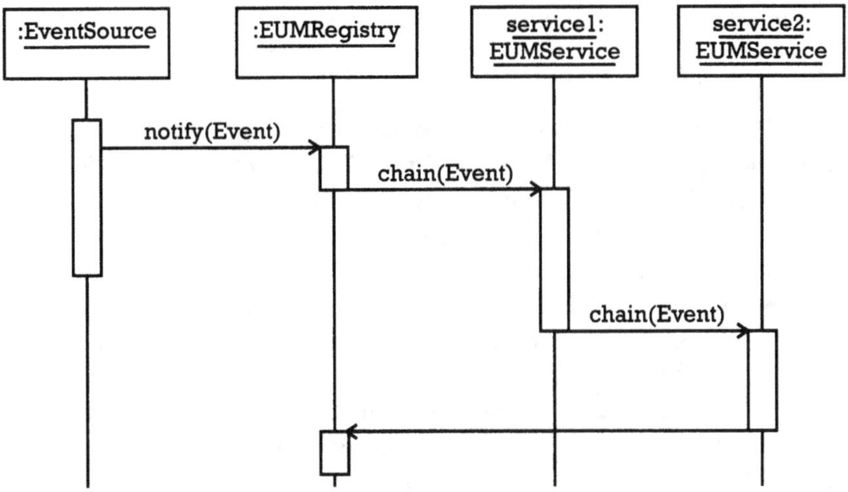

Figure 9.33 Event path with the chain of responsibility.

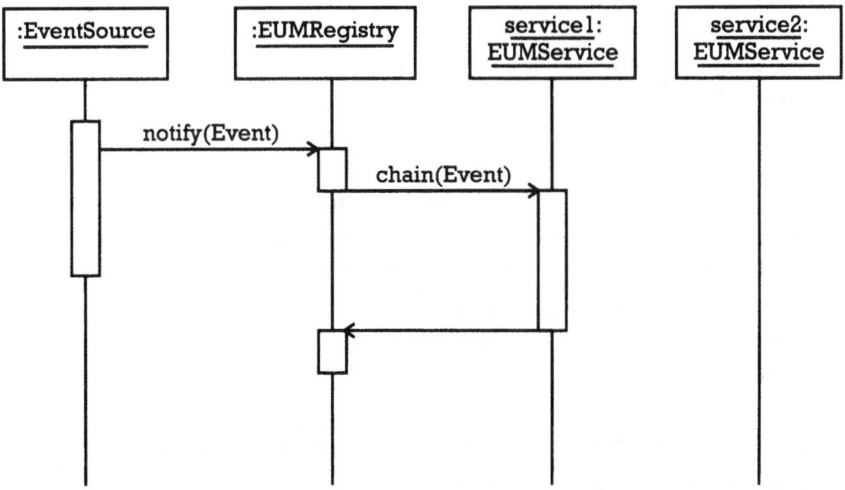

Figure 9.34 Event path with the chain terminated at the first step.

9.6.4 Browsable and searchable catalog of components in the domain framework

The components of the framework are under a configuration management system that allows browsing and retrieval of any version of the components from the component repository.

The catalog of the components is not presented here because of space restrictions.

9.6.5 Guidelines for developing applications using the framework

Two kinds of systems can be built using the framework: a system for simple connectivity and a system for advanced network services.

The system for simple network connectivity provides point-to-point or multipoint connectivity and has no knowledge of users, accounts, and services. The NCL 135 is an example of this system, providing wireless bridge functionality. The system for simple network connectivity is generally integrated in existing networks and poses very few constraints on the operation of the external systems connected to it. The development of such a system requires the embedding of suitable software in a piece of hardware. This software should comprise parts from the framework and parts custom built for the hardware. The framework already provides support for several types of hardware, so the development of the system may only require us to assemble existing parts of the framework. To allow easy integration of the system in existing systems, the development should study carefully the external interfaces of the systems, considering existing standards and requirements.

The system for advanced network services is based on four main concepts: network, accounts, users, and services. The framework already allows flexible topologies of the network and, to a certain degree, allows different network architectures. Accounts and users are common to most systems of this type. The main difference between these systems is in the services they provide. The framework supports plug-in capability of any services and a flexible mechanism for activating them according to different criteria.

The development of the system requires the integration of the framework with custom-built services that fit the requirement. Should the system be integrated in a larger system with similar functionality, suitable adapters need to be developed to make data and operation compatible. The complexity of these adapters depends on the differences between the systems involved.

The EUM, considered as a reference to describe the architecture of the framework, has been designed as a part in a system of the latter type. The EUM fits in an LMS system, providing connectivity to users in a complex wireless network. The advanced services of the EUM take advantage of the LMS system's features. The flexibility of the software embedded in the EUM is specifically designed to accommodate improvements and extensions of the LMS system.

It is conceivable that a simpler version of the EUM could exist, working as a bare wireless modem with no additional services. In this case the system would better fit into the category of systems for simple network connectivity.

9.7 Conclusions

Some final notes are necessary to explain what was learned during the WaveRider DA&E experience. The notes point out what in the experience was crucial, highlighting the difficulties and problems that we have encountered and that other DA&E practitioners should be aware of.

WaveRider's background for DA&E was very fertile. The firm was conscious of its potential and of its role in the market. WaveRider knew its competitors, the state of the art in technology, and, most valuably, the user needs that were not fulfilled by any of the previously available products. When the DA&E practice started (last quarter of 1998), a strategic plan was already in place and under implementation. Rather that starting from scratch, the approach of the DA&E practice was to build on what was already available.

Several issues were dealt with during the introduction of Sherlock at WaveRider. The issues, listed next, concerned the adaptation of Sherlock as a methodology to the working environment of WaveRider:

- *Development process.* The introduction of a methodology needs to tackle development process issues. A firm's commitment and proper understanding of the methodology's potential are necessary. WaveRider managed to get both through a two-phase approach. In the first phase, a group of six people representing the main competencies (from development to management) made a quick hands-on tour of Sherlock and performed in great detail the domain definition. The group had the authority to assess the usefulness of Sherlock in WaveRider and to decide whether to proceed to the second phase.

  In the second phase, the initial group worked as the champions to coordinate and train the rest of the people in the firm. In addition to this, one member of the initial group also worked as a reference person for the methodology, for the coordination of the deliverables, and for assessment of the results. The two-phase approach managed to introduce Sherlock progressively in the firm's development process. The approach addressed and solved the scalability issue of methodologies like Sherlock: It is easy to teach a few people something new, but it is very hard to change the way a large group of people works without some form of planning or coordination.

- *Object orientation.* Object-oriented development and C++ pervaded only one part of the development. A significant part of code was and still is written in C. Historically, object orientation has claimed to be applicable to analysis and design even if those object-oriented analyses and designs are not followed by an object-oriented implementation. This claim proved true in the sense that there were no problems in performing domain modeling—the equivalent of software analysis at domain level—using object orientation. Domain modeling mainly captures the users' view of the system. This view fits easily in object-oriented use case and analysis models. Sherlock has made clear that object orientation per se does not imply the usage of C++ or other object-oriented tools. Rather, developing code in a familiar language (C) gave the firm the opportunity to take full advantage of the developers' skills and of the existing domain libraries.

- *Software reuse.* WaveRider develops modular, scalable systems based on the integration of several components. This is typical in telecommunication systems. The opportunities for reuse are great and WaveRider is committed to fostering them. Sherlock's introduction did not conflict with existing reuse practices. This was possible because Sherlock leaves much freedom in the choice of the nature of the framework and of the design details. However, Sherlock does introduce a new perspective on reuse through variation points. Consequently, some portion of the DA&E practice was devoted to (1) explaining that reuse and variation points converge to the same results and (2) training people to use the new approach. The results have been better planning of reuse practices and better binding between strategic objectives, user needs, and software development.

The application of Sherlock in WaveRider has been extremely valuable. Among the interesting features that characterize this firm, the most noticeable and relevant for DA&E are as follows:

- WaveRider produces advanced technology in a quickly moving market.
- WaveRider works in a market—wireless telecommunications—where coordination and compatibility are critical but where standards for many features have not yet been established.
- WaveRider invests in planning its product line for several years in the future.
- Software reuse along the product line potentially provides high returns.

While WaveRider represents an almost ideal environment for the application of DA&E, we believe that many firms will find inspiration from this industrial case study. Many firms have structures similar to that of WaveRider. Also, many firms have a similar software engineering background.

Despite the kind and extent of the similarities, we can expect that adaptations—or tailoring—to any unique working environment will be necessary. For instance, the solutions to the scalability issues of the methodology will probably need to be revised. However, the WaveRider case study should provide enough motivations, explanations, and examples to serve as an inspiration for a large variety of DA&E practitioners.

References

[1] WaveRider Web site, http://www.waverider.com/company_overview/history.html.

[2] WaveRider Web site, http://www.waverider.com/company_overview/mission.html.

[3] WaveRider Web site, http://www.waverider.com/company_overview/tech.html.

[4] "Competitive Products," internal report version 3, October 22, 1998.

[5] WaveRider Web site, http://www.waverider.com/company_overview/index.html.

[6] Product Development Process Preliminary 0.0.

[7] http://andrew2.andrew.cmu.edu/rfc/rfc2138.html.

CHAPTER

10

Contents

Case study 2: Sherlock in a neural network domain[1]

10.1 Introduction

This case study involves the available neural network analysis tools currently on the market. The current prototype that has been developed is a neural network analysis module that plugs into an underlying mathematical analysis package: MATLAB. The rationale for the prototype's conception was to overcome the need to use specific function calls and parameter passing required in the current plug-in module called Neural Network Toolbox, produced by the same company that created MATLAB. This domain analysis case study entails the development of a software framework, which maps out the movement from a prototype front end to a neural network software application, to a variety of applications and reusable components. The domain has been defined through user requirements and

1. This chapter was written by Maj. William E. Curry.

market analysis (as of winter 1997–1998) as it compares with our current limited product. The competition has been defined through three products that include the ad hoc academic and library routines.

The study of this domain is particularly interesting, since we see that through the systematic application of Sherlock, a domain that may appear quite static can be reorganized and structured to take full advantages of network externalities and reuse. The UML notation adopted here is often the "compressed" one.

10.2 Domain definition

The domain definition is comprised of four parts: the domain vocabulary, which lays out the common terminology and corresponding definitions that will be used throughout this analysis; the classified information on the domain, which provides formal documentation defining the general domain in terms of the user, the market, and the technology base; the definitions of the feasible, strategic, and current domains; and the feasibility analysis.

10.2.1 DD1: Domain terminology

The following deliverable provides a working list of all pertinent terminology used in the domain analysis to ensure clarity and understandability across the project.

Artificial neural network. Basic generic descriptive term used for any type of neural network.

Neural network. A neural network is a computational construct that is modeled after the human brain. Essential elements that make up a network are neurons, representing neural cells of the brain, and synoptic weights, which are links between neural cells. Neural networks are intended to model the human brain through the act of information processing and learning. The process of learning is used to adaptively adjust the synoptic weights of the network based on certain rules in order to achieve the expected outputs, given certain inputs.

Learning. The process of iteratively changing the weights of a network so as to minimize the difference between the achieved results and the expected (target data) results, given known inputs.

Training data. Known data that is presented as input to the neural network to obtain results that will be compared to the expected (target) data.

Target data. Expected output values, given known input values. This data is used to compare with the actual results so as to allow the adjustment of the neural network parameters in the direction to minimize the difference between the two.

Topology. The type and structure of the neural network being used.

Learning algorithm. The specific type of algorithm used in the training of the neural network.

Weights. The weighting factor that is applied to an input of each individual node or neuron within the neural network. These are individually adjusted in the training phase to achieve the required results from known input data.

Hidden layer. Internal layer(s) of a neural network that interfaces between the input layer and the output layer. This is the area that conducts the complex calculations.

Transfer function. Specific function that is used within each layer of the neural network.

Configure neural network. The action of selecting the topology, the size, and learning algorithm of a neural network.

Train neural network. The action of setting the training parameters, inputting the training and target data to be used, and initiating the training of the neural network.

Evaluate data on trained neural network. The action of inputting data to be analyzed by a trained neural network.

10.2.2 DD2: Classified information on the domain

General user requirements for neural network analysis tool

The purpose of this section is to propose general requirements for the neural network analysis for the domain analyst and market expert based on the personal experience of the author as a user.

The required application family is to be used to support research and development activities. The requirement is to have an easy-to-use application that supports the full range of neural network topologies and standards, while being able to interface with simple input/output files and provide a graphical representation of the data.

Specific user requirements for neural network analysis tool

The purpose of this section is to provide further insights into the requirements of the neural network analysis for the domain analyst and market expert. This information is a summary of responses to a questionnaire that was answered by individuals involved in research using neural network software during the latter part of the 1990s.

A neural network analysis tool in the form of an integrated environment is preferred because it allows more effort to be focused on the building and training of the network while the outputting of results, the formatting of data, and the provision of feedback on results are handled automatically. An IDE or integrated environment usually provides the ability to graphically represent the network response to training, which is an important feature. To be able to implement the network into embedded systems, the ability to generate C/C++ code representations of a trained network is needed. Although a Windows versions of this type of tool is generally suited for smaller applications, Unix is more suitable for the much larger applications dealing with areas such as remote sensing, forecasting, and image processing.

Neural network analysis tool prototype: generic use case description

The purpose of this section is to provide high-level background information for the current work dealing with the neural network prototype. The source document is SENG 609.07, *Introduction to Software Reuse*.

Figure 10.1 reflects the general use case, which was used in the development of the prototype front end to the neural network engine. It has been included to provide a high-level view of the activities needed to use neural networks for modeling that have been incorporated into the current prototype. The three main activities identified are to (1) select and build a specific neural network for the required task **{configure neural network}**, (2) run historical data through the neural network until it is capable of providing a satisfactory generalization **{train neural network}**, and (3) analyze new data with the trained neural network **{evaluate data on trained neural network}**.

Requirements model for current prototype

The purpose of this section is to provide current design information that was used in the development of the current prototype. In the

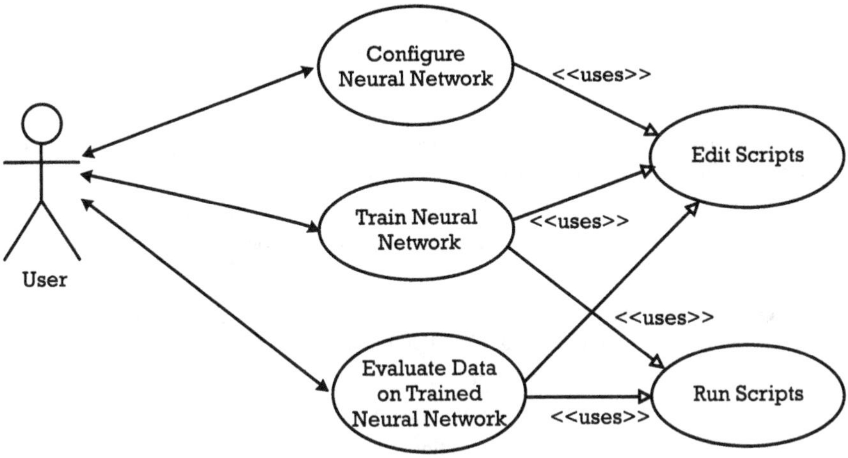

Figure 10.1 Generic use case.

development process used for the creation of the prototype, a requirements model was built using "use case" modeling techniques that represented the current neural network modeling process used in ongoing research. This was then followed by a robustness analysis of the created models.

The conclusions reached were that the modeled instances of Configure Neural Network, Train Neural Network, and Evaluate Data Use Cases could not be specialized any further. However, variability could be achieved in the model through a graphical use interface (GUI), which dealt with such things as setting the type of neural network, the number of neurons, and the type of training or type of plot. This is only a small subset of the parameter lists that could be provided though a GUI.

Competitive products

As of early 2000, three competitive products were available. The general characteristics of these products are summarized in Table 10.1.

The other competition for this market that is not mentioned in Table 10.1 is the myriad of Unix-based freeware routines that have been developed in academic circles around the world to meet the need for a readily available tool. A few software firms also offer a C++ class library of specific traditional neural network routines. Both of these types of products will be considered to be a single competitor for our purposes of analysis.

Table 10.1
Competitive Products

Application	Description
MATLAB Neural Network Toolbox by MathWorks	Plug-in toolbox for MATLAB environment. Must use MATLAB main application. Must use script commands in a math/function language. Graphical or text output dependent on commands used. Can generate C code. Will interact with C++ code using MATLAB computational engine. I/O difficult and not well documented. Unix or Windows based. Constructed networks are limited to three layers. Supports all traditional and standard topologies and algorithms.
Neuro Solutions by Neuro Dimension Inc.	Integrated stand-alone environment. Can generate C++ code. User customization of components using DLLs. User-definable macros. Built-in wizard helps to build network. Function calls can be made through OLE. Unix or Windows based. Supports all traditional and standard topologies and algorithms.

Information technology

The current prototype has been developed as a plug-in module for an existing analysis package (MATLAB) on a Unix platform. The prototype has been written in ANSI C++ using MATLAB-specific calls. Due to the nature of the analysis package, the topology of the user-defined neural network using the prototype is restricted to three hidden layers.

10.2.3 DD3: Definitions of the feasible, strategic, and current domains

The purpose of this section is to define the proposed short- and long-term placement of our products within the market. The source of this information is based on analysis conducted by the Corporate Think Tank. Figure 10.2 contains the corporate vision before complete domain analysis has been attempted.

The feasible domain consisted of providing a neural network analysis tool that is capable of generating code to embed the designed networks. Another option for this domain is to build plug-in neural network

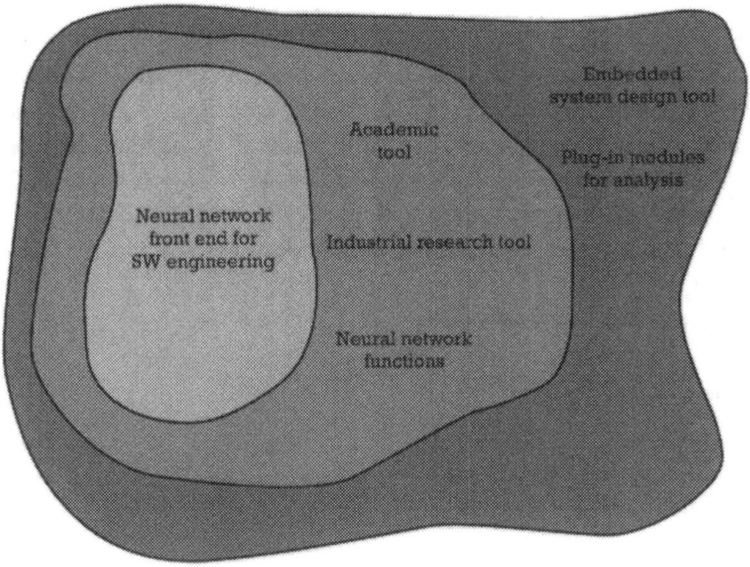

Figure 10.2 Current corporate view.

modules for other analysis tools such as Mathcad and Mathematica. This is a possible domain but is currently viewed as costly at this stage of our development.

The strategic domain consists of the two market segments: academic use and industrial use. In addition to this, the domain also includes the provision of library routines. All three competitors fall into this region. The two user communities should be easily catered to through costing and marketing. The provision of library functions also should be easily attained, but may have impact on other domain areas as discussed later in the section on domain scoping.

The current product domain is the provision of a plug-in neural network module to an existing analysis package.

10.2.4 DD4: Feasibility analysis

The current domain in which the prototype resides is in direct competition with the MATLAB Toolbox. It is believed that direct competition can be achieved successfully if focus is placed on such areas as ease of use, cost, and flexibility. Movement into the strategic domain is believed to be achievable primarily through marketing.

10.3 Domain characterization

This portion of the analysis is intended to describe the market within the target domain through the review of the competitors' organizations and products. The market is very large and includes many diverse research and industrial applications. The resulting market has great potential and is expanding. It is believed that due to this, initial entry into the market in a limited manner will be easily accomplished.

10.3.1 DC1: Diagrams of values

SERN plug-in module

Internal value

Features:

- Create, train, and utilize neural network model.
- Support all standard neural network types and topologies.

Quality:

- Ease of use;
- Flexibility;
- Ability to plug into existing analysis tools.

External value

Interoperability Between Users:

- Use of standard neural network architecture allows for consistent results as compared with other products.

Interoperability Between Products:

- Interoperable as a plug-in to the MATLAB analysis environment.

Our initial product is a plug-in that uses the MATLAB analysis environment. Due to this, there is a solid base of potential users. Because the MATLAB line of products has been on the market since 1984, there is confidence in the product and its availability in the future.

MATLAB Toolbox

Internal value

Features:

- Creation of up to a three-layered neural network;
- Support of all standard neural network types and topologies.

Quality:

- Fully integrated, using same format I/O as the MATLAB analysis software.

External value

Interoperability Between Users:

- Use of standard neural network architecture allows for consistent results as compared with other products.

Interoperability Between Products:

- Not applicable.

Expectations:

- This product has a solid base of potential users. Because the MATLAB line of products has been on the market since 1984, there is confidence in the product and its availability in the future.

Neuro Solutions

Internal value

Features:

- Support of all standard neural network types and topologies;
- Graphical building blocks to create a network;
- Wizard to assist construction and analysis.

Quality:

- Easy to use;

- Flexible;
- Stand-alone environment that is easy to install;
- Both training and analysis runs can be graphically represented.

External value

Interoperability Between Users:

- Use of standard neural network architecture allows for consistent results as compared with other products.

Interoperability Between Products:

- This product is capable of interacting through ActiveX with Microsoft products such as Excel.

Expectations:

- This product is not dependent on any other products or technology. It has the benefit of being able to use MS products for input and output and additional analysis. This provides a large potential compatibility base for users. The company has been in operation since 1991 and has marketed this specific product since 1994.

Ad hoc code

This type of product was created to meet a specific need. There is little expectation as to compatibility between products or users unless this specific need was identified when the code was written. There is also no guarantee as to adherence to specific standards.

10.3.2 DC2: Description of installed base

In Table 10.2, the current market is illustrated through the installed base of the various products. Neuro Solutions is the clear front-runner with its stand-alone tool. The MATLAB Neural Network Toolbox is next. It provides similar functionality, although it is a plug-in to the math analysis tool MATLAB. Ad hoc code has been considered because it has the largest installed base. It does, however, generally suffer from lack of ease of use and lack of standardization.

10.3.3 DC3: Tables of compatibilities

Table 10.3 represents the input and output compatibilities among the products on the market (including our prototype).

Table 10.2
Installed Base and Sales Trend

	Installed Base	Current Sales	Sales Trend	Expected Total Sales
Neuro Solutions	900	10/wk	Stable	1,400 end 1999
MATLAB Neural Network Toolbox*	500	2/wk	Stable	600 end 1999
SERN prototype front end	1	0	Stable	N/A
Ad hoc code	1000	0	Stable	N/A

* These values are rough estimates, because the company would not provide the information.

The common compatibility for MATLAB, SERN, and ad hoc code is through ANSI C/C++. There is one limitation, however, with the interaction between the MATLAB and ANSI C/C++. MATLAB will generate compilable ANSI C code based on a design modeled within the toolbox. As an input, it will interact with C++ code using embedded MATLAB language specific structured function and routine calls to the MATLAB computational engine. This use of C/C++ code is not clean and requires that the code used encapsulate specific MATLAB calls and routines.

Neuro Solutions interacts with all Microsoft products through ActiveX. This provides a very large potential user base. This, combined with its integrated environment, provides an easy-to-use tool. Both of the

Table 10.3
Compatibility Table for Data Input/Output

	ANSI C	ANSI C++	Active X	.M, .Mex, .MAT
Neuro Solutions	—	O	I/O	—
MATLAB Neural Network Toolbox	I/O	I/O	—	I/O
SERN prototype front end	I/O	I/O	—	—
Ad hoc code	I/O	I/O	—	—

strong contenders within the market provide tools that can be ported to Unix, MS Windows, or MS NT (Table 10.4). In the current form, the SERN tool is similar to the MATLAB Toolbox in that it requires the MATLAB analysis tool to function (Table 10.5).

10.3.4 DC4: User flow

Figure 10.3 contains a diagram of the user flows. The SERN neural network front end (plug-in) is the initial prototype produced by our company. There are three competitors: Neuro Solutions, MATLAB Neural Network Toolbox, and ad hoc code (including library functions). Our plug-in module is used in conjunction with the MATLAB analysis program. Complementary products that depend on the operating system are text editors such as emacs, notepad, MS Word, edit, and edlin.

The SERN neural network plug-in is intended to attract new users through its ease of use and price. Its primary focus is to provide an alternative to the MATLAB Neural Network Toolbox. The SERN plug-in is also intended to provide sufficient functionality that the current users of

Table 10.4
Compatibility Table for Operating System

	Unix	MS Windows	MS NT
Neuro Solutions	√	√	√
MATLAB Neural Network Toolbox	√	√	√
SERN prototype front end	√	—	—
Ad hoc code	√	—	—

Table 10.5
Compatibility for Input/Output to MATLAB Environment

	MATLAB Environment
MATLAB Neural Network Toolbox	√
SERN prototype front end	√

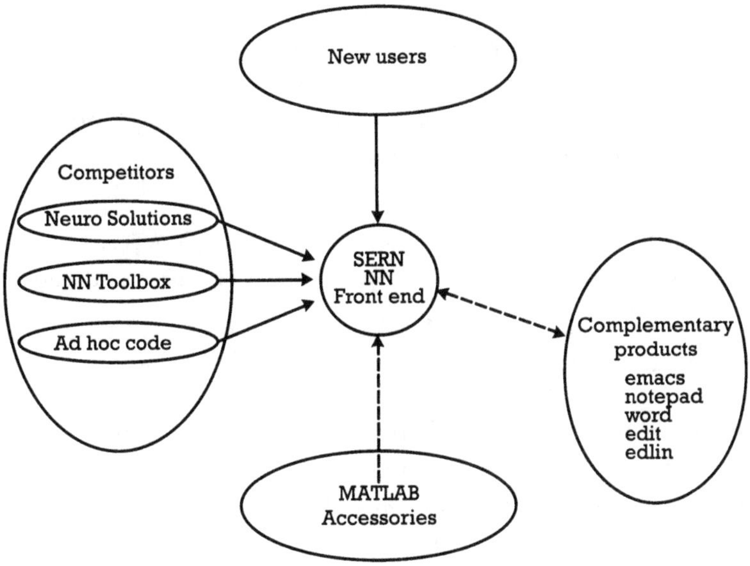

Figure 10.3 User flows.

either the Neural Network Toolbox or ad hoc routines will be willing to change to our product.

Our product requires access to a text editor. Because it is capable of reading any ASCII text file, complementary products consist of any text editor capable of generating ASCII text.

The SERN plug-in module requires the MATLAB analysis product to provide the underlying functionality for our product.

10.3.5 DC5: Market segments and pricing policy

The four market segments considered are as follows:

- Standard retail (including industrial users);
- Academic;
- Volume retail (including industrial users);
- Volume academic.

Based on the competitors' current prices, our product's pricing policy has been set to provide optimum access to the market. The pricing policy of our product is illustrated in Figure 10.4.

Based on the flows depicted in Figure 10.3 and a review of the pricing policies of the two major competitors, the following points are noted:

- Neuro Solutions is an integrated environment whose price is one-third lower than its major competitor, MATLAB Neural Network Toolbox, making it a strong contender in the market.
- SERN neural network provides a front end to MATLAB for neural network analysis similar to that of the Neural Network Toolbox.
- Ad hoc code and library functions have no defined pricing policy and suffer from standardization and usability issues.

Based on these points, the first issue to consider is that the SERN product can directly replace the MATLAB Toolbox. The user community that presently owns the MATLAB analysis package without the toolbox provides a potential user base that could be accessed. The integrated environment of the Neuro Solutions product has great appeal in its low price. The manner in which we could leverage our entrance into the market is to price our plug-in low, which would greatly reduce the tendency to purchase the integrated tool. The pricing policy set for our product is believed to provide the necessary leverage into the market while providing a sufficient profit margin.

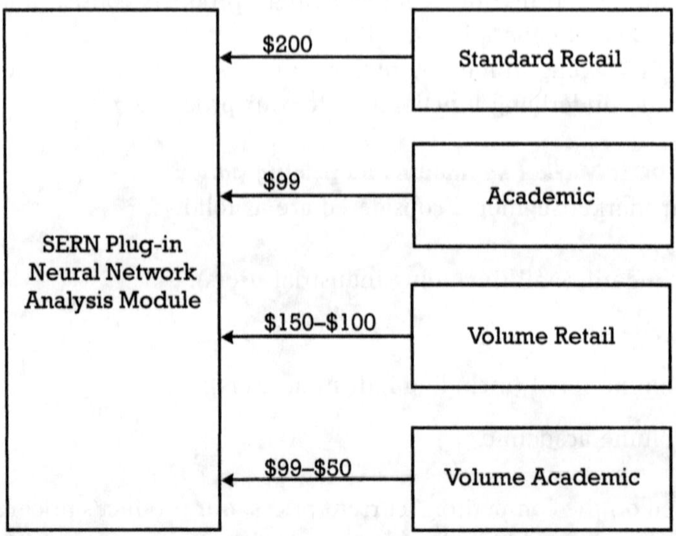

Figure 10.4 SERN plug-in pricing policy.

10.3.6 DC5: Plan of development of new products

Business interests in the domain

The business is currently entering the market with a plug-in prototype to be used in software quality analysis. This is viewed as the easiest point of entry due to the near completion of the product and the potential large expansion within this general market.

Objectives for the domain

The current objectives within the company are to complete the prototype product within the current product domain (see DD3) and expand from this point into an academic research tool followed by an industrial research tool and then possibly library functions.

Planned goals

Regardless of the application or family of applications, the initial intent is to obtain a foothold within the academic market in which to base expansion into the more lucrative industrial market.

Expected outcome

Initially it is expected that the prototype's entrance into the market will achieve a portion of the market share currently held by ad hoc routines. As the product evolves, movement into direct competition with the ad hoc code through the provision of library routines or entrance into the lucrative industrial market can be achieved.

10.4 Domain scoping

In this portion of the analysis, applications within the domain are identified and analyzed. From here their attributes are identified, from which variation points are then determined.

10.4.1 DS1: Variability space, attributes of products in the domain, and related constraints

Variability Space:

VP_1: Operating environment:

$V_{1,1}$: Windows/NT

$V_{1,2}$: Unix

VP_2: User group:

$V_{2,1}$: Academic

$V_{2,2}$: Industrial

VP_3: Type of application:

$V_{3,1}$: Plug-in module

$V_{3,2}$: Stand-alone development environment

$V_{3,3}$: Library routines

Attributes of the Products in the Domain

A_1: Performances:

Measured by the mean response time

A_2: Flexibility to make changes to an analysis model or run:

Ordinal Measure

Maximum: minimal effort to adapt (1 to 2 keystrokes or mouse clicks)

Medium: average effort to adapt (3 to 7 keystrokes or mouse clicks)

Limited: excessive effort to adapt (more than 8 keystrokes or mouse clicks or involves multiple applications or windows)

A_3: Ease of use:

Ordinal Measure

Easy: With neural network knowledge would require a B.Sc. less than 4 hours to be able to use this product.

Medium: With neural network knowledge would require a B.Sc. 4 hours to be able to use this product.

Hard: With neural network knowledge would require a B.Sc. over 4 but less than 8 hours to be able to use this product.

Constraints on the Attributes

A_1: Performances:

$C_{1,0}$: Do not care

$C_{1,1}$: Fast, mean response time below 1 second for all operations

$C_{1,2}$: Fair, mean response time below 10 seconds for all operations

A_2: Flexibility:

$C_{2,0}$: Do not care

$C_{2,1}$: Maximum

$C_{2,2}$: Medium

$C_{2,3}$: Limited

A_3: Ease of use:

$C_{3,0}$: Do not care

$C_{3,1}$: Easy

$C_{3,2}$: Medium

$C_{3,3}$: Hard

10.4.2 DS2: Definition of product strategies

Four main strategies are considered:

S_1: Academic users of an analysis plug-in for Unix-based machines;

S_2: Academic and industrial users of an analysis plug-in for Unix-based machine;

S_3: Unix/Windows NT industrial and academic library routines;

S_4: Integrated environment for academic/industrial users on Unix/Windows/NT-based machines.

S_1: Academic users of an analysis plug-in for Unix-based machines

This strategy considers a plug-in analysis module running on a Unix platform. It is intended for the academic user. This distinction is only controlled by way of marketing. This strategy provides an add-on tool to an existing analysis environment, specifically MATLAB. This general strategy is used by both our prototype product and a competitor, MATLAB Neural Network Toolbox. The differences in the approach to flexibility and ease of use are discussed further in DS3. The S_1 strategy is represented as follows.

Variants

VP_1: Operating environment:

$V_{1,2}$: Unix

VP_2: User group:

$V_{2,1}$: Academic

VP_3: Type of application:

$V_{3,1}$: Plug-in module

Attributes of Products in the Domain

A_1: Performances:

Measured by the mean response time

A_2: Flexibility:

Maximum

Medium

Limited

A_3: Ease of use:

Medium

Hard

Constraints on the Attributes

A_1: Performance:

$C_{1,2}$: Fair, mean response time below 10 seconds for all operations

A_2: Flexibility:

$C_{2,2}$: Medium

$C_{2,3}$: Limited

A_3: Ease of use:

$C_{3,2}$: Medium

$C_{3,3}$: Hard

S_2: Academic and industrial users of an analysis plug-in for Unix-based machines

This strategy is the same as that of S_1 except it includes the industrial users. Strategy S_2 is defined as follows.

Variants

VP_1: Operating environment:

$V_{1,2}$: Unix

VP_2: User group:

$V_{2,1}$: Academic

$V_{2,2}$: Industrial

VP_3: Type of application:

$V_{3,1}$: Plug-in module

Attributes of Products in the Domain

A_1: Performance:

Measured by the mean response time

A_2: Flexibility:

Medium

Limited

A_3: Ease of use:

Medium

Hard

Constraints on the Attributes

A_1: Performance:

$C_{1,2}$: Fair, mean response time below 10 seconds for all operations

A_2: Flexibility:

$C_{2,2}$: Medium

$C_{2,3}$: Limited

A_3: Ease of use:

$C_{3,2}$: Medium

$C_{3,3}$: Hard

S_3: Unix/Windows NT industrial and academic library routines

This strategy concentrates on the provision of library functions and routines to offset ad hoc code use. These routines are platform independent, and there are no constraints on their attributes. The strategy for this is defined as follows.

Variants

VP_1: Operating environment:

$V_{1,1}$: Windows/NT

$V_{1,2}$: Unix

VP_2: User group:

$V_{2,1}$: Academic

$V_{2,2}$: Industrial

VP_3: Type of application:

$V_{3,3}$: Library routines

Attributes of Products in the Domain

A_1: Performance:

Not specified

A_2: Reliability:

Not specified

A_3: Ease of use:

Not specified

Constraints on the Attributes

A_1: Performance:

$C_{1,0}$: Do not care

A_2: Flexibility:

$C_{2,0}$: Do not care

A_3: Ease of use:

$C_{3,0}$: Do not care

S_4: Integrated environment for academic/industrial users on Unix/Windows/NT-based machines

This strategy considers an integrated environment for academic and industrial users, running on either Unix or Windows/NT platforms. The constraints on its flexibility range between maximum and medium. This general strategy is used by a competitor: Neuro Solutions. The S_4 strategy is represented as follows.

Variants

VP_1: Operating environment:

$V_{1,1}$: Windows/NT

$V_{1,2}$: Unix

VP_2: User group:

$V_{2,1}$: Academic

$V_{2,2}$: Industrial

VP_3: Type of application:

$V_{3,2}$: Integrated environment

Attributes of Products in the Domain

A_1: Performance:

Measured by the mean response time

A_2: Flexibility:

Maximum

Medium

Limited

A_3: Ease of use:

Medium

Hard

Constraints on the Attributes

A_1: Performance:

$C_{1,2}$: Fair, mean response time below 10 seconds for all operations

A_2: Flexibility:

$C_{2,1}$: Maximum

$C_{2,2}$: Medium

A_3: Ease of use:

$C_{3,2}$: Medium

10.4.3 DS3: Identification of product strategies to develop in the future

Based on the corporate domain view as projected in DD3, the following sequence of strategies has been proposed:

Current status

As our product is coming on line, it is intended to take on strategy S_1 in direct competition with the MATLAB Neural Network Toolbox. Although limited to Unix platforms, a key area where our product can excel is by achieving a medium level of flexibility through pull-down menus versus the Toolbox's manual entry of new or modified function calls and parameters. The use of pull-down menus and pick lists will also move the ease of use attribute from the hard level for the Toolbox to the medium level with our product. The entry point into the market for our product is in the academic community. Due to our low development costs and user-friendly interface, our product should be capable of capturing a large portion of the student population involved in academic research.

Six months

Moving from the entry point in the market S_1 (our prototype), the first move would be into the industrial research market using the same product through strategy S_2. This is viewed as primarily a marketing move through aggressive advertisement. The previous use of our current product within the academic community is important to this stage because it exposes the product to new users who are moving from academia into the workforce. This move is dependent on the accomplishments of our initial S_1 strategy.

One to two years

The movement to S_3, the provision of source libraries in both academic and industrial markets, is considered a low-cost move that is virtually operating system independent. The strength of this move is through the provision of a standardized set of library routines to compete directly with the ad hoc market. The downfall of this is that these products may cut into our own potential market with a lower cost usable product. The timing of this move must be carefully considered.

Two years plus

A movement that may be considered later in the process is the porting of the products onto Windows/NT-based machines. The strategic domain therefore is with plug-in modules on Unix platforms within the academic and industrial community followed by the provision of library routines.

Not considered at this time

Movement to strategy S_4 is not considered at this time. The competitor Neuro Solutions has a fully integrated environment, which provides maximum flexibility and medium ease of use. This market will be difficult to break into due primarily to development costs to achieve these levels with a stand-alone environment.

10.5 Domain modeling

This portion of the analysis is responsible for assisting in factoring out all common aspects of the current domain, and producing both a use case and analysis model represented through the use of UML. This, as in the previous two stages, is iterative and dependent on feeding back information to those stages and readjusting based on their new outputs.

10.5.1 DM1: Product use case model

The first use case to consider is based on our prototype design (Figure 10.5). It is applicable to all products in the domain so this single use case figure will be used to represent them all.

At the high level, the use cases for plug-in modules are described as follows:

Use Case: Configure Neural Network **Description:** The **client** of the use case starts a **session** by **configuring the neural network** through the creation of a specific network to meet his or her current analysis needs. He or she does this through the selection of a specific **topology,** a **learning algorithm,** and by setting the actual **dimensions** (i.e., number of neurons, number of layers). In this instance, these parameters are set either through **editing** a **script** by **keyboard** entry of function and command line calls into a **script file** that will be **run** later, or through the use of selections made with a **pointing device** and **keyboard** from pull-down **menus, buttons,** and simple commands.
Use Case: Train Neural Network **Description:** The **client** sets the **training parameters** such as minimum error level required, number of cycles to train (epochs), location of **input data,** where to send the **output data** and in what format. Once the training session is set up, the neural network is trained through the activation or **running** of the **session.** These parameters are set either through **keyboard** entry of function and command line calls into a **script file** which will be **run** later, or through the use of selections made with a **pointing device** and **keyboard** from pull-down **menus, buttons,** and simple commands.
Use Case: Evaluate Data on Trained Neural Network **Description:** Once the training has been completed and the **client** has a trained neural network, he or she selects the **input data** to be processed, selects the destination for the **output data,** and determines the format. After these parameters have been set, the input data is processed through the activation or **running** of the **session.** These parameters are set either through **keyboard** entry of function and command line calls into a **script file** that will be **run** later, or through the use of selections made with a **pointing device** and **keyboard** from pull-down **menus, buttons,** and simple commands.

Now if we consider the two ancestor use cases Set Parameters and Run Session as they apply to the current plug-in prototype **{type of application}**, the following use case descriptions apply:

Use Case: Set Parameters
Description: The **client** requires a **session** to set the parameters to either configure, train, or evaluate data using neural networks. This **session** requires an **{operating environment}** which **is a** Windows/NT or Unix operating system. The **client** requires an **editor** to create a **script file** that will be run to accomplish the aforementioned tasks. Through the editing of the **script file** within the **session,** the **client** creates the **topology,** selects the **learning algorithm,** or selects what **input file** and what **output file** will be used.
Use Case: Run Session
Description: The **client** requires a **session** to run the **script file.** This **session** requires an **{operating environment}** which **is a** Windows/NT or Unix operating system. The **session** running the **script file** causes **specific operations** to occur based on the required **topology, learning algorithm,** or **training parameters.** Based on the **script file,** the **operation** imports the **input data file** and generates **results** that can be accessed by the **client.** These **results** can also be exported to an **output file** or **printer.**

Now if we consider the variation to this, using an integrated environment **{type of application}**, the following use case descriptions apply:

Use Case: Set Parameters
Description: The **client** requires a **session** to set the parameters to either configure, train, or evaluate data using neural networks. This **session** requires an **{operating environment}** which **is a** Windows/NT or Unix operating system. The **client** interacts with the **interface** to create the necessary neural network **topology,** select the **learning algorithm** to use, select and set the applicable **training parameters,** and select the **input** and **output data files.**
Use Case: Run Session
Description: The **client** requires a **session,** which is initiated by the **interface,** to run the analysis. This **session** requires an **{operating environment}** which **is a** Windows/NT or Unix operating system. The **session** causes **operations** to be conducted on the imported **input data file,** based on the **topology, learning algorithm,** and **training parameters.** The **operation** generates **results,** which can be accessed by the client through the display screen and through the data exported to the **printer** and the **output data files.** The client selects the **printer** and **input** and **output data files** through interaction with the **interface.**

10.5.2 DM2: Product analysis model

The corresponding analysis models for Set Parameters and Run Session for the current prototype or plug-in type product are illustrated in Figures 10.6 and 10.7.

The corresponding analysis models for Set Parameters and Run Session for the integrated environment are illustrated in Figures 10.8 and 10.9.

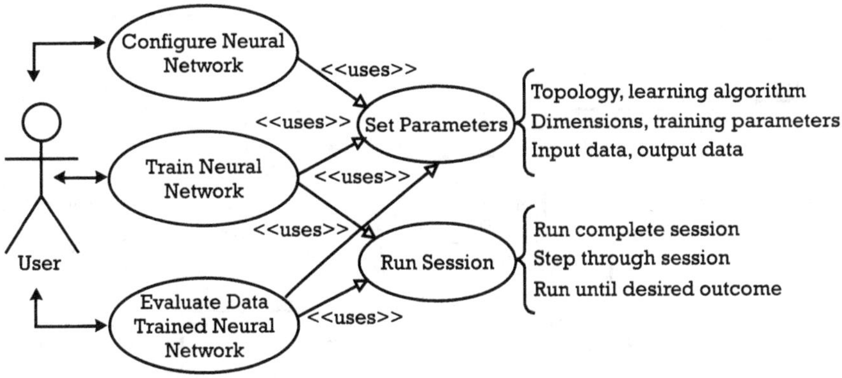

Figure 10.5 Prototype use case.

Figures 10.6 through 10.9 evidence the relations existing between objects and classes in the domain.

10.5.3 DM3: Domain use case model

Combining the two use case models and factoring out the variations give us the domain use case model of Figure 10.10.

Domain Use Case: Set Parameters **Description:** The **client** runs the current **session** that requires an **{operating environment}** which **is a** Windows/NT or Unix operating system. To set parameters, the **client** is required to **edit a script** or interact with a **user interface** dependent on the **{type of application}.**
Domain Use Case: Run Session **Description:** The **client** runs the current **session,** which requires an **{operating environment}** which **is a** Windows/NT or Unix operating system. The **session** either runs the **script file** to cause specific **operations** to occur or responds to the specific operation set by the **client's** interaction with the **user interface** dependent on the **{type of application}.**

10.5.4 DM4: Domain analysis model

The complete analysis model is shown in Figure 10.11. The two key activities have been identified through use case Set Parameters and Run

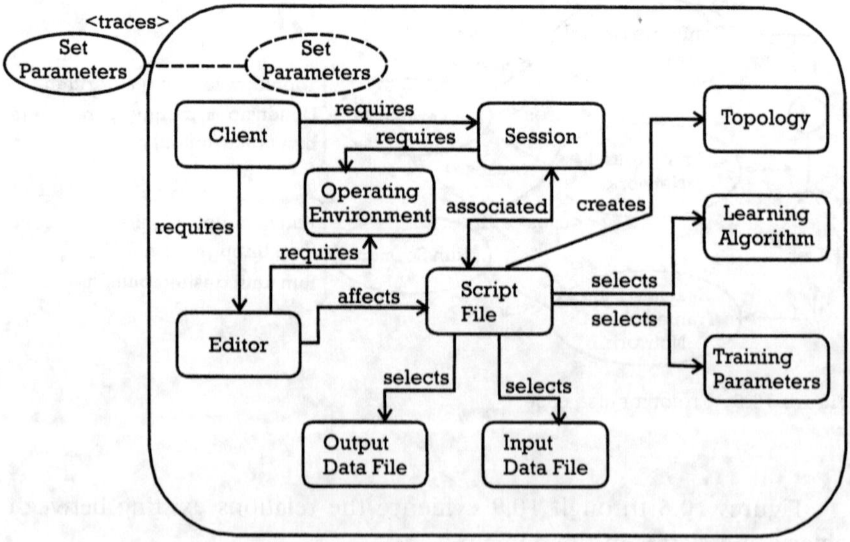

Figure 10.6 Plug-in module: Set Parameters analysis model.

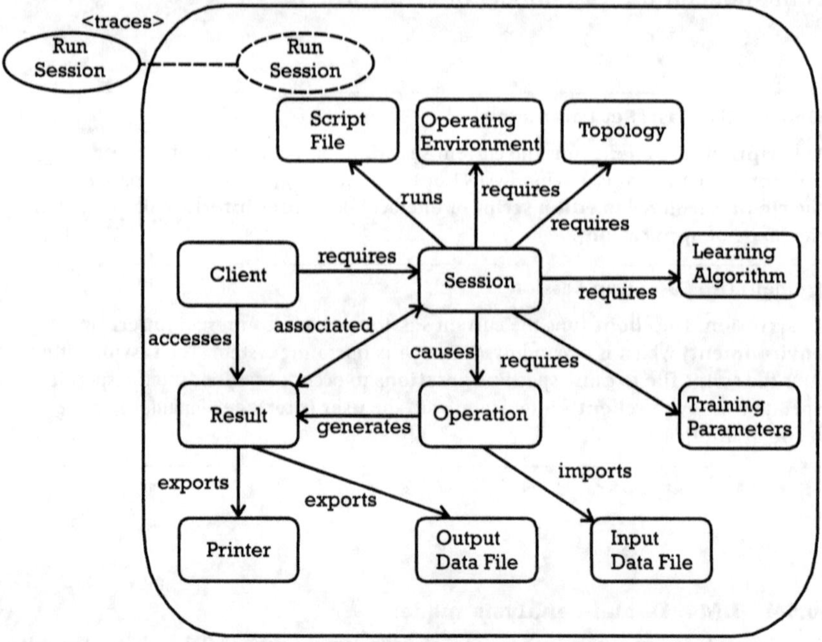

Figure 10.7 Plug-in module: Run Session analysis model.

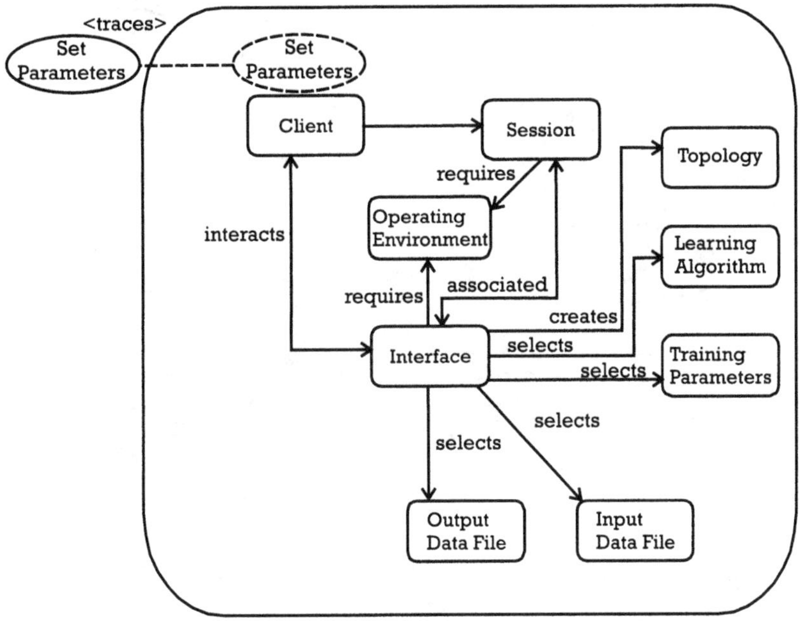

Figure 10.8 Integrated environment: Set Parameters analysis model.

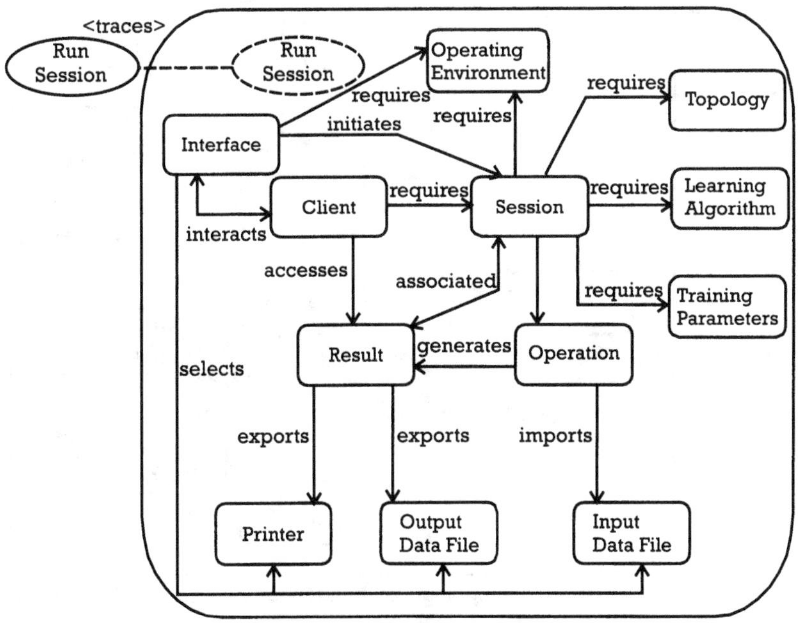

Figure 10.9 Integrated environment: Run Session analysis model.

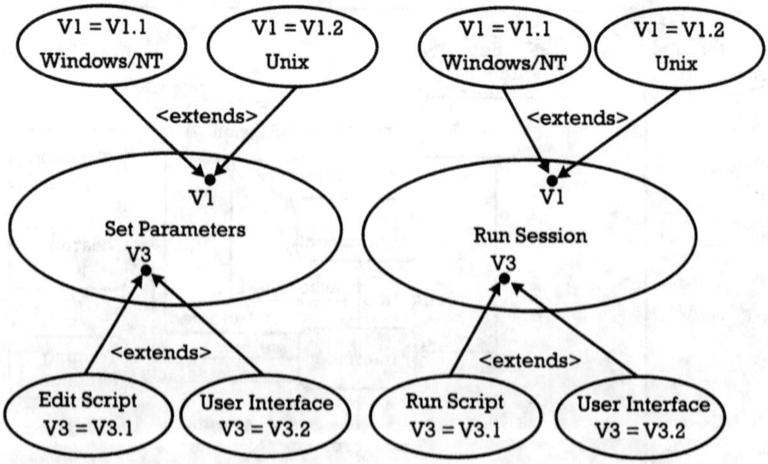

Figure 10.10 Domain use case.

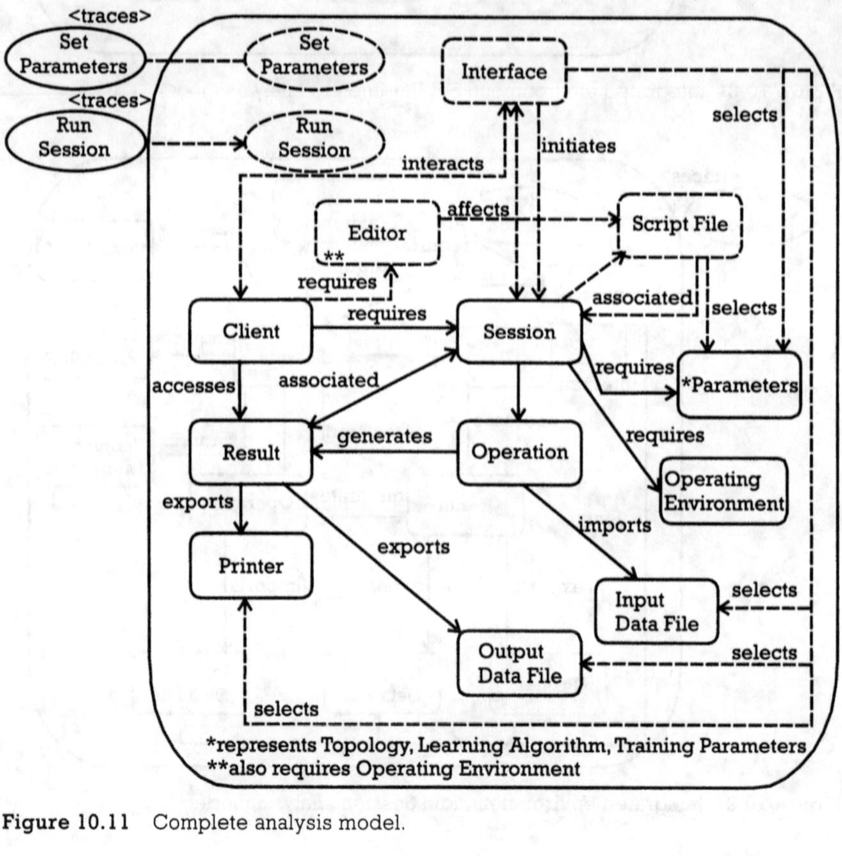

Figure 10.11 Complete analysis model.

Session. Within each use case, two variation points have been identified: **{operating environment V1}** and **{type of application V3}**. Although the editor is affected by the operating environment used, text editors are readily available in either environment considered and therefore are not required as a deliverable with any application. Due to this, the text editor will be referred to from this point onward as external. With both the commonalities and variations identified at this point in the analysis, a domain framework can now be considered that focuses on these aspects of the domain.

10.6 Domain framework design

10.6.1 DF1: Definitions of the nature of the domain framework

The framework is a passive entity that provides a plug-in to an analysis engine: MATLAB. The plug-in is used to create the neural network, train the neural network, and use this network to analyze new data. Through interaction with the user, the SERN plug-in creates a script file which is then processed by the analysis engine. All parameters, data files, inputs, and outputs are defined in the script file.

The nature of this framework (passive) has been driven by its role as a plug-in module.

10.6.2 DF2: Architecture of the domain

In its current form, the architecture is comprised of two core projections: packages and classes. Objects are not considered because only single instantiations are intended to be considered at this time.

Package projection

The framework has been broken into key discernable activity and variability groupings or packages. The following list presents the package composition of the designed framework.

- *SERN package.* This package contains all of the common core classes less those classes identified as interface or operating system (environment) related. This would include such classes as script or session classes.
- *Interface package.* This package contains the general interface classes, the command line interface classes, and integrated interface classes.

- *Operating system package.* This package contains the general operating system, Windows/NT, and Unix operating system classes.

Class and object projections

The class projection provides an overview of the general classes needed and their relationships. It presents the core framework complete with variants (Figure 10.12).

The object projections have been organized as to which application type is being implemented, since this poses the most significant differences within the projection.

Figures 10.13, 10.14, 10.15, and 10.16 contain the four main object projections. Through the illustrations of the interaction between each component and the variants, a basic domain framework design has been built.

Functional projection

The functional parts of the framework are as follows:

- Start session;
- Set parameters;
- Access script;
- Train network;
- Run network.

The links between the various functional parts are illustrated in Figure 10.17.

10.6.3 DF3: Documentation of components in the domain framework

Due to the limited nature of this analysis, our discussion of the documentation is restricted to the self-documented code in DF5.

10.6.4 DF4: Browsable and searchable catalog of the components in the domain framework

This is not available at this time.

10.6.5 DF5: Guidelines to develop applications using the components

The applications to be developed should initially be implemented using ANSI C++ primarily due to the interface standards used with the parent

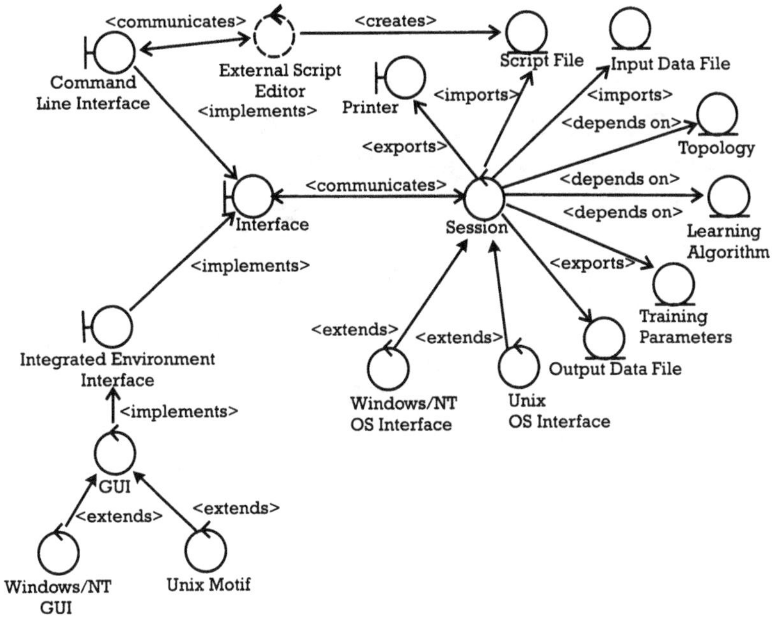

Figure 10.12 Class projection for the system.

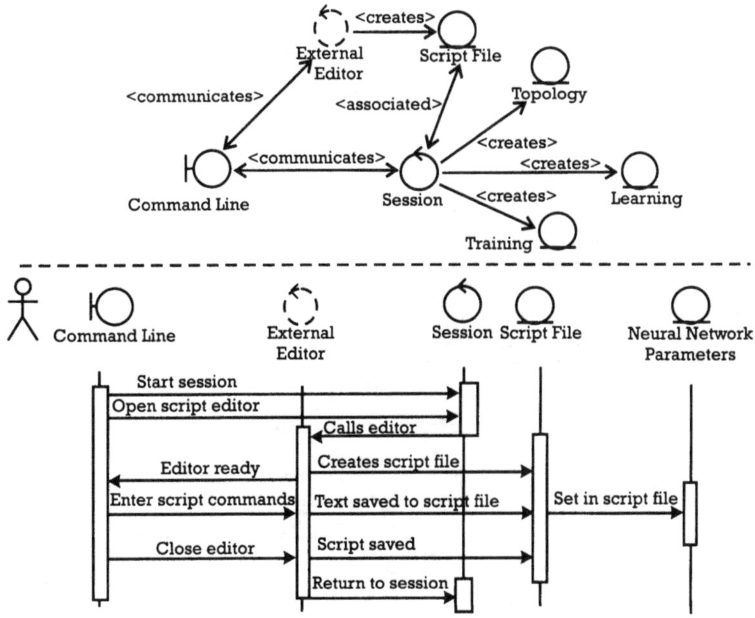

Figure 10.13 Object projections for the plug-in application.

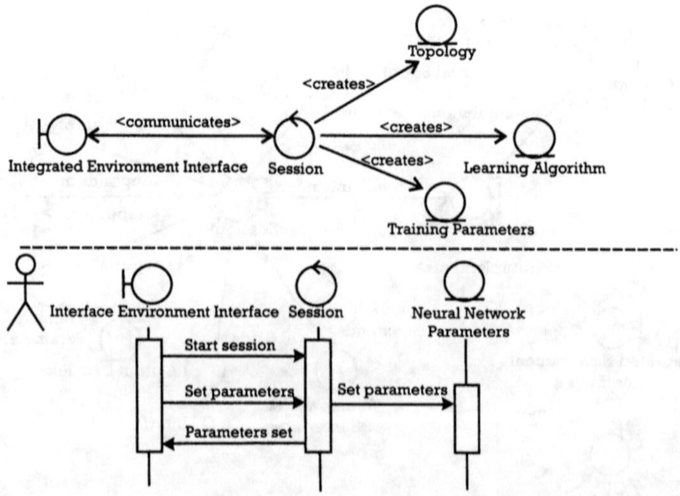

Figure 10.14 Object projections for the integrated environment.

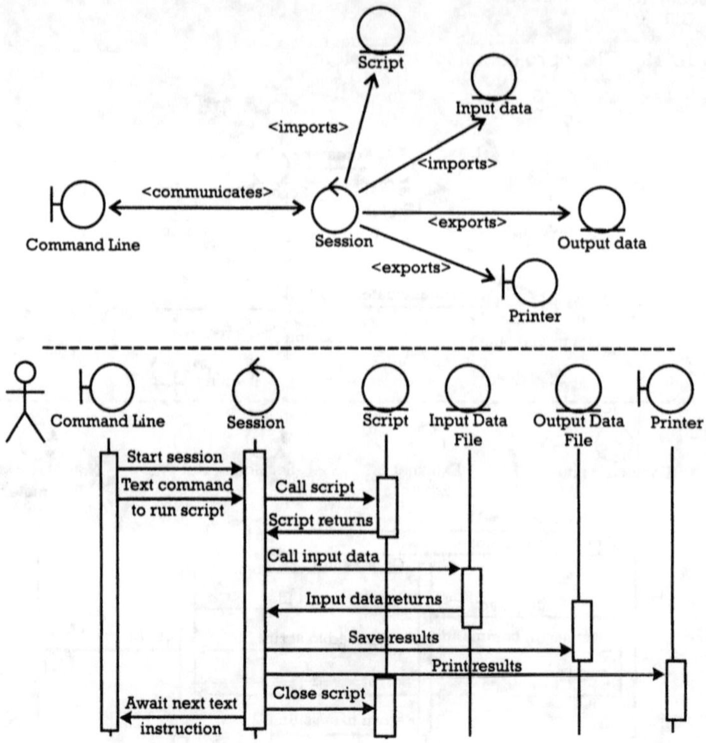

Figure 10.15 Object projections for running a session.

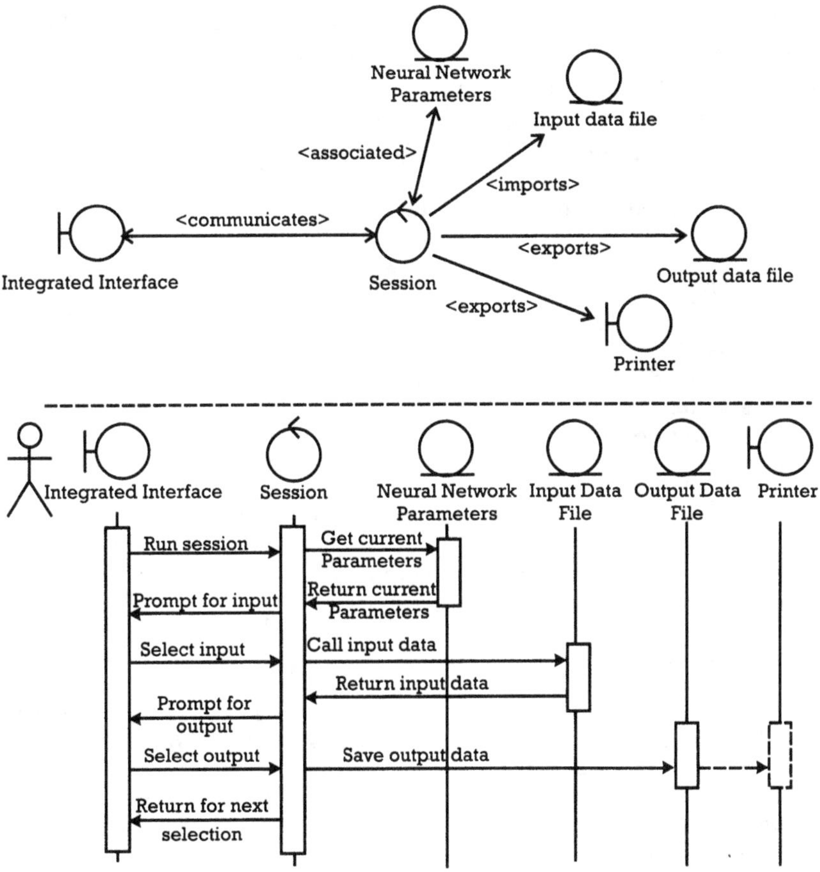

Figure 10.16 Object projections for permanent storage and printing.

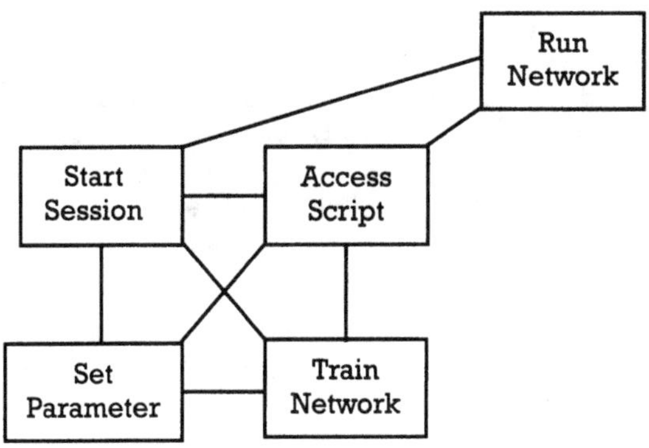

Figure 10.17 Functional projection.

applications and also the flexibility with interactions with the underlying system. As standards change, it is recommended that developers consider moving to Java once it is practical.

The following skeletal source code represents only those class projections that implement the variations within the application.

Type of Application Source Code:

```
class Interface{ //common framework for application interface
public:
  Interface( );
  ~Interface( );
  int* activeSession( ); //activates session and returns
  location
  int* activeDevice( ); //activates a device and rtns location
private:
  int source; //originator of activity
  int destination;//destination of activity
}
class IntegraEnv public Interface{ //variation using
integrated environment
public:
  IntegraEnv( );
  ~IntegraEnv( );
  void get_activeWidget(location); //goes to active widget
  int sessionAction( event); //passes request for an activity
  from current session
  int checkStatus( ); //returns status of specific client
private:
  int event;
}
class cmdLineInterface public Interface{ //variation using
command line interface
public:
  cmdLineInterface( );
  ~cmdLineInterface( );
  char* get_msg( );//gets text message from input
  void send_msg(destination);//passes message to destination
private:
  char* message;//text message string
}
```

Operating Environment:

```
class OSInterface{ //common framework for operating system
public:
  OSInterface( );
  ~OSInterface( );
```

```
  void systemCalls(systemType);//calls to system
  void deviceCalls(deviceType );//calls to devices
private:
  int systemType;
  int deviceType;
}
class WiNTos public OSInterface{ //variation for windows
environment
public:
  WiNTos( );
  ~WiNTos( );
 void someSpecialWindowsCalls( );//WindowsNT specific calls
private:
  int specialSecretWindowsFlag;
}
class UNICSos public OSInterface{ //variation for Unix
environment
public:
  UNICSos( );
  ~UNICSos( );
  void UNICSpecificCalls( );//Unix specific calls
private:
  int aUNICSflag;
}
```

Although the code given here is minimal, it provides a general idea as to the implementation of the variations within the developed framework.

10.7 Conclusion

This project entailed the development of a software framework that mapped out the movement from a prototype front end to a neural network software application, to a variety of applications and reusable components. These components have been identified and variations have been built to meet the best approach into the current market. The above framework has been developed, but will need further refinement before actual work on the applications and framework occurs.

From this study, it is apparent that the domain of neural networks has the potential to contain an entire suite of different products and to take advantage of externalities with lateral domains.

CHAPTER

11

Contents

Case study 3: Sherlock applied to Novatel Wireless, Inc.[1]

This case study involves the domain of wireless modems. Novatel Wireless, Inc. (NWI) is a developer and manufacturer of wireless modem products and solutions. The analysis focuses on configuration and diagnostic software developed for use with the family of wireless modem products.

11.1 Domain definition

11.1.1 DD1: Domain vocabulary

The domain vocabulary is comprised of the terms in the following list:

Advanced mobile phone service (AMPS). The analog cellular standard.

Air interface. The standard operating system or protocol of a wireless network; technologies include AMPS, TDMA, CDMA, and GSM.

1. This chapter was written by Mr. Jim Paulson.

Application suite. Refers to the suite of products we provide for configuring and diagnosing our product line of wireless modems. Includes applications such as Wireless Subscription Wizard, Wireless Modem Manager, and Wireless Modem Status.

Carrier. Refers to a telecommunications carrier (for example, AT&T, Telus, GTE).

Cellular digital packet data (CDPD). A wireless communication protocol for transmitting and receiving data over cellular networks.

Code division multiple access (CDMA). A wireless communication protocol.

Equipment identifier number (EIN). Used to track manufacturers of equipment. The EID is used to ensure security by assigning a unique ID number to every communications device.

Form factor. Refers to the general size, shape, and physical attributes of a device. For example, handheld PC form factor or palm-sized PC form factor.

Global system for mobile communications (GSM). A digital cellular or PCS wireless communication protocol used throughout the world.

Handheld personal computer (H/PC). A palmtop device or personal digital assistant that can wirelessly access e-mail, paging messages, and the Internet and intranets.

Original equipment manufacturer (OEM). Refers to a supplier that manufactures and provides equipment to a customer under the customer's brand name, or provides equipment that is integrated into the customer's product and sold under the customer's product name.

Personal communications services (PCS). A two-way, 1900-MHz digital wireless communication protocol being rolled out across the United States and previously available in other countries.

Personal digital assistant (PDA). A generic term used to describe any handheld device used to store and manipulate data.

Register/registration. Refers to when the wireless modem and the wireless base station have a valid connection.

Subscription. A process in which the user subscribes to a wireless data service.

Windows CE. A software platform for handheld personal computers developed by Microsoft Corp.

Windows 9x/NT. Refers to any of the following operating systems: Microsoft Windows 95, Microsoft Windows 98, or Microsoft Windows NT 4.0.

Wireless Internet/wireless IP. Also known as CDPD. Refers to a wireless communication protocol or system that provides access to Internet e-mail and the World Wide Web.

11.1.2 DD2: Classified information on the domain

History of the firm

Novatel Wireless, Inc. (NWI), is a leading edge developer and manufacturer of wireless communications solutions that provide mobile professionals with universal access to mission-critical information. In addition to the discussion here, information about Novatel Wireless can be found on the Web at http://www.novatelwireless.com.

The core technology expertise of NWI is its CDPD radio modem and application knowledge, as well as its 900-MHz spread spectrum radio design. The company leverages its cellular history into new wireless-based products that are in sync with the customer needs of the day, and a step ahead of the needs of tomorrow.

NWI's commitment to quality is unparalleled. The company's well-earned reputation derives from effective miniaturization of hardware coupled with solid yet flexible software—a winning combination!

Customers are considered the key to success and are a part of every decision the company makes. NWI's customers are considered valued partners, working together toward the mutual benefit and success of both companies.

NWI's product portfolio includes the CONTACT wireless H/PC, Minstrel wireless IP modem, Minstrel Plus wireless modem, Sage wireless IP modem, and the NRM-6812 wireless modem. CONTACT is the industry's only wireless Windows CE 2.0 handheld PC. Minstrel and Minstrel Plus are wireless IP modems for the PalmPilot, IBM WorkPad PC Companion, and Palm III. Sage is a versatile, external wireless IP modem. The NRM-6812 is an internal OEM modem.

Novatel Wireless is a privately held company, headquartered in San Diego, California. In addition, NWI maintains administrative and R&D facilities, in Calgary, Alberta, Canada, along with regional sales offices in Scottsdale, Arizona, and San Francisco, California.

Information from domain experts

The domain experts have provided a list of possible wireless communication air interfaces that our company could pursue. This includes CDPD, GSM, and CDMA.

Information from market experts

Available products: Novatel Wireless

The first step is to identify the products in the domain that Novatel Wireless provides. Novatel Wireless currently has four major product lines:

1. *CONTACT:* This is an H/PC with an integrated CDPD wireless modem running on the Windows CE 2.0 operating system.
2. *Minstrel:* This is an accessory to the PalmPilot H/PC that gives wireless functionality by adding a module with our CDPD wireless modem, battery pack, and charging system onto the PalmPilot. Applications written for this run on the Palm operating system.
3. *Sage:* This is a stand-alone module with a standard DB-9 serial connection for laptops and PCs. It gives desktop and laptop users wireless connectivity. Applications written for this run on the Microsoft Windows 9x/NT operating system.
4. *NRM-6812 (OEM):* This is our OEM module that we sell to third parties for industrial applications, integrated applications, and so on. It has a more robust form factor.

All of the above products have essentially the same CDPD (wireless IP) modem, and have similar if not identical configuration and diagnostic parameters. This means that the configuration and diagnostic applications are written for three types of operating systems:

1. Microsoft Windows CE;
2. Palm OS;
3. Microsoft Windows 9x, NT.

We currently produce three types of configuration and diagnostic software in some form for each of these platforms:

1. *Wireless Subscription Wizard:* A configuration application used to aid the user in the subscription process. The subscription process involves giving the wireless IP provider some information about the wireless modem, and entering some specific configuration information so that the modem can connect or register with the base station.

2. *Wireless Modem Manager:* A configuration and diagnostic application that shows the status of the wireless modem and its connections, and allows the user to configure more advanced parameters not found in the Wireless Subscription Wizard.

3. *Wireless Modem Status:* A diagnostic application that indicates the state of the wireless modem connection, and shows whether the modem is registered or not.

All products use some variant of the above three applications.

Available products: Competitors

The major competitors to our product line are Sierra Wireless, Motorola, and Uniden.

Sierra Wireless produces several products that compete directly with our product line, including a PC card CDPD modem for use on Windows 9x/NT platforms, a PC card CDPD modem for Windows CE platforms, and an OEM module for use with Windows 9x/NT platforms. Sierra Wireless uses a similar approach for their configuration and diagnostic software. They provide two applications for configuration and diagnostics. One is WirelessExpert, which is similar to the subscription wizard, an application that allows the user to set up and configure the wireless modem settings to successfully register with the wireless IP provider. The other application is the Watcher, a diagnostic and configuration application that allows the user to monitor the wireless modem and adjust settings in the modem. More information about Sierra Wireless and their products can be found at http://www.sierrawireless.com.

Motorola produces a PC card CDPD modem for use on both Windows 9x/NT and Windows CE operating systems. This product comes with a different configuration and diagnostic application for each operating system. The application for Windows 95/NT is called Personal Messenger Progtool, and allows the user to manually poll for registration information, and to set certain parameters in the modem. More about this application can be found at www.motorola.com. The other configuration and diagnostic application that is written for the Motorola PC card modem is bMobile Wireless. This application was written for Windows CE by a company called bSquare, a leading provider of Windows CE software products and services. More information about this product can be found at www.bsquare.com.

Although Uniden does produce a low-cost CDPD modem that competes with our Sage/OEM product line, it does not provide any configuration or diagnostic software other than an extension of the AT command set for modems. It is not considered in this analysis.

Current market trends

Future applications propose to expand our product line into the GSM communications protocol. GSM is a wireless communication protocol used throughout the world. Moving to a GSM product line would involve reworking the entire hardware design of the wireless modem, and the new products would require different configuration and diagnostic software, because the parameters for GSM are substantially different than CDPD. NWI is also interested in CDMA (another wireless protocol); however, the cost of licensing the CDMA technology may prohibit this direction.

A second application proposed was a remote diagnostics tool. At present, all configuration/diagnostic applications communicate via a serial port using a proprietary communications protocol. Certain customers have expressed interest in being able to diagnose modem status via the airlink interface. This is especially beneficial in remote telemetry applications, where many wireless devices are deployed. The proposed application would run only on the Windows 95/NT operating system, and would require modification to the embedded wireless modem software to handle status and configuration requests via the airlink interface.

The third area of interest is in the Palm PC. This is a different form factor than the H/PC, but runs the same operating system. Regardless of the hardware form factor, the configuration/diagnostic software will be very similar to that for the CONTACT H/PC, with modifications of the graphical user interface.

Firm's strategy

The firm's strategy is to create products and services that will allow users to access information anywhere and anytime. NWI plans to broaden its product strategy with future developments employing other wireless protocols such as GSM and CDMA.

11.1.3 DD3: Definition of the feasible, strategic, and current domains

The feasible domain comprises configuration, diagnostic, and remote diagnostic software for all operating systems and CDPD, GSM, and CDMA wireless modems. Figure 11.1 illustrates the three domains.

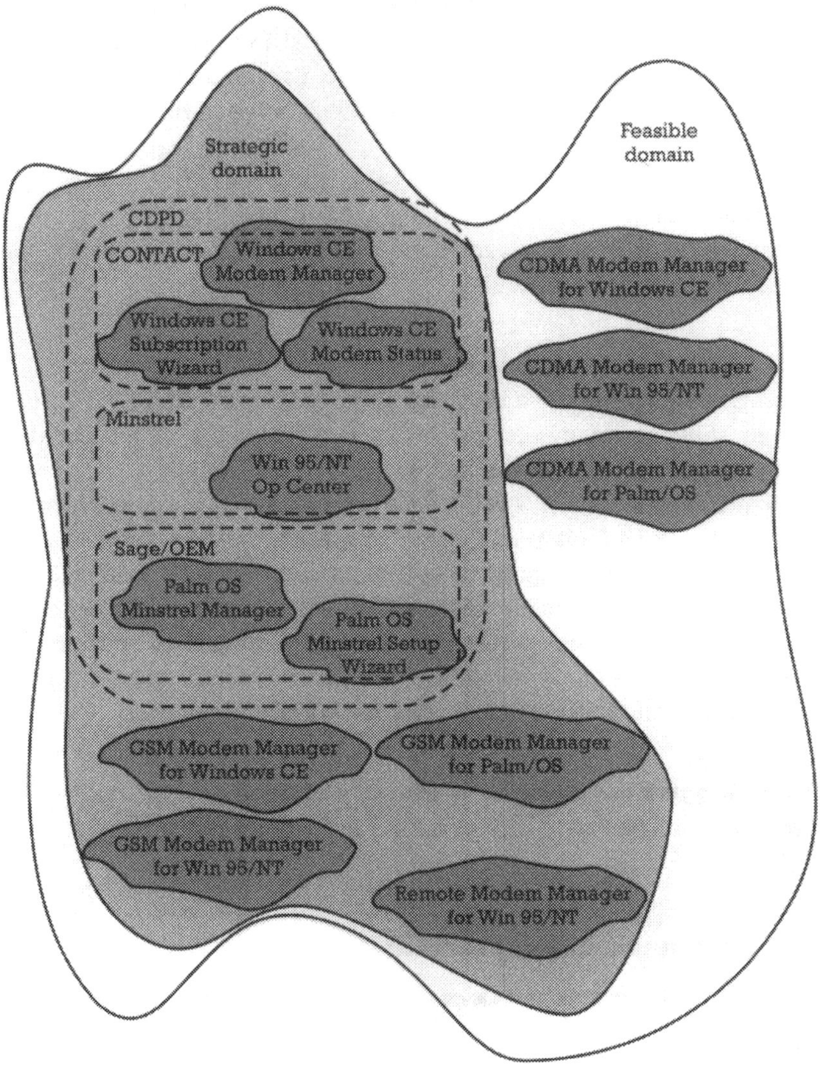

Figure 11.1 The feasible, strategic, and current domains.

Strategic domain

The strategic domain targets a GSM product line to take advantage of foreign markets, and to broaden our wireless communications experience. A CDMA product line may be attractive, but not feasible due to the associated licensing and initial development costs.

Also, strategically we will move toward the latest in H/PC/PDA products in which a strategic target is the new Palm PC form factor. In terms of software development, because the Palm PC uses the same OS as one of our current products, only portions of the GUI will change to meet the new form factor. We will also target remote diagnostic and configuration software for Windows 9x only, because this is only required for the OEM market.

Current domain

We are in the process of creating the configuration and diagnostic software for the CDPD product line.

11.1.4 DD4: Feasibility analysis

Although there are many differences between a CDPD and GSM wireless modem, there are many commonalities as well. Configuration and diagnostic software written for either will have many of the same components and functionalities. Because we are in the process of creating the software for the CDPD product line at present, we are uniquely positioned to design the components with a forward-thinking approach. The domain analysis and engineering will help us to implement those concepts into our existing development. The feasibility analysis has assessed that DA&E should go on and be used in the development phases of the configuration and diagnostic software for wireless modems.

11.1.5 Logging the evolution of domain definition

Table 11.1 summarizes the development efforts for this phase.

11.2 Domain characterization

11.2.1 DC1: Diagrams of values

Internal values

Features:

Table 11.1
Evolution of the Domain Definition

Author	Date	Action	Effort
Jim Paulson	1998-03-23	Domain analysis with domain expert, analysis of products, definition of terms	2 hrs 20 min
Jim Paulson	1998-03-24	Market analysis of products, definition of terms	3 hrs 30 min
Jim Paulson	1998-03-26	Definition of domains	3 hrs 0 min
Jim Paulson	1998-04-02	Feasibility analysis	1 hrs 50 min
Jim Paulson	1998-04-11	Update descriptions to reflect changes	0 hrs 30 min
Jim Paulson	1998-04-12	Update descriptions to reflect changes	0 hrs 30 min

- Easy configuration of essential modem parameters using a standard wizard approach;
- Ability to easily configure and diagnose modem operation through a graphical user interface;
- Ability to quickly view registration status while using other Internet applications.

Quality:

- Logical layout of configuration options with recommended settings indicated;
- Ability to restore default set of configuration options at any time;
- Constant and consistent feedback on the communications link between the wireless modem and the base station;
- Modular common components reduce the amount of testing and the possibility of failure.

External values

Interoperability Between Users:

- In general, wireless modems facilitate interoperability between users by giving them a wireless Internet connection. This gives them all the benefits of Internet access including e-mail and access to intranets through a variety of devices anywhere coverage is available. The configuration and diagnostic suite of applications enhances this interoperability by making wireless modems easier to use by all levels of the organization.

Interoperability Between Products:

- The software products in this domain are directly linked to their respective modem hardware interface. There is no standard for a standard interface proposed, and it is doubtful such a standard will be implemented in the near future. The modem interface for our product line is a proprietary communications protocol to configure and request data.

Expectations:

- The Wireless Modem Configuration suite has been completed for Windows CE, and Windows 95/NT, and the Palm OS. The suite is still under development.

Internal and external value will be improved as follows:

- Greater consistency in the graphical user interface between the versions for different operating systems;
- Additional diagnostic features in the Wireless Subscription Wizard to aid in the first time setup process;
- More division into components to allow reuse across the application suite.

11.2.2 DC2: Description of the installed base

Table 11.2 is an estimate of the installed base for comparison purposes between the three main competitors in this domain. Actual sales data is not available.

11.2.3 DC3: Tables of compatibility

As mentioned previously, because the configuration software is directly tied to the hardware, there is no compatibility between modems.

Table 11.2
Description of the Installed Base

	Novatel Wireless	Sierra Wireless	Motorola
Wireless modems for Windows CE devices	Medium	Low	Medium
Wireless modems for Windows 9x/NT devices	Medium	High	Low
Wireless modems for Palm OS devices	High	None	None

11.2.4 DC4: User flows

Novatel Wireless is going to attract new users by both its configuration tools and the features of its wireless modems (Figure 11.2). Unlike some of the previous examples, the hardware and software are firmly linked and cannot be separated in the analysis.

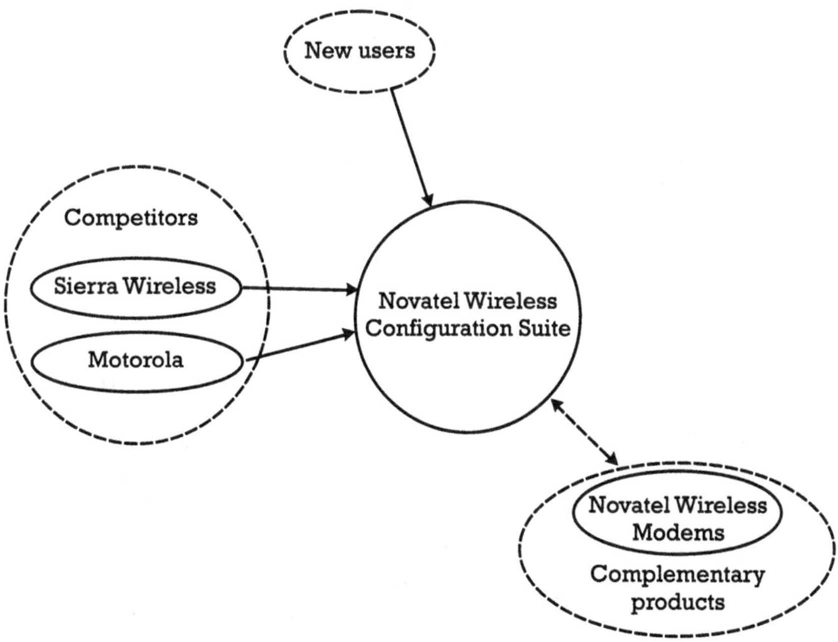

Figure 11.2 User flows.

Customers will consider both the aspects of the hardware modem itself, and the configuration and diagnostic software that is available for use with that modem.

Novatel Wireless will attract new users by a combination of its easy-to-use configuration software and the price of its wireless modems.

Novatel Wireless may be able to attract existing users of Sierra Wireless and Motorola products by providing a lower-priced alternative coupled with increased functionality of its configuration and diagnostic tools.

11.2.5 DC5: Market segments and pricing policy

Figure 11.3 shows the market segments we can target and how our pricing policy is affected. If we target the vertical markets (that is, sell to large firms as a solution provider), we can set our pricing policy higher and offer other benefits such as service and quality.

If we target the horizontal markets (sell directly to consumers), then we need to compete on a price level such that our pricing policy should be low. OEM markets are similar to vertical markets; however, the OEM market may be more sensitive to price per unit due to volume.

11.2.6 DC6: Plan for development of new products

The feasible horizon for this domain is 2 years. The plan is divided into 1-year periods, as described next:

Year 1: Deployment, use, and testing of the current version of our application suite for Windows 95, Windows CE, and Palm OS occur. We also plan to add a version of the application suite with remote diagnostic ability for OEM customers.

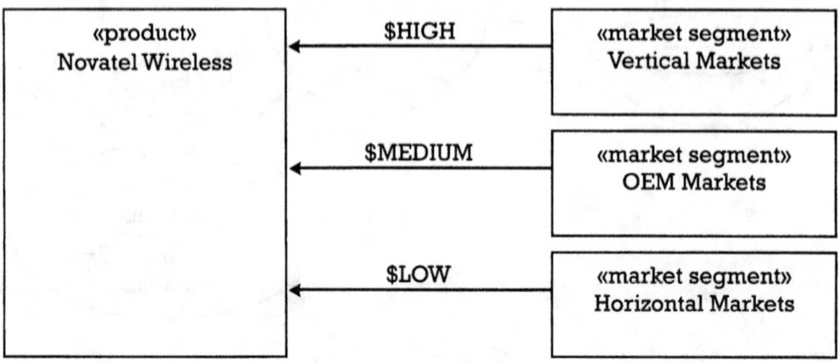

Figure 11.3 Market segments and pricing policy.

Year 2: In this year, we plan to expand current product line to GSM. This would allow us access to a broader market.

The field of mobile communication is changing so rapidly, it is not possible to predict what standards or protocols will be more than 2 years into the future. This is an uncertain time as telecommunications companies compete to provide the infrastructure necessary. Only time will show which standards will become the most widespread, and our plan will have to be adopted accordingly. For this reason, it is important that we make our software as configurable and modular as possible so we can respond to changes in the marketplace.

11.2.7 Logging the evolution of domain characterization

Table 11.3 summarizes the development efforts for this phase.

11.3 Domain scoping

11.3.1 DS1: Variability space, attributes of the products in the domain, and the related constraints

Variability Space

VP_1: User profile:

$V_{1,1}$: Nontechnical user

$V_{1,2}$: Technical user

VP_2: Wireless modem:

$V_{2,1}$: CDPD

$V_{2,2}$: GSM

Table 11.3
Evolution of Domain Characterization

Author	Date	Action	Effort
Jim Paulson	1998-03-28	Analysis of the values of our products	4 hrs 10 min
Jim Paulson	1998-03-29	Analysis of competitor products	4 hrs 0 min
Jim Paulson	1998-03-31	Users flows	2 hrs 40 min
Jim Paulson	1998-04-02	Analysis of the pricing policy	1 hrs 0 min
Jim Paulson	1998-04-11	Update analysis to reflect changes	0 hrs 50 min
Jim Paulson	1998-04-12	Update analysis to reflect changes	0 hrs 50 min

VP_3: Communications medium:

$V_{3,1}$: Serial

$V_{3,2}$: Airlink

VP_4: Operating system:

$V_{4,1}$: Windows CE

$V_{4,2}$: Windows 95/NT

$V_{4,3}$: Palm OS

The variation points have been chosen as follows:

1. *User profile:* Although our target market is the vertical market, it is a vertical market for horizontal customers. Therefore, we have essentially two user profiles: a technical user such as wireless service provider personnel who are interested in debugging any problems using their wireless communications service, and a non-technical user who does not require the detailed information, and is only interested in general information about the current connection.

2. *Wireless modem:* We have chosen only two variants for this variation point due to the cost and complexity of development for each wireless modem protocol. We already have an existing CDPD product line, and our second variant will be the GSM product line.

3. *Communication medium:* This refers to how the configuration/status information is accessed. Either it is accessed from the handheld device or PC via a serial communication link, or it is proposed that we access this same information via the airlink interface, that is, through the CDPD network.

4. *Operating system:* We currently have a product line varied across three operating system platforms, and we will continue to maintain this variation in future product development.

Attributes of the Products in the Domain

A_1: Performance:

Measured by the mean response time

A_2: Reliability:

Measured by the mean time to failure

A_3: Ease of use:

Measured on an ordinal scale:

Trivial (training required for a nontechnical person less than 4 hr)

Easy (training required for a nontechnical person between 4 and 8 hr)

Medium (training required for a technical person with at least a B.Sc. in the field less than 4 hours)

Hard (training required for a technical person with at least a B.Sc. in the field between 4 and 8 hours)

Very Hard (training required for a technical person with at least a B.Sc. in the field more than 8 hours)

Constraints on the Attributes

A_1: Performance:

$C_{1,0}$: Do not care

$C_{1,1}$: Fast, mean response time below 1 second for all operations

$C_{1,2}$: Fair, mean response time below 10 seconds for all operations

A_2: Reliability:

$C_{2,0}$: Do not care

A_3: Ease of use:

$C_{3,0}$: Do not care

$C_{3,1}$: Trivial

$C_{3,2}$: Easy

11.3.2 DS2: Definition of product strategies

There are three strategies:

S_1: CDPD strategy

S_2: CDPD OEM strategy

S_3: GSM strategy

S_1: CDPD strategy

This strategy is the present strategy implemented today. It consists of the variants shown below. It assumes nontechnical users will be using the software, and currently only CDPD is supported. The communication medium for configuring the modem is using a serial medium only. The software is written for three platforms.

Variants

VP_1: User profile:

$V_{1,1}$: Nontechnical user

VP_2: Wireless modem:

$V_{2,1}$: CDPD

VP_3: Communications medium:

$V_{3,1}$: Serial

VP_4: Operating system:

$V_{4,1}$: Windows CE

$V_{4,2}$: Windows 95/NT

$V_{4,3}$: Palm OS

Attributes

A_1: Performance:

Not specified

A_2: Reliability:

Not specified

A_3: Ease of use:

Must need minimal amount of training

Constraints

A_1: Performance:

$C_{1,0}$: Do not care

A_2: Reliability:

$C_{2,0}$: Do not care

A_3: Ease of use:

$C_{3,1}$: Trivial (training required for a nontechnical person less than 4 hours)

S_2: CDPD OEM strategy

This strategy provides OEM or value-added resellers with more features and abilities. Those aspects different from the previous strategy are support for technical users rather than just nontechnical users, and the ability to communicate with the modem either via the serial communication link or over the airlink.

Variants

VP_1: User profile:

$V_{1,2}$: Technical user

VP_2: Wireless modem:

$V_{2,1}$: CDPD

VP_3: Communications medium:

$V_{3,1}$: Serial

$V_{3,2}$: Airlink

VP_4: Operating system:

$V_{4,1}$: Windows CE

$V_{4,2}$: Windows 95/NT

$V_{4,3}$: Palm OS

Attributes of the Products in the Domain

A_1: Performance:

Not specified

A_2: Reliability:

Not specified

A_3: Ease of use:

Train a nontechnical person in less than 8 hours.

Constraints on the Attributes

A_1: Performance:

$C_{1,0}$: Do not care

A_2: Reliability:

$C_{2,0}$: Do not care

A_3: Ease of use:

$C_{3,2}$: Easy (training required for a nontechnical person is between 4 and 8 hours)

S_3: GSM strategy

This strategy would be an extension of the first strategy, to allow the application suite to work with a GSM family of products. It would be designed for nontechnical users and communicate via the serial port only.

Variants

VP_1: User profile:

$V_{1,1}$: Nontechnical user

VP_2: Wireless modem:

$V_{2,2}$: GSM

VP_3: Communications medium:

$V_{3,1}$: Serial

VP_4: Operating system:

$V_{4,1}$: Windows CE

$V_{4,2}$: Windows 95/NT

$V_{4,3}$: Palm OS

Attributes

A_1: Performance:

Not specified

A_2: Reliability:

Not specified

A_3: Ease of use:

Must need minimal amount of training

Constraints

A_1: Performance:

$C_{1,0}$: Do not care

A_2: Reliability:

$C_{2,0}$: Do not care

A_3: Ease of use:

$C_{3,1}$: Trivial (training required for a nontechnical person less than 4 hours)

11.3.3 DS3: Selection of the product strategies to develop in the future

According to the 2-year plan discussed in the domain characterization section, the decision was made to implement the following strategy sets:

Baseline, current situation: Σ_0

Year 1: Σ_1

Year 2: Σ_2

Σ_0 is the situation at the time of analysis. Σ_0 comprises S_1 and partially S_2. The variant for S_2, $V_{3,2}$, has not been implemented.

Σ_1 is the strategy set of S_1 and S_2. This finishes our application suite for CDPD with an OEM version released this year.

Σ_2 extends Σ_0 by providing a GSM version of the configuration suite.

11.3.4 Logging the evolution of domain scoping

Table 11.4 summarizes the development efforts for this phase.

11.4 Domain modeling

11.4.1 DM1: Product use case model

Figure 11.4 illustrates the product use case model. The use case description follows:

Wireless Modem Status and Configuration: Use Case Description: Use Case Model

Introduction

A graphical user interface running on an **{operating system}** platform will be used to allow the client of the use case to view the **{wireless modem}** status and configuration information, and configure the **{wireless modem}.**

Flow of events

The application is executed, and the graphical user interface running on the **{operating system}** is loaded.

Depending on the **{user profile},** the **{wireless modem}** status and configuration data is requested from the **{wireless modem}** via the **{communication medium}.**

The **{wireless modem}** receives the request from the graphical user interface, and responds with the requested information.

Table 11.4
Evolution of Domain Scoping

Author	Date	Action	Effort
Jim Paulson	1998-03-30	Variability analysis	3 hrs 10 min
Jim Paulson	1998-03-31	Variability analysis	1 hrs 10 min
Jim Paulson	1998-04-02	Strategy determination	0 hrs 50 min
Jim Paulson	1998-04-12	Update descriptions to reflect changes	0 hrs 40 min

Wireless Modem Status and Configuration (continued)
The graphical user interface receives the response, and displays the **{wireless modem}** information to the user in a form corresponding to the **{user profile}.**
The client will configure the parameters that are available according to the **{user profile}.** The configuration information will be validated upon entry. When the client is finished changing the configuration information on the graphical user interface, he or she will initiate a command to save the settings to the **{wireless modem}.**
The graphical user interface will send the configuration request to the **{wireless modem},** and the **{wireless modem}** will set the appropriate configuration parameters as requested.

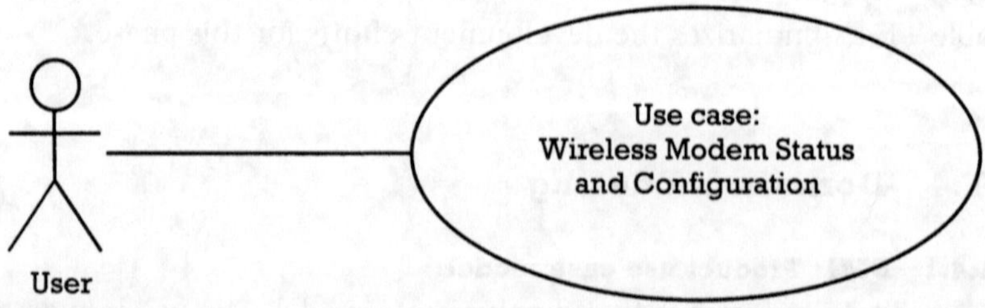

Figure 11.4 Product use case model.

11.4.2 DM2: Product analysis model

Figure 11.5 illustrates the product analysis model. The identifying objects and methods in the case model follow:

Identified Objects:

Graphical user interface;

Client;

Status information;

Configuration information;

{communication medium};

{user profile};

{wireless modem};

{operating system}.

Identified Actions:

Receive;

Transmit;

Display;

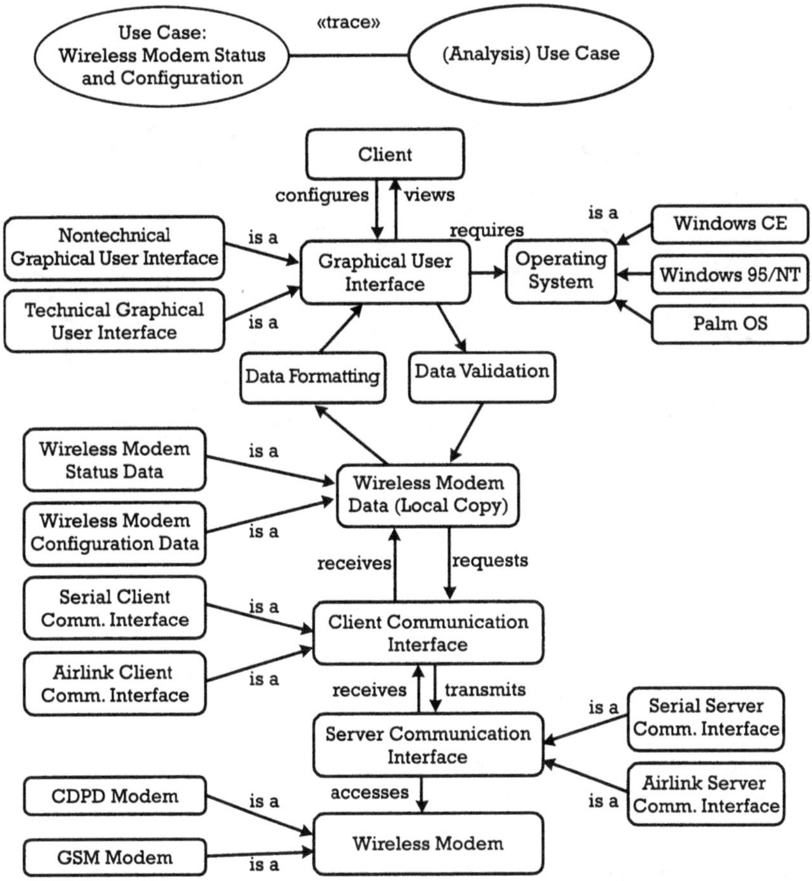

Figure 11.5 Product analysis model.

Validate;

Modify;

Save;

Poll.

11.4.3 DM3: Domain use case model

Figure 11.6 illustrates the domain use case model.

11.4.4 DM4: Domain analysis model

Figure 11.7 illustrates the domain analysis model.

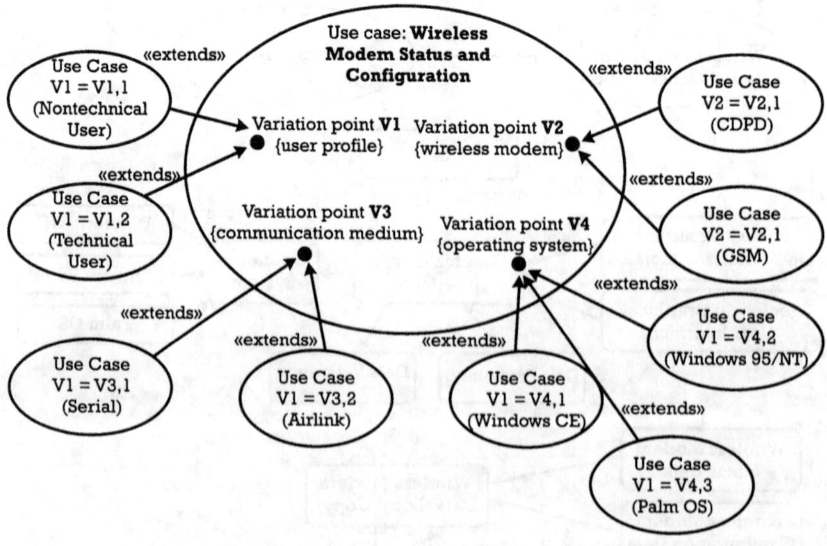

Figure 11.6 Domain use case model.

11.4.5 DM5: Traces between use cases and analysis classes

Tables can implement the traces between use case analysis objects. In this case study, the traceability is not easily identifiable since only one use case was used in this model.

11.4.6 Logging the evolution of domain modeling

Table 11.5 summarizes the development efforts for this phase.

11.5 Domain framework development

11.5.1 DF1: Definition of the nature of the domain framework

The framework used in this case study was a passive framework. This was chosen because the applications in the domain use a set of loosely coupled components in different ways to achieve the product variants.

11.5.2 DF2: Architecture of the domain framework

The architecture for this domain framework comprises the three core projections: module, class, and object dynamics projection.

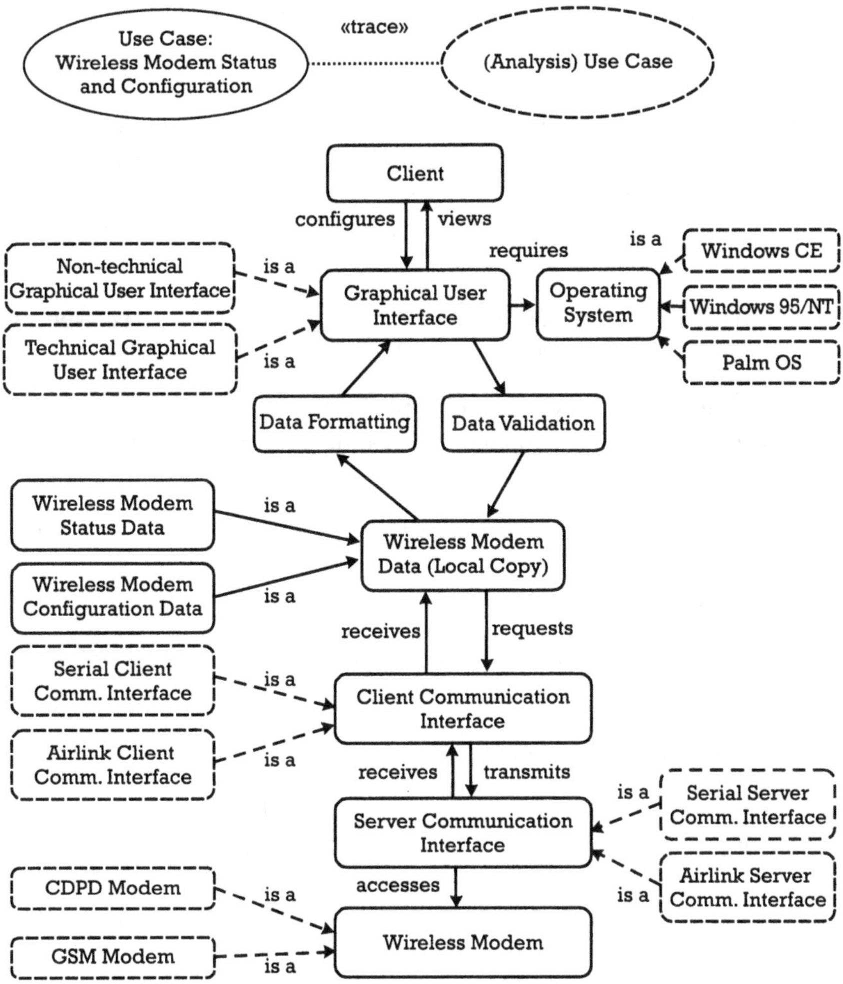

Figure 11.7 Domain analysis model.

Table 11.5
Evolution of Domain Modeling

Author	Date	Action	Effort
Jim Paulson	1998-04-01	Product use case model and product analysis model	3 hrs 10 min
Jim Paulson	1998-04-02	Product analysis model	0 hrs 30 min
Jim Paulson	1998-04-14	Domain models	1 hrs 10 min

Package projection

The following list describes the package decomposition of the framework:

- **wirelessmodem:** This package contains classes common to the whole system and regarding the communication between the client in the application, and the server in the wireless modem. This package handles generic functions such as request, response, and data.
- **wirelessmodem.server:** This package contains server-specific classes to manage requests from the application.
- **wirelessmodem.client:** This package contains the generic interface that all wireless modem applications must use to access the data in the wireless modem.
- **wirelessmodem.data:** This package contains all classes specific to managing and storing the data in the wireless modem itself, and in the local copy in the application.
- **wirelessmodem.gui:** This package contains classes to build the generic graphical user interface.

The packages are mapped into workpackages as follows:

- Workpackage 1 comprises **wirelessmodem, wirelessmodem.gui,** and the **wirelessmodem.client.**
- Workpackage 2 comprises **wirelessmodem.server** and **wirelessmodem.data.**

These groupings were created for the main reason that the server resides in the embedded software in the physical wireless modem, whereas the client and GUI reside in the host device's operating system. This grouping of the packages makes the implementation more logical.

Class projection

Class projection of the server side

Figure 11.8 shows the classes the framework provides to build a server in the embedded software of the wireless modem. This set of classes is self-sufficient and does not need any additional classes to make a running

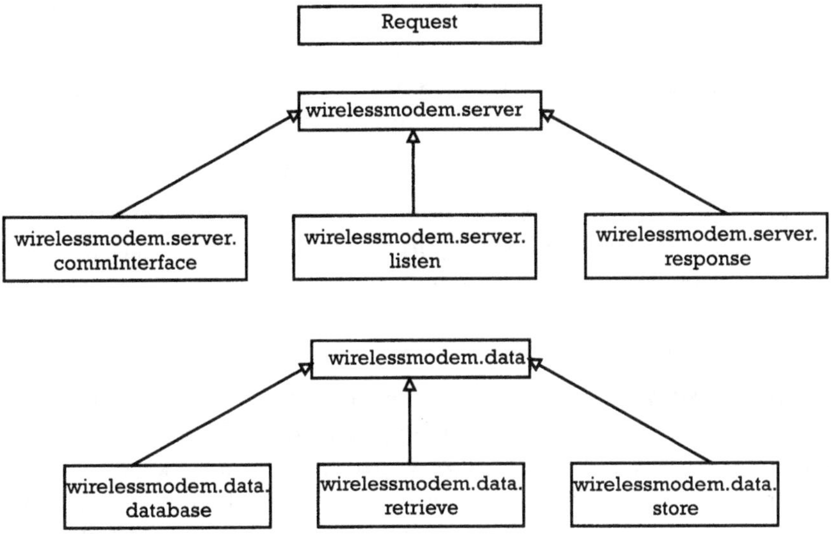

Figure 11.8 Server class projection.

server. However, additional classes can be added to provide custom features not provided by the framework. The diagram comprises classes belonging to the **wirelessmodem.server** and **wirelessmodem.data** packages.

The upper part of Figure 11.8 describes the classes of the **wirelessmodem.server** that obtain the request and send the response back to the client. The lower part describes the classes of the **wirelessmodem.data** that control access to the data and keep the working copy. Both classes are applicable to the embedded software physically residing in the wireless modem.

To build the wireless modem server, the product developer needs to do the following:

1. Install the **serial** or **airlink** communication interface class for the **wirelessmodem.server.commInterface** class as specified in the documentation. Both classes may be supported in some products.

2. Install the **CDPD** or **GSM** data class for the **wirelessmodem.data** class as specified in the documentation. This will determine what data is available for queries.

To extend the server, the product developer can do the following:

1. Subclass the **wirelessmodem.data** class to provide support for wireless communication protocols not specified by this framework.

2. Subclass the **wirelessmodem.server.commInterface** to provide communications support for other types of physical communication interfaces to the wireless modem.

Class projection of the client side

Figure 11.9 shows the classes the framework provides to build the client. The diagram comprises classes belonging to the **wirelessmodem.gui, wirelessmodem.client,** and **wirelessmodem.data** packages.

The **wirelessmodem.gui** class contains the **interface** class, the **validation** class, and the **formatting** class. These functions allow for variability in the complexity of the user interface.

The **wirelessmodem.gui** class also contains a **wrapper** class and a **toolkit** class. The wrapper allows the operating system-dependent classes to replace the **wirelessmodem.gui.toolkit** as needed without modifying the GUI itself.

The **wirelessmodem.data** class is the same as the class in the server. The client makes a physical copy of the database in the server object since the majority of parameters are static throughout the session. The **wirelessmodem.data** class has a **retrieve** and **store** class for accessing the data in the database, the same as on the server side.

The **wirelessmodem.client** class is similar to the **wirelessmodem.server** class in that it is comprised of a generic **commInterface** class, which allows variability in the actual physical medium over which the communication is performed. It has a **listen** class to process any responses from the server, and it has a **request** class to send out requests to the server.

The **wirelessmodem.client** package is not self-sufficient, because it requires the implementation of the specific GUI class depending on the product. Product developers who want to create a client need to do the following:

1. Select or implement the required **wirelessmodem.gui** class, which has the detailed interface layout and has the required formatting and verification methods to ensure integrity of the data.

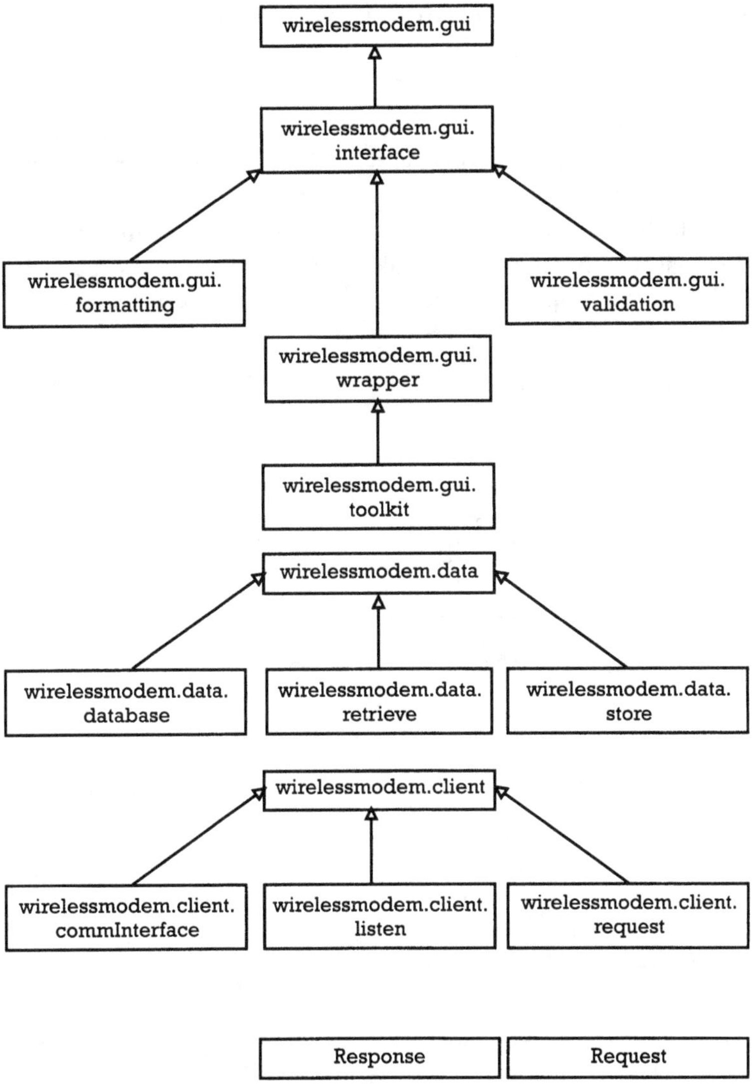

Figure 11.9 Client class projection.

2. Select or implement the appropriate **gui.toolkit** based on the operating system on which the client is to be run.

3. Select or implement the **data** class to represent the parameters that are available for this type of wireless modem.

4. Select the appropriate **commInterface** class to suit the physical communication medium.

Object projection

The object dynamics projection is very similar to the class projection since most classes are instantiated into a single object. Figure 11.10 shows more detail about the objects and the relationships between the objects.

The reason why the client makes a local copy of the data on the server is that the majority of the parameters in the wireless modem are

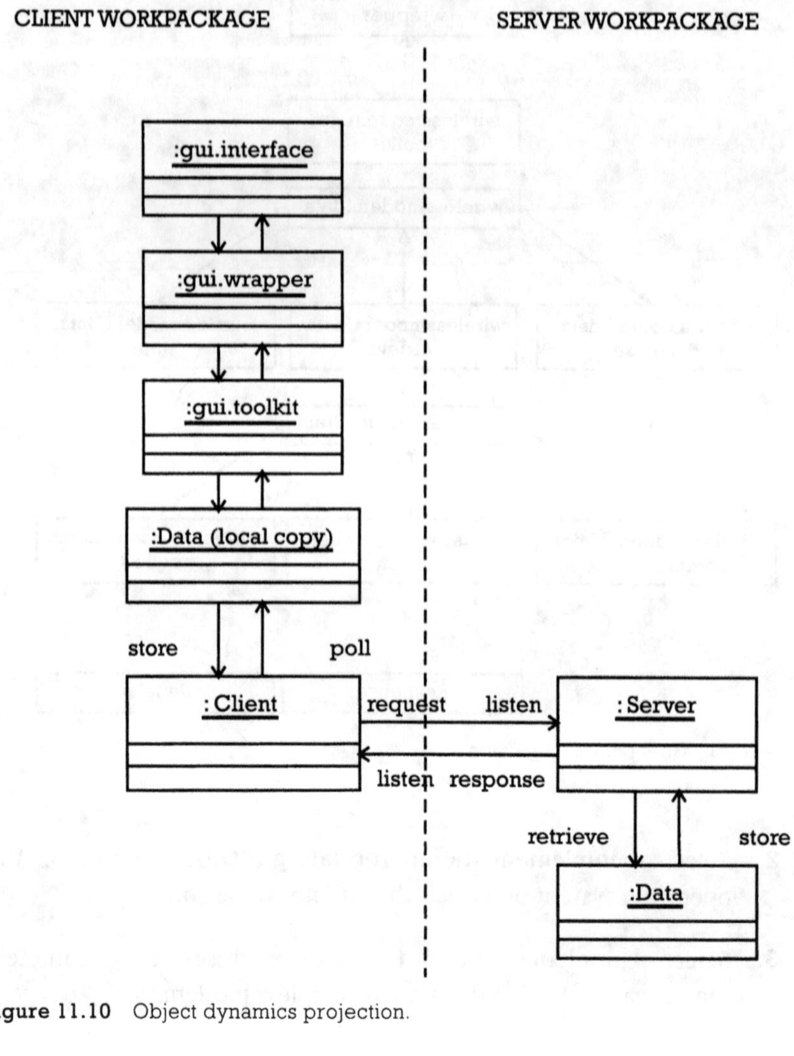

Figure 11.10 Object dynamics projection.

static throughout the life of the connection. And in the majority of cases the bandwidth across the communication medium is limited. Therefore, to reduce unnecessary traffic, the data object updates itself upon instantiation, and controls polling of the modem for nonstatic parameters. The **gui** object has no knowledge of the physical modem; it only has knowledge of the data object in its local space.

Functional projection

The functional projection is detailed and described in Figure 11.10.

Process projection

There are two processes on the client side that have not been previously discussed. The client object has two worker threads associated with it which are the classes of **Listen** (read thread) and **Request** (write thread). Together these classes control the asynchronous data transfers, and update the data object as required.

In this case study, the normal and preferred ratio of clients to servers is one to one. It is possible to have more than one client monitoring the status of the modem parameters, but the benefits of this would be minimal. The difficulty is that configuration requires the modem to be reset, which will tear down all the open sockets and would require all the clients attached at the time to reconnect.

11.5.3 DF3: Documentation of components in the domain framework

The framework is written in Visual C++ on the client side and in C on the server side. The server is written in C because it resides in the embedded code of the physical wireless modem. The documentation for each of the components in the framework is done in HTML. A sample of the documentation is shown in Table 11.6. In the actual documentation, the detailed description link provides a link to an HTML page with more detailed information on the component.

11.5.4 DF4: Browsable and searchable catalog of components in the domain framework

The catalog of components in this domain framework is relatively small; therefore, the catalog is simple. It consists of a list of the components sorted by alphabetical order, which link to the component summaries as shown in Table 11.6, and has a rudimentary search of the components based on the keywords as shown in the same table.

Table 11.6
Sample From the Component Library

Package: wirelessmodem.client **Class Summary**
commInterface
Location:
\library\comm\commInterface.cpp
Brief Description:
Handles the details of creating the socket over the physical communication medium. Creates the socket and connection on instantiation, and destroys the connection on destruction.
Detailed Description:
detailed description
Keywords:
Communication Socket Remote networking Serial Airlink
Request
Location:
\library\comm\request.cpp
Brief Description:
Creates a worker thread to listen for response messages from the server, and either stores the status responses in the data object, or notifies the client.
Detailed Description:
detailed description
Keywords:
Client Request Status Configuration Write
Listen
Location:
\library\comm\listen.cpp

Table 11.6 (continued)

Brief Description:
Creates a worker thread to listen for response messages from the server, and either stores the status responses in the data object, or notifies the client.
Detailed Description:
detailed description
Keywords:
Client Request Status Configuration Read

11.5.5 DF5: Guidelines for developing applications using the components

The framework can be used to generate a variety of products. The steps for developing an application using the components are summarized in Figure 11.11. A simple example of how a product can be built is described next.

Our example looks at a standard CDPD configuration and diagnostic application for Windows 9x/NT. The requirements for this product are summarized as follows:

- A graphical user interface for configuring and monitoring a CDPD wireless modem;
- Designed for a nontechnical user;
- Client is to operate on a Windows 9x/NT PC, and connect to the wireless modem using one of the PC's serial ports.

The steps for accomplishing this follow:

1. Either select one of the derived **gui** classes for a nontechnical user, or create your own from the generic **gui** class in the framework.

The class must implement the methods of formatting and verification. Note that certain methods may need to be implemented depending on the wireless modem type.

2. Either select one of the derived classes for the **gui** toolkit, or create your own from the generic **gui.toolkit** class provided. The **gui.toolkit** has the required operating system-dependent components to achieve the desired GUI functionality through the **gui.wrapper.** The **gui.wrapper** class should be implementable without modification.

3. Select the derived class of the **client.commInterface** class for serial communication. Two derived classes are provided with the framework, one for serial communication and one for airlink communication. An alternate form of this class for a new communications medium can be created if required.

4. Select the derived class of the **data** class for CDPD. Derived classes for the wireless modem type (protocol) need to be provided for

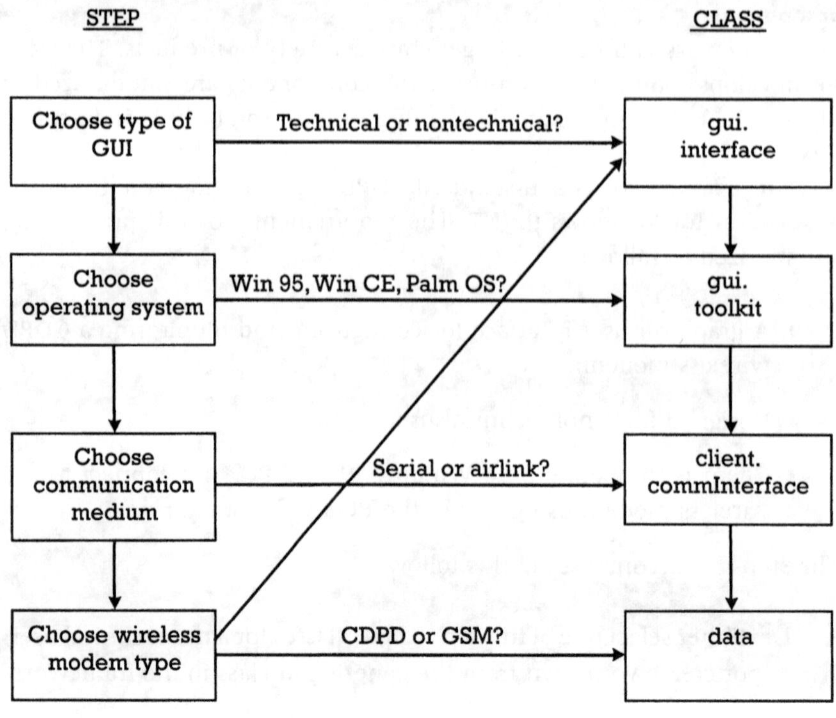

Figure 11.11 Guidelines for using the framework.

both the client and the server. The server "class" will be implemented in C.

5. Build the client as specified in the class projection, and install the client on the appropriate machine.

6. Create, compile, and download the wireless modem embedded code with the appropriate data object. Note that this step may be oversimplified for the purpose of this example. The specifics of the data structure and filling of the data structure need to be developed in the embedded wireless modem code for each protocol. The reuse comes from being able to design many configuration and diagnostic applications quickly and easily for a specific hardware product.

11.5.6 Logging the evolution of domain framework development

Table 11.7 summarizes the development efforts for this phase.

Table 11.7
Evolution of Domain Framework Development

Author	Date	Action	Effort
J. Paulson	April 10, 1998	Functional architecture	1 hrs 30 min
J. Paulson	April 10, 1998	Tracing services	1 hrs 20 min
J. Paulson	April 11, 1998	Class architecture	0 hrs 50 min
J. Paulson	April 11, 1998	Traceability	0 hrs 40 min
J. Paulson	April 14, 1998	Object dynamic architecture	0 hrs 50 min
J. Paulson	April 14, 1998	Interaction dynamic architecture	1 hrs 20 min

CHAPTER

12

Contents

Case study 4: Sherlock in a military domain[1]

12.1 Domain definition

12.1.1 DD1: Domain vocabulary

Control panel. A graphical user interface that provides the operator with control of the various functions of the ROV.

Control station. A computer, combined with RF data links, used to command, control, and receive sensor information from a remotely operated vehicle.

Data link. The link of data (usually provided via RF) between the unmanned vehicle and the ground control station.

Data link interpreter. CDL's terminology for the vehicle-dependent software component responsible for digital terrain elevation data (DTED). Map information providing elevation data as a function of latitude and longitude.

DND. Canadian Department of National Defense.

1. This chapter was written by Mr. Rob Morris.

Downlink. The stream of data flowing from the vehicle to the control station.

Global positioning system (GPS). The U.S. DoD high-accuracy satellite navigation system.

Ground control station (GCS). The control station located on the ground used to pilot the unmanned vehicle.

Ground probing radar (GPR). An alternate mine detection system that relies on the variation of electromagnetic return from a radar signal.

Inertial navigation system (INS). A navigation system that calculates a vehicle's position based on its moments of inertia.

Infrared (IR) camera. A video camera specifically designed to observe electromagnetic radiation in the infrared region.

Interactive map. The software component that allows users to interact with the ROV at a high level of abstraction.

Minimum metal mine detector (MMD). A low-content, metal detection system used in finding anti-vehicle and anti-personnel mines.

Mission planning. The ability to plan a mission represented by a series of geographical locations for an aerial vehicle.

Radio-frequency (RF). The data link of choice for communicating with remotely operated vehicles.

Remotely operated vehicle (ROV). Any vehicle remotely operated by a ground control station.

Remotely piloted vehicle (RPV). Synonymous with ROV. The term *piloted* more strongly suggests aerial vehicles.

Stare-point demand. A special feature of CDL software that allows operators to indicate a point on the ground of particular interest. The air vehicle and a gimbaled mounted camera are automatically controlled such that the same position on the ground is always under observation regardless of air vehicle roll, pitch, and yaw.

Synthetic aperture radar (SAR). An all-weather imaging system that can be carried as a payload instead of visible light or infrared cameras.

Tactical control system (TCS). The tactical control system is a system sponsored by U.S. DoD and NATO partners designed for interoperability between the numerous unmanned aerial vehicles.

Tactical UAV (TUAV). A UAV specifically designed for tactical situations. Typically this means the vehicle is used in reconnaissance and relays real-time data of some sort back to the ground station.

Target drone. A special type of highly maneuverable unmanned vehicle used to determine the effectiveness of various targeting and missile systems.

Target tracking. A feature of CDL software that allows artifacts to be identified in a video image and tracked as they move in the video image.

Thermal neutron activation (TNA). An advanced nuclear sensor used in mine and ordnance detection to determine the nitrogen (explosive) content found in a point location of the ground.

Vehicle control station (VCS). CDL Systems' terminology for its control station software.

Unmanned aerial vehicle (UAV). Most often used term when referring to remotely piloted aerial vehicles.

Uplink. The stream of data flowing from the control station to the vehicle.

U.S. DoD. United States Department of Defense.

12.1.2 DD2: Classified information about domain

CDL Systems (www.cdlsystems.com) is a small software company that markets control station software designed for the command and control of unmanned vehicles and for sensor information collection in both manned and unmanned applications. Most of these applications tend to be used by the military; however, potential markets extend beyond that of military applications. Because our size is limited, the software development focus has been directed by the award of contracts. This is in contrast to the more traditional approach of developing and marketing a specific product. Nevertheless, it is important for us to have knowledge of our feasible domain and identify the boundaries of the strategic domain. To this end, the more recent contract awards are listed in Table 12.1. These contracts identify points within our strategic domain.

Table 12.1
Products and Manufacturers in the Domain

Vehicle	Manufacturer	Description	Web Site Information
Vindicator	Bristol Aerospace	Air-based target drone	www.bristol.ca
Barracuda	Bristol Aerospace	Sea-based target drone	www.bristol.ca
Badger	Bristol Aerospace	Land-based target drone	www.bristol.ca
TLX-1	Hayes Targets	Towed target	Ourworld.compuserve.com/homepages/hayes_targets/
Outrider	Alliant Techsystems	Tactical unmanned aerial vehicle	www.atk.com
Shadow	AAI Corp	Tactical unmanned aerial vehicle	www.aaicorp.com
Rommids	Defense Research Establishment Suffield	Remotely operated metal mine detection system	www.dres.dnd.ca www.crad.dnd.ca/counter
ILDP	Defense Research Establishment Suffield	Improved land mine detection system	www.dres.dnd.ca www.crad.dnd.ca/counter

Competition

Remarkably, many of our competitors also tend to be good candidates for clients. In the remotely operated vehicle (ROV) market, companies tend to market a control station along with their vehicle. Our philosophy is to identify and implement the commonalities across the many control stations/ROV systems, then adapt the features specific to a particular ROV. In this way, software developed for earlier applications can be leveraged as it is applied to other ROVs. We can identify two categories of competitors.

1. The first is those competitors mainly in the ROV market, but who may also build a control station and write their own control station software specifically for their ROV. These "competitors" also have potential as clients if we can convince them that their system as a whole will be better if they use our software. There currently exist approximately 40 manufacturers worldwide in this category of which a few are listed in Table 12.2.

Table 12.2
Category 1 Competitors: Manufacturers of Air Vehicle Systems

Air Vehicle	Company/Organization
Outrider	Alliant TechSystems
Shadow	AAI Corporation
Spectre II	Northrop-Grumman
Ranger	Oerlikon-Contraves
Sperwer	Sagem
Seeker	Kentron
Prowler	Czech Republic
Scorpion	Freewing Systems
Predator	General Atomics Aeronautical Systems Inc.

2. The second involves corporations with the same market strategy as ours. They are solely in the control station software/hardware market and try to convince ROV manufacturers to use their product. To date, only two such competitors have been identified: Israel Aircraft Industries and Herley-Vega Systems, both of which target only the air vehicle market. In addition, the U.S. Department of Defense (DoD) has also realized the need for a common control station for their myriad of unmanned aerial vehicles. The U.S. DoD has recently introduced the TCS (tactical control system) program www.nswc.navy.mil. The goal of TCS is to provide a common interface and platform that can be used across all their unmanned aerial vehicles. Table 12.3 lists these competitors.

Classification of the collected information

User's perspective

The most natural method of classification by the naive user of the various ROVs is by sea, air, and land. The more educated user is aware of the various roles a ROV plays. For example, a tactical unmanned aerial vehicle (TUAV) is primarily used in reconnaissance and typically has some type of operator-controlled observation payload. Furthermore, the tactical definition requires data to be returned in real time. A strategic UAV might operate at high altitudes, have long endurance flights, with a low probability of detection, and be less susceptible to attack. Such a UAV may not return the

Table 12.3
Category 2 Competitors: Manufacturers of Ground Stations and Ground Station Software

Ground Control Station	Company/Organization
Unmanned air vehicles	Herley-Vega Systems
Unmanned air vehicles	Israel Aircraft Industries
Unmanned ground vehicles	U.S. Army

data in real time; instead, it might be stored within the vehicle to avoid detection and analyzed in a postmission fashion.

An aerial vehicle may also be used as a practice target for evaluating the effectiveness of missile systems. Such targets tend to be highly maneuverable, but also must have an ability to accurately reproduce specific avoidance patterns such that missile targeting systems can be evaluated objectively. Furthermore, the target systems should be low cost, since they are frequently hit and destroyed. Consequently as much functionality is placed in the control station as possible. Target systems may also be land based or sea based with similar characteristics as those of an air-based target.

Recently, ROVs have made inroads in the area of anti-vehicle and anti-personnel mine detection and clearance. The advantages of remote operation in land mine clearance and detection are clear. Having a land mine detonate under a manned vehicle is at the very least discomforting and potentially dangerous. Even with the recent worldwide ban on land mines, the "market" for land mine detection and clearance is quite large. Currently an estimated 100,000,000 land mines are buried in various countries around the world.

In addition, ROV land mine detection and clearance is politically attractive. Canada has always had a high profile in this area, but losing personnel in this humanitarian role is costly, both morally and politically. Using ROVs for this purpose, if it can be demonstrated as viable, is very attractive. CDL Systems has been contracted by the Defence Research Establishment in Suffield for their Improve Land Mine Detection Project (ILDP) to provide control station software for detection vehicles.

Market strategy perspective

The market strategy adopted by CDL is to adapt our existing suite of applications used in the command and control of new ROVs. This primarily requires two modifications to existing software. The first requires an adaptation to the client's specific vehicle. The second requires extending our existing software to address the wishes of the client and implement the additional functionality supported by the ROV. We then use the additional functionality as part of the suite. This additional functionality may play a role in the award of the next contract. These incremental increases in functionality cost us little because they are bid as part of the contract. Additional revenue can then be generated for additional copies of the software sold to the client. This can be justified since the client only contracted for the incremental addition to adapt our software to their vehicle.

Difficulties can arise when the additional functionality that may have been partially subsidized by one client is utilized in subsequent contracts that are awarded to the client's competitor. Sometimes, this requires exclusivity agreements for a specific duration. Often, this is not of too great a concern to the client since the contract award is from a contracting government and the government has already accepted the client's price through a lowest bid system. The client makes its profit by the contract award, and subsequent purchases by the government if the contract is successful. CDL maintains a market advantage through three avenues:

1. A relatively low-cost system (lower than if the client had to develop the software from scratch);
2. A system that, to a large degree, is tested by previous contracts;
3. A system that will not cause schedule slippage, which is often the case with software.

Through this approach a barrier to market has been established. Competitors wishing to take a similar approach would have to invest heavily to develop software to the level that is already available. Note that the approach relies heavily on software reuse. If the existing software cannot be adapted, the only advantages are previous ROV experience and a weak Canadian dollar for exports.

Information technology content

The technical perspective is concerned with the specific features each type of system will have. At CDL, the client funding the software often determines these features, but our competitive advantage is greatly enhanced by features that have been developed previously and, thus, are readily available. For example, some ROVs require one or more video channels to observe something of interest or to aid in controlling the vehicle. Such a feature is available providing the client is willing to choose a platform that can host the video cards supported by our software.

Many such technical perspectives exist and it is often the case that clients determine the technical directions that the software will take. One technical decision currently being considered is adapting our software to the Windows/NT platform. Previously, the operating system of choice tended to be Unix systems primarily based on HP and Sun platforms. More recently, the focus has been leaning more toward NT-based platforms. This market shift is a reflection of the popularity of the MS Windows-based OS. Training is always an issue, and the extra familiarity operators have with the operating system eases the training process.

12.1.3 DD3: Definitions of the feasible, strategic, and current domains

The feasible domain of "robot vehicle" control software is quite vast and can encompass many industries, such as oil exploration, mining, bomb disposal, law enforcement surveillance, forest fire detection, autonomous automobiles, and autopilots/auto-landing of commercial airliners to name just a few.

Our strategic domain has focused primarily on military applications, which can still be quite broad. Within this domain, our experience has been in the areas of target drones, reconnaissance and surveillance unmanned aerial vehicles, and land mine detection vehicles. Our company's limited size dictates that the number of active medium size projects is typically around two or three. Consequently, applications undertaken tend to be those in which contracts have been awarded. Nevertheless, proposals are generated only for those contracts that we believe we have a good chance of winning. Furthermore, teaming partners for these contracts are selected based on complementary skills, thereby creating an integrated product team synergy. Thus it is important to identify contracts that are within our capabilities and recognize areas where additional skills may be required through a product team approach. The three domains are shown in Figure 12.1.

12.1.4 DD4: Feasibility analysis

It is important when bidding on a contract to know as accurately as possible the level of effort necessary to address the requirements specified in the contractual statement of work. Equally important, but more difficult to quantify, is an estimate of the level of effort competitors will require. If the level of effort in-house is less than all competitors, it appears

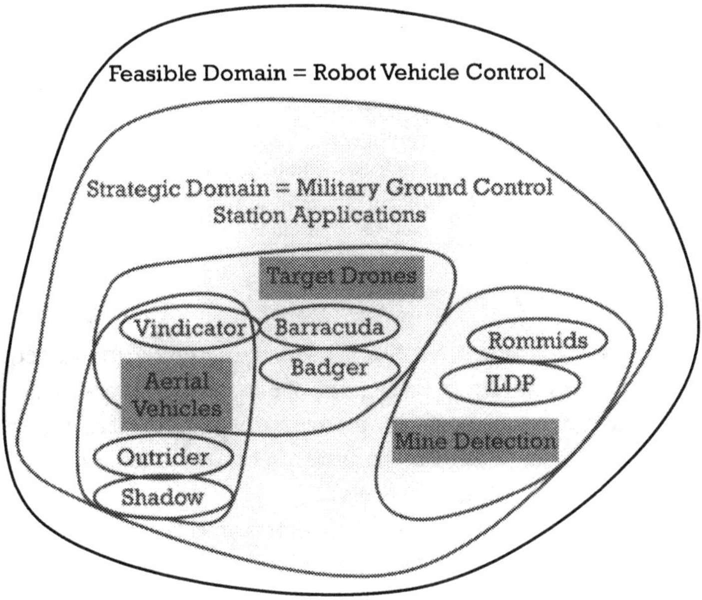

Figure 12.1 Current, strategic, and feasible domains.

favorable to proceed with the proposal. To maximize profit, the goal is to bid marginally lower than the nearest competitor. Estimating the level of effort to develop software is extremely difficult. Many factors play a role. Nevertheless, estimating accurately is the key for winning contracts. Consequently, it is envisioned that a domain analysis and engineering process could provide additional knowledge in identifying the domain "pockets" where contracts are likely to be won.

12.1.5 Logging evolution for domain definition

Table 12.4 summarizes the development efforts for this phase.

12.2 Domain characterization

12.2.1 DC1: Diagrams of values

Internal value

The success of CDL Systems lies in its ability to rapidly create custom vehicle control applications through the reuse of components that have been previously developed for other contracts. Time to market is critical.

Table 12.4
Evolution of Domain Definition

Author	Date	Action	Effort
RLM	1998-04	Technical/market analysis of products, definition of terms	12 hours
RLM/AS	1999-03	Update of technical/market analysis of products	8 hours

Often, as part of a competitive bid, a contracting government requires a technology demonstration to determine the credibility of a vehicle manufacturer to meet the needs of the government. Demonstrating a system that nearly fulfills the system requirements creates a competitive advantage in the contract selection process.

A scoring system is often used to determine technical compliance. The amount of development time prior to technology demonstration is limited; thus, the goal is often to develop a system prior to contract award that will score the highest technical compliance. Through software reuse, CDL Systems can generate a prototype system for a vehicle manufacturer in a limited amount of time. If the manufacturer wins the contract, follow-on work is generally required, which further enhances the suite of features available in subsequent contracts.

In addition to being able to rapidly develop a prototype system, additional advantages are gained through software reuse. Testing requirements for military-grade software are often extreme. Reusing software components that have been previously tested to these high levels leads to a more reliable product. Furthermore, software that has been reused may be classified as commercial off-the-shelf (COTS) software. This classification obviates the need for extensive testing, reducing our costs further and creating an additional competitive advantage.

The features of the software system are many, of which a few of the main ones are listed here:

- *Live video in a window.* Many systems need the ability to display live video. The live video can be used to locate targets or as an aid in vehicle control.
- *Video overlay annotation.* Overlaying graphics on top of the video provides many of the advantages associated with heads-up displays. The

operator is provided additional information without refocusing attention to other areas of the screen.

- *Target coordinate calculations.* It is often necessary to determine the location of an object in the live video. In the case of land mine detection, this may be the coordinates of a mine, whereas for UAVs, this may be the location of troop movements.
- *Customizable warnings.* All vehicles generate warnings when system failures occur. A means must be provided to notify the operator of these warnings in order to take appropriate action.
- *Map navigation.* Navigation via a map provides operators with the ability to relocate the vehicle simply by pointing on a map. This is far easier than having to remotely pilot the vehicle via the video imagery.
- *Mission planning.* The ability to plan the course and action of a vehicle ahead of time leads to a successful mission. Checks can be performed such as fuel requirements; intervisibility, that is, ensuring that line of sight is maintained so that communication with the vehicle is not lost; and terrain avoidance, that is, ensuring that the vehicle maintains a minimum clearance from the ground.

External value

A great deal of value is added to the vehicle control software by integrating to external systems. Key to CDL System's success is the ability to easily adapt the vehicle control software to command and control other vehicles. Customization to a particular vehicle requires the writing of a vehicle-dependent section of software we call the *data link interpreter* (DLI). The role of the DLI is to convert CDL Systems' proprietary command and control codes (VCS format) to the vehicle-dependent command and control codes (Figure 12.2).

Tactical unmanned air vehicles (TUAV) and land mine detection systems share the need to integrate with sensor payloads. With the land mine system, this entails controlling the sensor system and acquiring the sensor data to determine the probability and the location of a potential land mine threat. Typical sensor systems include metal detection, ground probing radar, and IR camera data. With TUAV the sensor data is typically in the form of a video signal from a visible or IR camera, but may also be synthetic aperture radar.

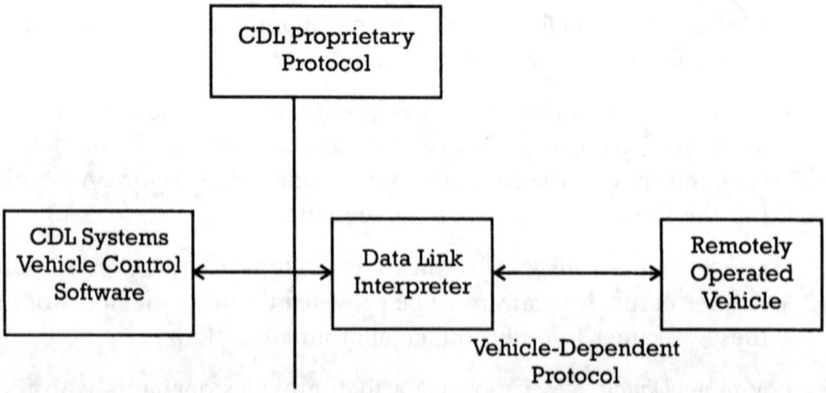

Figure 12.2 Integration of CDL software with external systems.

Being able to import Defense Mapping Agency maps and digital terrain and elevation model data (DTED) provides an association between ground elevation information and latitude/longitude coordinate data. With this information, ground clearance calculations can be performed along the air vehicle flight path in the mission-planning phase and also during flight. Real-time warnings can be announced if the air vehicle's altitude does not provide a suitable level of ground clearance.

One of the key advantages of unmanned air vehicles is the removal of the pilot from the system. This is only possible through the use of an auto-land system. The auto-land system is responsible for monitoring and adjusting the air vehicle's current position as it flies the final approach for a landing. Without auto-land, a skilled pilot is still necessary to land the aircraft through radio control. Recently, auto-land systems have been developed to land UAVs, eliminating the need for a ground-based pilot. Typically the vehicle control station software integrates with the auto-land system through an application program interface (API). The vehicle control station passes control of the vehicle to the auto-land system when the aircraft is to be landed.

Often the need arises to capture an image displayed in the video. Using a standard image format allows for the import of these images into other software programs. Images may be annotated with additional graphics and text with commercially available software. Currently, our software can capture images in JPEG and TIFF formats.

The ability to relay target information to command and control centers plays an importation role in increasing the external value of the software. Providing this feature allows systems using our software to become part of a larger aggregate known as the digital battlefield.

The external value features are summarized in Figure 12.3.

12.2.2 DC2: Description of the installed base

The description of the installed base can be considered from a number of perspectives, each playing a role in the generation of revenue. First, we can consider the number of teaming partners. The key to our success lies with convincing vehicle manufacturers to use our software rather than develop their own software in-house. Successfully teaming with an organization on one contract has led to additional teaming arrangements with the same organization. Presently, we have teaming agreements with

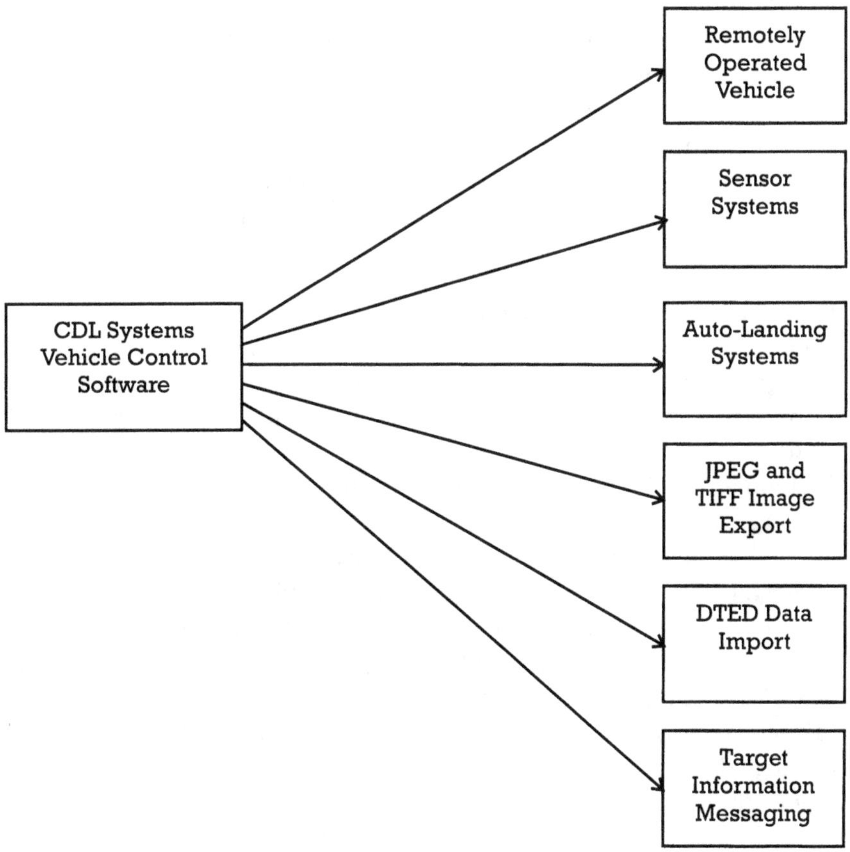

Figure 12.3 Summary of external value features.

five partners, all of which are currently generating revenue for us in various contracts. Of these five, three are repeat clients and two are first-time clients.

Second, we can consider our user to be the governments that procure the vehicle system. Ultimately, we must satisfy the government's military department if we want to be considered for additional projects. Our early role in the land mine detection projects has led to "sole source" awards. That is, contracts have been awarded to CDL Systems uncontested, since the early experience has placed them in the enviable position of being the only company capable of meeting the requirements. This situation happens frequently with multiphased government military projects.

Currently, we have a direct prime contractor relationship with the Canadian DND through its research establishments and indirect relationships as a subcontractor. The relationship with the U.S. DoD is as a subcontractor only.

Third, we must consider the end user of the software, the military personnel. Our situation is somewhat unique, in that the end user does not actually purchase the software. Nevertheless, end user satisfaction can inject pressures on procuring personnel, leading to additional contract awards.

12.2.3 DC3: Tables of compatibility

Two key features of the ground control station software are the ability to (1) import existing maps and (2) export the collected live imagery. For map display, we have the ability to import maps either in the United States Geological Survey (USGS) format or as a scanned GIF image. In addition, ground terrain elevation can be imported in the Defense Mapping Agency (DMA) format.

One of the primary roles of a UAV is to acquire imagery of an area of interest. It is therefore necessary to capture the video image data for subsequent analysis. Currently, this ability exists as image "stills." Operators can capture a frame of video and annotate it with other annotation software. The digital still imagery may then be sent to a command center for further analysis. The ability to transmit full-frame-rate, full-resolution live digital video does not yet exist, but is an area under active development. The leading candidate here is MPEG-2. We currently have the ability to export imagery in TIFF and JPEG formats. Virtually all image manipulation software can import these two formats. Tables 12.5 and 12.6 list these importing and exporting abilities.

Table 12.5
Map Import/Export

Product	Digital Elevation Models	United States Geological Survey	GIF
VCS land mine	I	I	I
VCS target drone	I	I	I
VCS TUAV	I	I	I

Table 12.6
Image Import/Export

Product	JPEG	TIFF
VCS land mine	O	—
VCS target drone	—	O
VCS TUAV	O	O

12.2.4 DC4: User flows

The software market that CDL operates in is different from the traditional software market where the purchase by an end consumer of a product causes a flow from a competitor's product. We try to convince ROV manufacturers to use our software rather than develop their own. Our argument is that we can adapt our software to meet the ROV manufacturer's needs much faster than they could develop their own. If we consider the ROV manufacturer who develops their own ground station software to be our competitor, then their decision to use our software creates a flow from this competitor. Once the decision has been made, the competitor now becomes our partner. New users acquired by this ROV manufacturer become our users as well. New end users are acquired through new partnerships. Figure 12.4 summarizes the user flows.

12.2.5 DC5: Market segments and pricing policy

The market pricing for software has been to charge a fixed price for the development of software required by a particular client to adapt our software to their vehicle, then charge a per-system license fee for each system fielded. The nature of the contracts typically does not require the purchase of a fixed number of licenses. The number of systems fielded is typically less than 10 and may only be 1 or 2. Consequently, we must

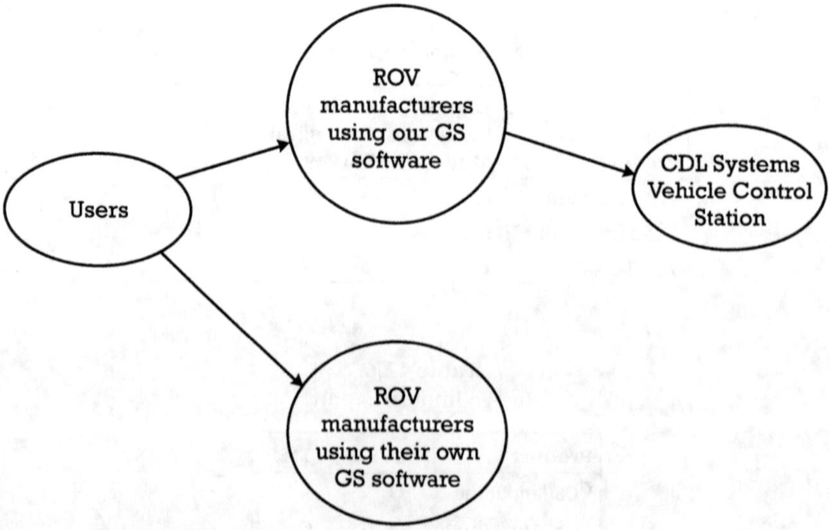

Figure 12.4 User flows.

recoup nonrecurring engineering costs through a fixed price mechanism for custom development.

12.2.6 DC6: Plan for development of new products

Since the work that is undertaken is primarily contract driven, the areas of development lean toward the areas where contracts are won. Nevertheless, a substantial amount of development and product direction is still under our control based on what is proposed.

All software to date has been developed for Unix-based operating systems, primarily due to their reliability. The popularity of the Microsoft Windows-based OS is so great that it can no longer be ignored. Consequently, a port of our software to Windows NT is planned. It is expected that approximately 70% of the software is nongraphics oriented, and as such should port with relative ease. The remaining 30% involves primarily GUI elements.

For these elements two approached are being considered: using standard MS foundation classes or using Java code. Java is particularly attractive since not only is it cross-platform portable, but code developed may also be included in Web pages in the form of applets. Elaborate configurations can be considered such as "distant" remote operation via the Internet.

The Windows operating system is also attractive due to the wide selection of available hardware. Leading edge hardware typically targets the Windows platforms first, with Unix lagging at least a year later. New technologies, such as DVD recording, could be taken advantage of today, if available.

Our immediate and short-term focus lies in primarily satisfying our current clients' needs. By reinvesting profits earned from these clients into the development of additional features, a more capable system is created.

12.2.7 Logging evolution for domain characterization

Table 12.7 summarizes the development efforts for this phase.

12.3 Domain scoping

12.3.1 DS1: Variability space, attributes of the products in the domain, and related constraints

Variation points and variants

VP_1: Vehicle types

For each manufacturer our software must be specialized to some degree to address the variations between vehicles. Currently we have adapted the software to three different vehicles that can be represented by variants $V_{1,1}$, $V_{1,2}$, and $V_{1,3}$. New contracts typically require the adaptation to new vehicles exposing new variants of a similar form. These are represented by $V_{1,4}$, $V_{1,5}$, ..., $V_{1,n}$.

Adapting to a vehicle type requires two considerations. First, the protocol must be implemented to communicate with the vehicle. This may be a significant undertaking if this is the first contract with the manufacturer. However, if a previous partnership has already been formed, a manufacturer tends to adopt a similar protocol, and as such, implementing the control protocol tends to be less of an effort even when the manufacturer decides to construct a completely new vehicle. Second, the GUI

Table 12.7
Evolution of Domain Characterization

Author	Date	Action	Effort
RLM	1998-04	Analysis of competitive relationships in the market	8 hours

must be modified to address the features of the vehicle. This typically requires some incremental modifications to incorporate additional controls, or vehicle status.

VP_2: Vehicle role

The role of the vehicle refers to how it is deployed by its end user. Some vehicles are used as targets to evaluate missile systems, others are used for information gathering in a reconnaissance role, while others may be used in a tactical environment where real-time information may be used for artillery corrections or laser targeting. We have adapted our software for each of these roles. In addition, we are considering other markets where our software may also be suitable. Some areas include crime fighting, as in aerial pursuit helicopters, Coast Guard drug enforcement, and early detection of forest fires.

$V_{2,1}$: Target

$V_{2,2}$: Reconnaissance

$V_{2,3}$: Tactical

$V_{2,4}$: Urban crime fighting

$V_{2,5}$: Coast Guard drug enforcement

$V_{2,6}$: Forest fire detection

VP_3: Operating systems

The vehicle control software must reside on a host running a particular operating system. Ideally, we would like to be able to accommodate all operating systems allowing potential clients to choose the platform most suitable to them. Currently we only support Solaris and HPUX, but we perceive market forces persuading us to port to the MS Windows environment. We would, however, like to avoid problems associated with maintaining multiple versions of software for each operating system. Some cross-platform development solutions (most notably Java) appear to aid with this problem.

$V_{3,1}$: Windows NT

$V_{3,2}$: Solaris

$V_{3,3}$: HP UX

$V_{3,4}$: Linux

VP_4: Video hardware solutions

Central to our software is a live video component used in vehicle navigation and targeting. In the past, it has been advantageous to be able to adapt our software quickly to a variety of live video hardware. The video board market is quite volatile, with companies going out of business, or discontinuing one product in favor of a more feature-laden product. Moreover, a cost-sensitive manufacturer may choose a video solution with fewer features at a reduced cost. Being able to offer multiple video hardware solutions has helped us provide better fit solutions for vehicle manufacturers.

$V_{4,1}$: Parallax Graphics SunVideo

$V_{4,2}$: MultiMedia Access Corporation Osprey

$V_{4,3}$: Visicom VigraVision

12.3.2 DS2: Definition of the product strategies

Attributes

Domain attributes that are identified include reliability, ease of use, multivehicle control, and cross-vehicle support. These attributes have an effect on the strategy in terms of cost/benefit. In general, software that exhibits high reliability, ease of use, an ability to control a large number of vehicles, and an ability to control many different types is preferred. Unfortunately, associated with these preferred attribute values is a higher cost of development. Consequently, the value selected is a function of contract requirements and client preferences.

Reliability

Many factors come into play when discussing the "reliability" of software. Unfortunately, software cannot be tested for reliability in the same manner as other engineering components. A mean time between failure (MTBF) measurement for software is meaningless. Consequently, software for UAV control must undergo extensive testing before being qualified as "flight ready." Such tests are known as *flight qualification testing* and are kin to regression testing within the software industry. A single change to software requires the flight qualification test to be repeated.

Military standards for software development may be required as a means to minimize the chance of a failure. However, strict adherence to these standards by no means guarantees high reliability software. Furthermore, development of these standards comes at a high price. Much effort is put into the documentation that verifies correct procedures have been followed.

Our experience has been that the greatest factor that plays a role in software reliability is the existence or independent development of a vehicle simulator. The role of the simulator is to test each and every command in the control software. Independent development decreases the likelihood that an identical software bug is introduced through protocol misinterpretation. It is less likely that two independent developers will misinterpret a protocol definition in the same way. Sometimes, only a protocol simulator is developed. This ensures proper communications, but does not address simulation of vehicle flight dynamics.

In essence, reliability can only be addressed by what measures have been taken to limit the chance of failure. The constraint for the reliability attribute then becomes whether or not the measure has been undertaken.

Ease of use

Ease of use is a subjective term, and as such is not measurable. Nevertheless, a number of factors can contribute to the creation of software that is easy to use. If the software is similar to other software that operators have used, the learning time is faster. To this end, development of a familiar operating system or window manager GUI interface may be required. This reduces the amount of operator training required.

Environmental constraints may have to be addressed. A hostile environment may require the operator to wear protective clothing or may make traditional pointing devices useless. Sometimes a compromise must be made between familiarity and environmental constraints. For example, the military environment may be unsuitable for the traditional mouse pointing device. An alternate, less friendly, but more robust device may be required. Certain operations, such as mouse dragging, may have to be avoided.

Multivehicle control

Another attribute of the vehicle control software is the number of vehicles a control station can operate. To date, all control stations (with one exception) have controlled a single vehicle. Experience has suggested that a control station could control multiple vehicles. As UAVs become more sophisticated, more effort is required to control the on-board camera and analyze the live video than to fly the aircraft. It is predicted that a two-person team will eventually command a squadron of UAVs. One operator will essentially play the role similar to that of an air traffic controller, while the other controls and interprets multiple live video feeds. The attribute here is the number of vehicles, which can take on values between 1 and *n*.

Cross-vehicle support

The logical extension to multivehicle control is cross-vehicle control. In this case, the control station may be controlling multiple vehicles of different types. Different vehicles may have contrasting advantages and disadvantages. For example, a vehicle may have a shorter or a vertical takeoff capability at the expense of extended range. The ability to support different vehicles from the same suite of control software eliminates operator retraining and provides the tactical advantage of being able to operate vehicles of different capabilities from the same platform. Here the attribute takes on the vehicles that the software can command and control.

Product strategy selection

Selecting a product strategy is usually a result of two forces. First, and foremost, CDL Systems selects strategies that are directly funded through contract awards. These strategies are represented by variation point VP_1. There is little incentive to adapt our software suite to a vehicle the manufacturer has no intention of using. Nevertheless, we do try to form partners with the vehicle manufacturers that we perceive to be most synergistic.

Second, when development is funded internally, we will choose a strategy that we perceive to be most profitable in the long term. This may involve development to capture a larger market in our current domain, or to consider expanding the domain into other roles. We would always consider the opportunity to adapt our software to a new role when funded through a contract, but we may also consider funding this development internally if we believe the cost and effort will lead to other contract awards and licensing revenue. All current awards have arisen from our ability to demonstrate a product that addresses most of the vehicle manufacturer's needs.

From the preceding arguments, we can identify three strategies (Figure 12.5) as discussed in the following sections.

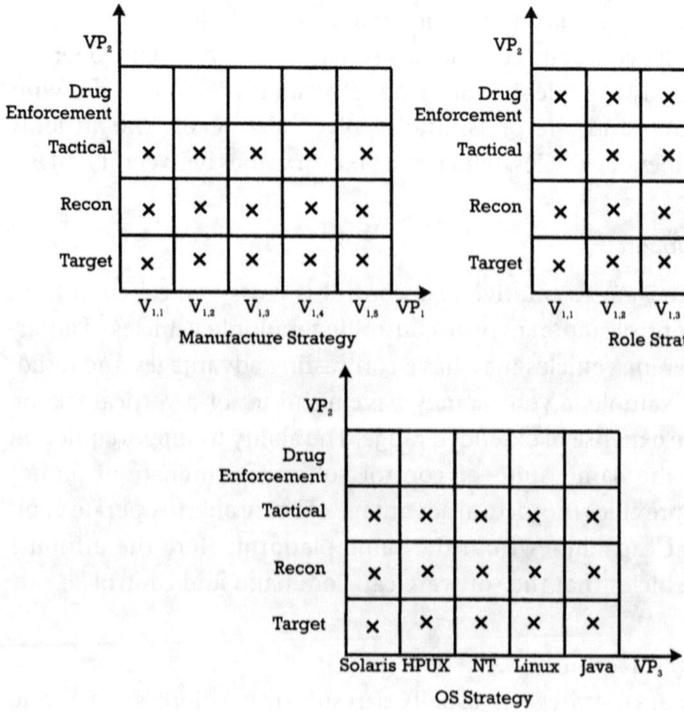

Figure 12.5 Identified strategies.

S_1: Manufacture strategy

Form alliances with as many vehicle manufacturers as possible. This strategy is most attractive since we acquire market share through teaming agreements. The cost to acquire this market share is minimal and, at times, even profitable. We also may venture into new roles without undertaking the risk of a failure. The downside is we have little to moderate control over the content of the new software development.

S_2: Role strategy

We may also try to expand the roles where our software is used. This may take place through a contractual award, internal funding, or a combination. We may perceive a new role to be lucrative enough to bid a contract at a loss with the intent that follow-on work or license revenue will make up for the loss. However, we are not of a sufficient size to undertake a venture into a new role completely on our own. For example, to expend effort adding the necessary features to address the role of forest fire detection when we do not have the support of a vehicle manufacturer is, for the most part, wasted effort.

S_3: OS strategy

We can also address an end user need by making our software available for multiple operating systems. Often a specific operating system is either specified or preferred during a request for proposal phase. For example, the U.S. Army uses Solaris and HPUX exclusively for mission-critical systems. Training and target platform costs also play a role. Users may already be familiar with a particular OS, and the cost of retraining and support for a second may be prohibitive.

Platform costs may play a minor role, but these systems tend to be ruggedized and as such the cost difference in relative terms tends to be minimal. However, state-of-the-art hardware may be available for one operating system much sooner than for others. This is almost always the case for Windows. For example, DVD-ROM, DVD-video playback, and DVD-RAM are readily available for the MS Windows environment, whereas for other operating systems, development in these areas is only beginning. When DVD recording becomes available, this will be a highly desirable feature over the current method of using VCRs.

In the manufacturer strategy, we currently have software in use for manufacturers that have funded us under contract. Although a manufacturer might not use its vehicle in the three roles depicted above, it would be a simple matter for us to configure our software for that role. The goal in this strategy is to adapt our current suite to new vehicles. In the role strategy, we consider adapting the existing suite to additional roles such as drug enforcement.

In the OS strategy we port the existing suite to new operating systems. Here we have included Java even though, technically speaking, Java is not an OS. Moving portions of our software to Java involves a port, and at the same time addresses many cross-platform issues.

12.3.3 DS3: Identification of product strategies to be developed in the future

The strategy selected is actually a combination of S_1 and S_3. Ideally, we would like to be fully employed adapting our software to new vehicles and thereby increasing market share. Unfortunately, this is not always the case. When a contract is completed and no other contract is available, effort focuses on adapting the current suite of software to the Windows platform. Currently a pilot project is in progress to port portions of the software to Java on a Windows platform.

12.3.4 Logging evolution for domain scoping

Table 12.8 summarizes the development efforts for this phase.

12.4 Domain modeling

12.4.1 DM1: Product use case model

The product use case model consists of three applications in the domain of remotely operated vehicles. The three applications are the control of target drones, control of reconnaissance vehicles, and the control of tactical vehicles. The target drone use cases are shown in Figure 12.6.

Use case: Mission Planning
Description: The mission planner devises a route and associated speeds for the target drone system. The routes are identified via a series of waypoints. The mission planner ensures various conditions in the plan in order to carry out the test of the targeting system. Conditions could include altitude clearance for a flight vehicle, avoidance patterns, and range of vehicle.
Use case: Drone Operation
Description: The operator of the drone for the mission is responsible for initiating the start of the mission, carrying out the mission, perhaps in-flight alteration of the mission, and aborting the mission if a dangerous situation is evident.
Use case: Mission Playback
Description: The mission analyst determines whether a missile system was successful. This requires more than checking to see if the drone was hit. The target drone must have performed the mission to the level required to test the missile system. The data from the mission is recorded, and the mission can be played back to check for the success of the test.

The reconnaissance use cases are shown in Figure 12.7.

The tactical unmanned air vehicle use cases are shown in Figure 12.8.

Table 12.8
Evolution of Domain Scoping

Author	Date	Action	Effort
RLM	1998-04	Domain scoping analysis	22 hours

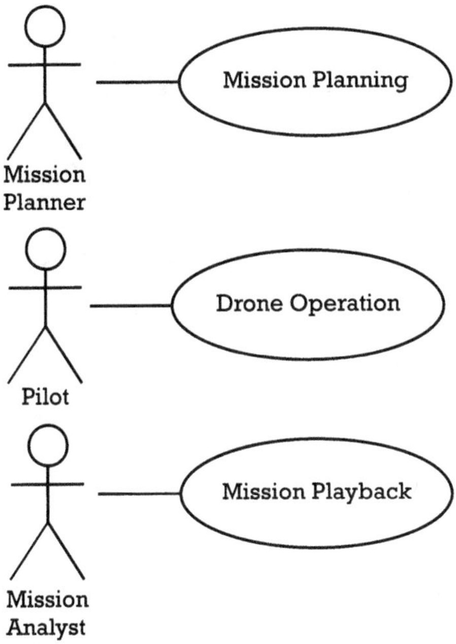

Figure 12.6 Target drone use cases.

Use case: Drive Vehicle

Description: The driver of the vehicle is responsible for guiding the reconnaisance through to an area where sensor information can be acquired. The driver makes use of the on-board camera for guidance. The camera may be panned, tilted, and zoomed to search for items of interest that might be in its path. The driver is also responsible for analyzing the output from the sensor suite and recording locations of interest. Additional information may be recorded by the operator and this information may be relayed for additional analysis. Telemetry information is relayed back to the operator indicating the current status of the vehicle including fuel, speed, heading, and electrical system status. This information is displayed on a set of gauges on an instrument panel.

Use case: Target Identification

Description: An IR (or payload) operator is reponsible for identifying targets within the IR camera video image. The target is identified and is automatically tracked within the image as it progresses to the other scanning system.

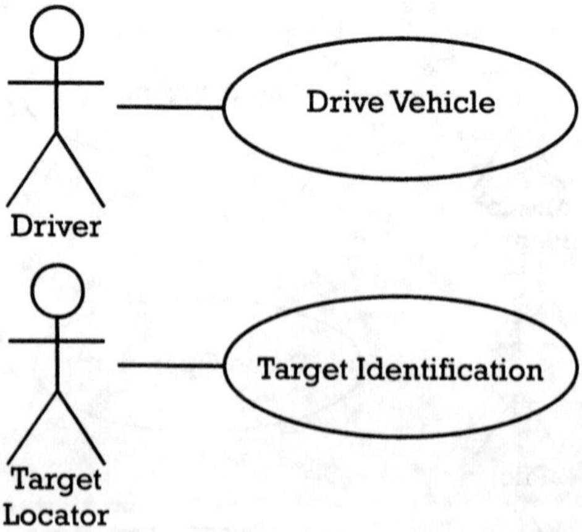

Figure 12.7 Reconnaissance use cases.

Use case: Mission Planning **Description:** The mission planner devises a route and associated speeds for the surveillance and reconnaissance aircraft. The routes are identified via a series of waypoints. The planner also must consider conditions of the flight such as air speed, fuel, clearance, and avoidance of obstacles. The mission planner also determines a variety of actions that are to take place at specified waypoints.
Use case: Vehicle Control **Description:** The pilot of the vehicle for the mission does not fly the aircraft. The aircraft is essentially autonomous. The pilot is responsible for initiating the mission, control of the observation payload, and in-flight retasking, that is, altering the mission for a particular purpose, and aborting the mission if it cannot be carried out. The pilot may decide to cause the aircraft to loiter at a particular location and redirect the IR camera or SAR payload to a particular location. The pilot may manually control the aircraft by pointing at a location on a map. The pilot may then invoke stare-point demand and initiate a loiter command to investigate a particular point on the ground further. Zoom controls may be used for closer observation. Instruments are also displayed to the operator to indicate the current status of the aircraft including fuel, speed, heading, electrical system status, and differential GPS operating mode. This information is displayed on a set of gauges on an instrument panel.
Use case: Information Relay **Description:** The pilot is also responsible for relaying information back to a command and control center. This information may be textual in nature notifying the location of a target, or that a path is clear, or may also be a still image captured on video.

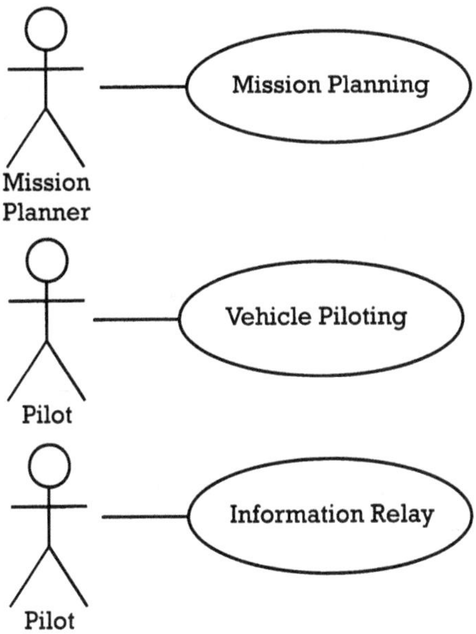

Figure 12.8 Tactical unmanned air vehicles use cases.

12.4.2 DM2: Product analysis model

Target drone analysis model

From the use cases for the target drone product we identify the analysis model shown in Figure 12.9.

Reconnaissance vehicle analysis model

From the use cases for the reconnaissance vehicle product we identify the analysis model shown in Figure 12.10.

Tactical unmanned aerial vehicle analysis model

From the use cases for the reconnaissance vehicle product we identify the analysis model shown in Figure 12.11.

12.4.3 DM3: Domain use case model

The mission planning use case for the target drone and for the TUAV share a high amount of commonality. To a large degree, they are quite similar. The main difference is that the TUAV mission planning use case is primarily an extension (Figure 12.12) of the target drone use case with some parametric variation (Figure 12.13).

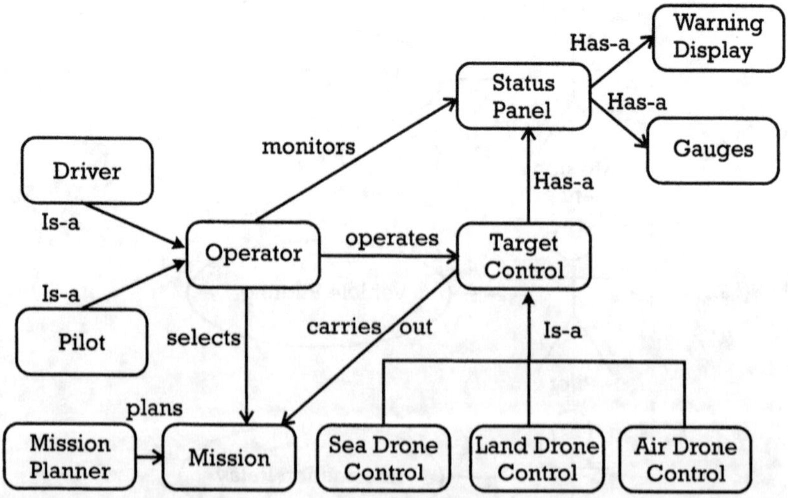

Figure 12.9 Target drone analysis model.

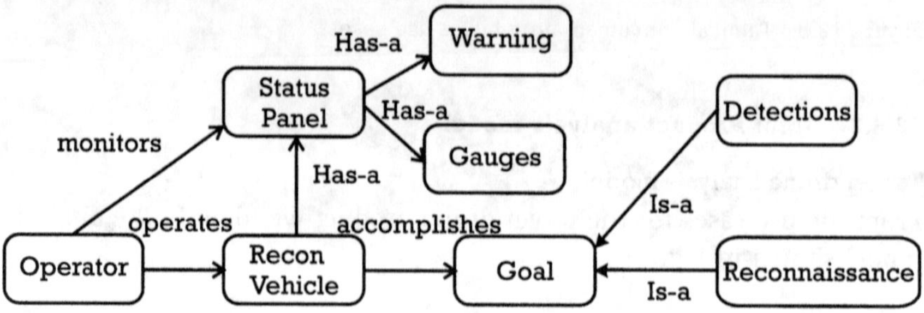

Figure 12.10 Reconnaissance vehicle analysis model.

The vehicle operation use case contains many similarities and many variations in the three target markets. Recall that within the target drone market there are the three types of target drones: air, land, and sea. The land and sea drones had the added functionality of live video, which is also found in the reconnaissance mine detection field, and the TUAV field. The commonality use case is modeled in Figure 12.14.

We can state a very general use case for vehicle operation:

> **Use case: Vehicle Operation**
>
> **Description:** The operator of the vehicle starts the vehicle and operates the vehicle to carry out a particular goal. The position and status of the vehicle are monitored.

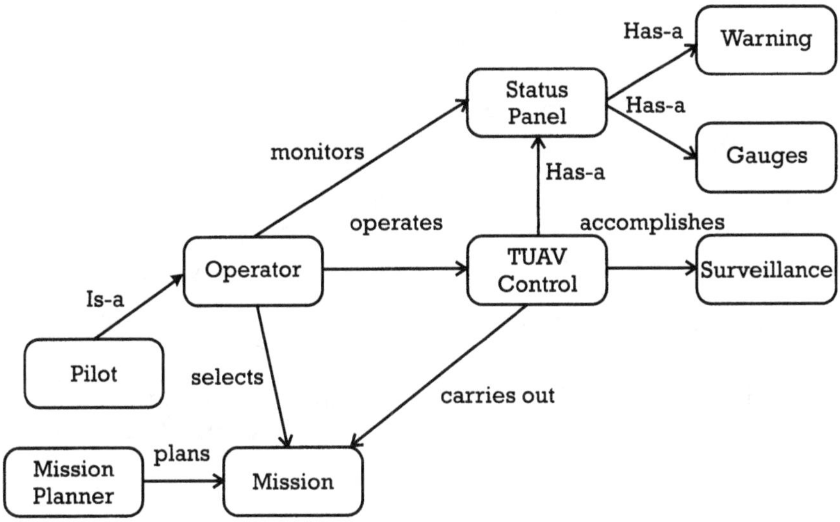

Figure 12.11 Tactical UAV analysis model.

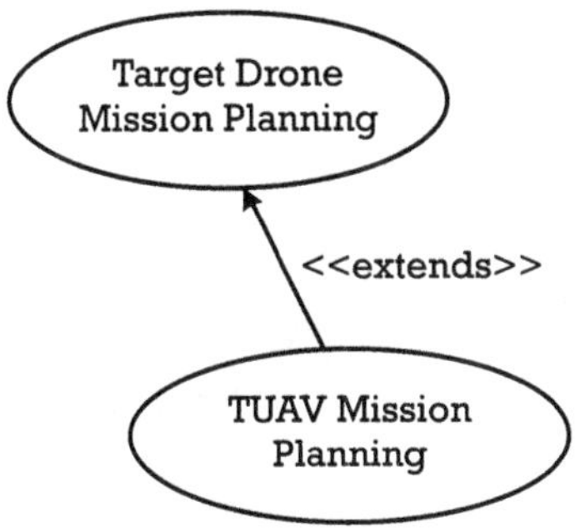

Figure 12.12 Relationship between target drone and TUAV mission planning.

12.4.4 DM4: Domain analysis model

The variations in the vehicle operation use case are many, as shown in Figure 12.15. In fact, every verb and noun in the general use case represent a variation.

12.4.5 DM5: Traces between use cases and analysis classes

For each use case identified in the domain modeling phase and each object in the analysis model, a cross-referenced table is composed that

Figure 12.13 Target drone mission planning as parameterization of TUAV mission planning.

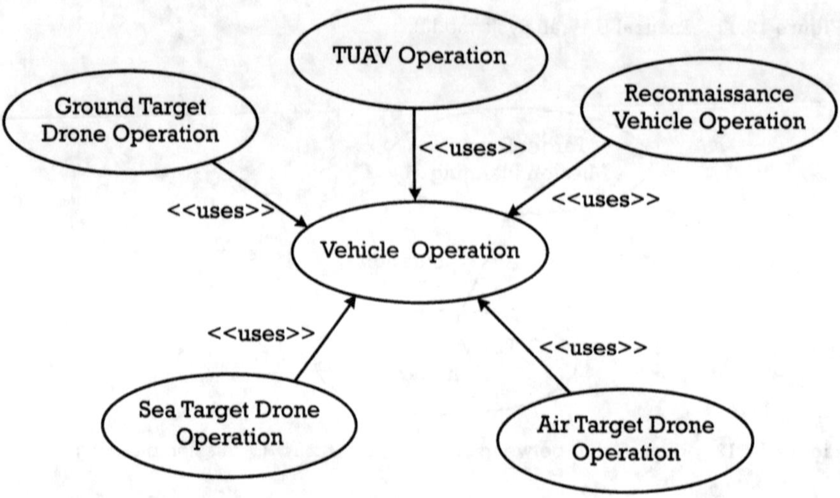

Figure 12.14 Domain use case.

identifies the components used in each of the use cases. This relationship is shown in Table 12.9.

12.4.6 Logging evolution for domain modeling

Table 12.10 summarizes the development efforts for this phase.

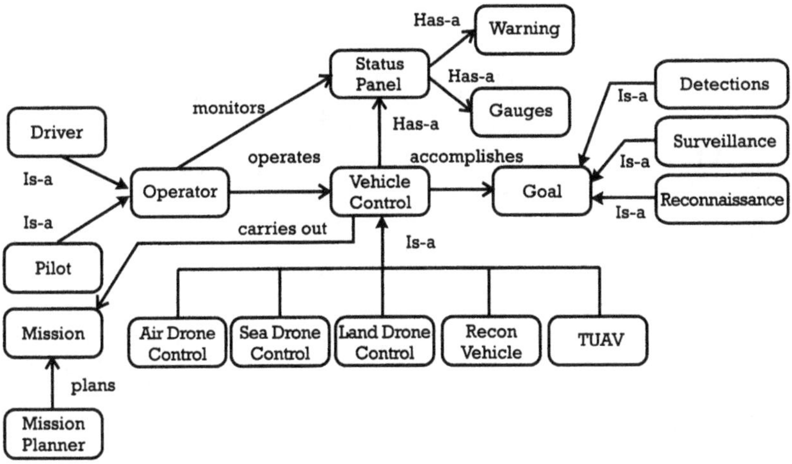

Figure 12.15 Domain analysis model.

Table 12.9
Use Case/Class Traces

	Driver	Pilot	Mission Planner	Operator	Mission	Status Panel	Warning Panel	Gauges
Drone mission planning	—	—	X	—	X	—	—	—
Drone operation	—	X	—	X	—	X	X	X
Drone mission playback	—	—	—	X	X	X	X	X
Recon vehicle operation	X	—	—	X	—	X	X	X
Recon vehicle target ID	—	—	—	X	—	—	X	—
TUAV mission planning	—	—	X	—	X	—	—	—
TUAV vehicle piloting	—	X	—	X	X	X	X	X
TUAV info relay	—	X	—	X	—	X	—	—

	Vehicle Control	Air Drone Control	Land Drone Control	Sea Drone Control	Recon Vehicle	TUAV
Drone mission planning	—	—	—	—	—	—
Drone operation	X	X	X	X	—	—
Drone mission playback	X	X	X	X	—	—
Recon vehicle operation	X	—	—	—	X	—
Recon vehicle target ID	X	—	—	—	X	—
TUAV mission planning	—	—	—	—	—	—
TUAV vehicle piloting	X	—	—	—	—	X
TUAV info relay	X	—	—	—	—	X

	Goal	Detection	Surveillance	Reconnaissance
Drone mission planning	—	—	—	—
Drone operation	—	—	—	—
Drone mission playback	—	—	—	—
Recon vehicle operation	X	X	—	X
Recon vehicle target ID	X	X	—	X
TUAV mission planning	—	—	—	—
TUAV vehicle piloting	X	X	X	—
TUAV info relay	X	X	X	—

Table 12.10
Evolution of Domain Modeling

Author	Date	Action	Effort
RLM	1998-04	Domain modeling analysis	17 hours

12.5 Domain framework development

12.5.1 DF1: Definition of the nature of the domain framework

The domain framework consists of VCS, a system of software components for the control of unmanned vehicles. A typical VCS configuration usually consists of (1) a map application, used for vehicle navigation; (2) a control application, used for status and control of the vehicles' systems; (3) a data link interpreter, used for the implementation of the vehicle-specific protocol; (4) a payload control application, used for monitoring the live video feed, camera control; (5) target identification; and (6) a mission planner, used for identification of waypoints that the vehicle is to safely fly.

The following sections present the details of the framework. The most relevant features include these two:

1. A client/server architecture. An application can serve the role of server, client, or both. A server application carries out requests on behalf of other processes, a client application makes the request, and an application performing both roles receives requests from clients that trigger requests to other servers.

2. Each new customization requires the development of a new data link interpreter to implement the vehicle's protocol, and a vehicle control/status panel to address the vehicle-specific behavior.

12.5.2 DF2: Architecture of the domain framework

The CDL functional architecture is basically divided into three layers as shown in Figure 12.16. At the lowest level are the operating system specific services. In general, we try to isolate the interface to the operating system from CDL applications as much as possible to increase portability. Slightly above the operating system is the X-Windows GUI software. There is very little interface to X-Windows. Most of the GUI interface is achieved through a third-party software library. This library is relied upon heavily and their lack of support for the NT platform is the prime barrier to CDL from moving into the NT market. CDL VCS applications

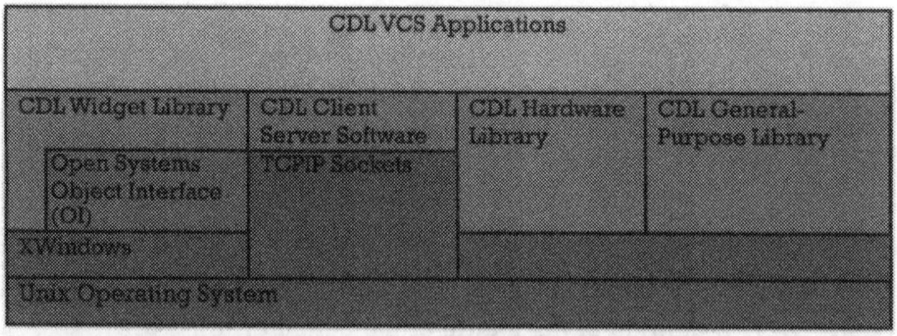

Figure 12.16 Component layers within the VCS system.

rely heavily upon the client/server model. CDL has developed Client and Server classes, which provide the backbone for IPC between CDL VCS applications.

Additional domain-specific software includes a widget library containing graphical objects primarily for user interaction and vehicle control and a CDL hardware support library containing objects used to interact with various hardware devices. This library includes an interface object for joystick interfaces, programmable button interfaces, VCR transport mechanism control, audio output, video-overlay control units, and video graphic cards (with JPEG extensions).

The general-purpose library is less domain specific and contains a variety of general-purpose objects such as lists, arrays, hash tables, and callback mechanisms. The VCS applications are client/server components that may be very "contract" specific, that is, they apply specifically to a single contract, or they may have a more versatile nature that can be reapplied to a number of contracts. Examples of general-purpose applications are VCS Map, VCR Control, Data Playback, VCS Control, VideoOverlay, WarningPanel, and ScrollingDisplay. Contract-specific applications almost always include a vehicle-specific data link interpreter and may include specific vehicle controls.

General-purpose package

The general-purpose package contains classes of a general-purpose nature that may be used in the development of components within the domain. This package consists of three subpackages: containers, numerics, and navigation. Container classes consist of classes used to hold a number of objects. These may be of a specific type, as in the case of

IntArray (an expandable array of integers), or more generic as in the case of ObjList (a list of objects of arbitrary type). The numerics package contains classes that perform mathematical operations. Because unmanned vehicle navigation requires a great amount of coordinate transformations, this package primarily deals with providing this support. The navigation package extends the numeric package one step further by addressing aspects of navigation such as waypoints and missions.

System package

The system package contains classes that deal with interfaces to the operating system or interfaces to other hardware. This package contains two subpackages, hardware and operating system interface (OS). The hardware package contains interface classes for joysticks, programmable buttons, VCRs, and serial ports. The OS package deals with OS-related classes concerned with interprocess communication and time.

Widget package

The widget package consists of classes that have a GUI aspect about them. Typical examples are gauges and user input widgets.

Application package

The application package contains large-scale classes that represent complete applications in their own right. These are used to develop an application suite used to control an unmanned vehicle.

12.5.3 DF3: Documentation of components in the domain framework

General package

Table 12.11 provides a brief description of the classes within the general package.

System package

Table 12.12 provides a brief description of the classes within the system package.

Widget package

Table 12.13 provides a brief description of the classes within the widget package. Figures 12.17 through 12.24 illustrate the contents of the various packages.

Table 12.11
Classes Within the General Package

ObjList	The ObjList is a general-purpose container object used to hold a list of objects of arbitrary type.
ObjArray	The ObjArray is a general-purpose container object used to hold a number of objects. The objects may be retrieved via an index. ObjArray will grow dynamically to hold an arbitrary number of objects.
HashTable	HashTable is a general-purpose container object used to hold a number of objects. The objects can be retrieved relatively rapidly by hashing on a key.
IntArray	The IntArray is a container object specifically designed for holding integers. The need for a dynamically growable array for integers is such a common occurrence that a class was implemented for this special purpose.
String	String is a container object specifically designed for holding characters and forming character strings. The need for a dynamically growable array for characters is such a common occurrence that a class was implemented for this special purpose. In addition, special concatenation and search operations are provided.
DblArray	The DblArray is a container object specifically designed for holding doubles. The need for a dynamically growable array for doubles is such a common occurrence that a class was implemented for this special purpose.
Angle	An angle object in many respects is similar to a double. However, valid values for angle objects range from –PI to +PI. Consequently, care must be taken when finding the difference between two angles or interpolating between angles. This class handles these types of common programming errors.
Orientation	Contains three angles representing the orientation of the vehicle, that is, the roll, pitch, and yaw.
IPoint2d	Integer-based two-dimensional point.
Point2d	Double-based two-dimensional point.
Rectangle	Integer-based rectangle, often used to manipulate images.
Point3d	Double-based three-dimensional point.
Rotation	3×3 rotation matrix optimized for vehicle roll/pitch/yaw calculations.

Table 12.11 (continued)

Transformation Rotation followed by a translation. Used to move Point3d from one coordinate system to another.
Image Two-dimensional array of image data.
JPEGImage JPEG compressed image data.
UncompressedImage Uncompressed image data.
UTMCoordinate Earth coordinate based on Universal Transverse Mercator Projection.
NavSolution Dynamic information about a vehicle at a point in time including its position, orientation (roll, pitch, yaw), velocity, and rotational velocity.
Histogram Number of bins representing the frequency of occurrence of some event, that is, a histogram.
WayPoint A particular destination of a vehicle given by a UTM coordinate, and an action to carry out at that position.
Task A sequence of WayPoints specifying the path of a vehicle.
Mission A sequence of Tasks to be carried out by a vehicle.

Table 12.12
Classes Within the System Package

Server A class used to carry out service on behalf of clients. The server class receives messages from clients via sockets and performs a function in response to the message. The response is a variation point handled in Server subclasses via virtual functions.
Client A class requesting a service from a server application through the sending of messages.
DualLinkServer A special kind of server class that can send messages to client applications asynchronously without the client having initiated a request.

Table 12.12 (continued)

DualLinkClient
A special kind of client class that can receive asynchronous message applications. Used in conjunction with DualLinkServer classes to respond to asynchronous events, such as serial communications from a vehicle.
DLI
The component primarily responsible for translating between VCS format and vehicle-specific format.
Button
A class that interfaces to a hardware button object. The button can have a downloaded bitmap associated with it. The button may also have multiple states and associated bitmaps for each state.
ButtonBox
A class that conveniently manages a number of buttons.
Joystick
A class providing a hardware interface to a two-dimensional joystick.
VCR
An abstract class providing transport mechanism control for a VCR.
Sony
A class providing transport mechanism control for a Sony VCR.
Panasonic
A class providing transport mechanism control for a Panasonic VCR.

Table 12.13
Classes Within the Widget Package

Gauge
An abstract class responsible for displaying a numeric value in some manner.
NumericGauge
A class that represents a value of some parameter as bar graph value.
TextGauge
A class that represents a value of some parameter in a textual format.
CircularGauge
A class that represents a value of some parameter in a circular gauge format.
HeadingGauge
A class specifically designed to show a vehicle's heading.
Slider
An interactive class that allows a user to specify a value for a particular parameter.
DrawBox
A class that allows graphic objects (rectangle, arcs, lines, etc.) to be drawn into it in various colors.

Table 12.13 (continued)

VideoBox A class designed to display a video image within a rectangular box.
ScrollBox A box that displays text from top to bottom, then scrolls text off the top. Can work in reverse, and also has a scrollbar allowing a user to scroll back through the text.
Transmission Similar to the transmission on a car, Park, Drive, Reverse, etc. Allows the transmission of the vehicle to be controlled.
TimedTest A convenience widget that provides a countdown while some test is being carried out. Convenient for things like calibration and built-in vehicle tests.
Map A digitized representation of a map and associated elevation information.
MapDisplay A box in which a map can be displayed.

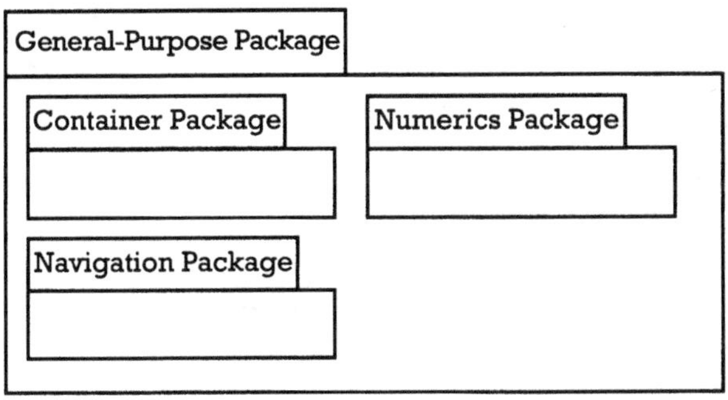

Figure 12.17 General-purpose package.

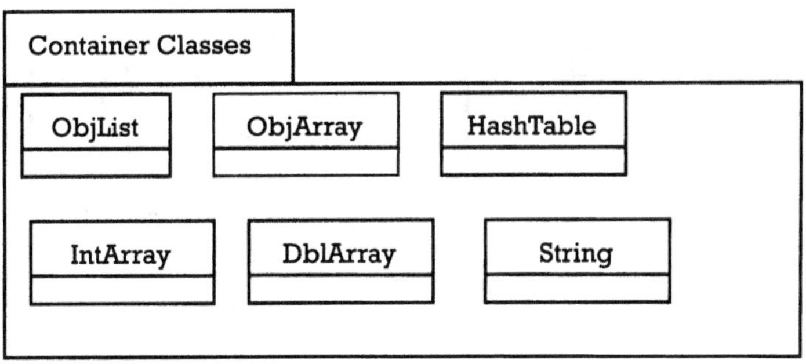

Figure 12.18 Container package.

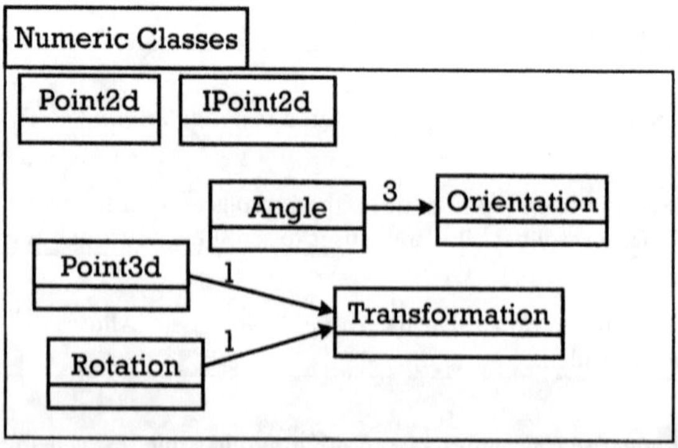

Figure 12.19 Numeric package.

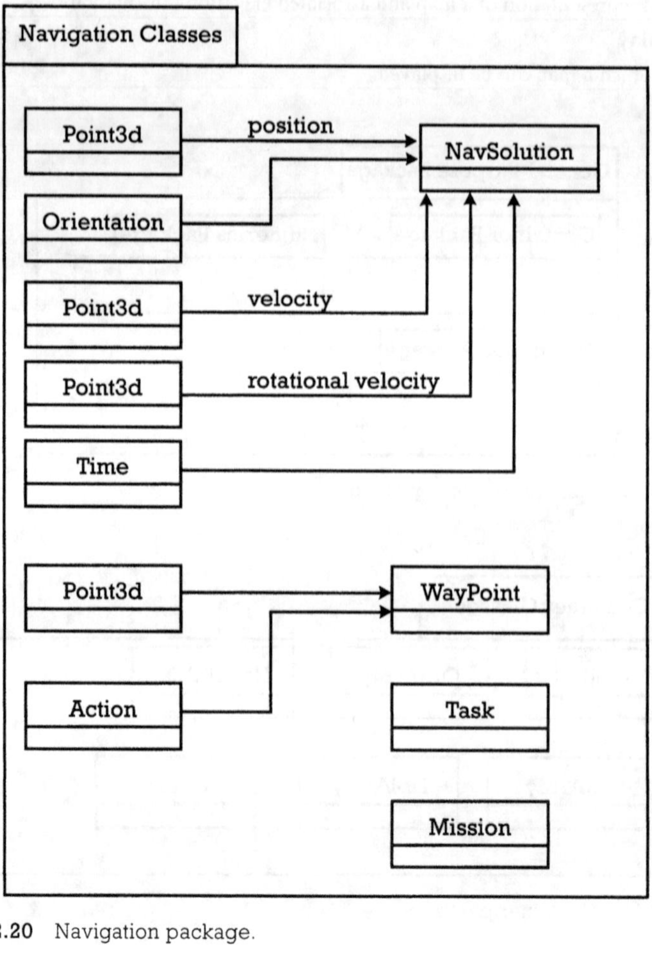

Figure 12.20 Navigation package.

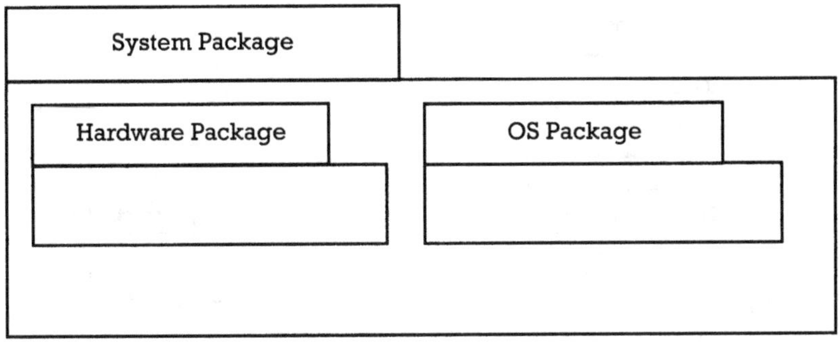

Figure 12.21 System package.

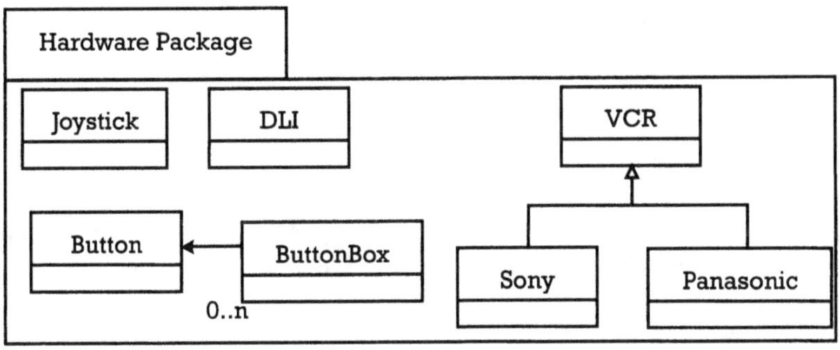

Figure 12.22 Hardware package.

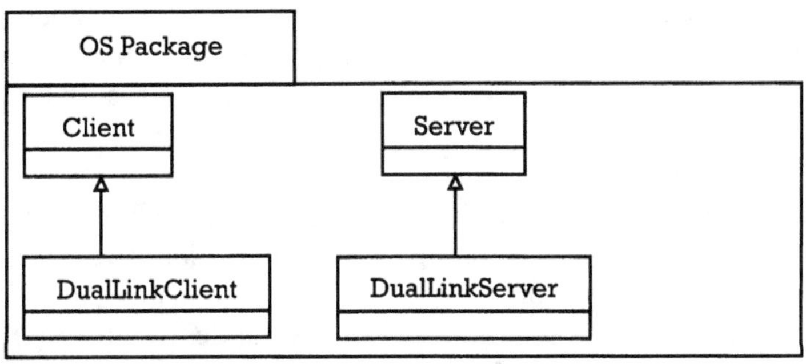

Figure 12.23 OS package.

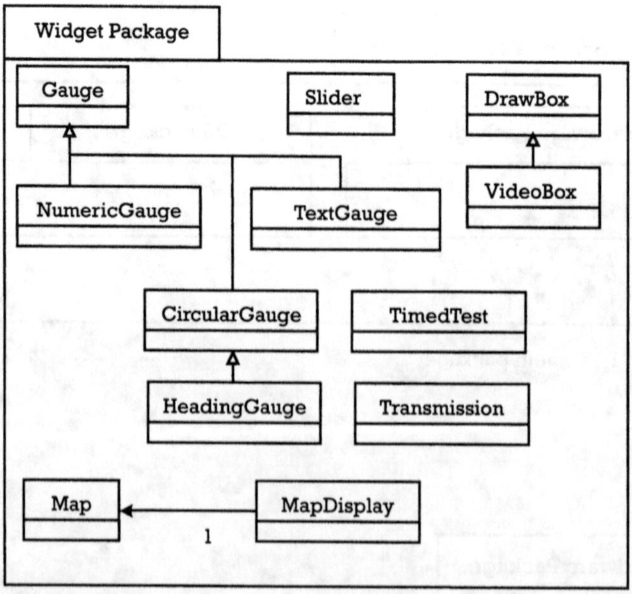

Figure 12.24 Widget package.

Applications components

Table 12.14 provides a description of the application components used in developing a VCS suite for a particular vehicle and Figure 12.25 shows the package.

12.5.4 DF4: Browsable and searchable catalog of components in the domain framework

Currently, the only "catalog" available is that used by our configuration management system. In this system, a hierarchy of "folders" is maintained, with each folder containing a number of files. By limiting one class per file, and naming each file the same as the class contained within it, a browsable hierarchy is achieved. In this manner, the files can be grouped, creating the equivalence of a package within the folder.

Final perspective

The Sherlock domain analysis methodology provides additional insight in developing both a better marketing strategy and a software engineering philosophy that focuses on the domain. In a company that survives through the contract award process, it is easy to develop a very narrow viewpoint focusing only on the contract at hand rather than considering

Table 12.14
Application Components Used in VCS Suite

Component	Description
VCSMap	Displays a map and allows a user to interact with it. Positions may be selected and referenced as latitude and longitude.
DataPlayback	Data from a mission is recorded and can be played back in a postmission analysis. Similar to the "black box" often referred to in aircraft crashes. Data may also be synchronized to recorded video.
VideoOverlay	An application in which shapes can be drawn as an overlay onto a video image. Useful for identifying targets and for displaying information in a heads-up display-like manner.
WarningPanel	A server application that runs allowing warning and alarm messages to be displayed to the operator.
ScrollingDisplay	A display that takes rows of data and displays them as an intensity image. As new rows of data are added, lower ones are scrolled off the screen.
VCRServer	Server application responsible for controlling a VCR. Clients can connect to the VCRServer and initiate video recording, playback, and other transport mechanism controls.
MissionPlanner	A non-real-time tool used as an aid in planning missions for vehicles.
BullnoseServer	A server application that allows clients to obtain button and joystick information.
ClockServer	A server application providing timing information and wake-up alarms to clients.
VehicleHistoryServer	A server application that maintains the location history of a vehicle such that other applications may query the position/orientation of the vehicle a short time ago.

the larger domain. It is usually easier and faster to develop software for the short term, addressing only the immediate requirements of the current contract.

Indeed, it has been the author's experience that many respectable software development corporations that do business through the contract award process employ minimal or nonexisting reuse strategies. Each contract award is very nearly a "from scratch" development process. CDL Systems maintains the philosophy that our clients are purchasing a

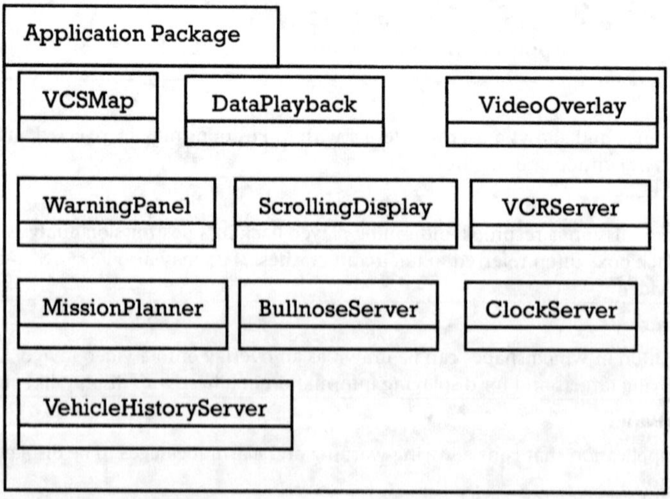

Figure 12.25 Application package.

highly customizable adaptable product rather than a team of software developers to address a particular need.

In Sherlock, the process of searching for different products and markets through the use of variation points fits in amazingly well with this type of approach. When considering a bid on a new contract, we "scope" our current domain to determine the level of effort required to fulfill the requirements of the contract under consideration. If the level of effort is sufficiently low (implying that the level of software reuse is high), there is a higher probability of a successful bid.

CHAPTER

13

Contents

Conclusions

Now, at the conclusion of this book, we would like to discuss our past and current experiences with Sherlock. We start with the motivations and some history behind the development of Sherlock.

Our first motivation for developing a DA&E methodology was to exploit reuse in our software projects. The projects were either our own projects or projects of our industrial partners. We were not aiming at building everything from scratch and then reusing it. We were more concerned about reusing what was already available in terms of ideas, experience, code, and documentation. Before reusing any asset, we needed to find all the information regarding it. Moreover, we needed to solve the problem of putting together software coming from different sources. What we were doing closely resembled the activities of domain definition and of domain framework development. More specifically, we were gathering and classifying information, as in domain definition, and we were struggling with the problems of architectural matching that derive from the construction of systems through composition, as in domain framework development.

In the meantime, we were considering the market aspects of software production. We were studying what determines the success of some products and the demise of others. This topic was interesting because many firms build systems using third-party products as building blocks, which is a form of reuse. Users of reusable software do not want to base their reuse practice on software that fails in the market. So, it was crucial to know what building blocks, among the many available, were going to be successful. Like many users, we were also surprised that some technically good products were not experiencing the success they deserved. A product that fails in the market gives very poor expectations of evolution and support to its users.

An answer to these concerns came from the study of network externalities, bandwagon, subsidization, standardization, and the other phenomena discussed in domain characterization. These effects were clearly visible in many markets, like those of DVD products, cell phones, and so on. The answer was that there is an external value of products that is as important as the internal value. So, the concept of "technically good" was only one side of the coin and thus unable to explain every case of product success.

Network externalities were an interesting subject. Oversimplifying, network externalities state that strong networks get stronger and weak networks get weaker. In the software industry this was evident. However, all discussions of network externalities that we found in the literature were focused on technologies, rather than on products. So, we were able, for instance, to understand why the Internet technology was booming, but we had little explanation of why a specific Internet tool was flourishing, and we had almost no guidance about how to build from scratch a successful product based in the Internet technology. Deeper analysis led to a definition of network externalities in terms of products and to the understanding of compatibility elements, the real key to network externalities in the software market. All of these concepts were summarized in domain characterization.

Domain scoping and domain modeling came almost together. Domain modeling, with different names, already existed in previous DA&E methodologies. The state of the art in domain modeling was quite advanced, due to existing industrial and academic experiences with modeling of large systems. Moreover, FODA was an example that domain modeling was practically possible in large, complex cases. Despite this, domain modeling was still not satisfactory in terms of how it handled variability. There was a tendency to focus on commonality and classification of features. What was missing was a satisfactory management of the differences: a product's most relevant features are those that make it different from the other products in the domain. Domain scoping and its variability space meet these needs and represent the overcoming of domain modeling's problems.

The conceptual division of the phases was also an issue. The identification of domain definition and of domain framework development is pretty natural. However, the distinction between characterization, scoping, and modeling is not trivial linguistically, let alone methodologically. Existing literature does not help because it provides too many discrepant definitions. While definitions are not the ultimate goal of Sherlock, a sound division in phases—or workpackages—is a prerequisite for any DA&E project. At the end we came up with the following division: Domain characterization deals with the market aspects, domain modeling deals with the technical aspects, and domain scoping works as the variability central.

13.1 More and better products?

We are often asked to explain, in a few words, what benefits can be expected from DA&E. The short answer is "more and better products." Clearly, four words cannot explain a methodology. To understand what "more" means, one would have to read the domain scoping chapter and all the discussions about variability and product lines. To understand what "better" means, one would have to understand first how we define the value of products in the domain characterization chapter. However, the short answer sets the right scope for the benefits of DA&E: products. If something about products does not happen, then DA&E is not successful.

If the short answer is not enough, the following is a list of benefits that our DA&E practitioners and we have achieved through DA&E:

- You realize that your products are an extremely important asset.
- You realize that you should consider your portfolio of products more carefully.
- You have an idea for a new product.

- You have an idea for an improvement of an old product.
- You realize that competitors are using the installed bases of their products against your products.
- You license technology for free to improve its adoption.
- You realize that your customers have difficulties assembling systems from your products.
- You decide that two products of yours should share more compatibility between them.
- You realize that making your products compatible with some competitor's product can be profitable.
- You realize that you are not tracking past versions of products properly.
- You realize that changing a product is difficult because variability was not designed up front.
- You discover many new variants that can be useful in the future.
- You decide to make an organic development plan for your product line.
- You realize that a common part can be factorized from two or more products.
- You evaluate more carefully the compatibility and the future perspectives of the reusable components you buy.
- You decide to produce reusable components.

We hope the readers will add their own achievements to this list.

13.2 Managers and developers get along well

Sherlock is neither only for managers nor only for developers. It is for both, although clearly managers and developers can have different perspectives. The unifying factor is the way in which variability is managed.

All issues regarding variability are treated in Sherlock in the same way. The same tool—namely, variation points—deals, for example, with the variability in the market and with the variability in software code. Of course, Sherlock does not manage variability as one single thing at all times; this would be impractical and contradictory with the effort to break down big problems into small ones. However, if there is a chance that two variation points, no matter how conceptually different, are related, then Sherlock makes the relationship evident.

We can think of variation points that pertain to managers only and variation points that pertain to developers only. However, the practice shows that there is a multitude of variation points that pertain to both. Sherlock spots them and requires both managers and developers to deal with them. As a matter of fact, many variation points have an impact, at the same time, on the market, on compatibility, on the development cost, on the product performance, and on reuse.

"We develop multiple products: variability is a major concern" has been the common motivation for many managers and developers to begin the DA&E process. Through Sherlock, those managers and developers have found a way to best integrate their competencies.

13.3 Sherlock at work

Our first applications of Sherlock were proofs of concepts. Existing literature and some reports of DA&E applications were available at that time. This was enough to start a DA&E experiment. However, there was little evidence that this could work for us too. The most critical issues that needed validation were the following:

- Variability is the core issue of a domain. Conceptually this is trivial. Practically this can be extremely hard to handle. Variation points and the variability space appeared as the right tool to approach the problem. Yet, the large number of variation points—almost 100 in some cases—created a problem of some complexity. Our first approach was to cut the number of variation points, eliminating those that were "not important." This led to keeping purposely only the half-dozen variation points that expressed the positioning of the products in the market. The approach seemed good because these variation points typically represent high-level aspects of variability. However, the approach failed because it overlooked the technical variation points, which oftentimes determine the critical characteristics of products. Moreover, the approach provided little input to the phase of domain framework development. Our second approach, which is the one presented in the book, was to keep all the variation points and to address the complexity problem through the use of projections. Practically this approach works, producing analyses that are complex but still usable and useful.

- Differences are as important as commonalities. Commonalities produce good abstract taxonomies of features. Taxonomies can be simple, clear, and understandable. Differences are usually much more complex and volatile. But without differences, real products become secondary. Differences are essential, especially when new products are designed.
- Market forces are as important as the technical qualities. Without this consideration it is impossible to explain why some products win or fail despite their technical qualities.
- Frameworks are powerful for reuse. Many software products start as stand-alone applications to solve the needs of specific situations. Then, as their applicability broadens to other situations and becomes consolidated, they move to the role of "infrastructure" software. This infrastructure software is usually in the form of a framework on which new applications can rely.

We check our progress in DA&E projects against this list. The better able we are to tackle these problems, the better the results of DA&E. The reader can use it to make a self-assessment of his or her DA&E practices.

When the DA&E projects became less exploratory and more established, we faced the problem of making Sherlock a process. This again comes to the issue of defining—or standardizing—the five phases. Sherlock's phases are sequenced as a preparatory phase (domain definition), an iterative core (domain characterization, domain scoping, and domain modeling), and a finalizing phase (domain framework development). In our experience, this order is usually respected. However, in most DA&E projects the whole set of five phases is iterated twice. The first iteration runs quickly through the phases and produces a first draft of the deliverables.

In the first iteration, only domain definition is performed thoroughly, identifying the exact borders of the domain, specifying the scope of the project, finding all useful sources of information, and performing the feasibility analysis. The second iteration performs the phases more systematically and generates an almost stable version of the deliverables. After the two iterations, DA&E enters a "maintenance" phase, in which the decisions made are enacted while changes in the domain are analyzed and reflected in the deliverables.

This kind of two-iteration approach has emerged in many applications of Sherlock. The conclusions of the WaveRider case study have given an explanation under a project management perspective: The first iteration involves a core group of DA&E practitioners of the firm, who plan the activities of DA&E and determine the expected benefits; the second iteration makes DA&E permeate the firm's development process and, generally, involves all the firm's employees. The two-iteration approach happens to be the basis of many personal DA&E practices, too.

At the time of this writing, Sherlock was running in several projects at software firms and several projects had been completed. Among the running ones, one is in the domain of information systems for nursing homes, another is in the domain of banking systems. From different perspectives, these two projects are challenging: The former domain is a recent market, the latter domain is a quite old, though quickly moving, market. The application of Sherlock in these domains will (1) highlight market opportunities, niches, and strategies; and (2) maximize the effectiveness of the software reuse investments undertaken by the DA&E practitioners.

Among the completed projects, there is a DA&E project on graphical user interfaces for public administration systems. Other applications of Sherlock have recently started to exploit DA&E in the domain of small and medium-sized enterprise information systems and in the domain of biomedical information systems.

APPENDIX

A

Contents

UML basics

Software engineering often requires knowledge to be formalized. Formal languages such as Z, Larch, and SDL serve such a purpose. However, software engineers often find them hard to understand and to use. A very common and attractive approach is to use graphic languages, that is, languages based on graphical notations. To be effective in software development, a graphic language should be usable throughout the entire development cycle. This means that the notation should be able to formalize requirements, design, and implementation.

In addition, the diverse nature of software development requires both flexibility and standardization. Flexibility ensures that a potentially infinite number of different situations can be handled. Standardization ensures that flexibility does not become chaos and that there is always a uniquely identifiable meaning for each construct.

The Unified Modeling Language (UML) fulfills all of these requirements [1]. UML is a graphic language for the description of systems, with a specific focus on software systems. UML is flexible in that it provides extension mechanisms for adapting itself to a wide range of circumstances. UML is standardized in that a core of concepts allows a UML expert to understand any situation, including those resulting from extensions.

UML is based on object orientation (see the Rational Web site and UML documentation). UML shares many commonalities with other object-oriented techniques, such as OMT [2], Booch's methodology [3], and OOSE [4].

As mentioned, UML is best suited to describe software systems, even though applications in other areas exist, such as Business Process Modeling [5]. UML is applicable also to DA&E, which is a particular approach to software development.

In Appendix A we demonstrate how Sherlock uses UML. In particular, we focus on the following usage of UML:

- *To characterize the domain:* UML's static structure diagrams describe the market situation, highlighting the products, the compatibility formats, the compatibility relations between the products, the converters, and the market segments.
- *To model the domain:* UML's static structure diagrams and use case diagrams formalize the products in the domain and their behaviors.
- *To develop the domain framework:* UML's package structures, static structure diagrams, and sequence diagrams support the design and implementation of the domain framework.

With these purposes in mind, the following sections briefly introduce the portions of UML used in Sherlock. More specifically, they discuss the structure of UML models, the organization of information in packages, and the diagram types used in the book.

A.1 Graphs and text

UML assumes that information can be represented as graphs of nodes connected through edges (Figure A.1). The meaning of the graphs can vary and depends on two factors, as discussed next.

First, the identity of the nodes and of the edges is important. The identity specifies to which physical or conceptual entity in the real world the nodes or the edges refer. The creator of the graph determines the

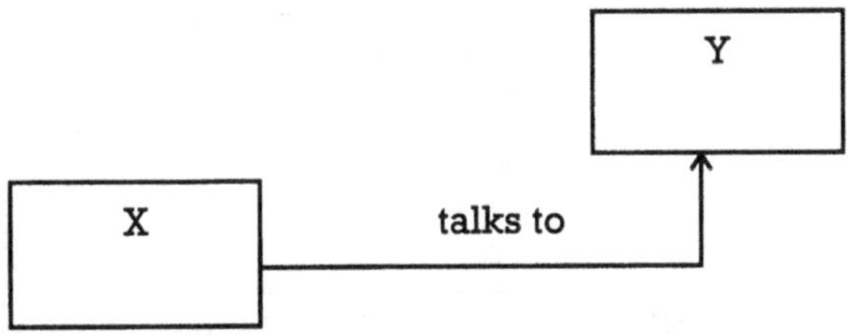

Figure A.1 Simple graph in UML.

identity. For example, the creator of a model may declare that a node named "Document" represents the category of electronic documents. Edges represent associations between nodes. Edges also have a direction, represented as an arrow, to show the direction of the association. For instance, if an edge represents a transitive verb, the direction tells which of the connected nodes is the subject and which is the object of the verb.

Second, also important is the diagram type to which the graph belongs. UML has several diagram types, each with a specific purpose: representing static relations, dynamic interactions, and so on. UML specifies how to interpret the meaning of each diagram type, that is, its semantics.

Textual information integrates the graphical notation. Text is a powerful and flexible tool because almost anything can be described through text. In natural languages, only grammatical rules put constraints on text. In UML, semantic rules frame text within the graphical notation. This structures text and makes it more readable and easier to retrieve and maintain.

A.2 Layers of models in UML

UML uses a four-layer scheme to represent the target system (Figure A.2). As mentioned, the target system can be anything, ranging from a software system to a business process. For the purposes of Sherlock, the domain is a system. Each layer contains information on the system at a different level of abstraction. The upper layers are the most abstract while the lower layers are the least abstract. Four layers may seem to provide an overcomplicated approach, but the four layers are the result of a deep analysis of the abstraction mechanisms and are actually needed to allow UML to model the diverse, complex situations of reality.

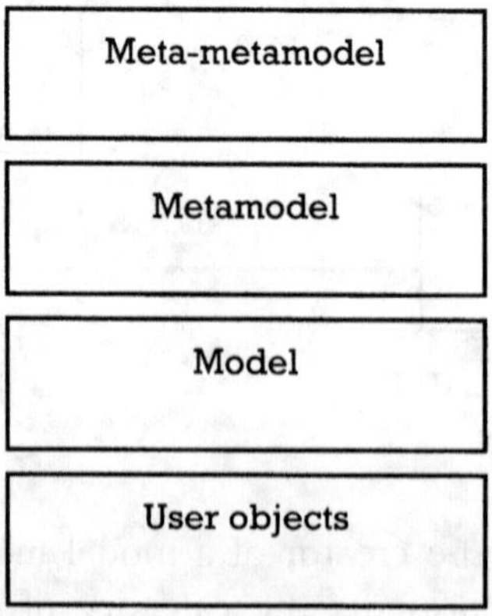

Figure A.2 The four layers of modeling in UML.

The lowest layer is the layer of user objects. User objects are concrete objects that live in a real—although not necessarily physical—world and that can be identified at a specific instant of time. "John Smith" and "the pen on my desk" are examples of user objects.

The layer on top of the user object layer is the model layer. A model contains classes of user objects. For instance, "person" and "pen" are adequate classes for the user objects considered before. A model is an abstraction of reality; it can state sentences like "there can be people," "there can be pens," or "a person is characterized by a date of birth." Models define the general shape of the reality without considering any specific configuration of reality.

The layer on top of the model layer is the metamodel layer. A metamodel defines the "classes of modeling." Without a metamodel, models would have no rule and could represent anything with no constraints. A metamodel shapes the models and binds them to a specific area of reality. Metamodels are the main extension mechanism of UML. Given an area of reality to model, we would first define a metamodel to focus our interest on that area, then we would find the classes (at model level) and the objects (at user object level) that fit our needs. An accessory task of a metamodel is to specify the graphical presentation of the elements in the model and user object layers.

The top layer is the meta-metamodeling layer. The meta-metamodel defines the whole structure of UML. The meta-metamodel is a small core of rules that show how metamodels can be defined. The meta-metamodel is the most abstract specification.

The meta-metamodel alone would be sufficient to define, implicitly, everything that can be done in UML. However, UML also has a default metamodel that makes UML adequate for modeling software systems. This means that, by default, UML focuses on software systems. There are extensions of UML—such as the UML extension for Business Process Modeling [5]—that focus on other areas of reality.

A.3 Packages

UML uses packages to organize the information in a hierarchy. The hierarchy is single rooted, with the package marked "system" being the root (Figure A.3).

The package hierarchy cannot represent the complex mechanisms and relations between the elements contained in the packages. However, it is flexible enough to handle the most common situations, such as the division of work into workpackages that are assigned to different working groups. Moreover, the package structure is adopted and supported in some programming languages including Ada and Java.

Once the package structure is in place, the elements in the packages can refer to each other. These relations do not have any package boundaries, that is, an element in package A can refer to an element in a

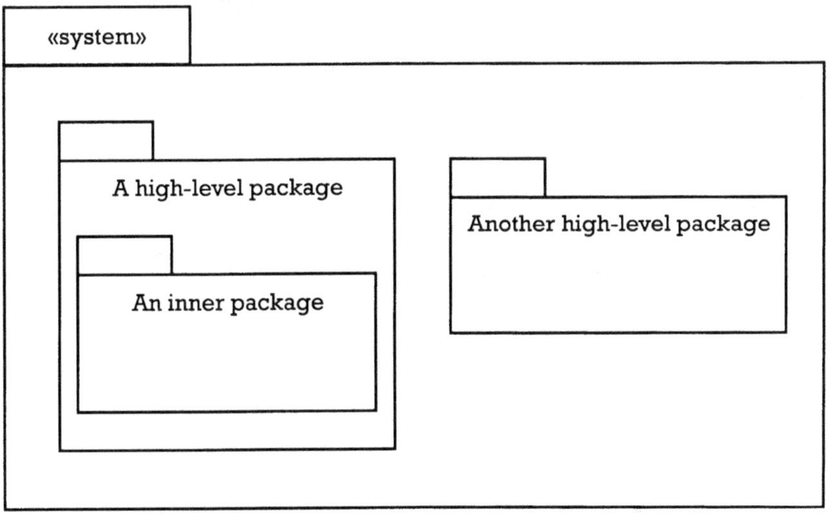

Figure A.3 A sample package structure.

different package B. In this case, however, package A "depends on" package B, and UML requires us to point out this relationship explicitly (Figure A.4).

A.4 Diagrams

A diagram is a graphical representation of a piece of information. The model is the repository of the information.

Diagrams are partial views of the model that make the model usable by people. Partial views are important because they reduce the complexity and the density of information in a diagram. Partial views are usually focused on a particular aspect or perspective of the model. The full collection of the diagrams gives the global view of the model.

In a diagram, some information can be invisible to a general examination, but can become visible if specifically required. Automatic software tools are a key factor to making partial views practical and efficient.

UML has several predefined diagrams: static structure diagrams, use case diagrams, sequence diagrams, collaboration diagrams, state chart diagrams, activity diagrams, and implementation diagrams. This set of diagrams is pretty extensive and can handle the majority of modeling requirements. The information some diagrams represent is overlapping. For instance, given a sequence diagram, a collaboration diagram can be obtained from it. In a context of software production, UML's diagrams serve effectively all the phases of a software life cycle.

The diagrams that are used in this book are the following: static structure diagrams, use case diagrams, and sequence diagrams. The following subsections give a brief overview of them.

A.4.1 Static structure diagrams

Static structure diagrams represent model elements without considering time. These diagrams can represent the following:

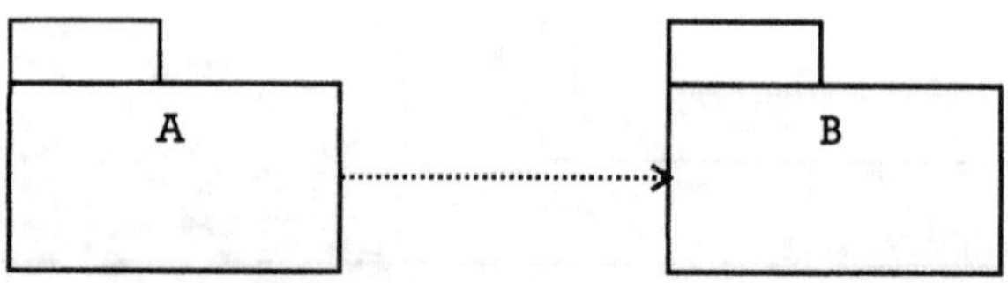

Figure A.4 Dependency relationship between packages.

- *Permanent, structural information:* The time variable is not present because the information exists regardless of time. Usually this is the case of diagrams in the model and metamodel layer (Figure A.5).
- *Snapshots:* Time is frozen at a given instant and the situation at that instant is depicted. Usually this is the case of diagrams in the user object layer (Figure A.6).

The representation of classes and objects is similar. The main difference is how they are uniquely identified. A class has a class name. An object is identified through a pair formed by the object name and the class name separated by a colon; usually the pair is underlined. The complete pair identifies one specific, well-defined object. Sometimes we only need to say that there is an object of a given class but we are not interested in the exact identity of the object. In this case we give the object no name and mention only its class. These objects are called *anonymous.* Figure A.6 showed an example of anonymous objects: the object identified as ":Pen."

A.4.2 Use case diagrams

Use cases are descriptions of the functionalities of a system. Use case diagrams contain two kinds of element: use cases and actors. An actor is an

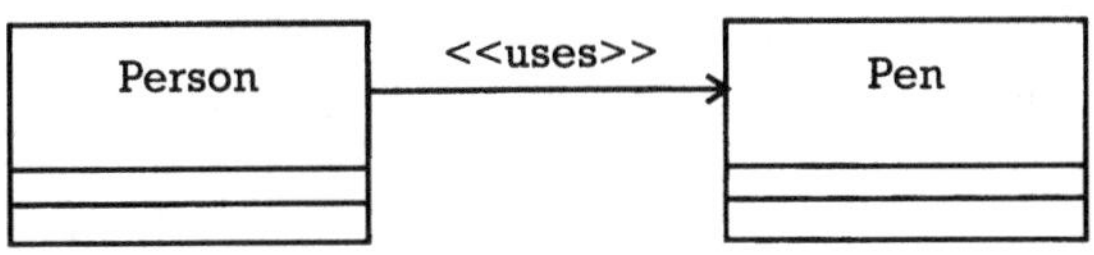

Figure A.5 Class diagram.

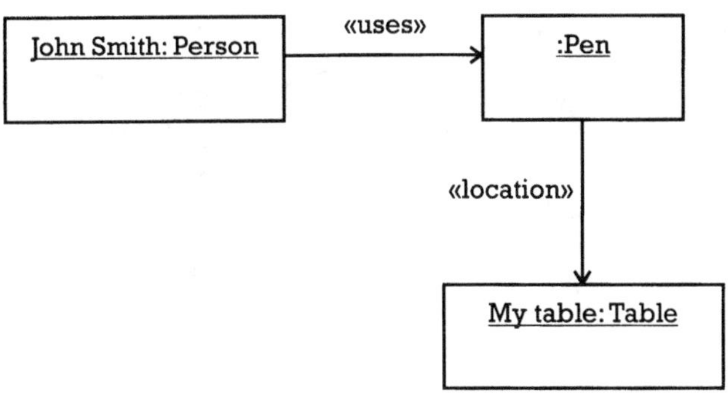

Figure A.6 Object diagram.

element that interacts with the system in a given "case of use" of the system. Typical actors are users, clients, and providers. Consequently, use cases describe a case of use of the system from the perspective of the actors.

Figure A.7 presents a use case diagram with two use cases (Access to database and Database administration) and two actors (User and Database Administrator). Note that one of the use cases "uses"—that is, exploits—the functionality of the other use case.

Each use case should have an associated textual description. This description shows how the actors interact with the use case and what is done during the interaction. Use case diagrams are a convenient way to express functionality:

- They consider functionalities from the real users' perspectives and express these functionalities in a format understandable to and verifiable by the real users.
- The description focuses on the functionalities and ignores the implementation details.

Sherlock's domain modeling uses use case diagrams extensively.

A.4.3 Sequence diagrams

Sequence diagrams represent interactions between objects taking time into account. Objects are usually arranged in a horizontal line. Objects

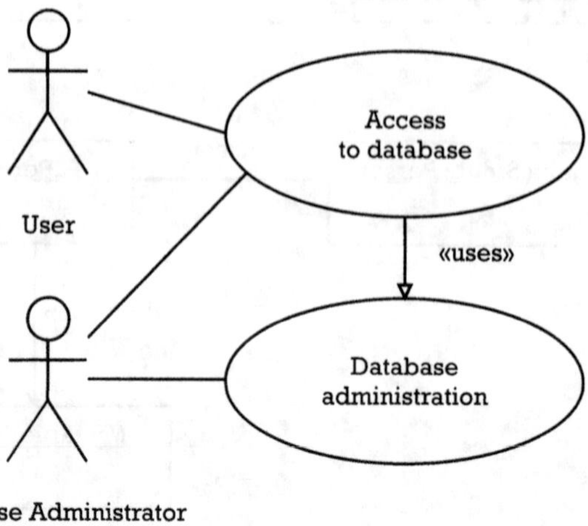

Figure A.7 Use case diagram.

have a "lifeline" that proceeds vertically and represents the time axis of the diagrams. A thick lifeline shows that the object is active, that is, performs some task. Interactions—or messages—between objects are represented as arrows connecting the objects that interact (Figure A.8).

The time axis is not necessarily proportional to actual time intervals; it just gives an ordering to the interactions. When adequate, the time axis can be marked with time labels.

A.5 Extensions of UML

Even if UML provides mechanisms for extending itself, extensions of UML are kept as minimal as possible in Sherlock to make the overall use of Sherlock easy. The few extensions follow:

- Domain characterization introduces new stereotypes to model products, compatibility formats, converters, and market segments.
- Domain modeling introduces "potential" associations. These represent associations that are present in the domain but may not be present in a specific product of the domain.
- Domain modeling also introduces a notation to represent variation points in use case diagrams.

The details and the motivation of these extensions are described in detail in the mentioned phases.

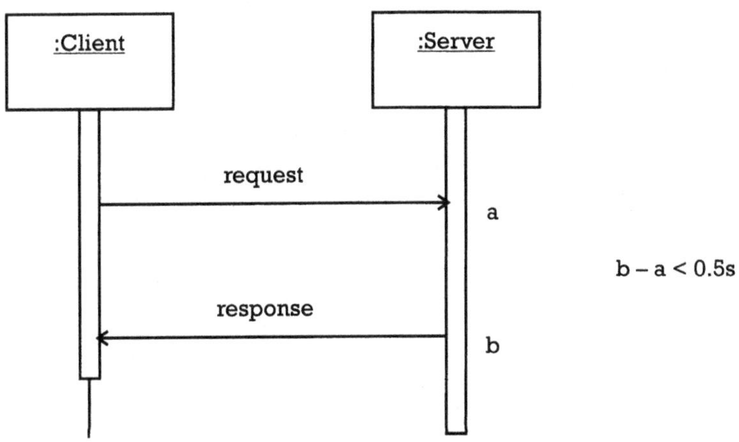

Figure A.8 Sample sequence diagram.

References

[1] Booch, G., J. Rumbaugh, and I. Jacobson, *The Unified Modeling Language User Guide*, Reading, MA: Addison-Wesley, 1998.

[2] Rumbaugh., J., et al., *Object-Oriented Modeling and Design*, Upper Saddle River, NJ: Prentice Hall, 1991.

[3] Booch, G., *Object-Oriented Analysis and Design With Applications*, Reading, MA: Addison-Wesley, 1994.

[4] Jacobson, I., *Object-Oriented Software Engineering: A Use Case Driven Approach*, Reading, MA: Addison-Wesley, 1994.

[5] Jacobson, I., M. Griss, and P. Jonsson, *Software Reuse: Architecture Process and Organization for Business Success*, Reading, MA: Addison-Wesley, 1997.

APPENDIX

B

Contents

Review of existing methodologies for domain analysis and engineering

Over the past few years, many authors have proposed different approaches to domain analysis and engineering. Each methodology has its own peculiarities. This is due to the specific problem to solve and the approach taken: problem driven or application driven, or, in other instances, reuse oriented or knowledge-representation oriented. The approach taken usually reflects the background of the authors of the methodologies to which one is attuned. For instance, Wartik and Prieto-Diaz [1] propose an interesting analysis based on a set of criteria suitable for comparing reuse-oriented domain analysis and engineering approaches. They emphasize that "comparing different domain analysis approaches requires considering the context in which an approach will be used." In particular, they propose five context factors: software process needs, existing software base, business objectives, state of domain knowledge, and intended use of information repositories.

In Appendix B, we survey some of the well-known methodologies. We discuss their limits and outline how Sherlock tries to overcome such limits.

B.1 Survey of existing DA&E methodologies

In this section we summarize the features of some of the most relevant methodologies proposed in the literature. Readers interested in a more comprehensive survey on domain analysis and engineering should consult [2].

Product-Oriented Domain Analysis [3] was among the first invented DA&E methodologies. It prescribes a phase of domain characterization in which the market is analyzed, but it does not detail the related activities. It does not contain explicit domain models.

Domain Analysis for Reusability [4] focuses mainly on creating a collection of components with a structured process for classifying both the entities in the domain and the components. The classification proceeds bottom-up and uses a faceted schema. Emphasis is placed on planning.

KAPTUR [5] and the related tool, Formal Alternatives Manager (FAM) [6], target the support of the decision process in DA&E from the initial phases onward. It provides a mechanism to link modeling and design through the concept of "features." The validation of the domain models and the documentation of the design rationale are emphasized.

Feature-Oriented Domain Analysis (FODA) is one of the most widely used methodologies for domain analysis and engineering [7]. It has been in development by the Software Engineering Institute of Carnegie Mellon University since the late 1980s. FODA is a model-driven approach centered on the analysis of different software systems with the intention of finding common "features." FODA employs entity-relationship diagrams and prescribes validation steps.

RAPID [8] gathers information on the domain from documentation and interviews with experts. This information is entered in a domain information database and is then used to create components that are easy to reuse.

Organon [9] and Organization Domain Modeling (ODM) [10] adopt a knowledge-based approach. Domains are "realms of discourse," a subject of study. The targets are organization domains, in which software is developed. There are no domain abstractions that are "absolutely" right, but the process of identifying the "right" variability in the domain models depends on several tradeoff decisions. Best results are achieved with an explicit multisystem perspective. The goal is to support the establishment of a DA&E methodology that is well grounded in the business objectives and the organization structure of the target firm.

Domain Specific Software Architecture (DSSA) defines a sequence of steps to go from users' needs to domain architectures [11]. It formalizes user needs, requirements, and implementation constraints and uses them to build architectural modules and reusable work products.

Proteus supports domain analysis activities in the context of evolutionary development putting strong emphasis on domain variability [12]. It uses OMT [13] to model the domain and its components, and takes advantage of features of object orientation, such as inheritance, to represent variability. Proteus prescribes an explicit documentation of domain models.

Domain Analysis and Reuse Environment (DARE) specifies in a clean and pragmatic way the steps for systematic elicitation and analysis of the information in the domain in the form of documents, code, or experts' knowledge [14, 15]. The information is classified using a multifaceted approach.

FeatuRSEB [16] and FODAcom [17] are extensions of FODA with object orientation in UML. They were originated by the fruitful cooperation between Martin Griss and John Favaro. In particular, FeatuRSEB augments FODA with the RSEB approach to object orientation in UML [18]. FODAcom integrates object orientation in FODA targeting telecommunication domains.

Several other methodologies are available for the DA&E process; we have merely focused on those most relevant for our work. It is also worthwhile to mention Draco [19] and DAGAR [20], which focus on generative reuse, which is outside the scope of the book.

B.2 Comments on the existing methodologies

Sherlock inherits lots of aspects from existing methodologies, especially ODM and FeatuRSEB. To understand the unique peculiarities of Sherlock, it is important to analyze the weaknesses of existing approaches:

- No methodology addresses the problem of extracting object-oriented frameworks that are considered to have high reuse potentials.

- In the preparation phase preceding data analysis, domain characterization and scoping are weak and domain modeling is emphasized too much. As a consequence, business analysis, feasibility study, project planning, and resource allocation are often performed just using personnel capability and experience. It lacks a clear description of the tasks to be undertaken and suitable guidelines that support personnel in carrying out these activities.

- Most of the proposed approaches are static; their process is mostly waterfall and leads to a "one-shot" result. It is hard to model situations when the model of the domain changes with time. However, changes in domains are very common in real life. DA&E should be able to identify and describe the possible evolutions of a domain, guiding the user through an interactive and cyclic process aimed at upgrading and improving domain understanding and representation at each successive step, maintaining domain models so they stay "alive," and following the dynamic changing boundaries of the domain. ODM is the exception, with an explicit provision for dynamic changes.

- DA&E should be part of the software process, by using the "usual" techniques and practices to the largest possible extent. Domain analysis and engineering needs to support software development without burdening the process by adding activities, practices, and deliverables that are not really needed. DA&E should strive to produce the same kinds of assets usually produced by "regular" software processes.

Last, but not least, as indicated by Arango [2], a useful method should be reliable, giving confidence to the user that by applying it, the desired results will be achieved. It should also be repeatable, ensuring that applying the same method in similar contexts will yield similar results. Moreover, it should provide verification procedures and validation criteria, enabling a user to evaluate her own work and decide whether she has accomplished her objectives.

Sherlock tries to address these limitations, as should be apparent after reading the book.

- Sherlock produces an object-oriented domain framework.

- Sherlock includes a careful study of the target domain, also from a market perspective. This involves business analysis, feasibility study, project planning, and resource allocation.
- Sherlock centers DA&E on the study of the variability in the domain and in the domain models.
- The deliverables of Sherlock include most of the "regular" deliverables of a structured software development process, making its introduction in a firm easy to accomplish. Sherlock adopts UML, which is the new emerging standard for software development.
- The maturity of Sherlock and its industrial validation ensure its reliability and its repeatability.

B.3 Components, frameworks, and architectures

Despite the fact that the terms *component, framework,* and *architecture* are considered to be the cornerstone of reusability, most DA&E methodologies do not define or use them. In contrast, Sherlock results in the production of a "framework" of "components" organized in a "domain architecture."

Sherlock adopts the definition of components that is given by Szyperski [21] and addresses the problem of "architectural mismatch" first evidenced in [22].

Sherlock follows the view of Bass et al. [23] that an architecture is composed of several views that Sherlock calls *projections.* These projections are somehow similar to the UML diagrams [24]. Bass et al. [23] identify nine major architectural projections; Sherlock is more flexible in its definition, limiting the required projections to three. Also, the selected projections sometimes differ from the original proposal of Bass et al. [23].

In the definition of the target object-oriented framework, special attention has been placed on the seminal work on the black box component framework [25].

References

[1] Wartik, S., and R. Prieto-Diaz, "Criteria for Comparing Reuse-Oriented Domain Analysis Approaches," *Software Engineering and Knowledge Engineering*, Vol. 2, No. 3, 1992, pp. 403–431.

[2] Arango, G., "Domain Analysis Methods," in *Software Reengineering*, W. Schaefer and D. Diaz, Eds., New York: Ellis Horwood, 1994.

[3] McCain, R., "Reusable Software Components Construction: A Product Oriented Paradigm," *Proceedings of 5th AIAA/ACM/NASA/IEEE Computers in Aerospace*, 1985.

[4] Prieto-Diaz, R., "Domain Analysis for Reusability," *Proceedings of COMPSAC 87: The 11th Annual International Computer Software and Applications Conference*, IEEE Computer Society, Washington, DC, October 1987.

[5] Bailin, S. C., et al., "KAPTUR: Knowledge Acquisition for Preservation of Tradeoffs and Underlying Rationales," *Proceedings of 5th Knowledge-Based Software Assistant Conference*, Rome Laboratory, September 1990.

[6] Knowledge Evolution Inc., "Tour Through FAM," (http://www.kevol.com/tour/tour1.html).

[7] Cohen, S., et al., "Application of Feature-Oriented Domain Analysis to the Army Movement Control Domain," Technical Report CMU/SEI-91-TR-28, 1992.

[8] Vitaletti, W., and E. Guerrieri, "Domain Analysis Within the ISEC Rapid Center," *Proceedings of 8th Annual National Conference on Ada Technology*, March 1990.

[9] Simos, M., "The Growing of an Organon: A Hybrid Knowledge-Base Technology and Methodology for Software Reuse," in *Domain Analysis and Software Systems Modeling*, R. Prieto-Diaz and G. Arango, Eds., Los Alamitos, CA: IEEE Computer Society Press, 1991.

[10] Simos, M., "Organization Domain Modeling (ODM): Formalizing the Core Domain Modeling Life Cycle," *SIGSOFT Software Engineering Notes*, August 1995.

[11] Tracz, W., and L. Coglianese, "DOMAIN (Domain Model All INtegrated): A DSSA Domain Analysis Tool," Technical Report ADAGE-LOR-94-13, 1995 (http://www.owego.com/dssa/lm-docs/LOR9411.ps).

[12] CAP SSP, CAP Gemini Innovation, CAP Sesa Telecom, Hewlett Packard, Intecs, Matra Marconi Space, Sintef, University of Lancaster, "Domain Analysis Method," Deliverable D3. 2B, PROTEUS ESPRIT project 6086, 1994.

[13] Rumbaugh, J., et al., *Object-Oriented Modeling and Design*, Upper Saddle River, NJ: Prentice Hall, 1991.

[14] Frakes, W., R. Prieto-Diaz, and C. Fox, "DARE-COTS: A Domain Analysis Support Tool," *Proceedings of 17th International Conference of the Chilean Computer Society,* IEEE Computer Society, 1997.

[15] Frakes, W., R. Prieto-Diaz, and C. Fox, "DARE Domain Analysis and Reuse Environment," *Annals of Software Engineering,* Vol. 5, 1998, pp. 125–141.

[16] Griss, M., J. Favaro, and M. Alessandro, "Integrating Feature Modeling With the RSEB," *Proceedings of 5th International Conference on Software Reuse,* 1998.

[17] Dionisi, V., et al., "FODAcom: An Experience With Domain Analysis in the Italian Telecom Industry," *Proceedings of 5th International Conference on Software Reuse,* 1998.

[18] Jacobson, I., M. Griss, and P. Jonsson, *Software Reuse: Architecture Process and Organization for Business Success,* Reading, MA: Addison-Wesley, 1997.

[19] Neighbors, J., "Draco 1.2 Users Manual," Department of Information and Computer Science, University of California, Irvine, CA, 1983, (http://www.bayfronttechnologies.com/manual.htm).

[20] Klinger, C., and J. Solderitsch, "DAGAR: A Process for Domain Architecture Definition and Asset Implementation," *Proceedings of ACM TriAda96,* 1996.

[21] Szyperski, C., *Component Software: Beyond Object-Oriented Programming,* Reading, MA: Addison-Wesley, 1998.

[22] Shaw, M., and D. Garland, *Software Architecture: Perspectives on an Emerging Discipline,* Upper Saddle River, NJ: Prentice Hall, 1996.

[23] Bass, L., P. Clemens, and R. Kazman, *Software Architecture in Practice,* Reading, MA: Addison-Wesley, 1998.

[24] Fowler, M., *Analysis Patterns—Reusable Object Models,* Reading, MA: Addison Wesley, 1997.

[25] Pfister, C., "Component Software: A Case Study Using BlackBox Components,"(http://www.oberon.ch/docu/case_study/index.html).

About the Authors

Paolo Predonzani is a researcher in Genova, Italy. He holds a Laurea degree in computer engineering, an MSc in computer science, and a Ph.D. in electrical and computer engineering, all from the University of Genova, Italy.

Dr. Predonzani serves as a consultant for several firms in the areas of software reuse, software systems development, especially Internet-based, and the design of information systems for biomedical environments. His research concentrates on domain analysis and engineering, with a focus on the pivotal role of network externalities and the consequent selection of compatibility strategies. He is also analyzing how compatibility can be used to predict the success of software systems.

Giancarlo Succi is a professor of software engineering at the University of Alberta, Edmonton, Alberta. He holds a Laurea degree in electrical engineering from the University of Genova, Italy, an MSc in computer science from the State University of New York at Buffalo, and a Ph.D. in electrical and computer engineering from the University of Genova.

Dr. Succi is a registered professional engineer in Alberta and in Italy, and an official consultant for the court of Genova, Italy, as well as for several North American and European firms and for the European Commission. He also serves as a reviewer for and is a member of the editorial boards of several international scientific journals and magazines. Dr. Succi is the author of more than 100 papers published in journals, conference proceedings, and books. He is also the editor of *Implementations of Logic Programming Systems* (Boston: Kluwer, 1994) and a soon-to-be-published book on extreme programming. Before joining the University of Alberta, Dr. Succi was an associate professor and the director of the Software Engineering Graduate Program of the Department of Electrical and Computer Engineering at the University of Calgary. He was also an assistant professor in the Department of Computer and Management Sciences at the University of Trento, Italy. Dr. Succi is also the owner and head of Eutec, a small software firm. Dr. Succi's current research involves software reuse, software metrics, object-oriented business modeling using UML and activity-based costing and management, and software engineering economics.

Tullio Vernazza is an associate professor at the University of Genova, Italy. He holds a Laurea degree in electrical engineering from the University of Genova. Professor Vernazza is also a registered professional engineer in Italy. He serves as a consultant for several firms and also acts as the director of the IT department for the Istituto Giannina Gaslini, one of the world's largest children's hospitals. Professor Vernazza is researching software reuse and electronic commerce, with a special interest in authentication mechanisms and biometric keys in the medical domain, including the use of smartcard and thumbs' code for authoring medical information. Professor Vernazza's research also includes hardware/software codesign, especially robotic systems, also in the medical domain.

Index

Recent Titles in the Artech House Computing Library

Advanced ANSI SQL Data Modeling and Structure Processing, Michael M. David

Advanced Database Technology and Design, Mario Piattini and Oscar Díaz, editors

Business Process Implementation for IT Professionals and Managers, Robert B. Walford

Configuration Management: The Missing Link in Web Engineering, Susan Dart

Data Modeling and Design for Today's Architectures, Angelo Bobak

Data Quality for the Information Age, Thomas C. Redman

Data Warehousing and Data Mining for Telecommunications, Rob Mattison

Distributed and Multi-Database Systems, Angelo R. Bobak

Electronic Payment Systems, Donal O'Mahony, Michael Peirce, and Hitesh Tewari

Future Codes: Essays in Advanced Computer Technology and the Law, Curtis E. A. Karnow

Global Distributed Applications With Windows® DNA, Enrique Madrona

A Guide to Programming Languages: Overview and Comparison, Ruknet Cezzar

A Guide to Software Configuration Management, Alexis Leon

Guide to Standards and Specifications for Designing Web Software, Stan Magee and Leonard L. Tripp

How to Run Successful High-Tech Project-Based Organizations, Fergus O'Connell

Information Hiding Techniques for Steganography and Digital Watermarking, Stefan Katzenbeisser and Fabien A. P. Petitcolas, editors

Internet Commerce Development, Craig Standing

Internet and Intranet Security, Rolf Oppliger

Managing Computer Networks: A Case-Based Reasoning Approach, Lundy Lewis

Metadata Management for Information Control and Business Success, Guy Tozer

Multimedia Database Management Systems, Guojun Lu

Practical Guide to Software Quality Management, John W. Horch

Practical Process Simulation Using Object-Oriented Techniques and C++, José Garrido

Secure Electronic Transactions: Introduction and Technical Reference, Larry Loeb

Security Fundamentals for E-Commerce, Vesna Hassler

Software Process Improvement With CMM, Joseph Raynus

Software Verification and Validation: A Practitioner's Guide, Steven R. Rakitin

Strategic Software Production With Domain-Oriented Reuse, Paolo Predonzani, Giancarlo Succi, and Tullio Vernazza

Systems Modeling for Business Process Improvement, David Bustard, Peter Kawalek, and Mark Norris, editors

User-Centered Information Design for Improved Software Usability, Pradeep Henry

For further information on these and other Artech House titles, including previously considered out-of-print books now available through our In-Print-Forever® (IPF®) program, contact:

Artech House
685 Canton Street
Norwood, MA 02062
Phone: 781-769-9750
Fax: 781-769-6334
e-mail: artech@artechhouse.com

Artech House
46 Gillingham Street
London SW1V 1AH UK
Phone: +44 (0)20 7596-8750
Fax: +44 (0)20 7630-0166
e-mail: artech-uk@artechhouse.com

Find us on the World Wide Web at:
www.artechhouse.com

www.ingramcontent.com/pod-product-compliance
Lightning Source LLC
LaVergne TN
LVHW011904200926
848484LV00002B/528
9781580531047